"Buy this book! Myth and the Movies *is a tremendous ass* [illegible] *process of building a script or needing a fix for story and str* [illegible] *I recommend it to all my clients."*

Marisa D'Vari, author of *Script Magic*
and Story Consultant

"Stuart Voytilla's Myth and the Movies *is a remarkable achievement: an ambitious, thought-provoking, and cogent analysis of the mythic underpinnings of fifty great movies. It should prove a valuable resource for film teachers, students, critics and especially screenwriters, whose challenge, as Voytilla so clearly understands, is to constantly reinvent a mythology for our times."*

Ted Tally, Academy Award®-winning screenwriter,
The Silence of the Lambs

"Myth and the Movies *is a must for every writer who wants to tell better stories. Voytilla guides his readers to a richer and deeper understanding not only of mythic structure, but also of the movies we love."*

Christopher Wehner,
Web editor, *The Screenwriters Utopia* and
Creative Screenwriting

"I've script consulted for ten years and I've studied every genre thoroughly. I thought I knew all their nuances—until I read Voytilla's book. This one goes on my Recommended Reading List. A fascinating analysis of the Hero's Myth for all genres."

Lou Grantt, Editor,
Hollywood Scriptwriter Magazine

"Myth and the Movies *is a work of remarkable depth, extraordinary research, and rare insight. Stuart Voytilla is an engaging writer who makes the film hero's journey as interesting for the reader as the protagonist. It is a must-have book for students of film, industry professionals, or anyone who loves the movies."*

Stephen Siegel,
Adjunct Professor of Screenwriting,
Department of Film & Television, Undergraduate
New York University

MYTH AND THE MOVIES

DISCOVERING THE MYTHIC STRUCTURE OF

50 UNFORGETTABLE FILMS

BY

STUART VOYTILLA

Published by Michael Wiese Productions, 11288 Ventura Blvd., Suite 821,
Studio City, CA 91604, (818) 379-8799 Fax (818) 986-3408.
E-mail: wiese@earthlink.net
http://www.mwp.com

Cover design by The Art Hotel
Interior layout by William Morosi
Printed by Sheridan Books, Inc.

Printed and Manufactured in the United States of America

Copyright 1999 by Stuart Voytilla

All rights reserved. No part of this book may be reproduced in any form or by any means without permission in writing from the author, except for the inclusion of brief quotations in a review.

Library of Congress Cataloging-in-Publication Data

Voytilla, Stuart, 1959-

Myth and the Movies : discovering the mythic structure of 50 unforgettable films / Stuart Voytilla.

p. cm.

Includes bibliographical references.

ISBN 0-941188-66-3

1. Motion picture--History. 2. Film genres. I. Title.

PN1995.V69 1999 99-27626

791.43'6 -- dc21 CIP

Michael Wiese Productions
OS/RE

TABLE OF CONTENTS

FOREWORD

BY CHRISTOPHER VOGLER

The book you are about to read is part of a long chain of reaction and response. This chain began with the response of the earliest humans to their environment, the frightening and wondrous world that confronted them on all sides. From their awe and fascination with the mystery of the world's grand design they forged the first mythic stories. The myths were attempts to explain, in an indirect, poetic, metaphoric way, the purpose and place of humans in the vast design. With the tools of myth, early people strove to answer the timeless questions, the questions we still have with us—Who made this world, and why? Where do we come from? Where do we go when we die? What does it mean and how are we supposed to behave? How do we relate to the great forces of life and death, female and male, creation and destruction, light and darkness?

This chain of thought expanded as humans enhanced the myths to reflect the distinct conditions of our living places and our unique experiences in the land. It stretched further, link by link, as we explored mythic dimension through dance, music, drama and all the other arts. With movies, we found a medium ideal to represent the fantastic world of myth. Movies embraced myth, both for story lines and for a deeper influence in structure, motifs, and style. A new and powerful link in the mythic chain was forged.

Other links were made in our own times as scholars and philosophers looked back at the myths of the ancient world. Among students of myth like Carl Jung, Mircea Eliade, Theodore Gaster, and Heinrich Zimmer, the work of a man named Joseph Campbell has particular relevance for our quest. He hammered out a mighty link of the chain, a set of observations known as The Hero's Journey.

In books like *The Hero with a Thousand Faces*, *The Power of Myth*, and *The Inner Reaches of Outer Space*, Campbell reported on the synthesis he found while comparing the myths and legends of many cultures. The Hero's Journey was his all-embracing metaphor for the deep inner journey of transformation that heroes in every time and place seem to share, a path that leads them through great movements of separation, descent, ordeal, and return.

In reaction to Campbell's work, a man named George Lucas composed what many have called a myth for our times—the Star War series, in which young heroes of a highly technological civilization confront the same demons, trials, and wonders as the heroes of old.

And that's where I come in, trying in my humble way to add something to the chain. Back in 1977 when the first Star Wars movie appeared, I was a film student at the University of Southern California School of Cinema. I had been on my own version of the heroic quest, seeking the golden key of storytelling. I found it in the works of Campbell, and saw it verified and validated by the unprecedented success of the Campbell-inspired Star Wars movies. I continued to test and refine my understanding of the Hero's Journey as I started to work for the Hollywood studios as a story analyst and consultant.

While working for the Walt Disney Company, I tried to formulate my reactions into a seven-page memo, "A Practical Guide to *The Hero with a Thousand Faces*." This memo took on a life of its own; it was photocopied and faxed all over town. It became part of Hollywood lore. In it, I attempted to translate Campbell's ideas into movie language. Where he illustrated the Hero's Journey with myths from various world cultures, I gave examples from classic and current Hollywood movies.

Following Campbell, but making adjustments to reflect the unique conditions of movie storytelling, I described the Hero's Journey as a twelve-stage adventure for the hero. The stages are:

1. The Ordinary World, in which the audience meets the hero, discovers his or her ambitions and limitations, and forms a bond of identification and recognition.
2. The Call to Adventure, when the hero is challenged to undertake a quest or solve some problem.
3. Refusal of the Call, when the hero hesitates or expresses fear.
4. Meeting with the Mentor, where the hero contacts some source of reassurance, experience, or wisdom.
5. Crossing the Threshold, at which time the hero commits to the adventure and enters the Special World.
6. Tests, Allies and Enemies—situations and people that help the hero discover what's special about the Special World.
7. The Approach, that phase when the hero prepares for a central battle of confrontation with the forces of failure, defeat, or death.
8. The Ordeal, the central crisis of the story in which the hero faces his or her greatest fear and tastes death.

9. The Reward, the moment in which the hero is reborn in some sense and enjoys the benefits of having confronted fear and death.

10. The Road Back, where the hero commits to finishing the adventure and leaves, or is chased out of, the Special World.

11. The Resurrection, a climactic test that purifies, redeems, and transforms the hero on the threshold of home.

12. Return with the Elixir, where the hero comes home and shares what has been gained on the quest, which benefits friends, family, community and the world.

I began to teach this approach to movie story structure and also had the opportunity to test it on movie projects, including the animated features *Beauty and the Beast, Aladdin,* and *The Lion King*. These became part of the endless chain of mythic inspiration and re-interpretation. Meanwhile I kept hammering on that memo, and in time it grew into a book, *The Writer's Journey: Mythic Structure for Writers.* This was both a description of the Hero's Journey idea and an observation of how the ordeals and challenges of mythic heroes can also be found in the daily experience of the writer.

The book enjoyed some success, being reprinted many times and translated into five languages. It became a guide for many writers and film students and another link in the chain of mythic reaction.

A couple of years ago, a young man named Stuart Voytilla approached me with the enthusiasm of a true mythic appreciator. A teacher and a screenwriter himself, Stuart had a great idea—to create a CD-ROM and a book that illustrated the many variations of the Hero's Journey with dozens of movie examples.

I loved this idea, a refinement of what I did in the original memo and had been doing in my classes and workshops. I had taught a class at the UCLA Extension Writer's Program called "Myth in the Movies, A Writer's Guide," in which I explored the fascinating permutations of the Hero's Journey in several film genres—thrillers, science fiction, adventure, romance, Westerns, and comedy. Stuart was proposing to cover these and more, with a multitude of examples to compare. He proposed analyzing a large number of films with the tools of the Hero's Journey, seeking out the stages and archetypes in these examples, and offering them up for comparison.

I liked the proposal because I was convinced that the act of comparison is the key to myth, and the power source of the Hero's Journey idea. The mythic impulse is driven by the very human tendency to learn about ourselves through comparison. The myths are metaphors, comparisons by which we hope to gain some useful insight into our condition and our place in the cosmos. In fact, we automatically read every story as a metaphor, and measure our own performance and behavior against those of the heroes and villains.

How great it would be to have a substantial collection of classic movie examples, each interpreted by the tools of the Hero's Journey. This could be a valuable resource for researchers, but also for screenwriters who are trying to grasp the mythic principles and apply them in their own work. It could be an entertaining book for a general audience of people who just want to enhance their enjoyment of the movies by understanding their mythic roots.

One of Joseph Campbell's greatest strengths as a speaker was the vast number of examples he had at his command. He had read deeply into thousands of patterns from different cultures, and was able to call up illustrations and insight on any subject. It was as if he could reach up into the jet stream of mythic thought that seems to swirl around the globe and pull down the perfect strand of story to weave into his design. With the book in your hand, Stuart Voytilla has assembled a collection of examples from the movies we all love, and has interpreted them through the lens of myth, offering you the beginnings of your own inventory of mythic examples. With these examples, you have tools to test your own thinking about the Hero's Journey, and perhaps find inspiration in the many ways mythic patterns are reflected in movies.

For screenwriters and development people, this book is a great inventory of solutions to story problems. Here, organized rationally and usefully, are dozens of ways great storytellers have guided their heroes through special worlds, into deadly inmost caves, through dramatically satisfying ordeals, resurrections, and returns. Having worked in the development of Hollywood films, I know how useful it is to have abundant examples of story solutions at your fingertips, to inspire you to create fresh and unique solutions, in combinations no one has ever seen before.

For people who just love movies and are curious about the mythic sources that inspire them, the book will give many hours of pleasure as they review their favorites through the lens of myth.

A great virtue of Stuart's efforts is that he has chosen examples from a wide range of genres and styles. It's fairly easy for people to grasp the presence and value of the Hero's Journey in adventure and fantasy movies, where we see a literal journey through a special world with tangible, physical ordeals. It takes a little more patience and imagination to find the Hero's Journey in less obvious genres, such as romance, film noir, comedy, and drama. There the trials, mentors, thresholds, and elixirs may be metaphorical, invisible, but nonetheless are a potent presence. This book goes a long way towards demonstrating that the patterns of the Hero's Journey still shape all forms of drama, and can be invaluable tools for writers working in any form of storytelling.

Obviously, this was a massive endeavor, involving many months of viewing, analysis, and organization. If you try to do a mythic analysis of even one film, you'll see how much mental labor is involved. I'm happy to report that the results are a worthy addition to the mythic chain of reaction, and will add significantly to your understanding and appreciation of the power of myth.

Of course, these interpretations are personal, as they must be. Every story can be interpreted in a multitude of ways, and myths are bottomless. You can never come to the end of the ways they can be read, of the metaphors that can be drawn from them. There is no Academy of Mythic Correctness, thank the gods, to pronounce exactly what every story means, what every character symbolizes, or what stage of the journey every scene represents. If there were such an Academy, it would mean the end of the long chain of reaction and reinterpretation. It would take all the fun out of it.

Fortunately, this book is wonderfully idiosyncratic and individual, with observations and conclusions which you are invited to disagree with or amend to suit your point of view. I don't agree with all of Stuart's interpretations, and am happy with the realization that we both can be right. There is no right or wrong about reading a story for its mythic meaning, except that it feels right for you and yields a useful insight in your life. It will mean something different in each culture and time period, to people of different backgrounds, ages, and genders. That's why, as Joseph Campbell suggests, the hero has a thousand faces.

So the chain will grow, link by link. Campbell reacts to myths and the scholars of his day, filmmakers react to the mythic storytellers who have gone before, I react to Campbell and the movies, Stuart reacts to all of it, and you react to this book. Go and compare. Find your own meaning from the movies, using Stuart's good work as a sounding board. Try out his readings of these beloved classic films, and see if they agree or not with your own instinctive reactions. Watch the movies with renewed pleasure. Tell your own stories with the tools of myth. Carry on forging links in this thankfully never-ending chain of myth and story.

INTRODUCTION

"The artist is the one who communicates myth for today."
—Joseph Campbell, *The Power of Myth*

When I suggested the idea of *Myth and the Movies* to Chris Vogler, I had no idea I was embarking on the most difficult, frustrating, bloody, rejuvenating, rewarding journey of my career. During this trek I've visited ten worlds bounded by genre. My guides have been some of our most cherished motion pictures, created by many of cinema's greatest storytellers. My map consists of the Stages and Archetypes of the Hero's Journey.

At the core of my journey is the art of storytelling. Delving into the inner workings of great cinema making means becoming immersed in the elements of a good story. And isn't that what we as screenwriters are trying ultimately to do, to tell a good story?

Movies serve the function of all storytelling, to entertain, inspire and perhaps even teach us to cope with problems. But the key here is that moviemaking can be considered the contemporary form of mythmaking, reflecting our response to ourselves and the mysteries and wonders of our existence. Many times we are blessed with a motion picture that elevates itself to true mythic stature and becomes such an important part of our storytelling tradition that it can transform lives and affect our culture. The Stages and Archetypes of the Hero's Journey provide a flexible, analytical tool to understand why *any* movie's story works or fails. But most important, the paradigm guides us to an understanding of why a story resonates on a universal level by answering our deepest mysteries.

In the process of writing the analyses of the films, I became aware of characteristics of the Stages of the Hero's Journey that distinguished one genre from another. Genres are important. They satisfy our basic instinct to classify and define, but they also allow us to better explain the type of story an audience is paying for. Genres are fascinating because they often describe a development in film that is in tune with and reflective of the unique tenor and experience of the age. The Western, a distinctly American art form, chronicles the journey into a new and dangerous land, an American land, the West. Part of my quest was to discover whether a genre like the Western uses the paradigm of the Hero's Journey in a distinctive way, a way that is different from say Romantic Comedy.

In these exciting storytelling times, we continue to blend and crossbreed genres creating stories that audiences can identify with yet hold a uniqueness that keeps the audience on the edge of their seats. I've chosen ten distinctive motion picture genres. Each genre contains five sample movies that have strong elements that fit within the particular genre. Each genre chapter begins with a discussion of the structural mythic characteristics of the individual genres. These are not hard and fast rules. There are no formulas intended. These are tools that you can use to better appreciate a particular cinematic journey as a viewer or to help the storyteller evaluate a genre when writing a script. The divisions of genre I chose are:

- ACTION ADVENTURE
- WESTERN
- HORROR
- THRILLER
- WAR
- DRAMA
- ROMANCE
- ROMANTIC COMEDY
- COMEDY
- SCIENCE FICTION AND FANTASY

I would like to emphasize that the movies chosen for the book are not intended to be a list of the fifty greatest films of all time. I leave you to debate that issue and hope that you will take what you learn here and make your own analysis of whatever favorite movie of yours was not included. Deciding was hard, but came down to the following list of criteria:

- The movie defined a particular genre (*High Noon, Halloween*), or is considered a classic of the genre (*Raiders of the Lost Ark, Some Like It Hot*).
- The movie challenged the genre, and pushed it into a new direction (*Dances With Wolves*), or may have started a new trend (*Die Hard*).
- The film's structure shows a unique spin on the Hero's Journey and its use of the Stages and Archetypes (*Annie Hall, Platoon*).
- The film was a blockbuster (*The Star Wars Trilogy, Home Alone*).
- The film tells a damn good story (*Notorious, The Bridge on the River Kwai*).

I hope this book will inspire you to write. I am a screenwriter and have the utmost respect for screenwriting as a creative process. As you'll see with the analyses, many of our most memorable movies follow the classic configuration of the Hero's Journey. Other movies can be interpreted in ways that break the rules or present new ways of looking at the Stages and Archetypes. And of course most of these movies were written without any intention of fulfilling the stages of the Hero's Journey. Joseph Campbell unearthed the Hero's Journey after studying centuries of storytelling tradition; these symbols, patterns and "truths" lie subconscious in the storytelling process.

Also, realize that each film is rich with mythic symbols and interpretation. *Casablanca* and *The Godfather* alone could support their own texts with their richly defined characters traveling their own journeys. To present every level of myth with each subplot takes much more space than this work allows. I hope this study is a threshold for further work, and analysis.

Finally, exploration into myths and storytelling, as in any creative art, is not an exact science and in fact can be a very personal journey. There's always room for re-interpretation. You may see the Road Back in *Platoon* differently than I have presented it. To quote one of our great movie mentors, Obi-Wan Kenobi, "You're going to find that many of the truths we cling to depend greatly on our own point of view." I value your point of view. At the very least, I hope that this material sparks discussion and argument. With adversity comes awareness and growth. And it shows that you are using the material.

So consider the Hero's Journey as a writing tool, an extremely malleable paradigm, that expands your intellectual and creative thinking, opening you to new avenues of exploration. Please accept this work as a springboard to an incredible world of writing and appreciation for the power of our movies.

HOW TO USE THIS BOOK

I assume that you were drawn to this book because of your awareness of the Hero's Journey either through Joseph Campbell's work (namely *The Hero with a Thousand Faces*, or *The Power of Myth* with Bill Moyers) or as presented by Christopher Vogler in *The Writer's Journey. Myth and the Movies* has been designed as a companion to Christopher's invaluable work. Although familiarity with *The Writer's Journey* will make the material in this volume easier to follow, it is in no means a prerequisite to appreciate the analyses. The beauty of the paradigm is its simplicity and the rich interpretations and varied applications of its simple truths. I include an overview of the Hero's Journey Stages and Archetypes in the following chapters. Those unfamiliar with the Hero's Journey can use these quick reference guides before tackling the chapters on genre. Refer to them and Christopher's book if you find any of the terminology confusing.

Myth and the Movies need not be read straight through. Jump into any genre you wish, or begin with a favorite film. In time I hope you will explore all the genres included here. Contemporary filmmaking continues to bend and blend its genres and important insights can be gleaned from the least likely resources. A writer specializing in Horror will find invaluable tools from studying good Thrillers, Comedy and even Romance.

Warning: Do not read the analysis without having seen the film first. I guarantee the analysis will ruin your viewing pleasure. So if you don't know who Rosebud is, or whether Annie Hall and Alvy Singer live happily ever after, see the film, and then study the analysis.

I hope that I've included some films that you haven't seen, or saw and didn't care for. Give them a chance and look at them in this new light. You may be surprised. I was.

HOW TO USE THE CHARTS

As a teacher and screenwriter, I've discovered that two of the most difficult aspects of screenwriting are rhythm and pacing. With the plethora of screenwriting texts in the marketplace, few if any show the pacing of a feature film. We judge pacing from the viewing experience, a pretty unreliable method. First and foremost, watching a movie is an emotional experience. The emotions that the filmmakers hope to elicit can distort — either condense or stretch —the real time of the filmed events and sequences.

In each chapter, I've included charts illustrating several of the sample films. Some show classic structure for the given genre; others may show a unique or radical spin on the paradigm. All are intended to show the pacing and rhythm of the stories. Key Stages are included with the time indicating the start time of the particular scene, or sequence. For your reference, 0:00 is the official start of the film *after* the studio "signature" (Leo completes his roar, the Universal plane buzzes around the world, etc.)

SPECIAL THANKS

This work would not be possible without the help and influence of many people. My thanks...

To the thousands who worked together and fought bitterly to create the movies that are included in this book.

To my mentor on this journey, Christopher Vogler, and to Ken Lee and Michael Wiese for this opportunity, and their constant advice and support.

To Mark Clements and his artistry in the creation of the icons used to represent the Stages of the Hero's Journey. And to Ken Schafer and the support of the entire staff at ScriptPerfection Enterprises, Inc.

To my parents, Nancy and Walter, who raised me with the conviction to see the journey to the end. To my life-partner, Barbara, whose support pushed me through the times when commitment wasn't enough. And finally to my hero, my daughter Elena Ann. May the stars learn how to shine from your smile.

THE STAGES OF THE HERO'S JOURNEY

All stories consist of common structural elements or Stages found universally in myths, fairy tales, dreams, and movies. These twelve Stages compose the Hero's Journey. What follows is a simple overview of each Stage, illustrating basic characteristics and functions. Use it as a quick-reference guide as you explore the genre and movie analyses. Since it cannot provide all of Christopher Vogler's insights upon which it was based, I recommend you refer to his book, *The Writer's Journey*, for a much more thorough evaluation of these Stages.

The paradigm that follows illustrates the "traditional" Hero's Journey as seen in the majority of stories. As you explore the film and genre analyses that follow, you'll find that the Hero's Journey provides a flexible and adaptable model with the potential for an infinite variety of shapes and progressions of Stages. The Journey's Stages may be avoided, repeated, or shifted about depending upon the needs of the individual story.

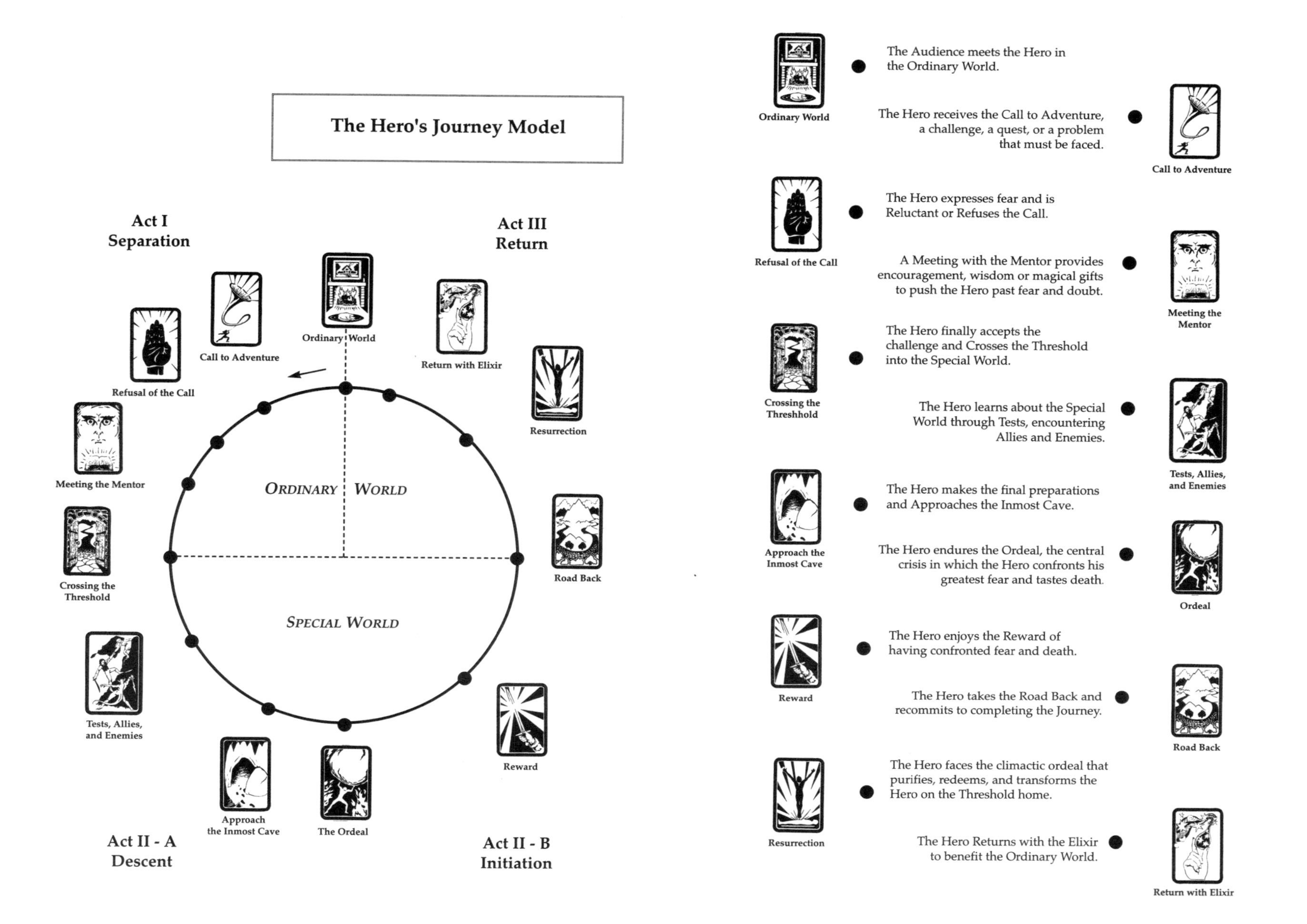
The Hero's Journey Model
Act I
Separation
Act III
Return
Ordinary World
Call to Adventure
Refusal of the Call
Meeting the Mentor
Crossing the Threshold
Tests, Allies, and Enemies
Approach the Inmost Cave
The Ordeal
Reward
Road Back
Resurrection
Return with Elixir
Ordinary World
Special World
Act II - A
Descent
Act II - B
Initiation
Ordinary World
The Audience meets the Hero in the Ordinary World.
The Hero receives the Call to Adventure, a challenge, a quest, or a problem that must be faced.
Call to Adventure
Refusal of the Call
The Hero expresses fear and is Reluctant or Refuses the Call.
A Meeting with the Mentor provides encouragement, wisdom or magical gifts to push the Hero past fear and doubt.
Meeting the Mentor
Crossing the Threshhold
The Hero finally accepts the challenge and Crosses the Threshold into the Special World.
The Hero learns about the Special World through Tests, encountering Allies and Enemies.
Tests, Allies, and Enemies
Approach the Inmost Cave
The Hero makes the final preparations and Approaches the Inmost Cave.
The Hero endures the Ordeal, the central crisis in which the Hero confronts his greatest fear and tastes death.
Ordeal
Reward
The Hero enjoys the Reward of having confronted fear and death.
The Hero takes the Road Back and recommits to completing the Journey.
Road Back
Resurrection
The Hero faces the climactic ordeal that purifies, redeems, and transforms the Hero on the Threshold home.
The Hero Returns with the Elixir to benefit the Ordinary World.
Return with Elixir

THE CHARACTER ARC

The symbolism of the Journey's Stages ("Crossing the Threshold," "Approach the Inmost Cave," "Return with the Elixir") can easily mislead us into seeing the paradigm as representing a purely physical journey. Indeed the Hero takes a physical, active part on the Journey to solve a problem or achieve a goal. But the Hero's Journey is as important an emotional or psychological journey as it is physical. A character's actions and decisions in response to the Journey's Stages can reveal the Character Arc, or phases of growth that a character experiences during the course of the story. The following illustrates the Character Arc using the icons representing the Journey's Stages for reference.

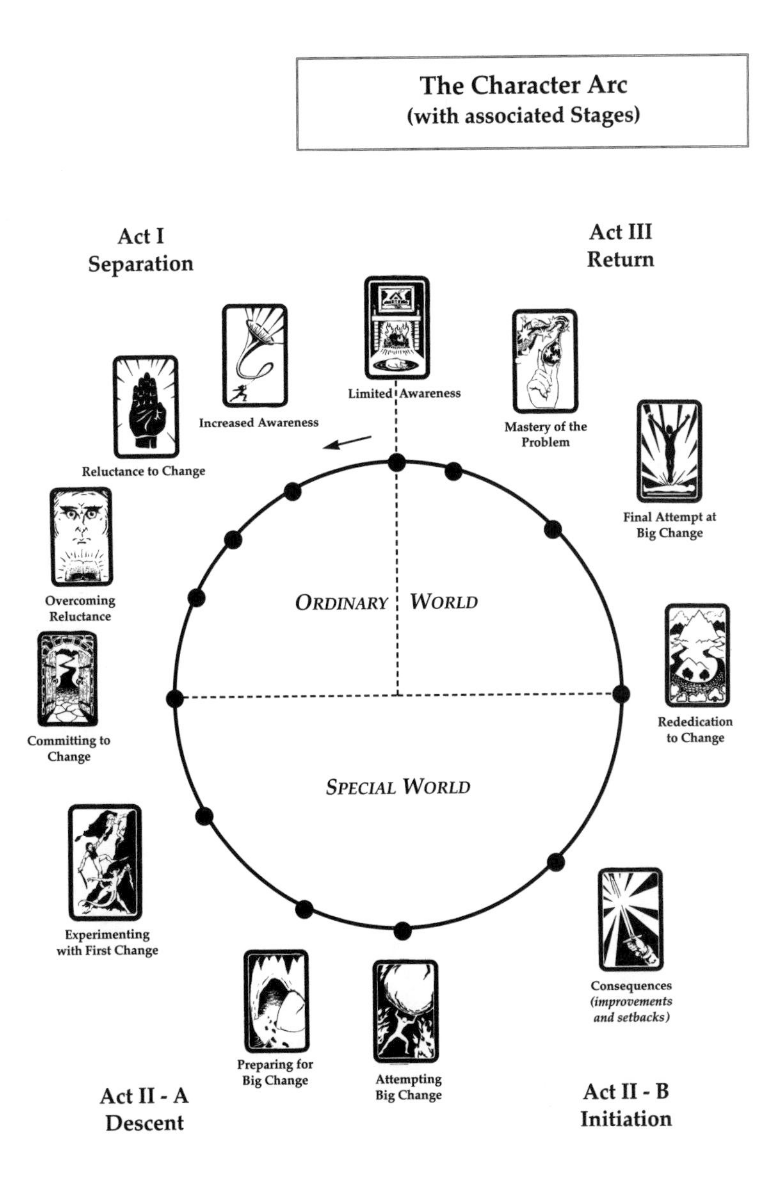

THE ORDINARY WORLD

The Ordinary World allows us to get to know the Hero and identify with him before the Journey begins. Since the audience usually experiences the Journey through the Hero's eyes, we must be able to relate to him. The Ordinary World gives us the opportunity to identify with the Hero's drives, urges, and problems, while showing unique characteristics and flaws that make him three-dimensional. The Hero's Inner and Outer Problems may be established, although these can change depending upon the demands of the Journey. Dr. Richard Kimble's problems in his Ordinary World change drastically when he enters his Special World as a fugitive of justice.

Every story involves a problem or Central Dramatic Question that disrupts the Ordinary World. The Hero must enter the Special World to solve the problem, answer the dramatic question, and return balance. The Ordinary World allows the storyteller to contrast the Ordinary and Special worlds. The Ordinary World is the Hero's home, the safe haven upon which the Special World and the Journey's outcome must be compared. Areas of contrast may include the Special World's physical and emotional characteristics, its rules and inhabitants, as well as the Hero's actions and growth while traveling through this Special World.

THE CALL TO ADVENTURE

The Call to Adventure sets the story rolling by disrupting the comfort of the Hero's Ordinary World, presenting a challenge or quest that must be undertaken. The Call throws the Ordinary World off balance, and establishes the stakes involved if the challenge is rejected. Often delivered by the Herald archetype, the Call to Adventure can take a multitude of forms, including: a message or announcement (*The African Queen*), a sudden storm (*Home Alone*), the arrival of the villain (*High Noon*), a death (*Jaws, Some Like It Hot*), an abduction (*Star Wars*), a man's dying words (*Citizen Kane*).

The Hero may need a Succession of Calls before finally realizing that a challenge must be met, or that his only means of escape is the Special World. Many times the Hero needs to choose between two Conflicting Calls.

REFUSAL OF THE CALL

A Hero Refuses the Journey because of fears and insecurities that have surfaced from the Call to Adventure. The Hero is not willing to make changes, preferring the safe haven of the Ordinary World.

The Refusal of the Call becomes an essential Stage that communicates the risks involved in the Journey that lies ahead. Without risks and danger or the likelihood of failure, the audience will not be compelled to be a part of the Hero's Journey.

Although an eager or Willing Hero may skip the Refusal Stage, the Hero's Allies or Threshold Guardians may still express the fears and risks involved (*Dances With Wolves*).

In Horror and Thriller, the frightening and forbidding nature of the Special World can lead the Hero to be repeatedly "called" to the Adventure that he continues to refuse. Each Call and Refusal must escalate the stakes, until the Hero has no choice but to accept the Call.

MEETING THE MENTOR

The Hero Meets a Mentor to gain confidence, insight, advice, training, or magical gifts to overcome the initial fears and face the Threshold of the adventure.

A Hero may not wish to rush into a Special World blindly and, therefore, seeks the experience and wisdom of someone who has been there before. This Mentor has survived to provide the essential lessons and training needed to better face the Journey's Tests and Ordeals. The Mentor may be a physical person, or an object such as a map, a logbook, or hieroglyphics. In Westerns and Detective stories, the Hero may hold an Inner Mentor, a strong code of honor or justice that guides him through the Journey.

CROSSING THE THRESHOLD

Crossing the Threshold signifies that the Hero has finally committed to the Journey. He is prepared to cross the gateway that separates the Ordinary World from the Special World. The Crossing may require more than accepting one's fears, a map, or a swift kick in the rear from a Mentor. The Hero must confront an event that forces him to commit to entering the Special World, from which there is no turning back.

The Event will re-establish the Central Dramatic Question that propels the story forward. The Event will directly affect the Hero, raising the stakes and forcing some action.

Outside forces may push the Hero ahead, such as an abduction of someone close to the Hero (*The Searchers*). A Chase may push the Hero to the brink, presenting no choice but to commit (*Some Like It Hot*). The Hero's place in his Ordinary World may be usurped by a penguin (*The Wrong Trousers*), or the Hero may cross the Threshold with guns blazing and whip cracking (*Raiders of the Lost Ark*).

Internal forces may also push the Hero to accept his Special World. Conrad finally decides to see a therapist (*Ordinary People*). Belle sacrifices herself in exchange for her father's freedom (*Beauty and the Beast*). Alvy and Annie agree to go out on their first date (*Annie Hall*).

TESTS, ALLIES, ENEMIES

Having crossed the Threshold, the Hero faces Tests, encounters Allies, confronts Enemies, and learns the rules of this Special World. This Stage is important for Hero and Audience alike. Whether entering the imaginary world of a future society or the emotional realm of romantic love, the Test Stage is our first look at the Special World and how its conditions and inhabitants contrast with the Hero's Ordinary World.

The Hero needs to find out who can be trusted. Allies are earned, a Sidekick may join up, or an entire Hero Team forged. Enemies and Villains are encountered. A Rival to the Hero's goal may reveal himself.

The Hero must prepare himself for the greater Ordeals yet to come and needs this Stage to Test his skills and powers, or perhaps seek further training from the Mentor. This Initiation into the Special World also Tests the Hero's commitment to the Journey, and questions whether he can succeed.

APPROACH TO THE INMOST CAVE

The Hero must make the preparations needed to Approach the Inmost Cave that leads to the Journey's heart, or central Ordeal. Maps may be reviewed, attacks planned, a reconnaissance launched, and possibly the Enemy's forces whittled down, before the Hero can face his greatest fear or the supreme danger lurking in the Special World. The confident Hero may bypass these preparations and make a bold Approach to the Inmost Cave.

The Hero has survived his descent into the Special World. He has earned his place and may need to take a break for a cigarette, a joke, or a romance, before facing the Ordeal. A Hero's Team may have hit setbacks during the Tests, and the Approach is necessary to reorganize the depleted ranks, remember the dead and wounded, and rekindle morale with a Hero's or Mentor's rally cry.

The Approach may signal a Ticking Clock or a heightening of the stakes. In Romantic Comedy, the Approach may force the lovers to question commitment; one partner may express the need for marriage.

THE ORDEAL

The Hero engages in the Ordeal, the central life-or-death crisis, during which he faces his greatest fear, confronts his most difficult challenge, and experiences "death". His Journey teeters on the brink of failure. Indy and Marion are sealed in the Well of the Souls; Annie and Alvy have broken up. And the audience watches in suspense wondering whether the Hero will survive. The Ordeal is the central, essential, and magical Stage of any Journey. Only through "death" can the Hero be reborn, experiencing a resurrection that grants greater powers or insight to see the Journey to the end.

The Hero may directly taste death, or witness the death of an Ally or Mentor or, even worse, directly cause that death. The Ordeal may pit Hero against Shadow or Villain, and the Hero's failure heightens the stakes and questions the Journey's success (*Die Hard*). The Hero may have the power to defeat a Villain in the Ordeal, only to have to face greater forces in the Journey's second half.

In Romantic Comedies, death can mean the break-up of the relationship. In Romance, a Crisis of the Heart can be a love scene—the physical act of love is a type of "death" or surrender. The Crisis of the Heart can also be a moment when a Shapeshifting lover suddenly reveals a dark side that attempts to destroy the Hero (*Casablanca*).

REWARD

The Hero has survived death, overcome his greatest fear, slain the dragon, or weathered the Crisis of the Heart, and now earns the Reward that he sought. The Hero's Reward comes in many forms: a magical sword, an elixir, greater knowledge or insight, reconciliation with a lover. Whatever the treasure, the Hero has earned the right to celebrate. Celebration not only allows the Hero to replenish his or her energy, but also gives the audience a moment to catch their breath before the Journey resumes to its climax and resolution.

The Hero may have earned the Reward outright, or the Hero may have seen no option but to steal it. The Hero may rationalize this Elixir theft, having paid for it with the Tests and Ordeals thus far. But the consequences of the theft must be confronted as the Shadow forces race to reclaim the Elixir that must not see the light of the Ordinary World.

THE ROAD BACK

The Hero must finally recommit to completing the Journey and accept the Road Back to the Ordinary World. A Hero's success in the Special World may make it difficult to return. Like Crossing the Threshold, The Road Back, needs an event that will push the Hero through the Threshold, back into the Ordinary World.

The Event should re-establish the Central Dramatic Question, pushing the Hero to action and heightening the stakes. Like any strong turning point, the action initiating the Road Back could change the direction of the story. The Hero may need a force to Chase her out of the Special World (*Thelma and Louise*). A Ticking Clock threatening destruction or death in the Ordinary World may be set in motion (*Home Alone*). The Villain may have recovered the Elixir and must be stopped (*Raiders of the Lost Ark*).

The Event may be an internal decision that must be made by the Hero. In Comedies, a Hero may be trying to juggle conflicting Journeys, and one must finally be sacrificed (*Some Like It Hot*). In Romance and Action Adventure, the Road Back may be a moment when the Hero must choose between the Journey of a Higher Cause versus the personal Journey of the Heart (*Beauty and the Beast*).

THE RESURRECTION

The Hero faces the Resurrection, his most dangerous meeting with death. This final life-and-death Ordeal shows that the Hero has maintained and can apply all that he has brought back to the Ordinary World.

This Ordeal and Resurrection can represent a "cleansing" or purification that must occur now that the Hero has emerged from the land of the dead. The Hero is reborn or transformed with the attributes of his Ordinary self in addition to the lessons and insights from the characters that he has met along the road.

The Resurrection may be a physical Ordeal, or final showdown between Hero and Shadow; however, the Ticking Clock of the Road Back has been set. This battle is for much more than the Hero's life. Other lives, or an entire world may be at stake and the Hero must now prove that he has achieved Heroic Status and willingly accept his sacrifice for the benefit of the Ordinary World.

Other Allies may come to the last-minute rescue to lend assistance, but in the end the Hero must rise to the sacrifice at hand. He must deliver the blow that destroys the Death Star (*Star Wars*), or offer his hand and accept the "magic" Elixir of love (*Sleepless in Seattle*).

RETURN WITH THE ELIXIR

The Return with the Elixir is the final Reward earned on the Hero's Journey. The Hero has been resurrected, purified and has earned the right to be accepted back into the Ordinary World and share the Elixir of the Journey. The true Hero returns with an Elixir to share with others or heal a wounded land. The Elixir can be a great treasure or magic potion. It could be love, wisdom, or simply the experience of surviving the Special World. Even the tragic end of a Hero's Journey can yield the best Elixir of all, granting the audience greater awareness of us and our world (*Citizen Kane*). The Hero may show the benefit of the Elixir, using it to heal a physical or emotional wound, or accomplish tasks that had been feared in the Ordinary World. The Return signals a time when we distribute rewards and punishments, or celebrate the Journey's end with revelry or marriage.

The Elixir may bring closure to the Journey and restore balance to the Ordinary World. Possibly it poses questions and ambiguities that continue the Journey beyond the final "fade out".

In most tales, the Return with the Elixir completes the cycle of this particular Journey. Story lines have been resolved, balance has been restored to the Ordinary World, and the Hero may now embark on a new life, forever influenced by the Journey traveled.

ARCHETYPES: THE ROLES CHARACTERS PLAY

> *"All the world's a stage*
> *And all the men and women merely players:*
> *They have their exits and entrances;*
> *And one man in his time plays many parts."*
>
> William Shakespeare (*As You Like It*)

Archetypes describe the function or role a character plays in a story. Think of the Archetype as a mask a character wears in a particular scene. One character may serve primarily as the Mentor of a tale, wearing that single mask for the majority of the Journey. But, just as we play many roles in our lifetime, or even change masks in a given day, a story's characters have the potential to wear any of the Archetypal masks depending upon the demands of the story. Obi Wan Kenobi is the Mentor throughout *Star Wars*, and yet he must wear the Hero's mask and sacrifice himself to Darth Vader in order to allow Luke to escape with the princess. In some stories, like the one told in *Casablanca*, a single Archetypal mask may be handed from one character to the next. Although Rick is the central character and can be considered our Hero, the Hero's mask is passed from Victor Lazlo to Ilsa before she gives it to Rick, who finally wears it to the journey's end.

What follows is an overview of the Archetypes that occur most frequently. The Archetypes and an action describing their primary function are:

1. Hero "to serve and sacrifice"
2. Mentor "to guide"
3. Threshold Guardian "to test"
4. Herald "to warn and challenge"
5. Shapeshifter "to question and deceive"
6. Shadow "to destroy"
7. Trickster "to disrupt"

When placing these masks on your characters, ask yourself the following:

- What is the character's function on the Journey?
- What is the character's goal?
- What action should the character take to achieve that goal?

THE HERO

"to serve and sacrifice"

The Hero is our protagonist, or central character, whose primary purpose is to separate from the Ordinary World and sacrifice himself for the service of the Journey at hand—to answer the challenge, complete the quest and restore the Ordinary World's balance. The Hero's Journey may be a challenge of personal growth: to win a competition, to heal a wound, or to find love. Heroes may also need to answer Calls to Adventure where physical lives and even the fate of the world are at stake. These Heroes must learn to accept the sacrifice of life and limb for the service of others.

Since we experience the Journey through the eyes of the Hero, we must be able to relate to him or her on some level. The Hero must be driven by universal needs: to find love, to succeed, to right a wrong, to seek justice. These drives are connected to the Hero's Inner and Outer Problems that need to be solved. The audience can relate to a Hero's idiosyncrasies, quirks, vices and deepest fears, while wanting to emulate the Hero's admirable qualities.

The Hero doesn't have to be all good. Some of our most endearing Heroes are actually Antiheroes, Outlaws and Loner Heroes who live by their own rules and consistently "buck the system."

The Hero usually grows and learns the most during the Journey. And although the Hero may be reluctant and make excuses, and even have to react to events that surround him, by the Journey's end he has become active, driven by his undying conviction to succeed.

MENTOR

"to guide"

An essential Archetype, the Mentor provides motivation, insights and training to help the Hero overcome his doubts and fears and prepare for the Journey. Often the Mentor has traveled the road before and can provide needed guidance to a Hero who is reluctant to face the unknown. If the Hero proves his commitment, the Mentor may reward him with magical gifts (a weapon, clothing, piece of advice, or a key) that will help him on the Journey ahead. The Mentor might present a powerful magical gift to lure the Hero to accept the challenge.

The Heroes of Westerns, as well as detective and noir Thrillers, may not have a physical Mentor, but instead may be guided by an Inner Mentor, a code of honor or justice that must be served.

THRESHOLD GUARDIAN

"to test"

Threshold Guardians protect the Special World and its secrets from the Hero, and provide essential Tests to prove a Hero's commitment and worth. The Hero must bypass these obstacles, and use any method available: ignoring, outwitting, overcoming, appeasing, or befriending.

Threshold Guardians may be characters, a locked door or secret vault, an animal, or a force of nature such as a tornado.

HERALD

"to warn and challenge"

Herald characters issue challenges and announce the coming of significant change. They can make their appearance anytime during a Journey, but often appear at the beginning of the Journey to announce the Call to Adventure. A character may wear the Herald's mask to make an announcement or judgment, report a news flash, or simply deliver a letter. The Herald can reside within the Hero in the form of dreams and visions that push the Hero to change his life. An external event, such as a declaration of war or a storm, can serve the Herald's agenda. Whatever the form, the Herald is needed to present the challenge, and get the story rolling.

SHAPESHIFTER

"to question and deceive"

The Shapeshifter mask misleads the Hero by hiding a character's intentions and loyalties. The Shapeshifter's presence surfaces doubts and questions in the Hero's mind, and can effectively infuse suspense. In Romance and Romantic Comedy, the Shapeshifter mask is often worn by the opposite sex.

SHADOW

"to destroy"

The Shadow can represent our darkest desires, our untapped resources, or even rejected qualities. It can also symbolize our greatest fears and phobias. To use *Star Wars* as an example, the Shadow is the Dark Side, personified by Darth Vader. Since the Shadow is a reflection of the Hero's qualities, it may represent positive qualities that the Tragic or Loner Hero may have suppressed or rejected. Shadows may not be all bad, and may reveal admirable, even redeeming qualities.

The Hero's enemies and villains often wear the Shadow mask. This physical force is determined to destroy the Hero and his cause. Or the Shadow may be an inner demon lurking within ourselves that must be accepted or purged. In *Unforgiven,* Will Munny constantly tempts his Inner Shadow as a bloodthirsty gunslinger.

TRICKSTER

"to disrupt"

The Marx Brothers are the embodiment of the Trickster. They relish the disruption of the status quo, turning the Ordinary World into chaos with their quick turns of phrase and physical antics. Although they may not change during the course of their Journeys, their world and its inhabitants are transformed by their antics. The Trickster uses laughter to make characters see the absurdity of the situation, and perhaps force a change.

The Trickster mask is often worn by the Sidekick in Westerns and the Mentor in Romantic Comedies (the best friend always offering comic advice to the lovelorn). In Action Adventure, the Hero may briefly don the Trickster mask to outwit or disarm a villain or enemy; while in Comedy, the Hero may rely on this mask throughout the Journey.

The Trickster's voice can be the most sane and reliable in the confusion of the Journey, as we see with the Trickster Old Mose in *The Searchers.*

THE MYTHIC STRUCTURE OF ACTION ADVENTURE

Danger lurks at every bend and the Shadow's Guardians abound to keep us from the Elixir. Whether our Special Powers are quick hands, a razor tongue, or just sheer determination, we will overcome the odds. We may have entered this Journey for personal desires but in the end we must make the selfless sacrifice or our Ordinary World will fall to the Shadow's ultimate plan of evil.

"I DON'T KNOW, I'M MAKING THIS UP AS I GO."

Action and Adventure lend themselves perfectly to the most important purpose of the movie-going experience: to escape into the screen world and live vicariously through the eyes and deeds of the Hero. Action Adventure satisfies the armchair adventurer in all of us, transporting us into exotic worlds where we accomplish unimaginable feats, win true love, cheat death and finally vanquish the Shadow, affirming our faith that, in the end, Good does indeed triumph over Evil.

We too easily attach the Hero's Journey paradigm solely to this genre, a myopia that spawns several problems. First, we limit the mythic power that transcends genre. And of course, exploring the universality of the paradigm is the purpose of this book. Secondly, we see the Journey's signposts as purely physical stages overlooking the emotional Journey that an Action Adventure Hero may need to accept. Character Arcs are not limited to Drama, Romance, and Thrillers. Although the recurring or series Action Adventure Hero (e.g., James Bond, Batman) does not require internal character change, some of our most memorable adventures show Wounded Heroes sacrificing themselves for the benefit of society *and* earning the personal Elixir of wholeness. Which brings us to the third problem, that as writers we tend to overlook the importance of character when creating the Action Adventure film. The writer focuses on the spectacle, the "wow" moments—essential moments in an *action* film. Or the writer turns the Hero's Journey into a rigid template for structure. A writer who builds story without regard to the influence of character fails to realize that two richly fleshed-out characters like Indiana Jones and John McClane will attack the same Journey in two very different ways. Story and character fuel each other to create your unique cinema vision.

THE WORLDS OF ADVENTURE AND ACTION

Although I bridge Action and Adventure as one genre, the two story worlds can be as different as Errol Flynn's *Robin Hood* is from *Under Siege.* No doubt you will find wonderful stories that effectively integrate elements from both worlds. Please use the following as guidelines to explore your story's world rather than rules that impede your storytelling.

The essence of the Adventure Film (including High Adventure):

- The story is set during historic periods in exotic locales.
- The Adventure Hero accepts a Quest that will bring greater good to his Ordinary World.
- The Adventure Hero has Special Powers that qualify him to be sought for the Journey. (Government Officials seek Indiana Jones because he is an archeologist and expert in the occult.) For the first-time Adventure Hero or Apprentice Hero, the Special Powers may be discovered along the Journey's road, or nurtured by a Mentor.
- The Hero's Quest is linked to and yet overshadowed by an overriding world conflict (i.e., war, revolution, or disaster.)
- The Elixir gained by the Hero solves the Journey at hand and *may* additionally contribute to solving the greater world conflict.
- Allies and love interests, all usually less qualified for the Adventure, may tag along with the Hero. These Allies can serve as Threshold Guardians, showing reluctance and reminding the Hero of the Journey's dangers.

The essence of the Action Film:

- Stories are set in contemporary times in lands that are closer to our Ordinary World (i.e., a 40-story high-rise, the dusty Oklahoma back roads, the urban streets.)
- The Action Hero is placed in a situation that he or she must escape. (John McClane did not choose to battle terrorists. Thelma never asked to be raped.)
- The Action Hero doesn't need someone to tell him how dangerous the Journey is. He knows the danger and he's not above showing fear or reluctance.
- The Action Hero's Journey usually does not have world ramifications. Instead, the Action Hero may have an additional inner Journey that involves personal awareness and healing.
- The Action Hero does not necessarily have Special Powers. Audiences enjoy identifying with the Ordinary Hero thrown into extraordinary circumstances and fueled by sheer will and unshakable conviction.

Within these worlds, a wide variety of stories can be told: the quest (*Raiders of the Lost Ark, Treasure of the Sierra Madre*), the chase (*Thelma and Louise*), defense (*Seven Samurai*), and revenge (*Braveheart*).

THE HERO'S TWO GOALS

The Action and Adventure Hero takes two Journeys:

1) The Journey of the Higher Cause is the Action or Adventure plot at hand. Will McClane defeat the terrorists? Will Thelma and Louise escape to Mexico? Will the samurai protect the village from the brigands?

2) The Journey of Personal Growth can be a romantic subplot that reveals itself during the Journey of the Higher Cause (*Raiders of the Lost Ark*). It could be the initial and intended Journey that is suddenly derailed by the demands of the Higher Cause (*Die Hard*). Sometimes, the Hero's Personal Journey becomes the Higher Cause by journey's end (*Thelma and Louise*).

Similar to the Romance Hero, at some point during the course of the Journey, the Action Adventure Hero may need to sacrifice the Personal Journey for the Higher Cause.

THE SELFLESS HERO

In order for the Hero to accomplish the Higher Cause, he must accept the sacrifice of his own needs, and perhaps his life, for the benefit of his Ordinary World. Only with this offering can one be Resurrected as a true selfless Hero. These sacrificial moments do not necessarily occur at Journey's end. Indiana Jones sacrifices love for the Ark several times during his journey. During the course of his physical ordeals, John McClane realizes how badly he's treated his wife. This Reward grants him the strength to now sacrifice himself for the Journey of the Higher Cause of foiling Gruber's plot. Samurai Kambei's selfless sacrifice to the Higher Cause earns the respect needed to secure his samurai team. Whenever the sacrifice happens, once committed to the Higher Cause, this Selfless Hero must be a driven warrior, ferociously determined to use all powers and resources to claim the Elixir.

ORDEALS . . . AND MORE ORDEALS

The stages of the Hero's Journey are typically Ordeals, brushes with death. The Hero may face death personally or taste death when an Ally or love interest dies along the road. The Hero may cheat death during the initial Call to Adventure (*Die Hard*), or when he or she passes through the Threshold (*Raiders of the Lost Ark*). The Test Phase may present a series of Ordeals that Test the Hero's commitment to the Journey, and question whether or not he is strong enough to defeat the Evil. But Action Adventure is not all Ordeals.

2194756

THE PREPARATION CAN BE JUST AS IMPORTANT AS THE THRILLS

Pacing can be one of the most important elements of the Action Adventure Film. The Action Adventure audience anticipates excitement and thrills. With greater, more sophisticated special effects, the audience is hungrier for greater action set pieces, daring-do stunts, and explosions. But explosions can be easily misused. A filmmaker who neglects characters we care for in favor of non-stop pyrotechnics can overwhelm, numb or nauseate an audience. Perhaps the "E-ticket" or Roller Coaster Ride is an appropriate metaphor. But a good theme ride gives you anticipation and suspense before the thrills.

The Approach and the Reward, the Stages that frame each Ordeal, are as important as the actual brush with death. Rewards from Ordeals yield greater awareness of the Goal, forcing new strategies that the Hero applies at the next Approach. As you explore these sample films, see how Approaches and Rewards are used to reveal characters, promote suspense and anticipation, or simply give the audience and the Hero a needed moment to recover.

THE FINAL CONFLICT OF GOOD AND EVIL

The Journeys of Action and Adventure end with a final physical battle of Good and Evil, Hero and Shadow. This showdown is the heart of the genre, for it meets the Audience expectations that in the end the Hero survives and the villain must be punished. Good triumphs over Evil.

Although Allies may have their moments of victory, Evil eventually falls by the actions of the Hero. A Hero may be thrust unwillingly onto a Journey where he must react to every move the Shadow makes, but in the end the Hero must take action and slay the dragon. John McClane alone saves his wife and defeats Gruber. Kambei and his samurai kill every brigand in order to protect the town. Thelma and Louise choose to drive into the Grand Canyon and freedom. Even Indiana Jones is smarter than his Shadow and keeps his eyes closed during the unveiling of the Ark.

GENRE CHALLENGES: ACTION ADVENTURE

1. The Action Adventure Hero can be Reluctant and show great fear. How does fear make you feel about the Hero? How is the Hero's fear established and effectively used in *Raiders of the Lost Ark* and *Die Hard*?
2. What does the ending in *Thelma and Louise* signify? What is their Journey's Elixir?
3. In *Seven Samurai,* the Mentor/Hero Kambei is a Gentleman Hero, dedicated to one single Journey: to protect the village because it is the right thing to do. Does the Gentleman Hero work today, or do today's heroes necessarily need a "wound" to heal?

4. In what ways are John McClane and Hans Gruber opposites, Hero and Shadow? How are their contrasts communicated with their speech, their backgrounds, the clothes they wear, and the way they fight their battles?
5. In *Treasure of the Sierra Madre*, do you identify with Fred C. Dobbs? Why, or why not? What are the Personal Journeys of each member of the Hero Team and how do they support or conflict with the Journey of the Higher Cause?
6. Using the sample films, how are Mentors used in Action Adventure?
7. Choose your favorite Action Adventure film and analyze it using the elements of the Hero's Journey. Are stages missing from your film's Journey? Are they missed? What are the memorable moments in the film? Do they represent a Stage of the Journey?

THE TREASURE OF THE SIERRA MADRE
(U.S., 1948)

"As long as there is no find, the noble brotherhood will last. But when the piles of gold begin to grow, that is when the trouble starts."

—Howard (Walter Huston)

Screenplay by John Huston
Based on the novel by B. Traven
Directed by John Huston

Two American drifters team up with an eccentric prospector on a search for gold in the Mexican mountains.

LANDMARKS OF THE JOURNEY

The Treasure of the Sierra Madre weaves the ultimate tale of greed, depicting how it destroys not only a man's soul but the Hero's Team. In other movies we see the Hero Team fight the physical Shadow on the quest to obtain the Elixir (see *Jaws, Unforgiven*). Allies may fall; others, turn back from fear. One Hero rises to vanquish the Shadow and share the Elixir for the benefit of the Ordinary World. Dobbs, Curtin, and the old prospector, Howard, face their share of physical enemies and shadows, but none more deadly than the inner Shadow of greed. The Hero Team begins to crumble when they discover gold, crossing the Threshold and becoming "men of property." Although the Mentor, Howard, tries to keep the Team together, he realizes that he's no match for this Shadow. On "traditional" Hero's Journeys, the Mentor must leave the quest, forcing the Hero to assimilate the Mentor's "gifts" and alone prove himself worthy of true heroic status. Here, in similar tradition, Howard regretfully leaves the team, presenting a final Test that sets the Road Back in motion. Without their Mentor, the Shadow of greed vanquishes Dobbs, allowing Curtin to rise as the Hero, forsaking the gold in favor of a greater Elixir to bring back to a richer Ordinary World.

THE JOURNEY

Mexico. February 1925. Fred C. Dobbs is a mangy, American drifter. His prospects haven't panned out, and now Dobbs resorts to panhandling and gambling what little he can afford on lottery tickets. Ashamed of his ORDINARY WORLD, Dobbs can't even look his benefactors in the eye, and he's pushed to change, a CALL TO ADVENTURE, when he "puts the bite" three times on the same man (the HERALD "White Suit").

Dobbs accepts a construction job offered by a contractor, McCormick, a CALL TO ADVENTURE, and soon meets a fellow drifter, Curtin. At the completion of the job, the

SHAPESHIFTER McCormick dupes them out of their pay, teaching them that nobody can be trusted.

Dobbs and Curtin pool what little money they have for a couple of beds in a flophouse where they overhear an eccentric old man, Howard, talking about his adventures as a prospector. He lures Dobbs and Curtin with his tales and knowledge that a nearby mountain is "waiting for the right guy to discover her treasure." But this CALL for wealth and adventure is a double-edged sword. The wise old MENTOR warns them of what lust for gold can do to a man's soul.

On a morning refreshed by dreams of gold-covered mountains, Curtin and Dobbs reject Howard's Warning that gold can curse a man's soul. They spot McCormick and corner him in a cantina, finally overpowering their ENEMY and taking the money owed them. They decide to use the money to prospect for gold. But before they can commit to the Journey, they need Howard's experience and knowledge and ask him to join the Team. The MENTOR eagerly accepts, but Curtin and Dobbs are still short on money. Dobbs' fortuitous winning lottery ticket provides the needed investment, which he gladly offers for his and Curtin's share in the stake. Dobbs shakes Curtin's hand, entering the THRESHOLD of partnership as they commit to finding the gold. But MENTOR Howard watches them, fully aware of what gold can do to this "brotherhood."

This Initial TEST PHASE is part of an extended THRESHOLD SEQUENCE as the HERO TEAM finally enters the SPECIAL WORLD as "men of property." First, Mexican Bandits led by "Gold Hat" attack their train. The TEAM bands together fighting off the ENEMY, killing several bandits. In Durango, they purchase supplies and burros, and the store-owner (THRESHOLD GUARDIAN) warns them of the dangers that lie ahead (a type of REFUSAL).

Later, Dobbs and Curtin are TESTED by the arduous work of the Journey; they can barely keep up with Howard. On their trail the TEAM also confronts nature's THRESHOLD GUARDIANS: fierce northern winds and dense jungles. These TESTS exhaust poor Dobbs, who wants to turn around. Howard mocks him and Dobbs threatens to kill this apparently crazed MENTOR. But the cackling HERALD finally announces they've found gold. Sure enough, he shows them the gold sand with his mining pan, and assures them that the mountain above them is rich. He finally asks them how they feel "to be men of property." This moment completes the THRESHOLD SEQUENCE.

The TEAM enters their Journey's second TEST PHASE, a series of physical and psychological trials testing the strength of their "brotherhood." Of course, they must begin by retrieving the gold from the mountain, and they build a sluice to do just that. That night, they watch Howard weigh their day's work—$5000 worth. Against the MENTOR'S warnings, Dobbs insists that they divide the gold as they go, making each responsible for his own share.

Curtin faces the next TEST when he sees the mine collapse on Dobbs. He knows Dobbs is trapped inside and hesitates a moment—TESTING his own greed. Curtin's humanity wins out, and he rescues Dobbs. His action lifts him above the TESTS and ORDEALS, allowing the audience to begin to identify with him as the Journey's HERO.

During a campfire scene (an APPROACH), their differences become more distinct as they discuss what they'll do with their ELIXIR of wealth. Howard plans to retire from prospecting and run a small business. Curtin wants to grow fruit trees. In contrast, Dobbs desires immediate pleasure—a Turkish bath, a great meal, and a woman.

Dobbs is failing the TEST PHASE, transforming him into Curtin's SHADOWY reflection. Overcome by paranoia and greed, he begins to talk to himself and REFUSES to ride alone into town for supplies, fearing the double-cross or bandits. Dobbs catches Curtin trying to roll the rock that hides his stash. He won't believe Curtin's story that he was trying to unearth a deadly Gila Monster and threatens to kill him. Howard and Curtin contain Dobbs and reveal the Gila Monster sitting atop Dobbs' gold.

In town to get supplies, Curtin meets another American, Cody, who asks about gold prospecting. Curtin tells this perceived ENEMY he wouldn't know—he's hunting animals. Cody doesn't believe this THRESHOLD GURADIAN and follows his trail.

Cody arrives at their campfire. Dobbs reluctantly invites him to enjoy the fire, but he wants him gone in the morning. Cody suspects their gold mine and refuses to leave. He gives them three options: to kill him, run him off, or take him as a partner. The three choose to kill him to protect their shares of the gold, an APPROACH. They go to the ridge to kill Cody, but the ENEMY dons the HERALD'S mask and warns them of the approaching Bandits. Faced with this impending ORDEAL, the TEAM needs as many guns as possible and enlists Cody as a scout (making him an ALLY).

Gold Hat and his bandits approach the camp and negotiate for guns. Dobbs rejects the leader, shooting a hole in his hat. Guns blaze, and Cody is killed during this ORDEAL. Before the Bandits can renew an attack, Federales chase them off. Dobbs is elated (their RESURRECTION).

They prepare to bury Cody and discover a letter from his wife swaying him to return home to his family, where "we've already found life's real treasure." Acknowledging Cody's REFUSAL of this ELIXIR, and having faced death in the ORDEAL, the TEAM'S REWARD is greater awareness that perhaps they've taken enough gold and can prepare for their ROAD BACK to civilization. Although this moment is a physical ROAD BACK, the TEAM must face a more difficult ROAD BACK further down the Journey of Greed.

That night, Curtin suggests giving a share to Cody's family, but Dobbs rejects this REWARD. The decision again delineates the polarity between gracious Curtin (HERO) and greedy Dobbs (SHADOW).

A band of Mexicans pulls Howard from the TEAM to save a little boy's life. He is treated as a HERO and medicine man (MENTOR), and receives the additional REWARD of the Mexicans' hospitality; however, he must trust Dobbs and Curtin with his share until the three can meet again in Durango.

Without MENTOR Howard, Dobbs and Curtin must make it back without his voice of experience to keep them together. The two face each other at the darkest moment of their Journey, the ORDEAL. Seeing his former friend as a SHADOW scheming to kill him in his sleep, Dobbs shoots Curtin. But now Dobbs wrestles with a new MENTOR, his conscience, a REWARD that is rejected by the SHADOW of Greed. Dobbs leaves Curtin's body until morning. But Curtin's wound isn't fatal and he crawls away (a RESURRECTION).

The TEAM'S initial THRESHOLD into this SPECIAL WORLD meant a binding of the three. Their ROAD BACK is the Team's unraveling, where one of them, greedy Dobbs, takes the gold and runs. Dobbs awakens to bury Curtin, and discovers the body gone. He tries to contain his paranoia and rationalizes that a tiger dragged the corpse away. Dobbs packs up all the loot and takes his ROAD BACK home.

Meanwhile, Curtin finds salvation at the Mexican village, his REWARD. He's taken to Howard who heals his wounds. Curtin tells the old man about Dobbs' treachery. The two are determined to retrieve their gold and must take the ROAD BACK. The CHASE begins.

Exhausted and parched, Dobbs finally stumbles onto some water where he confronts the ENEMY, Gold Hat and his bandits. Greed has finally taken Dobbs down the road to a lonely, pitiful death. The bandits kill Dobbs with a machete and dump his bags of gold, believing that it's sand. Wearing Dobbs' clothes, they try to sell the burros and are promptly arrested by Federales.

Howard and Curtin arrive as they hear the execution of the Bandits. They also find out that Dobbs is dead. They check his supplies, but there's no sign of the gold. A boy tells them where the bags are located.

Fighting fierce winds (Nature's THRESHOLD GUARDIAN), they find the torn bags but the Great Northern Wind has swept every ounce of gold back to where they found it.

Howard guffaws at the joke nature has played on them, and soon Curtin shares his laughter. Nature has destroyed the fruit of their hard work, their perceived ELIXIR, but the two are RESURRECTED with greater awareness of the poison of greed that killed Dobbs. Both will carry this true ELIXIR back to their ORDINARY WORLD. Howard can live with his Mexican family as their Medicine Man. He gives Curtin his share of supplies so Curtin can return to Cody's widow in time for the July fruit harvest. They exchange "good luck." Both return to a peaceful life, "rich" with "life's real treasures."

FADE OUT

SEVEN SAMURAI
(Japan, 1954)

"If you defend for all, each individual will be protected. He who thinks only for himself destroys himself."

—Samurai leader Kambei
(Takashi Shimura)

Written by Shinobu Hashimoto, Hideo Oguni, and Akira Kurosawa
Directed by Akira Kurosawa

The farmers of a small village hire samurai to defend themselves and their crops from brigands.

LANDMARKS OF THE JOURNEY

Rarely do we see the Gentleman Hero in contemporary Action Adventure. Not that Stallone, Willis, and Schwarzenegger are not gentlemen. But the Gentleman Hero of old has been resurrected into the Wounded Hero, a man (or woman) with a past, a ghost that drives him through the Journey. The Gentleman Hero is the Knight who slays the dragon and saves the princess because he stands by his Code of Honor, not because the dragon toasted his mother for breakfast. In Kurosawa's epic adventure, the Gentleman Hero, samurai leader Kambei, protects the village because it is the right thing to do. Nothing more. And it is his conviction and his honor that impress the other samurai to join his cause.

THE JOURNEY

16th Century. Japan is in the middle of a civil war. Every year, marauding brigands disrupt the ORDINARY WORLD of the villagers, who need to protect themselves, their homes, and their crops (their OUTER PROBLEM). Brigands arrive at the ridge overlooking one village. This SHADOW'S leader realizes they recently looted these farmers, and an attack now would be fruitless. They decide to come back after the barley harvest. A farmer overhears the brigands' plan to return (CALL TO ADVENTURE), and warns the village.

The villagers are RELUCTANT to fight the brigands. They seek advice from the Old Man who lives in the Mill. This MENTOR advises that they hire samurai to protect them. Although they are poor farmers, they can hire hungry samurai and offer three meals, a place to sleep, and the fun of fighting in payment for protection.

Two farmers enter this THRESHOLD and go to town to find samurai. They witness samurai Kambei rescue a young boy taken hostage by a thief. Impressed by Kambei's selfless act of heroism, they ask him to help protect their village. A HERO and MENTOR, Kambei considers their CALL TO ADVENTURE, but is RELUCTANT to do battle with the expected army of 30 brigands. He estimates that seven samurai would be needed to properly defend the village, and REFUSES their offer. Later, he learns that the farmers would be giving the samurai the last of their rice while they suffer eating millet. Moved by their sacrifice, Kambei agrees to their offer, initiating his THRESHOLD.

The initial TEST PHASE, the gathering of the samurai, is part of the overall THRESHOLD SEQUENCE which is completed when the samurai arrive in the village. Kambei and "disciple" Katsushiro enlist their band of seven HEROES: Kambei's old friend, Shichiroji; newfound friend, Gorobei; samurai-turned-woodcutter, Heihachi; master swordsman, Kyuzo; and finally the TRICKSTER HERO, Kikuchiyo.

The HERO TEAM soon passes THROUGH THE THRESHOLD, and arrives in an unsettling "empty" village. The farmers have closed themselves up in fear of the samurai. Although hired as HEROES to protect them, the samurai are also seen as ENEMIES who will lure away their daughters.

The samurai cannot coax the farmers out of their homes and Kikuchiyo sounds a false alarm that sends the farmers scurrying for the samurai's help. The TRICKSTER mocks the villagers for so quickly turning—treating them first as the "plague," and now worshipping them as saviors.

The main TEST PHASE of the Journey includes all the preparations the samurai make in defending the town against the threat of attack. The HERO TEAM must "enter the skins" of their SHADOWS to determine how the brigands will attack.

- They scout the terrain and layout of the village.
- They build fortifications: a fence, a moat.
- They train the villagers to defend themselves.
- They convince the villagers to sacrifice the Old Mill and several farms located outside the village's perimeter.

The barley harvest runs smoothly, and the farmers question whether the brigands will attack. But Kambei warns that "danger strikes when everything looks safe." With the preparations complete, they APPROACH THE INMOST CAVE.

The brigands send three scouts on horseback who spot the samurai and gallop off to warn the others. The samurai race after them, kill two of the scouts and question the third, securing important information about the weaknesses of the brigand's fort. The samurai decide to storm the fort to decrease the ENEMY'S numbers.

Three samurai, and farmer Rikichi, face this ORDEAL and burn the fort—killing several of the brigands—though Samurai Heihachi is killed.

The samurai and the villagers mourn Heihachi's death. The loss of the seventh samurai has plunged the village back into despair; the village's safety is in question. They are at the greatest distance from their ORDINARY WORLD. But Trickster Kikuchiyo snatches the samurai banner and displays it from the rooftop, rallying the samurai and villagers (a RESURRECTION) as the brigands approach. Farmer and samurai work together to man their battle stations (the REWARD).

The first major battle sequence TESTS the samurai's defenses. As MENTOR/HERO Kambei intended, the new fortifications redirect the brigands to the north where the samurai plans to lure the SHADOW'S forces, one by one, into the village.

Tragedy strikes when the brigands burn the mill, the ORDEAL. The Old Man perishes. Kikuchiyo tries to save the daughter but she's killed, leaving her son in Kikuchiyo's arms, a remembrance of his own ORDEAL as a child.

That night as the ORDEAL continues, the villagers rise to the battle, their RESURRECTION. Farmer Rikichi impresses the samurai by killing several brigands who try to cross the moat.

Surviving the night's ORDEAL, they successfully launch Kambei's plan and defeat several brigands (the REWARD). But they suffer a setback, the death of Samurai Gorobei.

Night. Only thirteen ENEMY remain. Kambei grants the REWARD of rest in anticipation of the morning's decisive battle. This ROAD BACK SEQUENCE is an emotional time of preparation, to spend time with loved ones and to respect those who have fallen. They will not be able to win the final battle if the villagers and samurai continue to mistrust each other, so the ROAD BACK becomes an important moment to set aside differences and recommit to the final leg of the Journey. At dawn, Kambei orders that they let all the remaining brigands through the gates, completing the ROAD BACK.

The decisive battle falls in the samurai's favor. The Brigand Chief slips past the ramparts and into one house, where he watches his men die. As the battle ends, master-swordsman Kyuzo is shot by the Brigand Chief. Seeing the death of the bravest samurai, Kikuchiyo rushes the house. He too is fatally shot but overpowers the Chief and runs him through. A farmer's son, Kikuchiyo dies a samurai HERO'S death, the RESURRECTION. At last only riderless horses gallop past; all the bandits have fallen.

The farmers celebrate with music and song as they plant the rice crops. They celebrate the ELIXIR of their survival, and the restored cycle of their crops.

The three samurai survivors, Kambei, Shichiroji, and Katsushiro, look on, alone. Kambei anticipated this response. Again they have survived—and again they have lost, Kambei tells his friend with renewed awareness. He stands by their commitment to the cause of others; the task itself is their ELIXIR. The village stands; the farmers again plant. The surviving samurai will Journey on to other noble causes.

FADE OUT

RAIDERS OF THE LOST ARK
(U.S., 1981)

"You and I are very much alike. Archeology is our religion, yet we have both fallen from the pure faith. Our methods have not differed as much as you pretend. I am a shadowy reflection of you. And it would take only a nudge to make you like me—to push you out of the light."

"Now you're getting nasty."

—Belloq (Paul Freeman) and
Indiana Jones (Harrison Ford)

Screenplay by Lawrence Kasdan
Story by George Lucas and Philip Kaufman
Directed by Steven Spielberg

Globe-trotting archeologist Indiana Jones must thwart Hitler's attempt to find the Ark of the Covenant and harness its mystical powers as a tool of mass destruction.

LANDMARKS OF THE JOURNEY

Great Action Adventure isn't solely action set pieces and thrills (although there's plenty of them here); it's the glue that holds the thrills together. The Action Adventure audience needs moments of reflection, of preparation, or simply to breathe before the next plunge on the roller coaster. And *Raiders* paces this beautifully. Approaches are laced with mystery and suspense (the poisoned dates). And the storytellers are not afraid to use the moments of Reward to grant greater awareness of Heightened Stakes while revealing the humor and humanity as the Journey takes its toll on our modern Swashbuckling Hero, Indiana Jones ("It's not the years, honey; it's the mileage.")

THE JOURNEY

The backdrop is 1936, before the outbreak of the Second World War, when the greatest of cinematic SHADOWS, Hitler and his Nazis, plot world domination.

Dr. Jones leads a double life as brilliant professor of archeology and globetrotting adventurer, his ORDINARY WORLD. Professor Jones is bespectacled and reserved, almost shy, an expert on the occult, yet refuses to believe in magic, "a lot of superstitious hocus-pocus." Indiana Jones is an "obtainer of rare antiquities," and stops at nothing to get a relic. He wields his bullwhip better than most bad guys can handle a gun. Unlike his RIVAL and SHADOW, French archeologist Rene Belloq, Indy believes in the preservation of antiquities.

The opening adventure in South America sets the roller-coaster tone of the entire film, and firmly establishes Indy's skills and determination in his daring-do ORDINARY WORLD. The mini-adventure distills the Hero's Journey to its essence. Indy and his ALLIES have already crossed the THRESHOLD into the SPECIAL WORLD of obtaining a Golden Idol. Since Indiana Jones begins the story as a fully-realized HERO and not an apprentice, there are few TESTS he has to overcome.

The team moves through the dense jungle. A native flees at the revelation of a horrifying stone statue (a REFUSAL that establishes the stakes and Indy's fearlessness.) Indy consults the map (a MENTOR), which unmasks one of the ALLIES. Indy disarms this ENEMY with his bullwhip.

Indy and Satipo pause outside the cave's entrance. During this APPROACH, Indy fills a small bag with sand and voices the dangers ahead. He leads the way into the cave with its spiders and booby traps (THRESHOLD GUARDIANS), finally coming face-to-face with the Golden Idol. Indy replaces the Idol with the bag of sand, the ORDEAL. But he misjudges the weight, triggering the booby traps (even Indy makes mistakes.)

Satipo double-crosses Indy and tries to leave him trapped in the cave. But Indy overcomes these obstacles using his trusty bullwhip. He finds Satipo, the careless victim of a booby trap (he neglected to heed his MENTOR's advice!), and reclaims the idol (the REWARD) just as a huge boulder rumbles toward him (the ROAD BACK) chasing him out of the cave.

Indy lands at the feet of Belloq and his native THRESHOLD GUARDIANS. Belloq takes the idol from Indy, but Indy uses this SHADOW'S need to display his power over the natives to escape. He barely makes it into his departing plane (his RESURRECTION), before finally revealing his greatest fear. He wrestles his pilot's pet snake. Indy's pretty human after all. He curses snakes as he flies off into the distance.

We quickly establish his ORDINARY WORLD in the university classroom. MENTOR Marcus Brody, the curator of the museum, meets Indy after class. Wearing the HERALD'S mask, Brody tells Indy that he's wanted by Army Intelligence.

Indy meets with the Army officials (HERALDS) who reveal that Intelligence has intercepted a Nazi communiqué about the Ark of the Covenant, Ravenswood (Indy's former MENTOR) and the headpiece of the Staff of Ra. They seek answers from Indy, the authority of antiquities. This MEETING WITH THE MENTOR raises their fear that Hitler wants to obtain the Ark of the Covenant and use it as a weapon of mass destruction.

That night, Marcus sees Indy and announces that the government needs him to find the Ark before the Nazis do, Indy's OUTER PROBLEM. Indy eagerly accepts the CALL TO ADVENTURE. Indy wonders if his Journey will cross paths with former lover Marion (a REFUSAL that reveals his INNER PROBLEM of longing for Companionship and Love.)

But MENTOR Marcus keeps Indy focused on his OUTER PROBLEM, and the greater dangers of securing this relic with its unknown powers. But Indy shrugs off these fears and tosses his gun into his suitcase.

The key to Indy's committing to the Journey is to secure the medallion, the headpiece of the Staff of Ra. Acquiring it is the THRESHOLD, and Indy must obtain it from his former MENTOR, Abner Ravenswood. Deep in the mountains of Tibet, Indy finds an isolated saloon run by Marion Ravenswood, Abner's daughter and Indy's former love interest. She informs him that Abner is dead. There will be no MEETING WITH THE MENTOR. Bitter about the way Indy had used her when she was younger, Marion becomes a SHAPESHIFTER/THRESHOLD GUARDIAN toying with Indy's need for the headpiece. Indy leaves her with an advance for the relic.

However, moments later, German thugs led by THRESHOLD GUARDIAN Toht threaten Marion if she doesn't hand over the same headpiece. Indy arrives to save the day. The gun battle leaves Marion's saloon burning to the ground, but Marion retrieves the medallion and offers it to Indy, with herself attached in the bargain. They have survived this THRESHOLD, and now can begin the search for the Ark of the Covenant.

Indy enters a TEST PHASE during which forces try to reject him from the Journey. Best friend Sallah (ALLY/SIDE-KICK) welcomes Indy and Marion to Cairo. As one of the laborers for the German's excavation, Sallah (wearing the HERALD'S mask) confirms Indy's fear that his SHADOW, Belloq, leads the Nazi search for the Ark. Sallah also expresses his fears of the Road ahead, that perhaps something as mystical as the Ark was intended to be buried (a type of REFUSAL).

In the marketplace, Indy and Marion must overcome a band of Sikh guards, THRESHOLD GUARDIANS intent on rejecting them from the SPECIAL WORLD. During this TEST, Marion's adopted monkey dons his ENEMY mask and reveals Marion's hiding place. As the Germans carry Marion away, Indy confronts the towering, sword-wielding warrior. He quickly takes care of this THRESHOLD GUARDIAN and races after Marion. The Germans dump Marion in a truck filled with explosives. Indy stops them, shooting the driver. The truck spins out of control and explodes, killing Marion. The taste of Marion's death pushes Indy off his Journey's road. He drinks, mourning the loss of his love. His SHADOW, Belloq, delights in seeing the HERO in such a vulnerable position. He uses the ORDEAL of Marion's death to sway Indy to join the dark forces. Indy would rather follow his lover into death and take his SHADOW with him. He pulls his gun but Belloq's THRESHOLD GUARDIANS surround him. Before they can kill him, Sallah's children intervene, granting Indy's RESURRECTION.

His confrontation with the SHADOW and the added support of ALLY Sallah give Indy renewed strength (a REWARD) to commit again to this Journey. Sallah takes Indy to an old seer, a MENTOR, who translates the inscriptions on the headpiece of the Staff of Ra.

This important and suspenseful MEETING WITH THE MENTOR confirms that the SHADOW is digging for the Ark in the wrong place, a REWARD.

Indy and Sallah now have the key to finding the Ark before Belloq and the Germans. But they must find the location, and sneak into the Map Room, APPROACHING THE INMOST CAVE. Indy uses his inner MENTOR, his knowledge of hieroglyphics, to place the Staff of Ra into the proper position, and allows this HERALD (with the help of the sun) to show him the Ark's location, a REWARD.

Disguised as one of the laborers, Indy accidentally stumbles upon Marion, bound and gagged. His discovery is her RESURRECTION, as well as the RESURRECTION of their Love. But Indy leaves Marion. He reveals the colors of the true Adventure Hero, choosing the HIGHER CAUSE of the Ark, and sacrificing his personal Journey of Love (for now, at least.)

Continuing the APPROACH SEQUENCE, Indy, Sallah and his men locate the burial place and dig throughout the night. They find the stone vault and remove the heavy lid. Sallah recoils from the stone serpents' warning passage into the Well of the Souls. Indy scoffs at Sallah's fear of these THRESHOLD GUARDIANS, only to face his own greatest fear. The vault floor is covered with hundreds of poisonous asps.

Indy and Sallah enter the Well of the Souls and use gasoline to ward off the slithering THRESHOLD GUARDIANS. The two find the Ark and prepare its removal.

Soon the Ark rises from the Well of the Souls, but the HERO'S possession of this ELIXIR is short-lived. His rope mysteriously dropped, Indy is stranded battling the snakes, beginning the HERO'S ORDEAL. SHADOW Belloq and the Germans leer down at him, gloating their victory. They now possess the ELIXIR of the Ark, and prepare to turn Indy into a relic. But the Germans won't let the HERO suffer his ORDEAL all alone, and seal Marion with him in the vault, against RIVAL Belloq's protests.

This moment is truly the HERO'S SUPREME ORDEAL. He had the ELIXIR and has lost it to the SHADOW. Indy is at the very depth of his SPECIAL WORLD, the furthest point from his ORDINARY WORLD. Using his resourcefulness, Indy muscles a statue and rides this battering ram through the vault's wall. Indy returns Marion to the light of day, granting their RESURRECTION.

Having escaped the SUPREME ORDEAL, Indy enters a second TEST PHASE, a SERIES OF ORDEALS and CHASES, as he tries to reclaim the Ark.

Indy and Marion thwart Belloq's plan to airlift the Ark, forcing the SHADOW to use a truck caravan. Indy overtakes them on horseback. During this suspenseful CHASE with its many REVERSALS, the HERO survives the ORDEAL (physically RESURRECTING himself from beneath the truck). Yet again, Indy cheats death and reclaims the Ark, his REWARD.

Sallah sets up passage for Indy, Marion, and the Ark on board a pirate ship. Safe in their cabin Indy licks his wounds. Marion tries to seduce him but this Journey has finally taken its toll on the HERO. The lovers will have to await another time to savor the REWARD of their renewed love.

The Germans take over the Pirate Ship, the ROAD BACK. Belloq reclaims the Ark and takes Marion. Indy keeps low until he can sneak off the pirate ship and stow away aboard the departing U-boat.

At the German U-boat base, Indy "wears the skin" of the ENEMY, using a soldier's uniform to follow Belloq's caravan and watch them perform the Ark's unveiling ritual.

Along the road, Indy threatens to blow the Ark unless they free Marion. But the SHADOW Belloq challenges the HERO'S archeological morality and dares Indy to blow up the relic, to blow up history. Indy cannot sacrifice the Ark (a RESURRECTION of the HIGHER CAUSE). He surrenders himself to protect the Ark, the ELIXIR of his Journey.

Bound to a post, Indy and Marion watch Belloq perform the Jewish ritual of the opening of the Ark. This signals the Journey's RESURRECTION. German soldiers witness the ceremony. Belloq opens the Ark, revealing sand—only sand. But before the SHADOW acknowledges failure, beautiful visions rise from this "sand" and entrance the witnesses. Quickly wearing the HERO'S mask, Indy warns Marion to keep her eyes shut. He sacrifices his witnessing of this ceremony and recognizes the possibility of "hocus-pocus" (a RESURRECTION), choosing instead to take responsibility for his and Marion's lives.

The visions turn deadly, burning through the eyes of Belloq, who refracts this death beam into the open eyes of each German witness. Bodies shudder, bodies melt, bodies explode. This ULTIMATE SHADOW FORCE of God sweeps the carnage and seals it shut in the Ark. Only Indy and Marion remain. Eyes closed. Alive (their RESURRECTION).

Washington, D.C. Army Intelligence quickly wraps up Indy's debriefing; however, Indy objects to the treatment of the Ark. This ELIXIR holds deadly powers, and was promised to the museum. However, the Army officer assures them the Ark is in good hands.

The crated Ark is placed in a huge government warehouse with hundreds of thousands of identical crates. Lost to Government bureaucracy, this ELIXIR may never see the light of the ORDINARY WORLD.

FADE OUT

DIE HARD
(U.S., 1988)

"Who are you then?"

"Just a fly in the ointment, Hans. A monkey in the wrench. A pain in the ass..."
—Hans Gruber (Alan Rickman) and
John McClane (Bruce Willis)

Screenplay by Jeb Stuart and Steven E. de Souza
Based on the novel *Nothing Lasts Forever* by Roderick Thorp
Directed by John McTiernan

An N.Y.C. cop comes to L.A. to reconcile with his wife at her corporate Christmas party, and ends up having to save her from a band of terrorists who have taken over the high-rise.

LANDMARKS OF THE JOURNEY

What makes *Die Hard* a rich, successful action picture is that John McClane travels two Journeys. We remember the main Journey of a lonely New York cop who must defeat a band of terrorists who have taken over a 40-story high-rise. Yet John gets into this situation when he arrives in Los Angeles to reconcile with his wife. This, his primary Journey, is interrupted at its worst moment by Gruber's Call to Adventure. The classic Reluctant Hero, McClane doesn't quickly answer Gruber's Call. In fact, he tries everything possible to avoid the situation until he has no choice but to act. However, through the physical ordeals of the Higher Cause, McClane learns to acknowledge his stubbornness with his wife. Interestingly, John's stubbornness (a quality that threatens his marriage) becomes a Special Power the Hero needs to thwart Gruber's plan.

Shapeshifters are effectively used in *Die Hard* to heighten suspense. Several of the Journey's Ordeals are key moments when the true identities of Shapeshifters are revealed. Two such moments include McClane's first face-to-face with the Shadow, and the Shadow's discovery that Holly is actually McClane's wife.

While McClane relies on resourcefulness and sheer determination, Gruber is the ultimate villain. This clever Shadow has his ingenious plot planned out to the very last detail. Everything has been anticipated (the police and FBI standard procedures) to work in his favor. Nothing is left to chance.

THE JOURNEY

A 13-year veteran of the New York city police force, John McClane has been separated from his wife, Holly, for the last six months. Her good job turned into a great career, and

Los Angeles became the new home for their two kids. McClane is stubborn, resourceful, and gutsy, yet human—he's afraid of flying. He needs to save his marriage, his initial OUTER PROBLEM, and to take wife and family back to his ORDINARY WORLD in New York, his INNER PROBLEM.

The story's Opening Image shows John McClane's plane landing at LAX. He passes through this THRESHOLD of his Journey to save his marriage, white-knuckling his armrests. A businessman, the MENTOR OF FREQUENT FLYING, suggests a cure for flight anxiety and layover: balling your bare feet into fists (a key setup for McClane's physical trials yet to come).

McClane's Journey to reconcile with his wife takes center stage as he enters its TEST PHASE. His limo driver, Argyle, becomes an ALLY, who offers to wait in the Nakatomi building's underground parking garage until McClane knows how things pan out with his wife, the impending ORDEAL.

McClane uses the building's computerized directory, an Electronic THRESHOLD GUARDIAN, to locate Holly, grimacing when he learns that Holly has been using her maiden name, Gennero.

McClane takes the elevator to the 32nd floor and the company Christmas party, APPROACHING THE INMOST CAVE. The C.E.O., Takagi, reveals himself as an ALLY, welcomes McClane and escorts him to Holly's office, where they interrupt Ellis, a RIVAL for Holly's heart. Holly arrives. They embrace awkwardly, and she takes him away to wash up.

Alone in a private office, Holly offers McClane the spare room at her house, confessing that she's missed him. McClane swiftly dashes the hope of reconciliation with his impulsive observation that she hasn't missed his name. Their argument (ORDEAL) is interrupted by Holly's assistant, a THRESHOLD GUARDIAN. Holly excuses herself to "address the troops," leaving their relationship in an awkward death-state.

At this worst possible emotional moment when McClane is the furthest from any reconciliation with his wife, the "action" plot kicks in, derailing him from his personal Journey. A SUCCESSION OF CALLS finally raises the stakes, forcing McClane to accept his darker Journey.

The Terrorists, led by SHADOW Hans Gruber, swiftly usurp the Nakatomi building. They effectively replace the building's security with their own THRESHOLD GUARDIANS (a SHAPESHIFTER terrorist becomes the front desk officer, elevators are limited, phone lines are severed).

A barefoot McClane, trying to relieve flight stress, hears gunfire as Gruber takes control of the party (CALL TO ADVENTURE). REFUSING to be a hostage, McClane quickly escapes to the stairwell to figure out his next move.

Gruber and his men take Takagi to the Conference Room where they try to get this THRESHOLD GUARDIAN to reveal the computer access codes. Takagi can't give them the codes. They shoot him and McClane witnesses it. Stakes have been raised, yet he flees (a REFUSAL).

Safely on an upper floor under construction, McClane berates himself for not stopping the murder. His REFUSAL is pretty reasonable; he'd be dead. He needs help from the outside and pulls the fire alarm. Gruber and his men quickly thwart his plan and use the building's security system to track down McClane.

McClane's anticipation of victory is crushed. The fire trucks turn away and the elevator bell signals the arrival of the bad guy, and the beginning of the THRESHOLD SEQUENCE.

John McClane has REFUSED the Journey for too long. He's run out of hiding places and must fight this bad guy. In the struggle, they tumble ass-over-kettle down a staircase, breaking the bad guy's neck. McClane has killed this THRESHOLD GUARDIAN, and now the HERO wants to send his own message to the SHADOW.

As Gruber announces the death of Takagi to the hostages, and his assurance that he and his cronies "have left nothing to chance," McClane's CALL arrives on the elevator. A dead terrorist with a message in blood: "Now I have a machine gun. Ho-Ho-Ho." His message is clear. McClane has committed to stopping them, completing the THRESHOLD SEQUENCE.

During the initial TEST PHASE, McClane must battle the terrorists while getting the proper help from outside. Both goals present overwhelming obstacles.

Hiding on the elevator roof, McClane overhears Gruber's conversation, scouting the situation, calculating the total number of terrorists, jotting down names. McClane doesn't realize that he has killed the brother of hot-headed Karl, who demands revenge (raising the stakes).

McClane sneaks to the rooftop and uses the dead terrorist's walkie-talkie to contact the police. This TEST almost turns disastrous. The police won't believe him, and Karl and his buddies trap him on the roof. The police finally hear the gunfire and send a dispatch, Officer Al Powell with his bag of Twinkies.

McClane avoids ENEMY gunfire and slips back into the building, finally using the building's air ducts to escape Karl.

Al Powell (ALLY / SIDEKICK) arrives at the plaza entrance. McClane spots him from the Conference Room and tries to smash the window to warn him of the terrorists. This ignites a shoot-out in the Conference Room. He kills two more terrorists (Tony and Marko) in this TEST.

Unaware of McClane's battle and confident that the building is safe and sound, Powell prepares to leave. A terrorist's body (courtesy of John McClane) smashes into his windshield. Leaving no room for misinterpreting his CALL TO ADVENTURE, McClane sprays gunfire at the retreating Powell, forcing him THROUGH THE THRESHOLD of his own Journey, and finally bringing in the authorities.

With the police come the media, led by the SHAPESHIFTER Richard Thornberg. Since he plays an important role during the Journey's ROAD BACK, his self-centered-everything-for-his-Pulitzer methods are quickly established.

McClane keeps Gruber aware of the odds, telling Gruber that he has killed Tony and Marko. McClane doesn't realize that he has raised the SHADOW'S stakes. McClane has the detonators.

Die Hard's APPROACH TO THE INMOST CAVE represents an important stage of the Journey, a "calm of preparation" before all Hell breaks loose. With police and media activity, everyone now knows that Terrorists have taken over the Nakatomi Building. The police surround the plaza and prepare their next move. Holly makes a BOLD APPROACH to Gruber to ensure the hostages' comfort.

Communicating by CB, McClane tells Powell all the facts and theories, infuriating the terrorists listening in. Gruber and his men are desperate to get this guy, and Gruber needs his detonators. McClane hands the mess over to Powell and the police.

But Deputy Police Commissioner Robinson is skeptical of Powell's source, and REFUSES to believe the seriousness of the situation. The Police initiate their own disastrous series of TESTS that leave the SWAT team at Gruber's mercy. McClane pleads for Gruber to let them pull back. The SHADOW refuses, and McClane sends a chair filled with explosives down the elevator shaft, blowing an entire floor. Now nobody wants McClane's help. The Deputy Chief berates him for spraying the police with glass, but McClane stands up to this MENTOR (setting up his upcoming ironic ORDEAL with glass.)

Hostage Ellis also wants McClane neutralized, and offers to hand him over to Gruber, in the Journey's second APPROACH. Pretending to be McClane's friend, SHAPESHIFTER Ellis tries to convince him to surrender the detonators. McClane knows the SHADOW better than Ellis and warns him not to get involved. Gruber sees that these negotiations are going nowhere and kills Ellis for everyone to hear. He demands the detonators.

Gruber finally speaks with the police and lays out his demands in exchange for letting the hostages escape via the rooftop. McClane begins to suspect Gruber's "smoke-and-mirrors."

Gruber goes to the building's roof to check the wiring for the explosives. He runs into McClane, and the SHADOW immediately feigns terror, pretending to be an escaped hostage, the HERO'S ORDEAL. McClane hands this SHAPESHIFTER a gun for protection. He turns his back allowing the SHADOW to reveal himself. Gruber fires at McClane—oops, the gun was empty, a REVERSAL and RESURRECTION. But Karl arrives and McClane barely escapes the gunfire, continuing the ORDEAL.

Karl and Hans trap McClane in an inner office. The SHADOW gains much from this ORDEAL. He retrieves the detonators and orders Karl to eliminate McClane by shooting out the glass. Karl fires on the office, an endless rain of gunfire and glass. Karl caps the ORDEAL with a bomb but he must leave without the satisfaction of seeing the proof of McClane's death.

Hans and Karl return to the hostages. Furious, Karl attacks a portable bar, a sign to Holly that McClane must still be alive. "Only John can drive a man that crazy." (A RESURRECTION).

McClane crawls into a bathroom, his bloodied feet covered with glass shards. He talks to Powell. He needs this ALLY to give him the strength to get through the RESURRECTION of his ORDEAL. We learn about Powell's past ORDEAL (accidentally killing a child) that has ruined his career. Powell also wears the HERALD'S mask to tell McClane that the FBI is now in charge, not realizing the FBI is precisely what the SHADOW wanted.

Guided by the "universal terrorist playbook," the FBI has cut the city's power, releasing the Vault's electromagnetic lock, and its contents, to the delighted SHADOW.

McClane has been REWARDED with Powell's friendship and with shared sympathy for their ORDEALS. Having faced death, McClane confesses that he's been a jerk to his wife and that he'll never have the chance to tell her. He asks Powell to apologize for him. Powell assures him he'll have to tell her himself. McClane also gains the REWARD of greater awareness of Gruber's plan. He realizes that Gruber had to be on the roof for a reason.

McClane returns to the roof and discovers Gruber's explosives, initiating the ROAD BACK SEQUENCE. He tries to warn Powell but Karl cuts him off.

Richard Thornberg sets the TICKING CLOCK, continuing the ROAD BACK. Having pushed his way into Holly McClane's home, he interviews daughter Lucy. Gruber watches Thornberg's news report and finally makes the connection: Holly Gennero is John McClane's wife. Gruber keeps her as a hostage and collects his bearer bonds, while his men herd the remaining hostages to the rooftop. Karl and McClane fight to the death. The FBI Helicopters move in.

McClane finally defeats Karl and rushes to the rooftop looking for Holly. But she isn't there. He needs to get the hostages off the roof and uses his machine gun to drive them back inside. But the FBI believe he's a terrorist and cut him off. Trapped on the rooftop, only seconds before the explosion, McClane uses a fire hose to leap from the roof and break back into the building. The rooftop explodes taking the FBI helicopter with it, completing the ROAD BACK.

With the hostages stampeding the terrorists for freedom, McClane must now focus on saving Holly from the SHADOW, Gruber. Our HERO has only two bullets left in his gun. He sees a roll of holiday packing tape and gets an idea.

McClane surrenders to Gruber, whose man now holds McClane at gunpoint. McClane learns that the entire terrorist plan was merely a fabrication to hide the robbery. Gruber prepares to shoot McClane, and the HERO laughs in the face of death. Soon we see why. McClane taped the gun to his back. McClane's RESURRECTION comes swiftly. He gets off his two shots perfectly, killing Gruber's thug and shooting Gruber, who falls backwards through the window. Gruber grabs Holly and threatens to take her down twenty floors with him.

McClane grabs his wife and unclasps her Rolex watch (the company's gift for a job well done), and Gruber falls to his death. McClane takes his wife into his arms and kisses her, their RESURRECTION.

McClane and Holly leave the building together. They have each other (ELIXIR of Love and Marriage Renewed), even if McClane can't get Deputy Police Commissioner Anderson's respect. And he doesn't need the formal respect from the L.A.P.D. McClane finally meets Powell (ELIXIR of Respect and Friendship). In a surprise RESURRECTION moment, Karl bursts from the building ready to shoot McClane and Holly. Powell rises to this HERO'S moment and kills Karl. He saves McClane, and redeems himself for the tragedy in his past.

Argyle bursts from the underground parking lot. As McClane and Holly prepare to depart, Thornberg questions the HERO and his wife. Holly gives the reporter his answer; she decks him on national television. McClane and Holly drive away into the distance.

FADE OUT

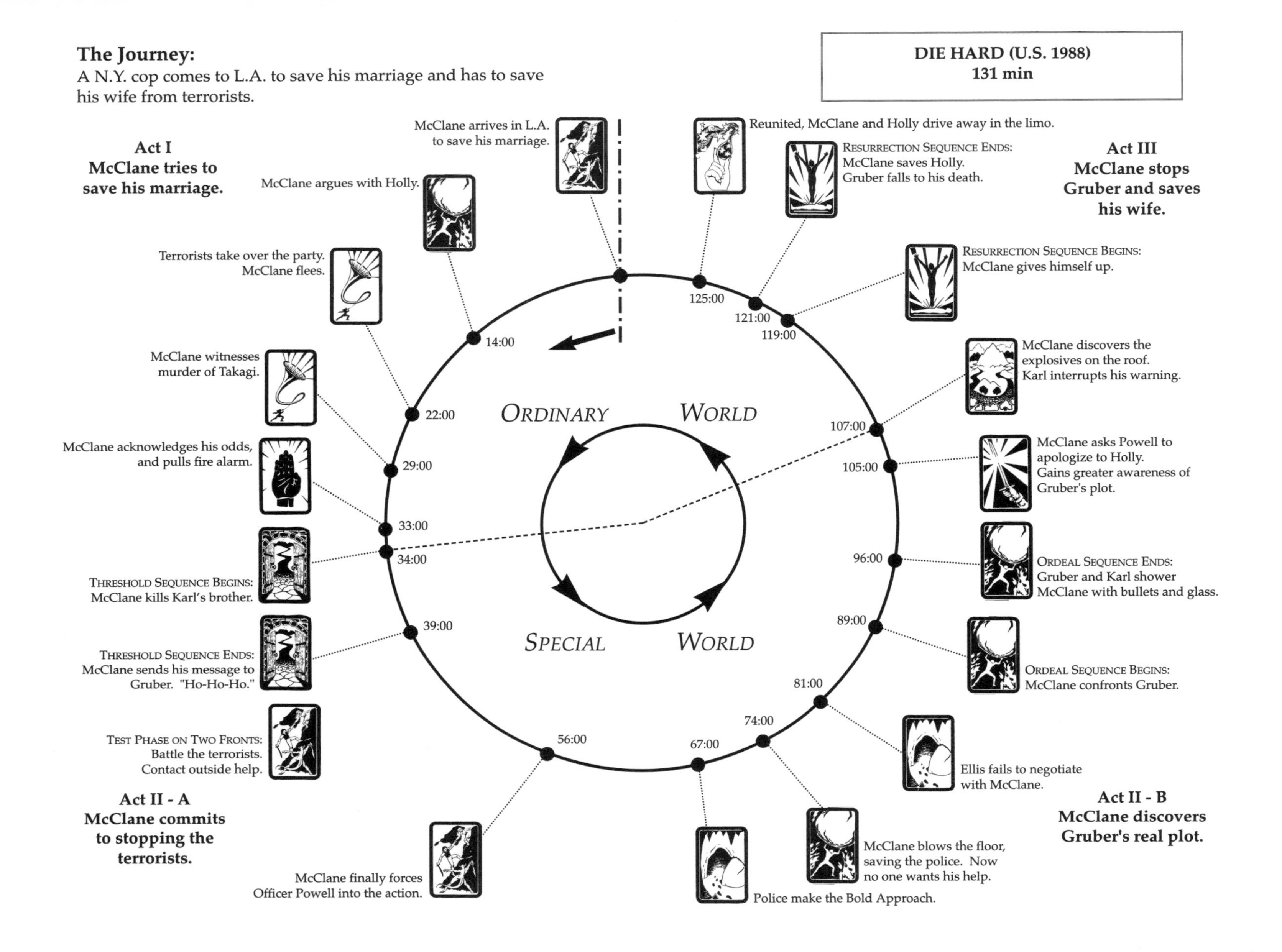

DIE HARD (U.S. 1988)
131 min
The Journey:
A N.Y. cop comes to L.A. to save his marriage and has to save his wife from terrorists.
Act I
McClane tries to save his marriage.
McClane arrives in L.A. to save his marriage.
14:00
McClane argues with Holly.
22:00
Terrorists take over the party. McClane flees.
29:00
McClane witnesses murder of Takagi.
33:00
McClane acknowledges his odds, and pulls fire alarm.
34:00
Threshold Sequence Begins: McClane kills Karl's brother.
39:00
Threshold Sequence Ends: McClane sends his message to Gruber. "Ho-Ho-Ho."
Test Phase on Two Fronts: Battle the terrorists. Contact outside help.
Act II - A
McClane commits to stopping the terrorists.
56:00
McClane finally forces Officer Powell into the action.
67:00
Police make the Bold Approach.
74:00
McClane blows the floor, saving the police. Now no one wants his help.
81:00
Ellis fails to negotiate with McClane.
Act II - B
McClane discovers Gruber's real plot.
89:00
Ordeal Sequence Begins: McClane confronts Gruber.
96:00
Ordeal Sequence Ends: Gruber and Karl shower McClane with bullets and glass.
105:00
McClane asks Powell to apologize to Holly. Gains greater awareness of Gruber's plot.
107:00
McClane discovers the explosives on the roof. Karl interrupts his warning.
119:00
Resurrection Sequence Begins: McClane gives himself up.
121:00
Resurrection Sequence Ends: McClane saves Holly. Gruber falls to his death.
125:00
Reunited, McClane and Holly drive away in the limo.
Act III
McClane stops Gruber and saves his wife.
Ordinary World
Special World

THELMA AND LOUISE
(U.S., 1991)

"I've always wanted to travel. I just never got the opportunity."

"You got it now."

—Thelma and Louise
(Geena Davis and Susan Sarandon)

Screenplay by Callie Khouri
Directed by Ridley Scott

A weekend escape for two women becomes a chase for their freedom.

LANDMARKS OF THE JOURNEY

Unlike many of their male counterparts, Thelma and Louise take time in their decision making. They consider the options and the ramifications before committing to their Journey, notably during the Threshold and Road Back Sequences.

Many Action Adventure Heroes are guided by Inner Mentors, past experiences and values that prepare them for the Tests and Ordeals of the Journey at hand. Thelma and Louise have awful Ordinary Worlds and past experiences with Shapeshifting men that they must learn to shake. These experiences drive them in their Special World, making them realize that the true freedom they need must last for more than a weekend. During the course of the Journey, both women also act as physical Mentors. Louise begins as the know-it-all Mentor who pushes Thelma to accept a weekend of freedom from her abusive husband. After she defends Thelma and shoots her rapist, Louise makes the decisions, guided by the Inner Mentor of her nightmare past in Texas. They pass the Mentor/Hero's mask after their Journey's Ordeal. Robbed of their "future" by J.D., Thelma uses Louise's strength and J.D.'s lessons to take their road to freedom.

THE JOURNEY

Thelma is the housewife of an abusive, self-centered husband, Darrell. Best friend Louise, a sassy coffee-shop waitress, has her own problems with men. Her current boyfriend REFUSES to commit to their relationship. At the initial stages of their Journey, both women need to escape this ORDINARY WORLD away from their men, their shared OUTER PROBLEM. Their INNER PROBLEM is to find themselves.

Thelma CALLS Louise to confirm plans for their weekend getaway. The RELUCTANT Thelma hasn't told her husband. But MENTOR Louise pushes her, so Thelma leaves her husband a note, entering the FIRST THRESHOLD. She dumps her stuff into Louise's convertible, and hands over a gun for safekeeping. After all there could be bears on fishing trips. The gun places a cloud over the comedic relationship of the two women, and warns the audience that this weekend Journey could be dangerous.

The two speed off. Initially, Louise is Thelma's MENTOR. She instigated this weekend escape. In a nice moment that foreshadows Thelma's transformation in the second act, she imitates her MENTOR as she smokes, "I'm Louise."

Thelma wants to eat, and she wants some fun. She convinces Louise to stop at the Silver Bullet for a meal. Thelma enjoys testing her new freedom and orders a drink. Initially surprised, Louise is lured by this MENTOR OF GOOD TIMES and orders a Margarita.

Handsome cowboy hunk, Harlon, tries to converse with the ladies. Although Thelma welcomes his CALL, Louise sees the overt seduction by this SHAPESHIFTER and sends him away, but not before Thelma promises him a dance. The alcohol and the dancing get Thelma sick; this type of freedom isn't sitting very well with her. Harlon quickly escorts her outside for fresh air where he lets down his HERO'S MASK and takes advantage of her. Louise comes to the rescue and shoots Harlon dead with Thelma's gun, initiating their THRESHOLD into a deeper SPECIAL WORLD.

Louise helps Thelma into the car and they flee the scene. The SPECIAL WORLD "on the run" leaves the two shocked, disoriented. During this THRESHOLD SEQUENCE, they face TESTS as they need to figure out what to do, and more importantly who are their ALLIES and ENEMIES.

Thelma wants answers, what are they going to do? Louise needs to think. Louise refuses to see the cops, who she insists won't see their side of the story. This SPECIAL WORLD strains their relationship, and we wonder if these two best friends will make it together to Journey's end.

Meanwhile, a police detective, Hal, takes in the murder scene. He represents the law, a SHAPESHIFTER ANTAGONIST, and his presence heightens suspense. Later his supervisor recommends that Thelma and Louise be questioned. Hal believes they've crossed state lines and now the FBI must be contacted, bumping the stakes even higher.

The THRESHOLD SEQUENCE continues. The women need money, so Louise calls her boyfriend, Jimmy, and convinces him with "no questions asked" to wire to her in Oaklohoma the $6,700 she has in savings.

Having entered this SPECIAL WORLD, Thelma and Louise begin to question their ORDINARY WORLD. Their INNER PROBLEM (finding themselves) becomes more conscious. Thelma acknowledges the crisis in her marriage. Louise wants to send Thelma back (a REFUSAL) and go on to Mexico, a CALL that would commit them to a deeper SPECIAL WORLD. Louise takes her to a gas station to call Darrell, and tell him she'll be back tomorrow.

Darrell demands that she come home now. Thelma realizes that this THRESHOLD GUARDIAN cares more about the football game he's watching than her safety. She tells him off and hangs up—an ORDEAL of her marriage. She leaves the phone booth and stumbles into her REWARD, handsome young J.D., a CALL TO ROMANCE. He asks for a ride, which interests Thelma but MENTOR Louise nixes the idea. In the car, Thelma asks how long before they're in Mexico, committing to Louise's Journey and completing the THRESHOLD SEQUENCE.

The TESTS continue. First they have to go to Oklahoma and then Mexico. But MENTOR Louise has rules for this SPECIAL WORLD. First, they have to travel the secondary roads to avoid the law. Second, they can't go through Texas. Thelma wants an explanation, but Louise refuses to discuss it. Soon, the two are singing on the road. Thelma and Louise are a team again.

Two key events happen during their APPROACH TO THE INMOST CAVE. First, Thelma spots J.D. waiting on the road. Whimpering like a puppy, Thelma sways Louise to pick up her "treat." They drive on to Oklahoma City where Louise picks up the wired money, but boyfriend Jimmy has tricked her and is waiting for her.

Thelma and Louise get hotel rooms for the night. Thelma has to send J.D. away, while Louise has to deal with Jimmy. In the privacy of Thelma's room, Louise gives her the $6,700, "their future." Louise returns to her room where the ORDEAL SEQUENCE begins for both Louise and Thelma. SHAPESHIFTER Jimmy waits for Louise with a rose, and an engagement ring. In the light of the ORDINARY WORLD, Louise wanted Jimmy's commitment. But the SPECIAL WORLD has created new circumstances. She REFUSES Jimmy's CALL, ending their relationship, an ORDEAL.

Meanwhile, J.D. knocks on Thelma's door. Seeing him soaked in the rain, Thelma invites him inside, committing to his CALL. Soon, they are playing on the bed. He takes off her wedding ring, pushing her toward freedom from marriage. When he confesses that he's a robber, Louise prods this MENTOR to show her how he does it. Soon they make love.

At breakfast, with one final passionate kiss, Louise sends Jimmy away, completing her ORDEAL. She confesses to him that she is happy, her REWARD. Thelma arrives and confesses her REWARD: she finally got properly laid. Both REWARDS are short-lived; J.D. split with their money. Louise can't face this ORDEAL, forcing Thelma to take charge, her REWARD.

Thelma robs a market while Louise waits in the car, sitting in Thelma's seat. Louise can't even smoke, as if she now wears Thelma's old mask. In minutes, HERO Thelma jumps into the car with the money and they speed away. In an innovative and funny technique of flashback and exposition for comic effect, Hal, the FBI, and Darrell watch the security videotape of Thelma's robbery and how she uses the lessons she learned from MENTOR

J.D. No longer on the run for a questionable crime, Thelma and Louise are Outlaws, with no turning back.

But they have to acknowledge their new Outlaw roles. After Louise finds out Hal knows they're running to Mexico, she gets furious with Thelma for telling J.D. their plans. "We're fugitives," she says. "Let's start behaving like it." This acknowledgment begins their ROAD BACK, and completes a transformation in both women as they accept their fate.

This stage of their Journey gives the women opportunities to take action against men who have sent them into this SPECIAL WORLD. They lock a highway patrolman in a trunk, warning him to treat his wife and family well. They also put an obscene trucker in his place, blowing up his gas truck.

But this stage also shows moments of true tenderness and friendship, as Thelma and Louise accept what they have done and how it has changed them. Louise regrets killing Harlon. Thelma isn't sorry Harlon's dead; she just regrets not doing it herself.

Louise has a moment of wanting to turn back. She calls Hal, hoping she can strike a deal. But MENTOR Thelma disconnects the call warning her not to "blow it." As they drive, Louise confesses that they are being charged with murder. Their ROAD BACK is complete.

Cops finally track them down and a CHASE ensues. Thelma and Louise escape, temporarily—and they brake suddenly before plummeting into the Grand Canyon. Surrounded by the law and blocked by the canyon, our HEROES acknowledge that there is no negotiation. Their freedom is what they choose, the RESURRECTION and ELIXIR. They hold each other's hand, and drive into the canyon. As their car sails to the peak of flight it dissolves to bright white.

FADE OUT

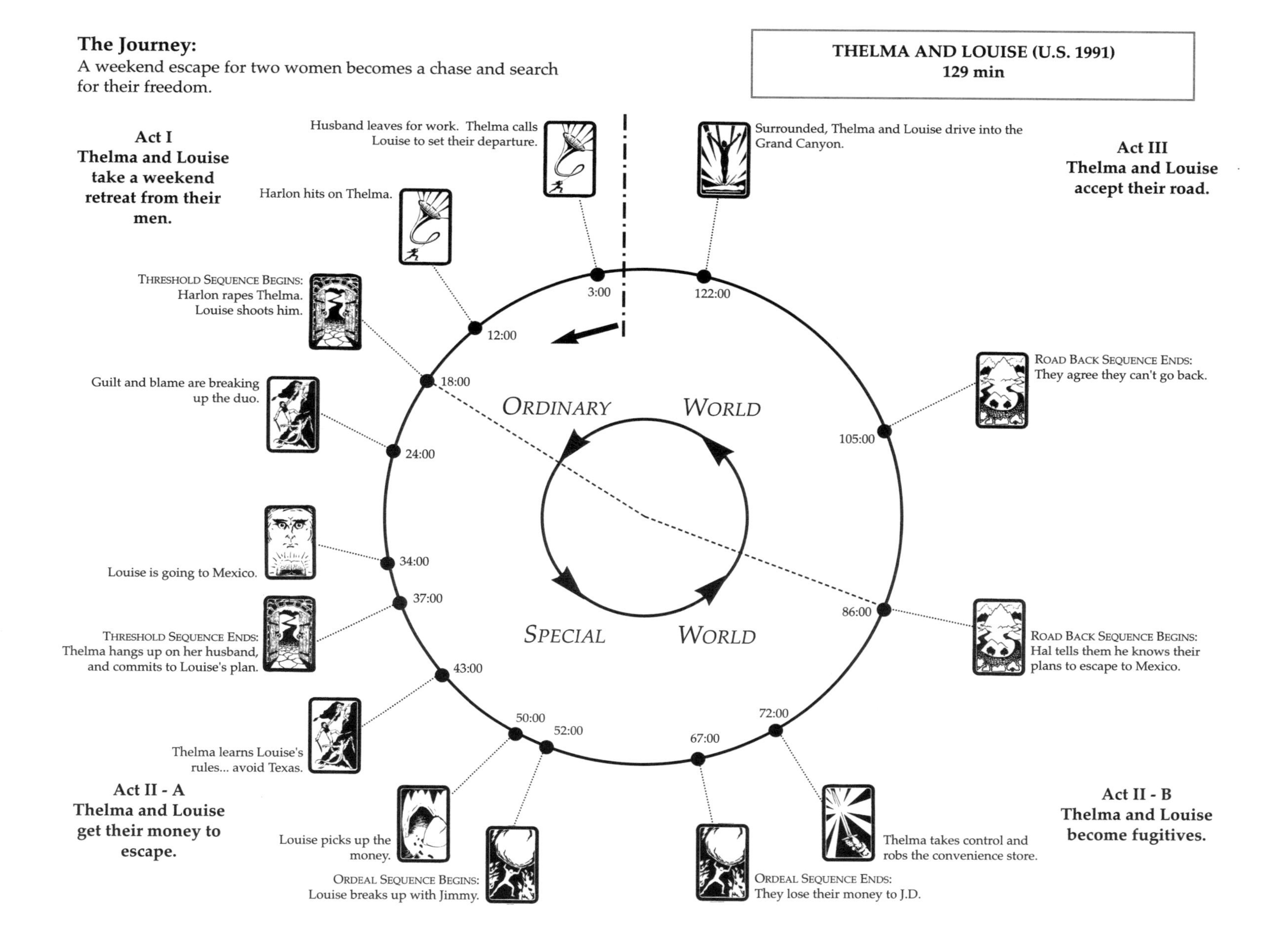

The Journey:
A weekend escape for two women becomes a chase and search for their freedom.
THELMA AND LOUISE (U.S. 1991)
129 min
Act I
Thelma and Louise take a weekend retreat from their men.
Husband leaves for work. Thelma calls Louise to set their departure.
Harlon hits on Thelma.
THRESHOLD SEQUENCE BEGINS: Harlon rapes Thelma. Louise shoots him.
Guilt and blame are breaking up the duo.
Louise is going to Mexico.
THRESHOLD SEQUENCE ENDS: Thelma hangs up on her husband, and commits to Louise's plan.
Thelma learns Louise's rules... avoid Texas.
Act II - A
Thelma and Louise get their money to escape.
Louise picks up the money.
ORDEAL SEQUENCE BEGINS: Louise breaks up with Jimmy.
ORDEAL SEQUENCE ENDS: They lose their money to J.D.
Thelma takes control and robs the convenience store.
Act II - B
Thelma and Louise become fugitives.
ROAD BACK SEQUENCE BEGINS: Hal tells them he knows their plans to escape to Mexico.
ROAD BACK SEQUENCE ENDS: They agree they can't go back.
Surrounded, Thelma and Louise drive into the Grand Canyon.
Act III
Thelma and Louise accept their road.
ORDINARY WORLD
SPECIAL WORLD
3:00
12:00
18:00
24:00
34:00
37:00
43:00
50:00
52:00
67:00
72:00
86:00
105:00
122:00

THE MYTHIC STRUCTURE OF THE WESTERN

We stand adrift on this great frontier, a solitary, reluctant hero. Ruled by a code of honor and a six-shooter at the side, we are the legend who has been called to bring virtue and justice to a lawless land. Violence cannot be avoided, and against the odds we must face the final shoot-out of right against wrong.

"WHEN THE LEGEND BECOMES FACT, PRINT THE LEGEND"

Western stories are the American mythology. The dime novel propagated the legends, a pulp version of the Greek Homer weaving tales of Wyatt Earp and Billy the Kid, transforming good guys and bad into epic heroes. These rich folktales and myths of the Wild West fueled the true American film genre.

Westerns are action. Images on the move. Images known and anticipated worldwide. Outlaws overtake a locomotive, six-shooters blazing. The cattle drive pounds the parched land. A family protects its isolated homestead against marauding Indians. A relentless chase takes Hero and Shadow over the rugged terrain by coach, horse, or on foot. The Western's action usually escalates to the final shoot-out when the Hero stands against many to impose his law on the land.

More than galloping horses and sweeping landscapes, the Western is a reflection of the American Identity. As our nation's identity changes with each decade, with each generation, and with domestic and world pressures, these shifts are reflected in the stories we tell. The classic tale of the Reluctant Hero, *High Noon* can be seen as a screenwriter's reaction to his isolation in the wake of the McCarthy hearings. During the late sixties and early seventies, filmmakers re-evaluated the western legends and the closing of the Frontier, looking through the embittered eyes of the Vietnam War experience. *Dances With Wolves* touched audiences with its themes of community and family, racism and the environment. Released during a time when society was surrendering its streets to violence, *Unforgiven* addressed the effect of revenge with the gun. Each generation brings the potential for reinterpretation of the Western, casting new light on the genre, and putting a new spin on its mythology.

THE WESTERN STORY

The Western weaves moral tales of good and bad, played out against the sweeping landscape of the American Frontier. Conflict is central, violence inevitable. Usually some overriding conflict looms over the "smaller" problems of the characters. This could be law versus lawlessness (*High Noon, Butch Cassidy and the Sundance Kid*), man versus the Frontier (*Dances With Wolves*), white settlers versus Indian natives (*The Searchers*), and on. Beneath this overriding conflict, the Hero faces his personal Journey. Several recurring Western stories include the following situations:

1) The Hero defends a town against Evil. The Hero may already be a member of the town (*High Noon*). He could be an outsider who stumbles upon the problem, or he's hired to cleanse the town of the Shadow's filth (Clint Eastwood's Man with No Name, *The Magnificent Seven*).

2) The Hero searches for someone who has been lost or abducted (*The Searchers*), or a fugitive of the law. The wilderness with its treacherous terrain, vengeful natives and wild animals plays an important part in these stories, where the Hero usually has some special affinity with this Special World.

3) The Hero is "on-the-run." These are Search stories taken from the opposite point of view. Here, the Antihero or Outlaw is the central character fleeing the law and being chased (*Butch Cassidy and the Sundance Kid, Lonely Are the Brave*).

4) The Hero seeks vengeance for a wrongdoing. The strongest vengeance stories affect the Hero on a personal level. The Hero may seek vengeance for the murder of a loved one (*The Outlaw Josey Wales, The Searchers*); or an Antihero could be a gun-for-hire and yet this Journey for Vengeance could tempt his inner Shadow (*Unforgiven*).

5) The Hero discovers himself in the Wilderness. These Journeys involve a Hero who wanders within various Special Worlds (white settlements, Indian villages, the wilderness) and eventually finds himself (*Dances With Wolves, Little Big Man*).

THE WESTERN HERO WALKS ALONE

A Western icon, the Loner Hero represents the constant movement westward that is the heart of Western mythology. Western stories romanticize this wanderer. The Hero arrives from the distant horizon, defends justice, and rides off into the sunset. Always on the move, the Loner Hero can't seem to settle down, and at times the need to settle down gets in the way of justice (*High Noon*). Or this Loner Hero can be portrayed in the tragic extreme of Ethan Edwards in *The Searchers*, who is incapable of finding his place, and wanders forever.

Loner Heroes can be willing or reluctant to accept the Journey. Allies and sidekicks, possibly Tricksters for comic effect, may lend a hand along the way, but eventually, the Hero rises above the rest to face the danger on his own.

Remember there are no hard and fast rules, and the Western genre offers wonderful exceptions to its mythology. In a poetic turn, *Dances With Wolves'* John Dunbar finds solitude on the prairie only to realize how alone he truly is in his Ordinary World and seeks companionship, acceptance and finally family with the Sioux.

THE RELUCTANT HERO

Many early Western heroes willingly leaped on horseback and rode headlong into the Journey, yet the Reluctant Hero has evolved into an important archetype within the Western genre (*High Noon*). An important landmark of the Journey, the Hero's Refusal, reminds the Hero and the Audience of the dangers that lie ahead, raising the stakes of the Journey. Coping with fear makes that Hero more human, and more identifiable.

THE MORAL CODE: THE MENTOR WITHIN

The lonely Western Hero must rise to take the law into his own hands. In many Western Journeys, the Loner Hero is without a physical Mentor, relying instead upon his Inner Mentor, his moral code, his integrity, his uncompromising belief of right and wrong. The Hero may have acquired this integrity from past experiences and Mentors, former lawmen (*High Noon*), even good wives (*Unforgiven*).

The strength of this moral code may be what is at stake during the Hero's Journey. A Hero, Antihero or Wounded Hero could be in moral conflict, yet the Ordeals of his Journey resurrect this Inner Mentor, and he finally serves Justice. On the other hand, the moral code that pushes the Hero to serve the greater community may be in conflict with a more personal need such as Love (*High Noon*).

THE VIOLENT WEST

Violence cannot be avoided in the Western. The Western audience anticipates violence, and even relishes it. The essential moment expected in the Western is the final shoot-out, where the Lawman faces the Outlaw, each serving his own "justice" with a pair of six-shooters. As tension builds along the Hero's Journey, the final confrontation between Hero and Shadow can evoke a much-needed and desired catharsis for audience and Hero as he is cleansed and resurrected by violence.

Generally, Westerns serve a swift, decisive violence. Without speedy "justice" the outlaw could eventually be pardoned by the court system and return to haunt the Hero (*High Noon*). A particularly nasty Shadow may be deserving of an agonizing death, or the storyteller could use a drawn-out painful death to make an important statement about the nature of violence (*Unforgiven*).

HERO AND SHADOW

Few genres show as clear a polarity of character archetypes as the Western. Lawman and Outlaw. Hero and Shadow. Polar Opposites. Shadows of one another. With its moral tales set against the underlying theme of man civilizing a savage frontier, the Western can easily explore this polarity of law versus lawless, even exploiting the Kane and Abel theme. Two brothers, or best friends, begin on the same side of the law; however, an Ordeal pushes them to opposite sides of the mirror and eventually they must face each other for the final showdown at Journey's end.

The conflict of polar opposites may exist within the Hero or Antihero, forcing him to walk a fragile line between good and evil. When facing the Ordeals of the Journey, a Hero may be overcome by the mask of his Shadow, and yet possibly only through this violence can the Hero purge himself of his Shadow. In a brutal act, Ethan Edwards scalps Chief Scar, but through this bloodletting he's able to accept his niece and bring her back home.

The Hero's Shadow may be his dark past for which he seeks redemption. William Munny tempts his Shadow self and finally resurrects it, but after a vicious shoot-out he, like Ethan, purges himself of his Shadow. He finds redemption, and a new life of non-violence.

THE LANDSCAPE AS SPECIAL WORLD

The landscape is a constant reminder of the overriding conflict between Man and Nature, and the vulnerability of man in this Special World. The austere backdrop dwarfs the Lone Hero, the isolated homestead, the one-street wooden town, exposed to all manner of dangers.

The audience expects this Special World of beautiful mountains and stark prairies, regardless of the physical or psychological Special World the Hero must enter on the Journey. The audience wants to be transported, to live the freedom and romance of the Frontier through the visuals and the actions of the characters.

GENRE CHALLENGES: WESTERN

1. In *High Noon*, Sheriff Will Kane's Mentor is his integrity. Can integrity and honor be a strong enough Mentor and motivator for today's stories?
2. Watch *The Searchers* through the eyes of the "Journeyman Hero" Martin Pawley. Does he experience stages in his Journey which are different from Mentor Ethan's? What does he learn from his Mentor?

3. The comic sidekick or buddy is an important archetype for the Western story. Take a look at the Sundance Kid, Old Mose in *The Searchers*, or Munny's best friend, Ned, in *Unforgiven*. Why are sidekicks essential characters? What important roles can they play on the Hero's Journey?
4. Lt. Dunbar is a willing hero in *Dances With Wolves*. How are reluctance and fear of the Journey revealed throughout his epic Journey of self-discovery?
5. Look at the Antihero (Ethan Edwards in *The Searchers*, William Munny in *Unforgiven*, Butch and Sundance.) Do you like them? Why or why not? Can you identify with them? What pivotal moments or actions make them identifiable? Are they heroic? Why?
6. The Western Landscape is as important as the characters inhabiting it. Pick any one of the analyzed films and see how the environment plays a role in the Hero's Journey. In what ways does it assist or obstruct the Journey?
7. *High Noon* and *The Searchers* show the traditional role of the woman in the classic Western story, representing home and hearth, and the completion to the Hero's lonely Journey. Take a look at *Butch Cassidy and the Sundance Kid, Dances With Wolves*, or *Unforgiven*. How do women serve these journeys? What roles do they play: Mentors? Shapeshifters? Heralds? Heroes? Shadows? Are there sacrifices made, and why? How do these recent stories expand and enrich the role of the woman in this male-dominant story-form?

HIGH NOON
(U.S., 1952)

"Don't try to be a hero. You don't have to be a hero. Not for me."

"I'm not trying to be a hero. If you think I like this, you're crazy."

—Amy (Grace Kelly) and
Will Kane (Gary Cooper)

Screenplay by Carl Foreman
Based on the magazine story "The Tin Star" by John W. Cunningham
Directed by Fred Zinnemann

On his wedding day, retired marshal, Will Kane, feels honor-bound to protect the town from a revenge-seeking gunslinger. But as High Noon approaches, no one in town will help their marshal.

LANDMARKS OF THE JOURNEY

High Noon denotes a turning point in the psychological development of the Western Hero. We don't see the dashing Hero dressed in white of the genre's earlier stories, but a weatherworn Gentleman who will fight for what is right but is terrified of his fate.

Told in real time, Kane's Journey is selfless, dedicated to his responsibility to the town and his people. His Allies do not join him on his Journey. They aren't killed; they don't fall trying to help the Hero. Simply they refuse to travel this road; they forsake their Hero. However, they are quick to reap the Elixir when the Hero triumphs in the end, a bitter Elixir that Kane must learn on this Journey.

THE JOURNEY

1870s. The small western town of Hadleyville. This ORDINARY WORLD is a safe place for women and children, now that Marshal Will Kane has established law and order. Five years earlier, the ruthless Frank Miller ruled the town. It took Kane and a dozen deputies to finally break Miller's gang and imprison Miller for murder.

Well respected by the townspeople, Will Kane is courageous and proud, unafraid to stand up for what's right. Now retiring, Kane plans to marry Amy Fowler, a beautiful Quaker girl, and leave Hadleyville to begin a new, quiet life. This is his OUTER PROBLEM at the beginning of the Journey. But once word hits that Frank Miller is returning for revenge, Will Kane's OUTER PROBLEM is to protect the town, to muster a posse to defeat the SHADOW. Kane's INNER PROBLEM is to do what is right, and uphold the law.

High Noon opens with the gathering of the three surviving members of Frank Miller's gang. With determined faces, they ride down the main street. The townspeople recognize this CALL TO ADVENTURE with dread and fear.

Meanwhile, Kane and Amy marry, passing through the THRESHOLD of Kane's Journey of Romance. For the second half of the "ceremony," Kane must retire as the town's marshal. As soon as Kane relinquishes the Tin Star, the Station Master, a HERALD, interrupts with a telegram announcing that Frank Miller has been pardoned and is returning to town on the noon train seeking revenge. The TICKING CLOCK is set in motion.

The selectmen convince Kane to REFUSE this CALL TO ADVENTURE and leave town with his new wife. Although he believes he should remain to do his job, he takes their advice and rides off with Amy. But he stops on the road. He can't run from this problem and must return to Hadleyville, even against his wife's protests. Kane's integrity, his inner code of honor, and past experience serve as his MENTOR. He assures Amy that he'll swear in some new deputies and quickly take care of the matter. Amy REFUSES to wait to find out whether she'll be a wife or a widow, and prepares to leave on the noon train. Kane must stay, and they go their separate ways. This ORDEAL of Kane's Journey of Romance pushes him through the THRESHOLD to commit to his Journey of Duty.

During Kane's TEST PHASE, he tries to muster support from the cowardly and reluctant townsfolk.

- Judge Mettrick is fleeing town and fails to convince Kane to do likewise.
- Harvey Pell, Kane's former deputy and RIVAL, refuses to help.
- Kane appeals for deputies at the saloon, but these men are Miller's supporters, THRESHOLD GUARDIANS.

Each failed TEST gradually isolates our HERO and pressures Kane to abandon the impending showdown and flee town. This phase can also be seen in a positive light as TESTS of Kane's integrity; regardless of the REFUSALS, Kane's integrity wins out and he stands up for what is right.

Kane interrupts the town's church service. He uses this gathering, APPROACHING THE INMOST CAVE, to solicit volunteers, again meeting rejection. The former marshal, Martin Howe, warns Kane that the town just doesn't care about justice. This MENTOR gives Kane one last warning to leave town alive.

The townsfolk's rejection and Howe's words strike home; Kane goes to the stables and considers fleeing. Kane is at the furthest point in his Journey, the ORDEAL. His integrity has weakened and he's ready to run. When Deputy Harvey Pell "pushes" him onto the horse, Kane lashes back. He's tired of being pushed. The two fight; Kane knocks Harvey out. Kane survives this physical ORDEAL, and his moral code has won out (his RESURRECTION from his psychological ORDEAL.)

Kane gets himself cleaned up at the barber, a type of RESURRECTION. The barber quiets the undertaker who is busy building the needed coffins for the noon showdown. Kane leaves and tells them to resume making the coffins. Having learned his lessons from the TEST PHASE and the ORDEAL, Kane is REWARDED with the awareness that he must do this alone. Kane completes his last will and testament, as the whistle announces the approach of the noon train, beginning his ROAD BACK.

Kane enters a deserted main street. His bride, Amy, passes him on a buckboard heading out of town to catch the train. Kane finally faces the fear of his fate and his isolation.

The noon train arrives. There is no turning back.

The Third Act focuses on the final showdown, an extensive RESURRECTION sequence. As the noon train prepares to depart, a burst of gunfire pulls Amy from the train. Fearing the quick death of Kane, Amy races to the main street, where she finds Miller's brother dead. Kane must still be alive.

After a long shoot-out, Miller's gang traps Kane in a burning stable. Kane escapes, shielded by maddened horses, a RESURRECTION. Now only Miller and Pierce remain from the gang. But the odds are still against Kane.

Amy finds shelter in the marshal's office as Pierce positions himself outside the window. She can't face seeing Kane shot down. She enters this SPECIAL WORLD of violence and shoots Pierce dead. This gives Kane the upper hand, but Frank Miller quickly turns the tables, using Amy as a hostage. HERO and SHADOW stand off in the middle of the street. In the final stage of the RESURRECTION, Kane offers himself in exchange for Amy's safety. However, Amy claws Miller's face, freeing herself and allowing Kane to shoot his SHADOW dead.

Eager to claim their ELIXIR, the townsfolk return to the streets made safe again by their marshal. Kane stood by his moral duty, and by accepting his responsibility becomes a true HERO. He faces death, and emerges victorious, but the ELIXIR of this victory is a bitter one. Disgusted, Kane discards the Tin Star in the dusty street. He and his wife must move on (their ELIXIR). Without looking back, they leave the town that has forsaken Will Kane.

FADE OUT

THE SEARCHERS
(U.S. 1956)

"So we'll find 'em in the end, I promise ya. We'll find them just as sure as the turnin' of the earth."

—Ethan Edwards (John Wayne)

Screenplay by Frank S. Nugent
From the novel by Alan LeMay
Directed by John Ford

An outcast launches an obsessive five-year quest for his niece, who was abducted by Indians.

LANDMARKS OF THE JOURNEY

This dark tale transforms the simple Western plot of "the Search" into a rich psychological study of an obsessed Indian-hater, bent on revenge for the death of his only love and the abduction of his niece. What better actor to play Antihero Ethan Edwards than the quintessential Western icon, John Wayne. We desperately want to identify with Wayne, and yet are pushed away by Ethan's savagery.

We also embrace Martin Pawley, the part Cherokee "journeyman" Hero seeking the guidance of his adopted Uncle Ethan. Although Ethan is respected as a Mentor of Indian customs and the wilderness, Martin sees the obsessive revenge and prejudice beneath Ethan's Mentor-Hero mask, and realizes that the search for Debbie could ultimately bring her death at Ethan's hands.

THE JOURNEY

Texas. 1868. An unstable ORDINARY WORLD of white settlers attempting to civilize a hostile land. Three worlds clash in *The Searchers*: Settlers, Indians, and Wilderness. Settlers and Indians cannot interact except with hostility and destruction. Both vulnerable to the Wilderness. One man holds the Special Powers to wander amongst these three worlds: Ethan Edwards.

Ethan is a man of the wilderness and an obsessed Indian-hater, yet knows their language and customs better than his Indian nephew. He is a tragic loner; an outsider to his family, his community and his culture. Although deeply in love with Martha, Ethan has chosen to wander, refusing the homestead and allowing his brother Aaron to marry Martha and settle down. Ethan's INNER PROBLEM is to seek vengeance for Martha's death and to redeem himself for not being there to save her and Aaron. Ethan's OUTER PROBLEM is to find his niece.

The adopted son of Aaron and Martha, Martin Pawley was found by Ethan, yet Ethan refuses to accept this one-eighth Cherokee as family. Martin's OUTER PROBLEM is to save his adopted sister, Debbie. He too wants vengeance, but Martin has the additional INNER PROBLEM of finding love and a home with girlfriend Laurie.

In Revenge stories, a wrong disrupts the natural order of things and must be set right. In *The Searchers,* this CALL TO ADVENTURE is the massacre of Aaron's family and abduction of young Debbie. This CALL can be broken down into two stages:

- Lars Jorgensen's cattle are stolen, a Comanche ploy to get the men to leave their homesteads vulnerable, allowing...
- Chief Scar's murder raid on Aaron Edwards' homestead.

Ethan returns to the burned ruins of Aaron's home. He protects Martin from the horror of the butchered, defiled bodies of Martha, Aaron and their son. The discovery of Debbie's doll confirms that she and sister Lucy have been abducted. This brutal act forces Ethan and Martin THROUGH A THRESHOLD with no opportunity for REFUSAL. The Search for the girls and vengeance must begin. So determined to enter this SPECIAL WORLD, Ethan puts an abrupt end to the funeral and pushes the Reverend Captain Samuel Clayton and his posse THROUGH THE THRESHOLD. They initiate the Journey's TEST PHASE during which many will willingly bow to the challenges ahead and return to the ORDINARY WORLD. Some will perish along the Journey's trail, and two HEROES will rise to the challenge and see the Journey to its end.

The posse erodes under the conflict of RIVAL MENTORS. Clayton (a SHAPESHIFTING MENTOR representing the Bible's Laws and Society's Laws—as Reverend and Texas Ranger, respectively) and Ethan (MENTOR of the Wilderness and the Indian Culture) clash over what action to take. Ethan finally rejects Clayton and his posse. He moves on with only Martin and Lucy's boyfriend, Brad Jorgensen. Soon Brad too cannot survive the Journey's TESTS. Upon Ethan's news of Lucy's death, Brad makes a mad suicide ride into the Indian camp.

Ethan and Martin continue their search for the next two years without success, yet Ethan remains undaunted. The TEST of time has insured Debbie's safety. She'll be raised as an Indian until she is of age to be a wife. They return to the Jorgensens' place, where Martin reunites with Laurie.

The Jorgensens give Ethan a letter from Futterman with a swatch of clothing from Debbie's apron. This CALL pushes Ethan to resume the search—this time alone. He REFUSES Martin's participation in the Journey, arguing that Debbie isn't his blood relative, and leaves without him.

Laurie also tries to keep Martin from continuing the search, pushing him to remain with her and commit to his Journey of Love and Family. But Martin warns that the stakes of

Debbie's search have been raised. Since Ethan believes that Debbie has been defiled by the Indians, Martin fears his uncle will kill Debbie when he finds her. Laurie can't argue with Martin's stubbornness and pushes him back onto the Journey's road.

Futterman provides the first substantial clue to Debbie's whereabouts, telling Ethan that she is with a Comanche tribe led by Chief Scar. When Ethan refuses to reward Futterman until Debbie is found alive, the greedy THRESHOLD GUARDIAN plans to ambush Ethan and Martin while they sleep. Ethan anticipates Futterman's treachery and kills him. This act raises the stakes as Ethan is now wanted for murder.

Years pass and the TESTS continue for Ethan and Martin as they follow Futterman's lead. These events are described in a letter Martin has sent to Laurie.

- A SHAPESHIFTER Indian woman, Look, leads them to a Comanche village, the site of a cavalry raid.
- Debbie is neither amongst the dead nor one of the cavalry's prisoners, hysterical white girls. (Ethan reveals his racism when he refuses to accept the girls as white any longer, foreshadowing Debbie's danger in his hands.)

Laurie finishes Martin's letter. Its completion closes the TEST PHASE of Ethan and Martin's Journey. Distraught by the letter's formal ending, Laurie concludes that their relationship has ended; the ORDEAL of their Journey of Love and Family is complete. Laurie will choose a RIVAL rather than wait for her true love to return. If Martin continues, he will find himself on the same tragic Journey that Ethan travels, without commitment to the hearth.

At last Ethan and Martin APPROACH THE INMOST CAVE. With no further leads to Debbie's whereabouts, fate takes Ethan and Martin into a New Mexico bar, where they find old Mose. This HERALD knows where Debbie is and sets up a meeting with Figueroa (ALLY/THRESHOLD GUARDIAN). Figueroa leads them to Scar's camp disguised as traders. Chief Scar emerges from his teepee. Ethan faces him—nose to nose, reflections of one another, HERO and SHADOW.

They enter Scar's teepee, the INMOST CAVE, where Scar shows Ethan the scalps he has taken in retaliation for the massacre of his two sons. Horrified, Ethan and Martin look up and see Debbie holding these symbols of death, and wearing clothing that represents the SHADOW's people. Ethan's worst fear is realized: Debbie is Scar's squaw.

At their camp, Ethan and Martin try to anticipate Scar's next move. Debbie descends from the ridge, a visual RESURRECTION—we share Martin's hope that Debbie has been set free. But this is a FALSE RESURRECTION, a REVERSAL; Debbie warns Martin to leave. At one time she prayed that Martin would be her HERO, but now the Indians are her people. Hearing her confess the unspeakable, Ethan threatens to kill Debbie, the ORDEAL. Martin protects her, drawing his gun on Ethan. Ethan will shoot Martin if he has to, but Scar's men attack, wounding Ethan. Ethan and Martin flee without Debbie, and find refuge in a cave.

Martin heals Ethan's wounds; yet having faced death, Ethan presents his last will and testament. He has failed to kill Debbie and prepares for his ROAD BACK, even if it means accepting his death. Ethan bequeaths everything to Martin and disowns Debbie. Ethan's REWARD is his acknowledgment that Debbie is no "blood kin." This is the DARK REWARD that Martin fears. Martin rejects his MENTOR'S gift, and nearly stabs him with a knife, hoping to see the MENTOR die. But Martin's threat gives Ethan the strength to pull through (a RESURRECTION). Their relationship is at its furthest point. Fully aware of Ethan's motives, Martin now sees Ethan as his SHADOW. This ORDEAL initiates their ROAD BACK.

They return to the Jorgensens homestead, and interrupt Laurie's marriage to RIVAL Charlie McCorry. Martin drags Laurie away and vows his love to her. Having denounced his MENTOR, Martin's deeper REWARD is the awareness that he will not follow in Ethan's footsteps. He will commit to his love and the hearth. However, the RESURRECTION of Laurie and Martin's relationship is interrupted by Clayton's demands that Ethan and Martin serve time for Futterman's murder. But this too is interrupted. This time by a Cavalry soldier requesting support to attack Scar's camp that the HERALD old Mose discovered. Every time Ethan's trail is lost, the TRICKSTER FOOL seems to get the Journey back on track.

Usually the ROAD BACK pushes the HERO homeward; however, this ROAD BACK pushes the HEROES back into the SPECIAL WORLD. They failed the ORDEAL and now Ethan and Martin must renew the Journey and see it to the end. Suspense is heightened because we know where HERO and MENTOR stand. Instead of supporting his MENTOR'S actions, Martin must stop them.

As they await the dawn attack, Martin pushes his own Journey and convinces Clayton and Ethan to let him sneak in and take Debbie away, beginning the RESURRECTION SEQUENCE. He finds Debbie in Scar's teepee. She embraces her HERO, the answer to her prayers. Scar finds them and Martin shoots the Indian Chief dead. His gunshots signal Ethan and Clayton's attack.

Ethan finds Scar's corpse and scalps him. Although vicious, Ethan's act mirrors Scar's belief in taking a scalp for the death of his own. This is Ethan's only recourse in revenge for Martha's death. He becomes his SHADOW and scalps his enemy. (This cathartic act actually purges Ethan's SHADOW allowing him to accept Debbie.)

Ethan chases Debbie down. He lifts his niece forcefully and in a beautiful gesture of acceptance carries her away in his arms. (Ethan's PSYCHOLOGICAL RESURRECTION as well as Debbie's PHYSICAL RESURRECTION.) This emotional catharsis of his acceptance completes the Journey's RESURRECTION.

Ethan and Martin return Debbie to the Jorgensen homestead; her reintroduction to her "family" is the ELIXIR. Martin reunites with Laurie, shows his commitment to her and they share their ELIXIR OF LOVE.

Ethan is left outside, framed by the doorway, the tragic Loner Hero in awkward hesitation. He refuses the THRESHOLD leading to comfort of family and turns to continue his wanderings into the Wilderness. In a poetic image that bookends with the film's Opening Image, the door slams shut and the screen goes dark.

FADE OUT

BUTCH CASSIDY AND THE SUNDANCE KID
(U.S., 1969)

"Every day you get older—that's a law."

—Butch Cassidy (Paul Newman)

Written by William Goldman
Directed by George Roy Hill

Two legendary outlaws refuse to change with the times of the Turn-of-the-Century West while staying one step ahead of a Superposse.

LANDMARKS OF THE JOURNEY

The ultimate Refusal is to run, and Butch and Sundance run throughout their story. From Butch's introduction in the "state-of-the-art" bank until their "fade out" in Bolivia, Butch and Sundance constantly refuse to accept that the times are changing. They must change their Outlaw ways or die; yet, their realization that they cannot change makes their Journey all the more poignant. Goldman has created a classic study of revealing character "on-the-run." Character is action; a character reveals himself by the actions he makes. What better way to reveal the essence of a character than to place him in the worst position imaginable, confronting his worst fears? Enter the most frightening Shadow Butch and Sundance could ever imagine.

THE JOURNEY

Teamed with gunslinger, The Sundance Kid, the legendary Butch Cassidy leads The Hole-in-the-Wall Gang, the last great outlaw gang of the Wild West. Butch specializes in bank and train robberies, but the changing times are putting pressure on his ORDINARY WORLD. American banks are using higher security measures, and Butch and Sundance aren't getting any younger, the OUTER PROBLEM. Preferring the old days and old ways, Butch wants to recapture the past, his INNER PROBLEM.

Butch's initial CALL TO ADVENTURE is an INNER STIRRING. While riding back to Hole-in-the-Wall, Butch tells Sundance his latest plan, to move to Bolivia. Sundance shrugs it off as yet another one of Butch's fantasies, a REFUSAL.

Butch's gang is stirring as well. They want change, and Harvey Logan challenges Butch for leadership, a CALL. At first RELUCTANT to fight, Butch uses his wily skills to fell the giant man. Regaining his position as Leader and MENTOR, Butch agrees to use Logan's plan to rob the Union Pacific Flyer.

Butch and the Gang resume the legendary ways of their ORDINARY WORLD, successfully robbing the Union Pacific Flyer, and again on its return trip, easily tricking Woodcock, the devoted THRESHOLD GUARDIAN protecting E. H. Harriman's safe. Using a bit too much gunpowder, Butch blows the safe and its cash. As Butch's Gang scrambles for the cash, another train approaches. The "Superposse," a SHADOW, bursts from a train car and thunders toward them. This CALL leaves no time for REFUSAL. Several of Butch's men are killed. The rest flee, and the long, grueling CHASE begins.

The entire Superposse Chase is the THRESHOLD that finally pushes Butch and Sundance to leave for Bolivia. This THRESHOLD SEQUENCE consists of a series of TESTS that propel our heroes to face a memorable ORDEAL at the top of a cliff.

In the first TEST, Butch and Sundance hope to divide the Superposse. The two split from the rest of the Gang and take their own road. But the Superposse follows Butch and Sundance in full force, visually establishing the SHADOW'S sole goal: to hunt down Butch and Sundance.

Hiding out in a brothel, Butch and Sundance use Sweetface, an ALLY, to send the Posse in the wrong direction. Sweetface fails, giving up the heroes. And the CHASE continues.

Butch and Sundance try tricking the Superposse, riding on one horse, but this is only a temporary diversion. The two see Sheriff Ray Bledsoe, a MENTOR. Showing their desperation and fear, Butch and Sundance try to REFUSE the Journey they've been thrown into. They ask for Bledsoe's help to enlist in the Army and fight the Spanish. But Sheriff Bledsoe can't help them. Wearing the HERALD'S mask, he warns them that there's going to be a bloody end for the outlaws, foreshadowing their death. And the CHASE continues.

Butch and Sundance try to recognize the Superposse. By attaching some human identity, they can better face this SHADOW and make it more vulnerable. This is their APPROACH TO THE INMOST CAVE. Abandoning their horses, Butch and Sundance climb higher and higher into more treacherous terrain, the Superposse nipping their tails. Butch finally recognizes the Posse's leader, Lefors.

Trapped on a cliff overlooking a river, Butch and Sundance confront their Journey's ORDEAL. Spent, beaten, desperate, they can fight or they can surrender. They're outnumbered if they fight. And they'll go to jail if they surrender. Butch offers a third option: jump. Sundance balks confessing his greatest fear: he can't swim. Butch laughs it off—the jump will kill them. They jump. And survive, cheating death.

They return to the home of Sundance's girl, Etta Place. She welcomes them, relieved that they aren't dead, their RESURRECTION. Butch reads a news article confirming his worst fear—the Superposse will not stop until the outlaws are dead. They decide to go to Bolivia, their REWARD. Etta will join them but she refuses to see them die.

In a lively THRESHOLD SEQUENCE, Butch, Sundance and Etta leave America for Bolivia with high expectations... only to arrive in a dump. Furious, Sundance detests the SPECIAL WORLD of Bolivia.

But Butch believes he'll get over it after they rob a bank. This begins a new TEST PHASE. Butch and Sundance can't speak the local language and fail to rob a bank, so MENTOR Etta teaches them Spanish.

Success returns quickly to the old outlaws. Butch and Sundance—Bandidos Yanquis—become legends again. However, their boon is short-lived. During dinner (an APPROACH), Butch spots Lefors. The SHADOW has tracked them down. While Sundance prefers the bold APPROACH and wants to take on Lafors and finish it, Butch decides they'll go straight, to "outlast the bastard" (a sort of REFUSAL).

They get jobs as payroll guards for Percy Garris. But on the trail, Bandits ambush them and kill Percy, the ORDEAL. Surrounded, Butch and Sundance question which side of the law they are on. Butch confesses that he's always been an Outlaw. They give up the payroll to save themselves, a RESURRECTION.

They return to the Bandits' camp to retrieve the payroll bags, the second stage of the ORDEAL. But the Bandits won't give the bags up without a fight. Already outnumbered, the odds become overwhelming when, in the face of death, Butch admits that he's never killed anyone before. The Bandit Leader laughs off Sundance's final plea to leave. Gunfire. The bloodbath. Only Butch and Sundance remain standing, shattered, yet RESURRECTED with the awareness of their ROAD BACK.

They've failed at going straight, and don't know what to do next. At their campfire, Etta can't convince them to try other ways of going straight. Their silence confirms their REWARD, that there is only one road for Butch and Sundance.

Etta tells them she's going back home. Butch and Sundance let her in a quiet, powerful ROAD BACK moment. Butch is well aware of the significance of Etta's departure; this HERALD warns of their impending deaths.

Butch and Sundance quickly commit to their Outlaw ways, and are soon trapped and wounded in an adobe building by the Bolivian police, beginning the RESURRECTION. As more than a hundred members of the Bolivian Cavalry surround them—shot up and bloodied, Butch and Sundance REFUSE to accept the death that awaits them outside. Butch offers his latest great idea, to go to Australia. Finally, Butch realizes their SHADOW, Lefors, isn't out there. Relieved that this is merely a TEST and not an ORDEAL (a final REFUSAL of death), they emerge from the building ready to fight.

The hail of gunfire is heard over the final freeze-frame of Butch and Sundance. Their death is likely, but the frame dissolves to sepia-tone like the opening newsreel, RESURRECTING their legend. And granting Butch and Sundance the ELIXIR of immortality.

FADE OUT

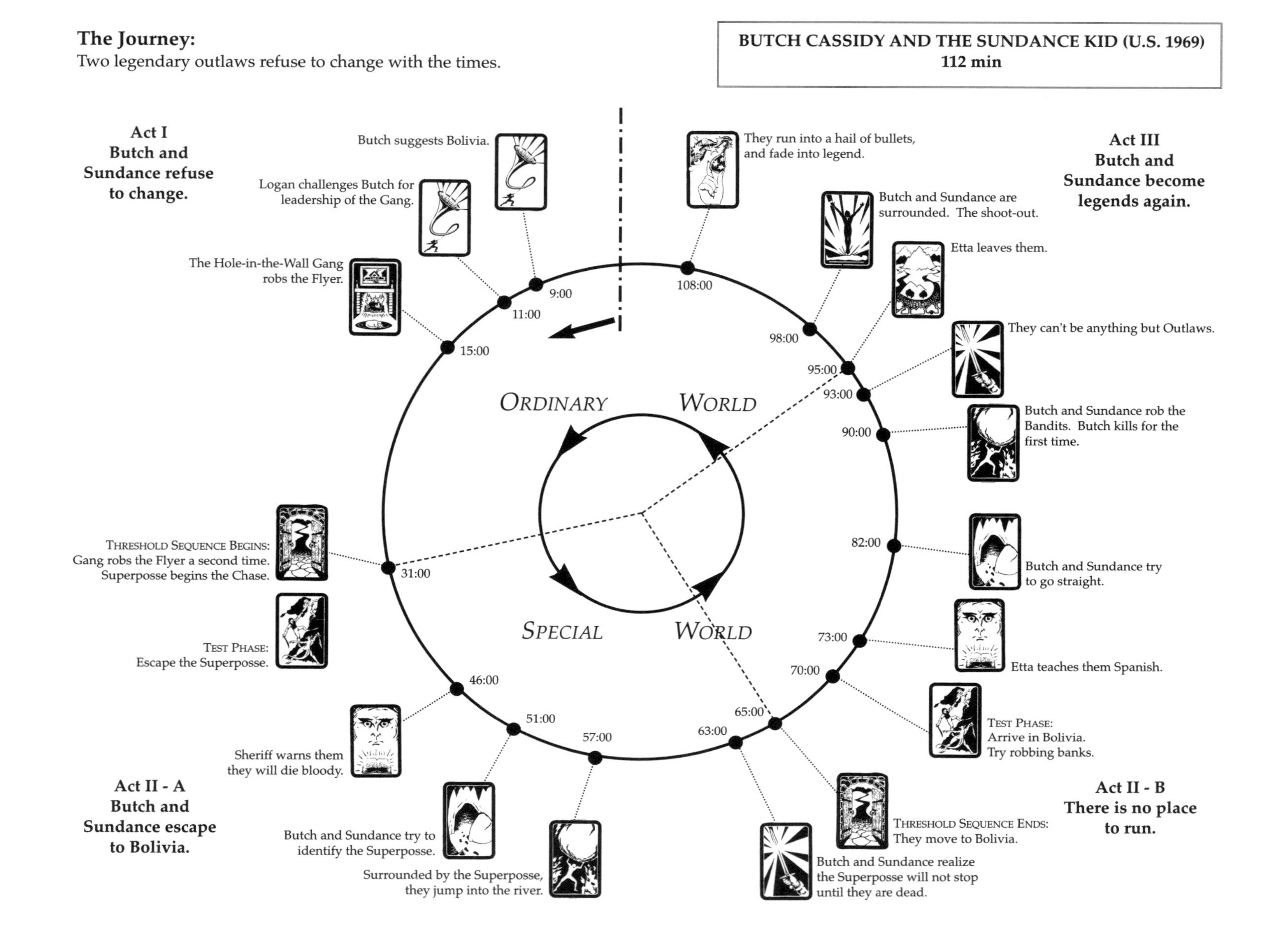

The Journey:
Two legendary outlaws refuse to change with the times.
BUTCH CASSIDY AND THE SUNDANCE KID (U.S. 1969)
112 min
Act I
Butch and Sundance refuse to change.
Butch suggests Bolivia.
Logan challenges Butch for leadership of the Gang.
The Hole-in-the-Wall Gang robs the Flyer.
9:00
11:00
15:00
THRESHOLD SEQUENCE BEGINS:
Gang robs the Flyer a second time.
Superposse begins the Chase.
31:00
TEST PHASE:
Escape the Superposse.
46:00
Sheriff warns them they will die bloody.
51:00
Butch and Sundance try to identify the Superposse.
57:00
Surrounded by the Superposse, they jump into the river.
Act II - A
Butch and Sundance escape to Bolivia.
ORDINARY WORLD
SPECIAL WORLD
63:00
Butch and Sundance realize the Superposse will not stop until they are dead.
65:00
THRESHOLD SEQUENCE ENDS:
They move to Bolivia.
70:00
TEST PHASE:
Arrive in Bolivia.
Try robbing banks.
73:00
Etta teaches them Spanish.
82:00
Butch and Sundance try to go straight.
Act II - B
There is no place to run.
90:00
Butch and Sundance rob the Bandits. Butch kills for the first time.
93:00
They can't be anything but Outlaws.
95:00
Etta leaves them.
98:00
Butch and Sundance are surrounded. The shoot-out.
108:00
They run into a hail of bullets, and fade into legend.
Act III
Butch and Sundance become legends again.

DANCES WITH WOLVES
(U.S., 1990)

"Of all the trails in this life, there is one that matters more than all the others. It is the trail of a true human being. I think you are on this trail and it is good to see."

—Kicking Bird (Graham Greene)

Written by Michael Blake
Based on his novel
Directed by Kevin Costner

Civil War hero Lt. John Dunbar leaves the insanity of war-torn civilization and "finds" himself in the Frontier with the Sioux.

LANDMARKS OF THE JOURNEY

Dances With Wolves shows a man who searches for the Frontier, but ends up finding himself. Dunbar passes through several physical and emotional Thresholds of self-discovery as he realizes his loneliness in the Ordinary World of the white culture and the military. Each Threshold Crossing initiates a new series of Tests, Ordeals and Rewards as Dunbar passes deeper into his Special World with the Sioux, gradually casting off the "skin" of his old self, embracing his Resurrected self and finding friendship, love and family with the Sioux.

The story's structure is a wonderful example of the malleability of the Hero's Journey. To prepare for his Journey, Dunbar goes through an Ordeal/Resurrection in the opening moments of the story. Elevated to heroic status in the Civil War, Dunbar chooses his Reward: to see the Frontier before it disappears. He leaves the white man's Ordinary World, and enters a Special World: a world of Shadows feared and subsequently destroyed by white civilization. By Journey's end, Dunbar becomes a Hero in this Special World, the polar opposite of what he was in the Ordinary World. He discards the Hero's mask of the Ordinary World and is resurrected as Dances With Wolves, now seen as white man's Shadow who must be destroyed.

THE JOURNEY

1863. The American Civil War. The striking opening image effectively introduces our hero, Lt. John J. Dunbar, in a chaotic, crazy ORDINARY WORLD. Dunbar seizes the agonizing opportunity to escape the amputation of his leg as doctors take a much-needed coffee break. He would rather face a heroic death with both feet.

Dunbar joins a fellow Union soldier at St. David's Field, where Confederates and Federals square off on opposite sides of the field. Nobody will make a move. Dunbar rides a lone suicidal charge, miraculously dodging enemy fire and unwittingly rallying his fellow soldiers. This is Dunbar's RESURRECTION, a moment usually faced at the end of a Hero's Journey. The Union wins the battle, and Dunbar survives, a Hero. His leg spared by General Tide's surgeon, Dunbar is REWARDED a horse, Cisco, and a transfer to any post away from the war's front lines. An additional REWARD is his awareness or INNER STIRRING that he needs to leave this ORDINARY WORLD and see the Frontier "before it's gone," his OUTER PROBLEM. Dunbar reports to Fort Hays, on the border or THRESHOLD of the Frontier. Major Fambrough, the crazed outpost commander and THRESHOLD GUARDIAN, assigns Dunbar a "knight's errand" to Fort Sedgewick, the CALL TO ADVENTURE.

Dunbar willingly seeks the adventures that await him on the Frontier. Major Fambrough first expresses the Journey's dangers (a type of REFUSAL). Driven mad by his post on the edge of the Frontier, Fambrough salutes Dunbar's departure by committing suicide.

The FIRST THRESHOLD sequence encompasses Dunbar's travel to the Frontier and arrival at Fort Sedgewick. Along the way, Teamster Timmons (a THRESHOLD GUARDIAN) introduces Dunbar, with white man's eyes, to the savage Frontier with its "goddamn Indians" and "stinking buffalo" (a REFUSAL). They arrive at Fort Sedgewick and find the outpost abandoned. Timmons tries to persuade Dunbar to REFUSE his crazy Journey and return to Civilization. But Dunbar forces him at gunpoint to unload the supplies for "his post."

Dunbar settles into his new world with several TESTS. He makes ALLIES and confronts ENEMIES. He builds a corral for Cisco, cleans up the polluted water, and befriends a wolf, Two Socks. While Dunbar washes clothes, a Sioux Medicine Man, Kicking Bird, scouts out the fort. Dunbar runs off this perceived ENEMY, yet this "magnificent fellow" impresses him. Encounters with the ENEMY continue. The Sioux twice fail to steal Dunbar's horse, Cisco. On the second attempt Dunbar faces Wind In His Hair. The warrior shouts his challenge and gallops off. Dunbar stands up to this ENEMY, passing the TEST, and faints.

Fed up with waiting for the next meeting, Dunbar finally takes action and makes a bold, decorated APPROACH to the Sioux village. He encounters a Sioux woman, Stands With A Fist, bleeding from a self-inflicted wound, and takes her to the Sioux village. Dunbar's arrival frightens the Sioux, and Wind In His Hair rejects the white man from their SPECIAL WORLD, a REFUSAL.

Yet Dunbar's CALL stirs the Sioux' curiosity as they try to fathom its meaning; Kicking Bird and Wind In His Hair pay a visit to Dunbar's fort. The TEST of communication proves difficult, but they eventually understand "buffalo." They exchange gifts and

Dunbar accepts Kicking Bird's invitation to the village. They share a pipe, an important ritual that binds ALLIES.

One evening, a buffalo stampede awakens Dunbar. He knows that this bears good news and rushes to the Sioux village, the APPROACH TO THE INMOST CAVE. Dunbar interrupts their ceremony, offending the Sioux, but Kicking Bird understands Dunbar's announcement and they quickly accept the white man as a HERALD of good news.

He joins the Sioux on their search for the buffalo. They find a field littered with rotting carcasses of skinned buffalo, and the tracks from white men's wagons. Having entered the Sioux' world, Dunbar sees the Frontier through their eyes, and the white man as their ENEMY.

They encounter the buffalo herd. Dunbar joins their hunt and saves one young warrior, Smiles A Lot, from a charging buffalo. On the field of their ORDEAL, Dunbar and Wind In His Hair share a buffalo liver, symbolizing Dunbar's acceptance as an ALLY. This is Dunbar's REWARD and THRESHOLD into another deeper SPECIAL WORLD.

At the buffalo feast, Dunbar exchanges gifts with Wind In His Hair, giving him his military coat and accepting the warrior's breastplate. Dunbar's physical RESURRECTION as a Sioux has begun. But Dunbar must return to his outpost and quickly realizes how completely lonely he feels in his white culture, the greatest REWARD from this first ORDEAL.

The Sioux prepare a war party on their ENEMIES, the Pawnee. Dunbar offers to fight, but he's REFUSED, since he is not a Sioux warrior. However, Kicking Bird requests that Dunbar watch over his family while he is gone. Dunbar accepts this CALL with honor. And Kicking Bird addresses Dunbar with his Sioux name, Dances With Wolves.

Dances With Wolves sees Stands With A Fist, who teaches him how to speak Sioux. Attracted to her, he discovers that Stands With A Fist is in mourning. He decides to give her time and leaves her, but the separation from the SPECIAL WORLD only makes man and woman realize their love for each other. They finally pass through this THRESHOLD at the stream when they kiss and make love.

The Sioux prepare for a counter-attack by the Pawnee, an APPROACH, and welcome Dances With Wolves' gift of rifles. The Sioux have now accepted Dances With Wolves as one of their warriors. With his help, the Sioux overpower the Pawnee, the ORDEAL.

Dances With Wolves' heroic commitment yields two important REWARDS. First, he no longer thinks of himself as his old name but as Dances With Wolves. Second, Kicking Bird releases Stands With A Fist from mourning and she marries Dances With Wolves, a REWARD and THRESHOLD.

Dances With Wolves has committed himself to the SPECIAL WORLD, his new family and community, and gives his best friend, Kicking Bird, his REWARD. He answers a question that had been plaguing the Sioux since first meeting Dunbar. He warns that the white man will come to the Frontier in numbers "like the stars." This begins Dances With Wolves' ROAD BACK; however, instead of taking a REWARD or ELIXIR back to his ORDINARY WORLD, as seen in many heroes' journeys, Dances With Wolves uses his knowledge of the ORDINARY WORLD to warn his new family in the SPECIAL WORLD. The chief, Ten Bears, agrees with this HERALD, and decides that they will move to their winter camp. But Dances With Wolves must return to the ORDINARY WORLD to retrieve his Journal, a type of MENTOR, that would lead the white man to the Sioux. Soldiers ambush Dances With Wolves at Fort Sedgewick. These new ENEMIES kill Cisco, and hold the former officer as a traitor. This moment completes the Journey's ROAD BACK.

The Soldiers offer Dunbar better conditions if he helps them against the Sioux. Speaking Lakota, Dances With Wolves rejects them and their world. Psychologically Dunbar has completed his RESURRECTION as Dances With Wolves, a Sioux Hero, and SHADOW to his white world.

As Soldiers transport Dances With Wolves to Fort Hays, they are ambushed by Wind In His Hair and his rescue party. Dunbar is freed, his physical RESURRECTION, and returned to family and friends, an ELIXIR.

Fearing that his status as traitor with the whites threatens the Sioux, Dances With Wolves decides to leave the Sioux. He must sacrifice himself, a second RESURRECTION, separating from his new family in order to protect them. As the Army approaches, Dances With Wolves and Stands With A Fist leave the valley and their Lakota family. They hold within their hearts the ELIXIR of family and friendship.

The Army arrives but the Sioux village is gone, the ELIXIR of Safety and Peace for now. The Epilogue confirms that their safety is short-lived. The time of the Horse Culture and the Great Frontier will finally pass into history.

FADE OUT

UNFORGIVEN
(U.S., 1992)

"Just because we're going on this killing doesn't mean I'm going back to the way I was."

—William Munny (Clint Eastwood)

Written by David Webb Peoples
Directed by Clint Eastwood

Desperate to help his family, a reformed murderer comes out of retirement and tempts his inner Shadow.

LANDMARKS OF THE JOURNEY

Unforgiven is a story about revenge and its effect on the people that seek it. *Unforgiven*'s administrator of revenge is a retired gunslinger, a murderer who has been reformed by his good wife. But after her death, he's afraid to leave his failing pig farm, as if it's the penance he must serve for his Shadow past. For the benefit of his family, he must re-enter the Valley of Death to serve vengeance: to kill a pair of cowboys who disfigured a prostitute. On a psychological level, Munny must take this Journey to prove that he is a reformed man. But can Munny tempt his Shadow side (while upholding his wife's lessons) and rise from this Journey unscathed? As long as Munny is the instrument serving another's vengeance, his Journey's end seems assured. But that's much too easy. What if on the Journey's trail, an Ally's death makes vengeance more personal? Instead of shunning the Shadow's mask, now the gunslinger must wear it.

THE JOURNEY

Ex-murderer turned pig farmer William Munny lives in his ORDINARY WORLD guided by the memory of his recently deceased wife, Claudia, who reformed him of his wickedness. It's been eleven years since he's taken a drop of whiskey or fired a gun at a man. But the farm's failing and Munny needs to provide for his son and daughter, Munny's OUTER PROBLEM. His INNER PROBLEM is to honor his wife's lessons and not become the bloodthirsty killer he was.

Unforgiven is a Revenge Story. The CALL TO ADVENTURE is the offense that disrupts the natural order of things and must be set right. Big Whiskey, Wyoming. 1880. Two cowboys disfigure a prostitute's face with a knife. Sheriff "Little Bill" Daggett punishes them only by imposing a "fine": a number of horses must be delivered to the Saloon/Flophouse proprietor in exchange for his "damaged property." The outraged prostitutes seek justice and pool together a $1,000 bounty on the two cowboys' heads.

A young gunslinger, "The Schofield Kid," solicits Munny to join him in killing the cowboys and splitting the bounty, the CALL TO ADVENTURE. This HERALD knows the legend of this bloodthirsty gunslinger and seeks help from the MENTOR. Although he needs the money, Munny's REFUSAL is quick, "I ain't like that no more." He returns to wrestling pigs and eating mud. Munny watches the Kid ride off into the distance, beginning the THRESHOLD SEQUENCE.

Resolved to accept the Journey, Munny puts aside the picture of his wife, Claudia, the MENTOR of his "good ways," and picks up his gun, the symbol of his killer ways. Before he sets forth on his Journey, Munny places flowers on his wife's grave, respecting the lessons she has given him. He clumsily mounts his horse and leaves his son and daughter, completing Munny's entrance THROUGH THE THRESHOLD.

Munny enlists an ALLY, his old partner, Ned Logan, to join the hunt. They meet up with the Schofield Kid, but have to convince the Kid to allow Ned on the Journey, a TEST. Suspicious of the Kid's eyesight, Ned TESTS him on the trail. The Kid finally admits he can see a distance of only 50 yards, and Ned doubts his benefit as a killer. But Munny keeps the team together; 50 yards is all you need to kill someone.

Back in Big Whiskey, "Little Bill" Daggett refuses to let the bounty disrupt the town's ORDINARY WORLD. He posts a sign banning all firearms in the town's district. When English Bob arrives seeking the bounty, Daggett beats him and runs him out of town as a warning to other would-be assassins.

Along his Journey to Big Whiskey, Munny is TESTED by his past, his SHADOW self. He assures himself of the strength of his wife's lessons, proud that he's a changed man who hasn't touched a gun or a drop of whiskey in eleven years. Their final night on the trail, the three bounty hunters sit around a campfire, the APPROACH TO THE INMOST CAVE. The Schofield Kid wants to hear stories of Munny's killings. But the old gunslinger suppresses the past, claiming that he "can't recollect."

Munny, Ned, and the Kid ride into the INMOST CAVE of the town. The driving rain prevents them from seeing the Sheriff's sign prohibiting all firearms.

The three go to Skinny's Saloon where the first of a series of ORDEALS occurs. Sick and drenched, Munny waits at a table, while the Schofield Kid gets the information about the cowboys from the prostitutes upstairs. Ned excuses himself to spend some time with the prostitutes. Daggett enters the saloon with his deputies and confronts Munny. He finds Munny's gun, and beats him senseless. The prostitutes rush Ned and the Schofield Kid out the upper window, their RESURRECTION. The sadistic Daggett lets Munny crawl out of the saloon, into the mud and rain where Ned and the Kid quickly get him out of town.

Hovering at the edge of death, Munny claims that he has seen the Angel of Death and confesses his fear of dying. Delilah, the disfigured prostitute, nurses Munny. She offers him a "free one." But he declines on account of his wife. Munny is RESURRECTED maintaining the lessons of his MENTOR of Peace and Goodness, a REWARD of this first ORDEAL.

Munny, Ned and the Kid find the first cowboy, the second ORDEAL. Ned shoots the cowboy's horse, pinning the young man, but Ned loses his nerve and REFUSES to murder him, a REVERSAL. Munny takes charge and shoots the cowboy. The bounty hunters listen to the cowboy's pleas, as he dies a slow, agonizing death. This ORDEAL yields the painful lesson that killing a man is not easy.

Shaken by the ORDEAL, Ned can't finish the Journey (his REWARD), and leaves Munny and the Kid only to face another ORDEAL. Daggett's posse captures Ned.

Meanwhile, Munny and the Kid stake out the second cowboy's hideaway. It is the Kid's turn to face death. His MENTOR, Munny, covers him as he shoots the Second Cowboy in the outhouse. Munny and the Kid escape, their RESURRECTION, completing this FINAL ORDEAL.

On the outskirts of town, Munny and the Kid await their bounty. Paying the emotional price of murder, the Kid finds comfort in a whiskey bottle. He confesses that this was the first man he ever killed. His MENTOR tries to ease the Kid's pain with words of advice and a swig of whiskey. Both are ready for their return home, itching to leave this world of death.

A prostitute delivers their bounty, the REWARD, and the news that Daggett killed Ned. This HERALD tells them that Ned's dying words warned of Munny's wrath. The news shocks Munny. He takes a swig of whiskey. Eyes burning with vengeance. His SHADOW overcomes him, the ROAD BACK. That night, again in the driving rain, Munny tosses the empty whiskey bottle and rides into town.

Munny passes the display of Ned's corpse outside the Saloon. He enters, interrupting Daggett's celebration with his men. Munny quickly kills Skinny for allowing the display of his friend's corpse. In a bloody gunfight, Munny outsmarts Daggett and shoots him and several of his deputies. Munny's RESURRECTION amazes the pulp writer, Beauchamp. As Munny takes a drink, Daggett—still living—struggles for his pistol but Munny stops him and without mercy shoots him in the head.

Munny leaves the Saloon and heads out of town. The terrified townsfolk refuse to shoot this "Angel of Death." He warns them that he'll return if they don't bury his friend properly or if they should cut up any more whores. He uses the threat of violence to force morality on the town and prevent further violence, the first ELIXIR.

Has this Journey of Death reverted Munny back to his bloodthirsty ways? In the Epilogue, we learn that Munny has moved to San Francisco with his children where it is said he prospers in dry goods. In a savage act of revenge, Munny has purged himself of his SHADOW, his ELIXIR. Redeemed and RESURRECTED, he at last can leave his wife's grave, and the pig farm, and return to the world of the living.

FADE OUT

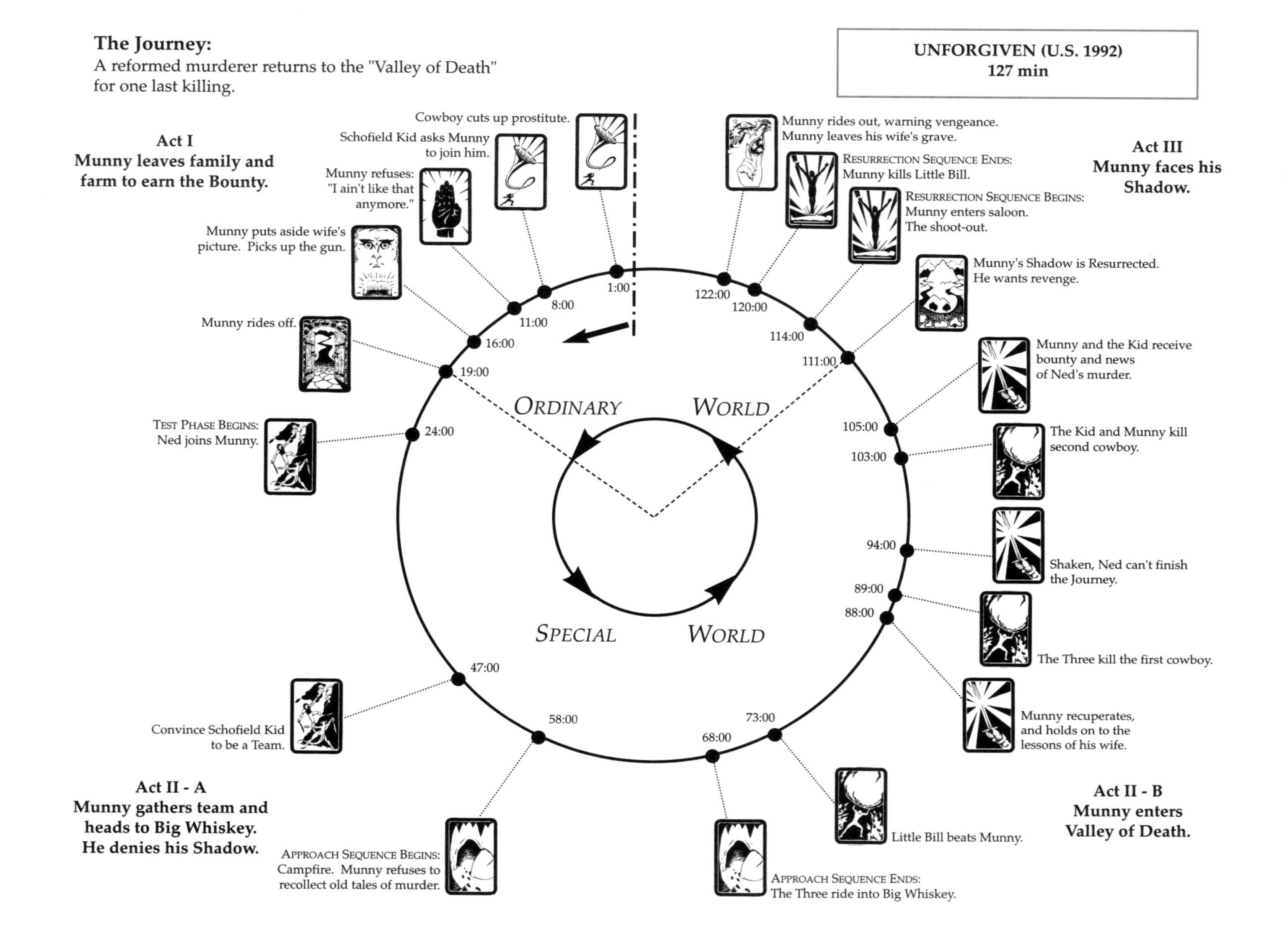

The Journey:
A reformed murderer returns to the "Valley of Death" for one last killing.
UNFORGIVEN (U.S. 1992)
127 min
Act I
Munny leaves family and farm to earn the Bounty.
Cowboy cuts up prostitute.
1:00
Schofield Kid asks Munny to join him.
8:00
Munny refuses: "I ain't like that anymore."
11:00
Munny puts aside wife's picture. Picks up the gun.
16:00
Munny rides off.
19:00
TEST PHASE BEGINS: Ned joins Munny.
24:00
Convince Schofield Kid to be a Team.
47:00
Act II - A
Munny gathers team and heads to Big Whiskey. He denies his Shadow.
APPROACH SEQUENCE BEGINS: Campfire. Munny refuses to recollect old tales of murder.
58:00
APPROACH SEQUENCE ENDS: The Three ride into Big Whiskey.
68:00
Little Bill beats Munny.
73:00
Act II - B
Munny enters Valley of Death.
Munny recuperates, and holds on to the lessons of his wife.
88:00
The Three kill the first cowboy.
89:00
Shaken, Ned can't finish the Journey.
94:00
The Kid and Munny kill second cowboy.
103:00
Munny and the Kid receive bounty and news of Ned's murder.
105:00
Munny's Shadow is Resurrected. He wants revenge.
111:00
RESURRECTION SEQUENCE BEGINS: Munny enters saloon. The shoot-out.
114:00
RESURRECTION SEQUENCE ENDS: Munny kills Little Bill.
120:00
Munny rides out, warning vengeance. Munny leaves his wife's grave.
122:00
Act III
Munny faces his Shadow.
ORDINARY WORLD
SPECIAL WORLD

THE MYTHIC STRUCTURE OF HORROR

Gothic manors, fog-shrouded graveyards, monsters lurking in the shadows; this is not a world we tread willingly, yet the alarum has sounded. The curse has stricken this town. Friends have fallen and we alone must face our worst fear, vanquish the Shadow, and bring our world back to light.

"BE AFRAID, BE VERY AFRAID."

Horror preys on our fears. Effective horror preys on our most primitive fears: the unknown, powerlessness, alienation, dehumanization, mutilation, death. When a Hero's Journey taps these base fears, it unsettles the horror audience at its primal core and invokes identification with the Hero's plight. The more universal the fear (dark basements, crowds, heights, bugs, chain saws), the stronger the audience's identification, and the more effective the horror.

While films in other genres address these same fears (e.g., *Home Alone, Fatal Attraction*), the Horror film plays with these fears for one effect: to terrify, horrify, and many times just plain gross out their audience. Which is what the Horror audience expects: to live through this horrifying Journey, to face our own fears from the safety of our Cineplex chairs. Horror audiences relish a good scare.

THE ROOT OF HORROR: POWERLESSNESS

Man is an organized being who seeks structure, order, and understanding. Horror throws organized man into chaos by placing him in an unpredictable world where he must face the unknown. Nothing is as it should be in this Special World. No one can be trusted, not even ourselves.

Man feels powerless in light of this unknown monster. As the Hero in a Horror film gradually learns to understand the monster, he gains power over it, and dissipates his fear.

The fear of powerlessness is a major theme in the many Horror stories about mutation and animalization. In these tales we fear we are losing ourselves, that we are becoming something more primitive than man, or tipping Darwin's scale in the other direction, that animals are becoming more than animals. Whether the stories involve werewolves, vampires, Mr. Hyde, or, in the case of these analyses, Seth Brundle's mutation into a fly, man fears that he has lost control of his own humanity.

Many times the worst fear is not the understood monster, but the Shadow that cannot be comprehended. Sure, it's terrifying for an individual to face death or mutilation or loss of identity; however, effective horror threatens not merely the individual but the very foundations of our civilization. In *Halloween*, the Shadow isn't simply a knife-wielding boy, but the Boogie-Man. The alien seedpods in *Invasion of the Body Snatchers* threaten not only our Hero, but the town—and they are spreading!

Regardless of the level of powerlessness we experience, the forces of chaos must be defeated. The horror audience anticipates that the Hero will bring the unknown to light, vanquish the Shadow, and return our world to normalcy. Many times the Hero succeeds, but happy endings are not always the case in horror films.

THE THREE TYPES OF HORROR STORIES

Horror stories generally fall into one of the three following categories:

1) Man battles an outside monster that has come to pay a visit. These stories include demons, vampires, diseases, alien visitors (*Invasion of the Body Snatchers*), monster sharks (*Jaws*).
2) Man creates the monster, seemingly with good intentions, that gets out of hand and must be destroyed. The classic story is Mary Shelley's *Frankenstein*. We can also include genetic experimentation and inventions that have turned disastrous (*The Fly*).
3) Man is the Monster. These stories address the wickedness of man. Man confronts the dark side of his nature. The Hero can face the Shadow within himself as in *Dr. Jekyll and Mr. Hyde*, or this Evil may be externalized or personified (*The Silence of the Lambs, Halloween*).

Each of these stories provides a central thrust or action that propels us to the end of the film. Horror thrills aren't enough to make a successful film; those terrifying sequences need to be structured around the central action.

THE SPECIAL WORLD IS NOT ONE WE WILLINGLY WISH TO ENTER

In Horror, the Special World is usually not a place the Hero would gladly enter. While the adventure Hero seeks to save the world or the romantic Hero desires the object of affection, the horror Hero needs to escape the threat of the Shadow. The Hero's Journey can be seen as a continual loss of means of escape, until there is no choice but to enter the Special World and confront the Shadow. In *Jaws*, Chief Brody would rather close the beaches and hope that the Shark swims away than hunt it down. Seth Brundle's Journey in *The Fly* wasn't desired or even planned. Laurie's "reluctant" Journey in *Halloween* illustrates the most extreme example of a Hero escaping the Special World until the last possible moment.

Not that the Horror genre doesn't have its share of willing Heroes. In *Invasion of the Body Snatchers,* Dr. Miles Binnell needs to find out what is happening to the townspeople. Some Heroes forge ahead even with the knowledge of the evils that lurk ahead. Although Clarice Starling is an eager Hero in *The Silence of the Lambs,* her supervisor Crawford warns her not to let Hannibal Lecter enter her mind. Yet that is the deal she must make with Lecter in order to catch "Buffalo Bill."

IT TAKES MANY CALLS TO PUSH THE HERO ON THE JOURNEY

Since Horror deals with man's primal fears, the Hero has a lot of reluctance to overcome before he is pushed through the Threshold of the Special World. Many Calls to Adventure are needed, and the stakes must be raised with each Call.

Even the "mad scientist" can start the Journey with the best intentions—to play God and create life from death (*Frankenstein*), or to "change the world as we know it" with a teleportation device (*The Fly*). This driven scientist is reluctant to see the danger in the experimentation until something goes horribly wrong finally setting in motion a dark and often tragic Journey.

IF YOU DON'T START OUT AS A LONER HERO, YOU WILL BE SOON

Either the Hero will begin the Journey as a Loner Hero (Brody in *Jaws;* Brundle in *The Fly*) or the Hero will eventually become isolated and fearfully alone (Laurie in *Halloween;* Miles in *Invasion of the Body Snatchers;* Clarice in *The Silence of the Lambs.*) On either course, the Horror Journey's trail is marked with the corpses of Allies; each loss heightens the stakes, surrounding our Hero with death. Equipped with courage and the lessons of the slain, the Hero, alone, must overcome his fears and face the Shadow.

GENRE CHALLENGES: HORROR

1. Screenwriter Kevin Williamson pays homage to *Halloween* with his screenplay for *Scream*. Take a look at *Scream* and analyze it according to the elements of the Hero's Journey. How does the structure of *Scream* compare to or differ from that of *Halloween*? How do the differences reflect an evolution in this type of Horror story?
2. *Jaws* is analyzed here as two consecutive journeys that Chief Brody must travel. How would you analyze Brody's Journey if instead it were only one large trek that he must travel, realizing that many of the elements of the first Journey (e.g., Ordeals, Thresholds, Tests) could now be considered Calls to Adventure. With this analysis,

how many Calls to Adventure does Brody receive? How are stakes raised with each Call? How are the Calls refused?

3. A Shadow may be the hero of his own myth. Analyze *The Silence of the Lambs* as if it were Hannibal Lecter's Journey. How does Lecter's Journey support or conflict with Clarice Starling's Journey?
4. How are the Special and Ordinary Worlds contrasted in *Invasion of the Body Snatchers*? How are the Ordinary World and the use of Shapeshifters used to promote terror?
5. Compare Seth Brundle's tragic scientific Journey with the classic "Mad Scientist" journey of Dr. Frankenstein or Dr. Jekyll. These earlier scientists were given redemption because they were men of higher society or knowledge. Are we this forgiving today? In what ways is Seth Brundle a sympathetic hero?

INVASION OF THE BODY SNATCHERS
(U.S., 1956)

"I'd hate to wake up some morning and find out you weren't you."

"How can you tell?"
(He kisses her)

"You're Becky Driscoll."

—Dr. Miles Binnell (Kevin McCarthy) and
Becky Driscoll (Dana Wynter)

Screenplay by Daniel Mainwaring
Based on the *Collier's* magazine serial by Jack Finney
Directed by Don Siegel

A small town doctor discovers that alien seedpods are assimilating the townsfolk, and he must warn the outside world.

LANDMARKS OF THE JOURNEY

The timeless theme of powerlessness and dehumanization in the face of an indestructible force elevates this Journey to a myth that continues to touch generations, evidenced by the numerous remakes. This horror goes beyond a plague on the individual or society. It consumes the essence of humanity. The Shadow steals our capacity to be human, bleeding us of our emotions—notably love, the very Elixir that the Hero tragically fails to reclaim.

Relying on little gore and violence, the horror rises from the ceaseless building of tension and paranoia as the alien force overtakes society. Shapeshifting Allies and Mentors play an important part to fuel the paranoia by repeatedly de-railing the Hero's Journey, pushing Miles to Refuse the Calls to Adventure and return to his Ordinary World. Only when Miles finally commits to the Journey does he reveal a Shadow that has been lurking in the very normalcy of the Hero's (and our) Ordinary World.

Invasion of the Body Snatchers was originally released with a studio-mandated prologue and epilogue to soften the story's doomsday message. Taking these "bookends" away, we can see the entire movie as a frightening, futile Call to Adventure. A Call to Beware.

THE JOURNEY

Dr. Miles Binnell is a levelheaded, well-respected doctor in his ORDINARY WORLD, the small town of Santa Mira, California. Miles is divorced; his commitment to medical science ruined his marriage. Miles' OUTER PROBLEM is to find out what's happening to the townspeople. His INNER PROBLEM is to find love.

The events of the film are told in flashback. A Doctor confronts a raving Miles, a HERALD/HERO, who convinces him to hear his story (the ELIXIR) "before it's too late." And so Miles begins his tale.

Miles had been called back early from a medical conference. But this initial CALL leaves the MENTOR HERO unsettled in his apparently ORDINARY WORLD. Townsfolk who had demanded to see him have now suddenly canceled their appointments. Their apparent maladies have disappeared.

In a second, more intimate CALL TO ADVENTURE, Becky Driscoll asks Miles to see her cousin Wilma, who believes that Wilma's Uncle Ira is an impostor. Since Becky is a former lover who has recently returned from England, her arrival is also a CALL FOR ROMANCE. Miles sees Wilma, but according to his assessment, Uncle Ira seems like Uncle Ira. He REFUSES to believe that anything strange is going on.

Becky agrees to Miles' dinner invitation, easing them THROUGH THE THRESHOLD of the Journey of Romance. In the restaurant's parking lot, Miles discusses Wilma's delusion with psychiatrist, Dr. Dan Kauffman. This MENTOR attributes the rash of cases to some mass hysteria that has been spreading through the town. Nothing more. He halts Miles' Journey into the mysterious SPECIAL WORLD (a REFUSAL).

Miles escorts Becky into the restaurant and voices his fear of waking up to find out that "you weren't you." She asks how he could tell. He kisses her, a mutually passionate kiss, tasting the ELIXIR of their love, and foreshadowing the story's horrifying climax.

An urgent phone call from friend Jack interrupts dinner and pushes Miles forward. Miles and Becky arrive at Jack and Teddy's home, where a human body lies on their pool table. Apparently dead. Perfectly—too perfectly formed in the weight and build of Jack. The town's psychological "stirrings" have now become physical. Miles warns them to watch the body carefully while he takes Becky home.

Later that night, the strange body "awakens" (a CALL). It is Jack, in every detail, down to the recent cut on Jack's hand. Concerned for Becky, Miles rushes to her house where he finds Becky's "double" in her basement. He sneaks the real Becky safely out of the house. Miles has passed a THRESHOLD showing commitment to Becky, and to his OUTER PROBLEM that indeed something strange is going on.

Dr. Kauffman arrives at Jack's, but the strange body has disappeared. Miles and Jack take Kauffman over to Becky's basement, but her double too has vanished. Again, Kauffman explains it away as hysteria and delusion. For now, our HERO accepts the MENTOR'S pat answers, and halts the Journey.

Miles finally crosses the THRESHOLD at an evening barbecue. The two couples (Miles and Becky, Jack and Teddy) witness seedpods hatching into goo-covered duplicates of themselves.

Miles fails the TEST of getting an outside line to warn the Governor; the operator can't patch him through. Miles suspects that the seedpods have control of the operator and the phone lines; this blocked THRESHOLD will make sending warnings and messages difficult. Now aware that everyone is suspect, Miles destroys the pods in the greenhouse, leaves the phone off-hook, and takes Becky away.

The TEST PHASE continues as Miles and Becky soon discover that they are all alone in a town overrun by Pod People. Miles thwarts a gas attendant's attempt to plant seedpods in his car trunk. They race to Nurse Sally's hoping to find an ALLY, only to discover a gathering of Pod People and "Sally" preparing to place a seedpod next to her daughter's bed.

With the police in pursuit and everyone an ENEMY, Miles and Becky find sanctuary in Miles' office, where they can plan their next move. Miles gives them stimulants, MENTOR'S GIFTS, to keep them awake. During this APPROACH TO THE INMOST CAVE, the two share a moment of tenderness, the ELIXIR of their love. They realize the sacredness of being human now that they have to fight for it (a REWARD).

The following morning, they watch through the window as the townsfolk gather and distribute truckloads of seedpods, the DARK ELIXIR.

Jack knocks on the door and Miles lets him in, immediately realizing the mistake of his impulsiveness. Jack is now a Pod Person. Jack and Dr. Kauffman, HERALD/THRESHOLD GUARDIANS, try to lure Becky and Miles to join them. Kauffman promises them a simple life without love, desire, ambition. They lock the couple in the office with two seedpods beginning to metamorphose (the ORDEAL.)

Determined to escape or die rather than join a world without love, they ambush Jack and Kauffman, and flee (Freedom as RESURRECTION) with the knowledge of the seedpods' plan to take over humanity (the REWARD). The threat is spreading; the stakes are raised. Miles and Becky must warn the outside world.

Miles and Becky "wear the skin" of the Pod People, and pretend to be automatons without love and warmth. But Becky screams when a dog is almost hit by a truck, revealing herself. They are chased out of town, the ROAD BACK, and find safety in a mining cave.

Later, Miles leaves Becky to investigate music too beautiful to be anything but human. He finds Pod People harvesting the seedpods, listening to a radio. His hopes crushed, he returns to Becky who has collapsed with exhaustion. Miles has to keep her awake, and he kisses her. In a deliciously horrifying moment, he withdraws from the kiss realizing that this isn't Becky. His lover is one of them. And Miles is alone. She warns the other Pod People as he flees (his RESURRECTION.)

The Pod People let Miles escape to the main road on the outskirts of town. Who's going to believe him? Sure enough, he screams his warning, the ELIXIR OF TRUTH, but drivers honk and wave the HERO/HERALD off as some delusional fool. Miles finds a truck filled with seedpods leaving town, the DARK ELIXIR is spreading. He wanders the middle of the highway screaming to deaf ears.

Which takes us back to the present, where the Doctor REFUSES to believe Miles' story until an emergency victim is wheeled in. An accident involved a truck filled with strange seedpods. The Doctor finally believes Miles' story, the ELIXIR OF TRUTH and calls for action...

FADE OUT

JAWS
(U.S., 1975)

"Gotta close the beach, call the mayor."

"You've got a bigger problem than that, Martin. You've still got a hell of a fish out there."

—Chief Martin Brody (Roy Scheider) and
Matt Hooper (Richard Dreyfuss)

Written by Peter Benchley and Carl Gottlieb
Based on the novel by Peter Benchley
Directed by Steven Spielberg

Teamed with shark expert Hooper and shark hunter Quint, Police Chief Brody must track down and destroy a monster shark terrorizing a summer resort town.

LANDMARKS OF THE JOURNEY

This brilliantly crafted scarefest exploits the most primal of man's fears—what lurks beneath the water's dark surface. Martin Brody takes two successive Journeys. He begins with the need to close the beaches and protect Amity from a Special World inhabited by a monster shark. But Brody butts heads with the mayor and Amity's businesses which cannot survive without summer tourist dollars. Their consistent Refusal of the Call dooms Brody's Journey. When this Journey fails, and Brody's personal world is threatened, he must face his greatest fear and accept a second, higher Journey: to enter the waters and hunt down the beast. Brody's second Journey, the hunt, is reminiscent of the fearless vampire hunters tracking down Count Dracula, with Chief Brody as "apprentice hunter" Jonathan Harker and Quint, the mythic Van Helsing of shark hunters.

During his Journeys, Brody juggles three important Mentors. He unmasks the first, Mayor Vaughn, as a false Mentor, a Threshold Guardian more protective of tourist dollars than tourist lives. The two "true" Mentors, shark hunter Quint and shark expert Matt Hooper, become rivals on the hunt. At polar opposites, Quint uses brawn and cunning, while Hooper relies on expensive gadgetry. Each Mentor pushes his Gifts/Tools while denouncing the other's in a bid to be the true Hero of the Journey. Although the team finally works together in the end, both Hooper and Quint fail the Journey; yet Brody uses the gifts of both Mentors to finally destroy the monster.

THE JOURNEY

Amity's new Chief of Police, Martin Brody, recently relocated with his wife and two sons from New York. Brody's job is to protect this island township and its beaches, his OUTER PROBLEM. He prefers the small-town problems of Amity, where one man can make a difference, his INNER PROBLEM. Brody may never be able to fit into the ORDINARY WORLD of this island community—he hates the water for fear of drowning.

Many Journeys begin with two distinct CALLS TO ADVENTURE. One strikes the society or ORDINARY WORLD as a whole. A second CALL is directed at the Hero. The initial CALL in *Jaws* is one of the most terrifying moments in cinema. A young woman's moonlight swim is shockingly interrupted by the unseen SHADOW. It yanks and drags Chrissie, finally pulling her to her death beneath the surface of this SPECIAL WORLD.

The following morning, Chief Martin Brody receives a SUCCESSION OF CALLS. While investigating the beach, Brody answers Deputy Hendricks' choked whistle and finds Chrissie's remains. The Medical Inspector confirms a shark attack. This second CALL forces Brody to close the beaches, barring entrance to the SPECIAL WORLD. However, Mayor Vaughn (a SHAPESHIFTING MENTOR) cautions Brody's quick actions, and prompts the Medical Inspector to recant his conclusions. Instead of giving our HERO a swift kick into the adventure, this MEETING WITH THE MENTOR stalls Brody, swaying him to REFUSE THE CALL.

Brody remains uneasy and watches the beach. He witnesses the horrifying death of young Alex Kintner, which pushes Brody THROUGH THE THRESHOLD of his first Journey. But Amity's townspeople must be pushed as well. Brody tries to take control of the community meeting announcing the closure of the beaches, but Mayor Vaughn snatches the Hero's mask from Brody and assures his people that the beaches will be closed for only 24 hours. The meeting also introduces one of Brody's future MENTORS. Making a spine-jarring entrance, Quint, the salty shark hunter, offers himself as MENTOR and "LONER" HERO. He promises to kill the shark but it'll cost more than Mrs. Kintner's $3,000 bounty. Vaughn brushes this MENTOR off with saccharine assurance that the council will take his offer under advisement (a REFUSAL).

The TEST PHASE in full force, Brody deals with the jammed docks, as fishermen pack the waters fighting for the bounty. During this melee, Brody meets his second MENTOR, oceanographer and shark specialist Matt Hooper. Hooper examines the remains of Chrissie, confirming Brody's initial fear that death was indeed caused by a large predator shark.

Later, Hooper warns Brody that the enormous tiger shark caught by fishermen may not be the predator; the bite radius is too small. They'll have to open the shark's slow-working digestive tract to make sure. Mayor Vaughn REFUSES this TEST, protecting his town from the possible sight of the Kintner boy's remains spilling onto the dock.

That night, Brody and Hooper APPROACH THE INMOST CAVE. They cut open the shark's carcass, confirming that their Rogue Shark still roams the SPECIAL WORLD. Brody wants to call the mayor, and close the beach. But his MENTOR warns him of a HIGHER CALL: there's a hell of a big fish out there.

Hooper forces Brody (drunk enough to pass this MENTOR'S TEST) to face his fear of the water and the two patrol the shark's SPECIAL WORLD where they discover Ben

Gardner's wrecked fishing boat. Hooper dives into the water leaving Brody alone on the boat. During this ORDEAL, Hooper discovers the large tooth of a Great White lodged in a hole in the hull, but he loses this REWARD at the sight of Gardner's corpse.

REWARDED with the awareness of what they are up against, Brody and Hooper plead for Mayor Vaughn to close the beaches. Without the shark tooth as proof, Vaughn won't be swayed, denying the danger to his town. Brody can patrol the beaches but they will remain open for the Fourth of July, the ROAD BACK of Brody's First Journey.

The Fourth of July tourists pack the beaches and begin to test the waters. After two kids play a practical joke with a fake shark fin, a FALSE ORDEAL, the Shark enters "the pond," and threatens Brody's eldest son. A fisherman is killed; Brody's son is pulled from the waters alive, his RESURRECTION.

Brody looks out at the water. He has earned the ELIXIR of his First Journey, the awareness that he must face his greatest fear (the water) and finally accept the Higher Journey in store for him. He forces Vaughn to hire Quint, a second ELIXIR.

To enter his new Journey, Brody denounces one MENTOR, the Mayor, and teams up with two RIVAL MENTORS, Quint and Hooper. During the MEETING WITH THE MENTOR in Quint's lair, Quint TESTS Hooper of his worthiness, trying to strip down his RIVAL MENTOR. The clash of the MENTORS continues at dawn as the shark hunters board Quint's boat, initiating the THRESHOLD SEQUENCE. Armed with harpoon and rope, Quint ridicules Hooper's high-tech equipment (devaluing these MENTOR'S GIFTS). We watch through the bony jaws of one of Quint's trophies, as the Orca heads out to sea. This final image of the THRESHOLD SEQUENCE foreshadows *Orca*'s eventual destruction.

Completely unfamiliar with this SPECIAL WORLD as shark hunter, Brody becomes a HERO TRAINEE, serving now as Chief of "Chumming." In addition to teaching Brody the RULES of the SPECIAL WORLD, the TEST PHASE must bring the two MENTORS in alliance or the HERO TEAM will fail.

In a rich moment weaving exposition, character and foreshadowing, Brody accidentally topples Hooper's air tanks. Hooper warns Brody that the tanks could blow up. Quick to criticize Hooper's techno-gadgets, Quint jokes that the shark might eat the tanks. (Brody will use these two lessons to finally kill the Shark.)

The Shark finally rears its gnashing maw at Brody. This first encounter with the SHADOW begins to band the Shark Hunters together. Quint, the hunter, readies his harpoon, while Hooper, the scientist, prepares a tracking device. Both stubbornly focus on using their own tools, yet finally get the shot off, barely passing the TEST. The shark escapes a second harpoon as the day ends.

That night, the three APPROACH THE INMOST CAVE. They drink. The MENTORS compare scars from past battles, finally earning each other's respect. The HERO TEAM may pull together after all. Quint tells the horrifying story of the sinking of the *Indianapolis* and the slaughter of the crew by tiger sharks. Since sharks prefer to feed at night, his tale is a bitter reminder of their vulnerability as the three sit "in the belly" of Quint's boat, reliving the ORDEAL of Quint's tale of death. The three hunters finally unite in song, but the Shark makes it clear that the battle has only begun. It disrupts the moment, pounding the boat's hull. Brody faces his greatest fear as "death" waits on the other side of the leaking hull (the ORDEAL.) Pistol in hand, he rises, moves to the main deck and stares petrified into the darkness.

The next morning, the three work together as a team, the first REWARD of their ORDEAL. They shoot the Shark with a second barrel and fasten the ropes to *Orca*'s cleats. Quint wants to drag his REWARD inland but the Shark drags *its* REWARD further out into its own world. The cleats rip free, and the hunters chase the Shark, shooting a third harpoon. The Shark submerges, befuddling both MENTORS (neither has faced this challenge, raising the stakes).

And then the Shark chases them! The ROAD BACK begins. Quint leads the shark inland, trying to out-race the monster, straining the engine's bearings. Quint won't back down. The engine explodes, leaving the shark hunters stranded at sea.

Admitting the failure of his tools, Quint finally acknowledges his RIVAL MENTOR, asking Hooper what he can do with his techno-gadgets. Hooper suggests his anti-shark cage. Echoing his ORDEAL confronting Ben Gardner's corpse, Hooper re-enters the SPECIAL WORLD armed with a harpoon of strychnine. His tools also fail, and he narrowly escapes the SHADOW'S jaws.

The Shark now enters its hunters' world, rising from the water and smashing upon the *Orca*'s stern. Brody and Quint scramble to keep from slipping into the deadly jaws. Quint loses the battle (with the help of a MENTOR'S GIFT turned lethal) and slides to his death.

In the final RESURRECTION SEQUENCE, Brody, alone, surrounded by death, is trapped in the cabin of the sinking boat. Brody uses the lessons he learned from both MENTORS (with a bit of improvisation). He shoves one of Hooper's air tanks into the Shark's bloody jaws and scrambles out of the cabin.

Armed with a rifle, Brody climbs the mast, symbolically claiming Quint's position in the Crow's Nest. But as Brody's mast sinks, the Shark swims at him. Brody fires several shots before striking the air tank, blowing the shark into a rain of chum, Brody's RESURRECTION.

Moments later, Hooper surfaces alive. The two share a moment of sorrow that Quint wasn't as fortunate. Soon, they swim back to shore with the ELIXIR of their lives, and the tale of their success. They have saved the town from the beast. Brody returns with an additional, personal ELIXIR; he has conquered his fear of the water.

FADE OUT

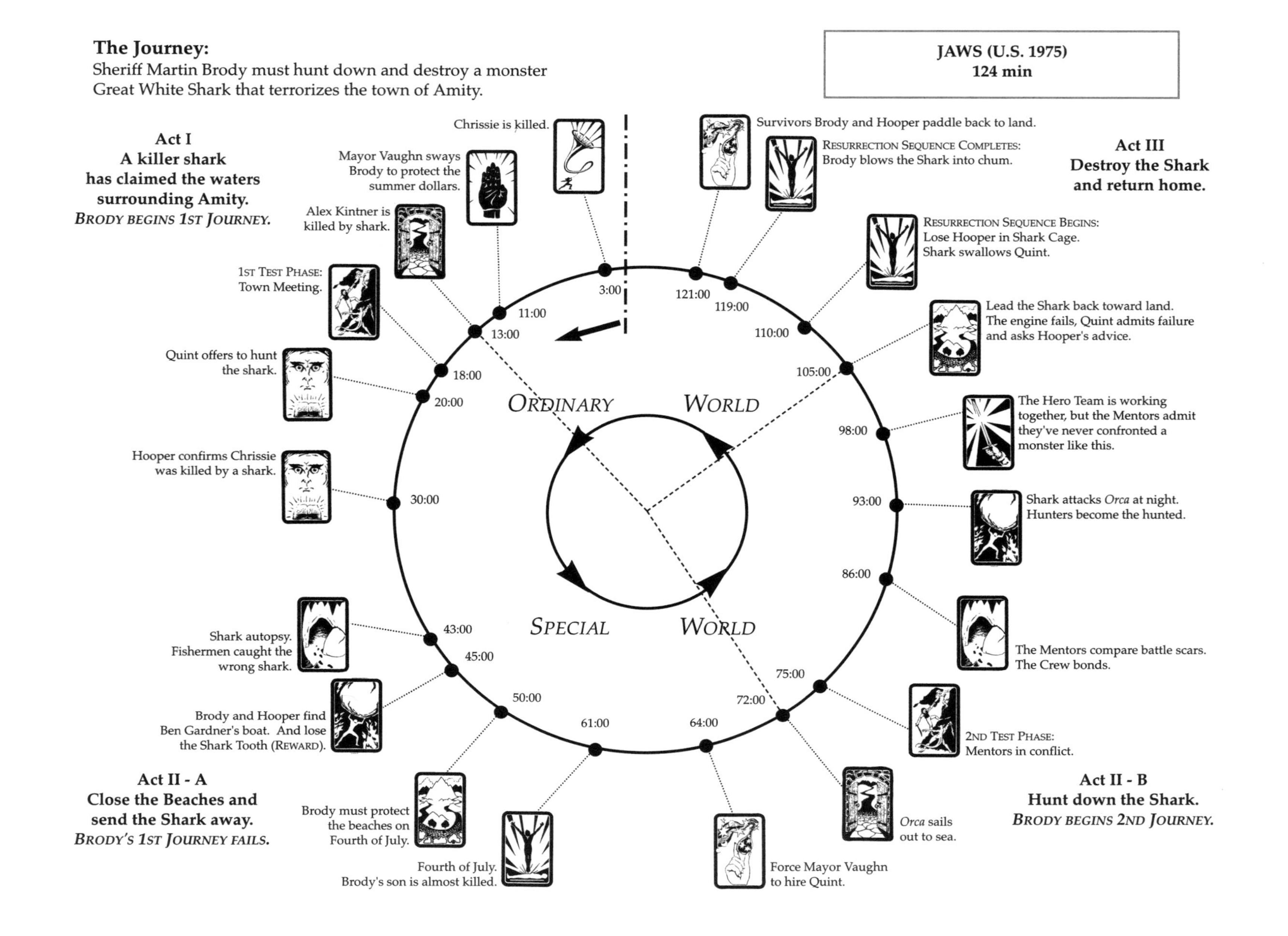

The Journey:
Sheriff Martin Brody must hunt down and destroy a monster Great White Shark that terrorizes the town of Amity.
JAWS (U.S. 1975)
124 min
Act I
A killer shark has claimed the waters surrounding Amity.
BRODY BEGINS 1ST JOURNEY.
Chrissie is killed.
Mayor Vaughn sways Brody to protect the summer dollars.
Alex Kintner is killed by shark.
1ST TEST PHASE: Town Meeting.
Quint offers to hunt the shark.
Hooper confirms Chrissie was killed by a shark.
Shark autopsy. Fishermen caught the wrong shark.
Brody and Hooper find Ben Gardner's boat. And lose the Shark Tooth (REWARD).
Act II - A
Close the Beaches and send the Shark away.
BRODY'S 1ST JOURNEY FAILS.
Brody must protect the beaches on Fourth of July.
Fourth of July. Brody's son is almost killed.
Force Mayor Vaughn to hire Quint.
Orca sails out to sea.
2ND TEST PHASE: Mentors in conflict.
Act II - B
Hunt down the Shark.
BRODY BEGINS 2ND JOURNEY.
The Mentors compare battle scars. The Crew bonds.
Shark attacks Orca at night. Hunters become the hunted.
The Hero Team is working together, but the Mentors admit they've never confronted a monster like this.
Lead the Shark back toward land. The engine fails, Quint admits failure and asks Hooper's advice.
RESURRECTION SEQUENCE BEGINS: Lose Hooper in Shark Cage. Shark swallows Quint.
RESURRECTION SEQUENCE COMPLETES: Brody blows the Shark into chum.
Survivors Brody and Hooper paddle back to land.
Act III
Destroy the Shark and return home.
ORDINARY WORLD
SPECIAL WORLD
3:00
11:00
13:00
18:00
20:00
30:00
43:00
45:00
50:00
61:00
64:00
72:00
75:00
86:00
93:00
98:00
105:00
110:00
119:00
121:00

HALLOWEEN
(U.S., 1978)

"Death has come to your little town, Sheriff. You can either ignore it, or you can help me to stop it."

—Doctor Loomis (Donald Pleasence)

Written by John Carpenter and Debra Hill
Directed by John Carpenter

A boy murders his teenage sister on Halloween night. Fifteen years later, he returns to his hometown to strike again.

LANDMARKS OF THE JOURNEY

How many times can you tell the Hero that she is in danger before she finally takes action? This granddaddy of the contemporary teen-age slasher film is crafted with a long Succession of Calls to Adventure. While many Calls are directed to the Hero, Laurie, just as many happen behind her back, making the audience uneasy and jumpy, and effectively build tension. Taut, suspenseful storytelling at its finest.

THE JOURNEY

Two Heroes take the Journey's road to stop Michael Myers before he kills again. The MENTOR/HERO Dr. Loomis is the psychiatrist who has been treating Michael Myers since he has been institutionalized. While his OUTER PROBLEM is to stop the killing, Loomis sees Michael Myers as pure Evil. He must put this Evil away forever, his INNER PROBLEM.

The Second Hero, Laurie, is an intelligent, clean-cut high school student, and career baby-sitter. Her immediate goal is to baby-sit Tommy. But when she finally accepts the Journey, her OUTER PROBLEM is to survive and protect the children. Her INNER PROBLEM is to have fun like her girlfriends and get a date with Ben Tramer.

Laurie's small-town ORDINARY WORLD of Haddonfield would rather forget the horrible murder of Judith Myers fifteen years ago. However, the neighborhood kids have turned this Ordeal into legend and believe the boarded-up Myers' house is haunted by the Boogie-Man.

Like many Horror films, *Halloween* begins with the establishment of the SHADOW. In a brilliantly eerie prologue, young Michael Myers murders his sister, Judith. Structurally, her murder is a mini-Journey we experience through the eyes of the SHADOW...

Michael watches Judith retire upstairs with her boyfriend, and soon her bedroom lights turn off symbolizing their lovemaking, the CALL TO ADVENTURE. Michael enters the kitchen and takes a butcher knife, the THRESHOLD. He waits for the boyfriend to leave, and ascends the staircase, APPROACHING THE INMOST CAVE, pausing at the doorway to put on a Clown Mask (hiding himself behind a mask representing his SHADOW). He sees proof of his sister's indiscretion: strewn bed sheets, and a half-naked sister brushing her hair. And he stabs her to death, an ORDEAL and REWARD. He leaves the house as his parents arrive, the ROAD BACK. They pull off Michael's mask, a RESURRECTION revealing their DARK ELIXIR, a psychotic little boy holding the butcher knife dripping with sister Judith's blood.

The prologue foreshadows the pure evil Michael Myers is capable of when he returns to Haddonfield, the Journey's SPECIAL WORLD. Fifteen years later...

Michael Myers' escape from the State Hospital sets the Journey in motion. MENTOR Dr. Loomis knows "the Evil" is returning to Haddonfield; however, nobody will listen to his warnings. Setting Loomis aside until he returns at the end of the story, our focus is on Laurie, where Synchronicity of Fate and a long, tense SUCCESSION OF CALLS ultimately push her forward. Some of the more significant CALLS:

- Laurie drops off the Myers' house key, against the warnings of young Tommy, an ALLY and MENTOR of Children's Fears. Both are unaware of Michael Myers' watchful eye.
- During English Class (appropriately about Fate), Laurie sees the masked Myers (hereafter referred to as the SHADOW) standing next to Loomis' State Hospital station wagon. Mysteriously, he disappears.
- The station wagon stalks Laurie and her two TRICKSTER SIDEKICKS, Annie and Lynda. It brakes suddenly in response to Annie's taunting, and drives away.
- Laurie sees the SHADOW appear briefly behind a hedge, and again later, standing amidst the blowing sheets on the clothesline.
- At dusk, Laurie and Annie drive to their baby-sitter jobs, unaware that the station wagon follows.
- They see Annie's dad, the Sheriff, outside the hardware store. Someone broke in and stole Halloween masks, rope and several masks. The audience realizes the significance of this CALL.

As the sun sets, Annie and Laurie arrive at their respective baby-sitting jobs, across the street from one another. Like it or not they've entered the SPECIAL WORLD. It's Halloween night and Michael Myers watches Annie enter the Wallace home. But the CALLS continue:

- Tommy sees the SHADOW approach the Wallace house, but Laurie insists that the Boogie-Man doesn't exist.

- The SHADOW kills the Wallace's dog, a positive THRESHOLD GUARDIAN protecting Annie and the little girl, Lindsay.

The REFUSAL of all these CALLS finally leads to tragedy as Michael Myers strikes. He kills Annie in the Wallace's car, followed by Lynda and her boyfriend after they make love.

Finally, Laurie receives the gasping phone call from Lynda. At first believing it's a joke, Laurie becomes suspicious. She looks at the Wallace's house. The lights flicker out (yet another CALL). She investigates.

She cautiously enters the dark house believing that this is all a prank—until she finds the bodies of her friends in the upstairs bedroom, an ORDEAL as THRESHOLD. Laurie is now committed to her Journey to survive. The SHADOW lunges at her. The knife cuts her arm and Laurie falls down the staircase, escaping his attack, completing her THRESHOLD into a frightening SPECIAL WORLD.

She breaks the back door window, removes the rake barricade and flees, passing her first TESTS. She runs to the neighbor's yard and yells for help. She won't find any ALLIES here as curtains are closed and lights turned out to her. So she awakens Tommy, her only ALLY, and he lets her inside.

In the APPROACH TO THE INMOST CAVE, Laurie prepares for the SHADOW. She sends Tommy back upstairs. Tries the phone. Dead. Michael springs from behind the couch. Laurie reacts quickly in this ORDEAL and stabs him in the neck with a sewing needle. Apparently, she's killed the SHADOW.

She takes a moment to catch her breath and then goes up to check on the kids. But Tommy, wearing his MENTOR'S mask, takes back Laurie's REWARD with a warning that she can't kill the Boogie-Man. Sure enough, the SHADOW approaches from the top of the staircase.

Now equipped with the knowledge of what she's up against, Laurie locks the kids in the bedroom and rushes into the master bedroom. The ROAD BACK begins. She opens the balcony door hoping to trick the SHADOW into leaving the house, and she hides in the walk-in closet. But this SHADOW isn't that stupid. It rips through the closet door. Although Laurie faces death head-on, she's quite resourceful and jabs a coat hanger into the SHADOW'S eye, and stabs it with the butcher knife. The SHADOW falls dead.

Laurie checks on the children and sends them out of the house to get help. As She collapses in the bedroom doorway and rests, the SHADOW rises behind her, its RESURRECTION. She gets to her feet, unaware of the danger.

The kids rush out of the house screaming, alerting Dr. Loomis (who's been wandering around for the right house).

The SHADOW strikes, strangling Laurie, as Dr. Loomis, wearing his HERO/MENTOR mask, comes to the rescue. In a heroic act, Laurie rips off the SHADOW'S mask, revealing Michael Myers (a RESURRECTION of his humanity). He releases his death grip and Laurie falls away, her RESURRECTION. Michael re-attaches his mask, resuming his SHADOW self. Loomis empties his gun into the SHADOW, sending it over the balcony, to its apparent death. When he looks, the SHADOW is gone, confirming his worst fear. The Evil won't die, the DARK ELIXIR of this tale. This open ending leaves the characters and audience terrified, wondering where the Evil will appear next.

FADE OUT

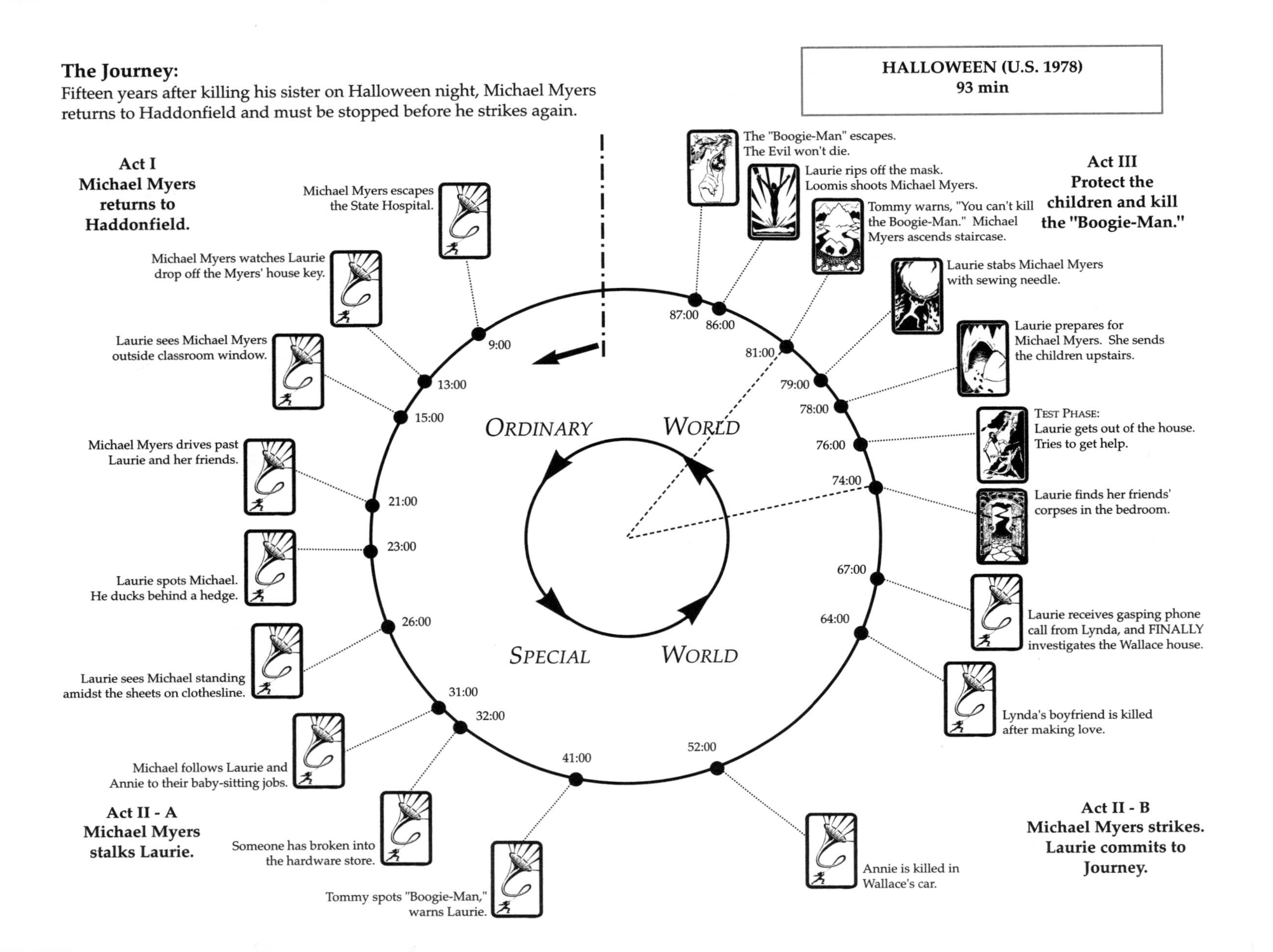

The Journey:
Fifteen years after killing his sister on Halloween night, Michael Myers returns to Haddonfield and must be stopped before he strikes again.
HALLOWEEN (U.S. 1978)
93 min
Act I
Michael Myers returns to Haddonfield.
Michael Myers escapes the State Hospital.
9:00
Michael Myers watches Laurie drop off the Myers' house key.
13:00
Laurie sees Michael Myers outside classroom window.
15:00
Michael Myers drives past Laurie and her friends.
21:00
Laurie spots Michael. He ducks behind a hedge.
23:00
Laurie sees Michael standing amidst the sheets on clothesline.
26:00
Michael follows Laurie and Annie to their baby-sitting jobs.
31:00
Someone has broken into the hardware store.
32:00
Tommy spots "Boogie-Man," warns Laurie.
41:00
Act II - A
Michael Myers stalks Laurie.
Annie is killed in Wallace's car.
52:00
Lynda's boyfriend is killed after making love.
64:00
Laurie receives gasping phone call from Lynda, and FINALLY investigates the Wallace house.
67:00
Laurie finds her friends' corpses in the bedroom.
74:00
TEST PHASE:
Laurie gets out of the house. Tries to get help.
76:00
Laurie prepares for Michael Myers. She sends the children upstairs.
78:00
Laurie stabs Michael Myers with sewing needle.
79:00
Tommy warns, "You can't kill the Boogie-Man." Michael Myers ascends staircase.
81:00
Laurie rips off the mask. Loomis shoots Michael Myers.
86:00
The "Boogie-Man" escapes. The Evil won't die.
87:00
Act II - B
Michael Myers strikes. Laurie commits to Journey.
Act III
Protect the children and kill the "Boogie-Man."
ORDINARY WORLD
SPECIAL WORLD

THE FLY
(U.S., 1986)

"I'm an insect who dreamt he was a man, and loved it. But now the dream is over and the insect is awake."

—Seth Brundle (Jeff Goldblum)

Screenplay by Charles Edward Pogue and David Cronenberg
From the story by George Langelaan
Directed by David Cronenberg

An eccentric scientist's research on teleportation goes horribly wrong when he accidentally transports himself with a housefly.

LANDMARKS OF THE JOURNEY

Romance is the heart of this Journey, elevating it above most B-movie fodder. The elements of great romance are here (see the chapter on Romance): the Forbidden Love, the Love Triangle, the Rival, the Noble Sacrifice.

Seth Brundle is the Journey's soul. After his experiments go horribly wrong, Seth's humanity battles the cold insect Shadow that he is becoming. Suspense and horror build as we question which side will ultimately wrest control of Seth's Journey and fulfill its Resurrection at the road's end.

THE JOURNEY

Seth Brundle's initial Journey and OUTER PROBLEM—to make a teleportation device—is solved fairly soon in the story. In Horror stories, HEROES don't always get what they intended—their greatest fear comes true. After Seth discovers that he has spliced himself with a housefly, he must find a way back to his human form. This is his main Journey: to re-gain his humanity.

Seth's second Journey is the subplot that involves Veronica. Dedicated, eccentric scientists usually don't get out much. Seth's lack of intimate experience with the "flesh" proves to be the key to his experimental failures. He needs to be a whole man and "know the flesh," his INNER PROBLEM. Enter beautiful Veronica, MENTOR of the flesh and potential romantic partner.

At a cocktail party, Seth uses the mystery of his research to lure investigative reporter Veronica Quaife to his lab. Veronica is won over by the MENTOR'S demonstration of his telepods and questions him for her story (her OUTER PROBLEM), but Seth REFUSES her CALL to enter society with his invention. He only wanted to impress this beautiful woman with his achievements. He requests her interview tape; Veronica REFUSES and runs with her story.

Fearing that Veronica's premature magazine story will kill his research, Seth invites her to lunch where he suggests that they work together, CALL TO ADVENTURE. She'll monitor his research as he works to achieve his goal: to transport himself from one telepod to the other.

Together they cross the THRESHOLD and continue his experimentation, but they fail the initial TEST, teleporting a baboon into a fleshless screaming mass. Seth blames himself, and confesses that the teleportation computer (an important THRESHOLD GUARDIAN) doesn't know the flesh. How can Seth teach it something that he doesn't know himself? Answer: Veronica seduces him. This MENTOR teaches the flesh and takes him through the THRESHOLD of their relationship, where Seth achieves new awareness, a REWARD. Rejuvenated from their lovemaking, Seth teaches the computer to be "made crazy by the flesh." Soon they celebrate the success of transporting a second baboon. The goal of teleporting himself is now in sight. However, they must APPROACH THE INMOST CAVE with caution; preparations must be made. The baboon must be thoroughly examined.

Since Seth's "jump" could be postponed for weeks, Veronica proposes a vacation, pushing them to APPROACH THE INMOST CAVE of their relationship. As Seth prepares a romantic dinner, Veronica discovers the magazine cover art sent by her editor and former boyfriend Stathis—a warning that this RIVAL is running with a magazine article that threatens Seth's research. Veronica leaves Seth to get rid of her "personal bullshit" once and for all.

Questioning Veronica's abrupt departure and jealous of her relationship with Stathis (a CRISIS OF THE HEART), Seth TESTS himself in the telepod. A pesky fly slips into Seth's telepod moments before the jump. The computer monitors as Seth and fly are zapped from one pod and "Resurrected" in the next, an ORDEAL that pushes Seth through a THRESHOLD into a SPECIAL WORLD not anticipated. This ORDEAL is an extended sequence that begins with Seth's teleportation. It ends when Seth finally realizes his DARK REWARD, that he has been genetically spliced with the fly.

Veronica returns and Seth confesses that he made the jump. She realizes he risked his life because of jealousy and assures him that Stathis is not a threat, RESURRECTING their relationship.

After making love, Seth discovers his "new powers": quick reflexes, incredible physical strength. He relishes this TEST PHASE of the new SPECIAL WORLD. Over coffee, Seth concludes that the "jump" has purified him, granting him a chance to realize his true potential. He's more energized, almost manic, dumping sugar into his espresso, as he pitches his ELIXIR. Yet Seth suffers an inflated ego. He challenges the world with his new powers: "Catch me if you can."

And he challenges Veronica, who can no longer keep up with his lovemaking. Seth demands that she join him in his SPECIAL WORLD, but she REFUSES his DARK CALL. She discovers his strange back hairs and snips them off for analysis, fearing that something has gone wrong in the teleportation process. In denial, Seth discards Veronica, seeing her as an ENEMY, and seeks someone who can keep up with him.

Seth's Journey of the Flesh is in crisis as human touch irritates him. He demands that Tawny, a prostitute, make the jump but she's afraid to APPROACH THE INMOST CAVE. Veronica interrupts them with her warning: insect hairs are sprouting from his back. Seth denies it and throws her out of the lab, closing the door on their relationship, and completing its ORDEAL. And ending the overall ORDEAL SEQUENCE.

Seth's REWARD is his acceptance of what he has become. After his face hairs jam his razor, and his fingernails begin to fall off, Seth finally acknowledges that something is wrong. Computer data confirm that he was genetically fused with a housefly, his DARK REWARD.

Veronica returns to the lab and witnesses Seth climbing the walls like a fly. He acknowledges that he's metamorphosing into Brundle-Fly, and explores the NEW RULES of this SPECIAL WORLD. He videotapes his disgusting eating habits which are later viewed by Stathis, foreshadowing his confrontation with Seth. But Veronica reveals her own DARK REWARD to Stathis; she's pregnant with Seth's baby.

Alone in the lab, Seth solves his problem of returning to a more human state, beginning his ROAD BACK. He must decrease the percentage of fly by genetically splicing himself with a pure human specimen. Enter Veronica.

Seth sees this beautiful human specimen that Brundle-Fly wants to sacrifice. He clasps onto his humanity, the true ELIXIR, long enough to expose his SHADOW and warn her that Brundle-Fly will hurt her. Horrified, she leaves his SPECIAL WORLD. Stathis is waiting for her outside. From the rooftop, Seth overhears Veronica demand the abortion tonight (the CHASE begins).

In an act of desperation, Seth abducts Veronica from the hospital. Although Seth pleads for her not to kill the last bit of Brundle that exists inside of her, INTERNAL SHADOW Brundle-Fly realizes its own ROAD BACK...

Stathis temporarily wears the HERO'S mask to rescue Veronica but he's ambushed by Brundle-Fly. Brundle-Fly presents Veronica his plan to splice (RESURRECT) Brundle-Fly, Veronica and their baby into one genetically fused whole. She adamantly REFUSES this DARK ELIXIR, as Brundle's metamorphosis into the Fly comes to quick, horrifying culmination. It throws her into the telepod, and sets the TICKING CLOCK in motion. The Fly enters the second pod as Stathis regains consciousness.

Stathis shoots the telepod cables, saving Veronica, her RESURRECTION. However, time runs out before the Fly can break out of its pod, and it is RESURRECTED into a grotesque amalgam of Brundle-fly and telepod.

Seth's humanity, the TRUE ELIXIR, realizes that there is no return for him. He places the rifle's muzzle to his head, pleading for Veronica to shoot him. At first rejecting his CALL, she finally gathers the inner strength to destroy the SHADOW, granting mercy to the last vestige of Seth's humanity.

FADE OUT

THE SILENCE OF THE LAMBS
(U.S., 1991)

"You think if you saved poor Catherine you could make them stop, don't you? You think if Catherine lives you won't wake up in the dark ever again to that awful screaming of the lambs."

—Hannibal Lecter (Anthony Hopkins)

Screenplay by Ted Tally
Based upon the book by Thomas Harris
Directed by Jonathan Demme

An FBI trainee creates an alliance with an imprisoned serial killer to stop a string of gruesome slayings.

LANDMARKS OF THE JOURNEY

The film's success can be attributed to the deftly drawn (and brilliantly acted) characters of the Willing Hero, Clarice Starling, and her Shadow-Mentor, Hannibal Lecter. The power of these characterizations at times overshadows the poignancy of Clarice's Journey. Clarice's Journey is a Rite of Passage which works on both psychological and physical levels. Clarice must face the psychological force of Lecter's mind in order to physically defeat serial-killer "Buffalo Bill."

THE JOURNEY

The FBI Academy in Quantico is the ORDINARY WORLD of Cadet Clarice Starling. Determined and smart, Clarice aspires to work for Jack Crawford in the FBI's Behavior Science Division after her graduation, her OUTER PROBLEM. She worshipped her father, a town marshal, and felt abandoned when he was murdered when she was ten. Clarice's INNER PROBLEM is to come to terms with her father's death by accomplishing a worthy deed.

Meanwhile, Jack Crawford's ORDINARY WORLD is in turmoil. A serial killer, nicknamed "Buffalo Bill" because he skins his victims, continues to elude the FBI.

Impressed by her academics and her aspirations, Crawford offers Clarice an "errand," to convince convicted serial killer Hannibal Lecter to fill out a questionnaire. She willingly accepts his CALL, but this MENTOR leaves her with an important warning: "You don't want Hannibal Lecter in your head." (The stakes are raised.)

Clarice meets Dr. Chilton, a THRESHOLD GUARDIAN, who quickly drills the Rules for communicating with "the Monster" Lecter. He shows her a photo of one of Lecter's victims, a warning if the Rules are not met.

Clarice makes an unsettling trek past shadowy inmates, hissing insults at her, before facing Dr. Hannibal "the Cannibal" Lecter. Although Clarice impresses this SHADOW MENTOR, she fails her errand; Lecter refuses to fill out Crawford's questionnaire, rejecting Clarice from the SPECIAL WORLD. As Clarice leaves, an inmate flings semen in Clarice's face. An incensed Lecter apologizes and offers Clarice advancement with a TEST: to see one of his old patients, Miss Mofet.

Clarice solves Lecter's cryptic CALL. She locates "Your Self Storage" and a unit belonging to Miss Hester Mofet. Inside, she discovers a car where she finds a headless female mannequin and a man's head preserved in a jar.

Lecter admits the head belonged to a former patient, Raspail, and Clarice senses a connection with Buffalo Bill. Before Lecter will reveal more, he offers a psychological profile of Buffalo Bill, in return for a room with a view away from Dr. Chilton, Lecter's OUTER PROBLEM. Lecter presses urgency: Buffalo Bill must be searching for his next victim.

Sure enough, Buffalo Bill lures Catherine Martin into his van, setting the TICKING CLOCK in motion.

Lecter's offer is put on hold while Clarice willingly accepts Crawford's HIGHER CALL to go to West Virginia to attend an autopsy of a Buffalo Bill victim. She has now crossed the THRESHOLD into the SPECIAL WORLD; Clarice is actively on the Buffalo Bill case. Crawford quickly initiates Clarice with the details of the case. She presents her profile of Buffalo Bill, to Crawford's approval. Her TESTS continue in the autopsy room. Clarice spots an insect pupa lodged in the victim's mouth, and takes it to two entomologists, ALLIES who successfully identify this important clue as a rare Death's Head Moth.

Back at the Academy, Clarice watches the news report announcing that Catherine Martin has been kidnapped by Buffalo Bill. Catherine's mother, U.S. Senator Ruth Martin, pleads for her release. This CALL has "stirred the government to its highest levels." The stakes are raised, forcing Crawford (using Clarice as his agent, making a swift bold APPROACH) to make a deal with Lecter: a room with a view in exchange for a profile on Buffalo Bill. Lecter accepts on the condition that Clarice answer *his* questions, quid pro quo. She must tell him things about herself, allowing Lecter to get into her mind. She accepts, confessing her worst childhood memory: the death of her father.

Dr. Chilton reveals the FBI's bogus deal to Lecter, and kills Clarice's relationship with Lecter, an ORDEAL. In a move to RESURRECT their relationship, Clarice gives Lecter back his drawings as an apology, but she also stands up to her MENTOR and demands the truth. Lecter directs her to the case files. He presents one simple revelation about

Buffalo Bill's nature: we begin by "coveting what we see every day." Before he will tell more, Lecter gets her to confess her childhood ORDEAL when she failed to save the spring lambs from slaughter. She still wakes up in the dark with the screaming lambs, and admits that if she could save Catherine, the screaming would stop, her INNER PROBLEM.

Clarice presses Lecter to reveal Buffalo Bill's name, but Dr. Chilton interrupts. Clarice breaks free from the guards and grabs the case file from Lecter's outstretched hand. Lecter's fingers linger on hers—the only time the two have physically touched. Knowing Lecter's wicked ways, this simple moment in the film is a tense ORDEAL. She literally touches death, and he sets her free.

Surviving this ORDEAL gives Clarice new insight to solve the answer to Lecter's clue, "covet what you see every day." Buffalo Bill knew his first victim, Frederica Bimmel. Clarice has seized her REWARD.

Clarice visits the home of Frederica Bimmel, and finds her sewing room. The diamond-shaped darts on an unfinished dress match the shape of the skin flayed from the recent autopsy victim. This discovery is Clarice's ROAD BACK. She phones Crawford with her news, but he tells her they already know the identity of Buffalo Bill, Jamie Gumb, and are on their way. Clarice offers to drive to Chicago (to conclude her Journey to catch Buffalo Bill), but Crawford needs her to remain where she is and connect Jamie Gumb to Bimmel.

As the FBI move in on the suspected home of Jamie Gumb, Clarice stumbles upon his actual home. She sees a Death's Head Moth, a warning that initiates Clarice's RESURRECTION sequence. Clarice pursues Gumb into the house, discovers Catherine trapped in her chamber, and stumbles upon Gumb's skinning room as Gumb cuts the lights. Surrounded by darkness and death, Clarice is unaware that Gumb pursues her with infrared goggles. He taunts her and raises his gun. But Clarice hears the metallic click of the gun's hammer and spins, shooting Gumb dead, completing her RESURRECTION.

Clarice's Journey yields several ELIXIRS. The case is solved, Buffalo Bill is dead, and Catherine is rescued. Clarice graduates and earns the ELIXIR of her MENTOR'S respect. At the reception, Crawford assures her that her father would have been proud. Clarice gets a phonecall from another proud MENTOR. Lecter assures her that she is not in danger now that he is free. The world is more interesting with Clarice in it. Lecter grants Clarice the ELIXIR OF LIFE.

FADE OUT

THE MYTHIC STRUCTURE OF THE THRILLER

Dark forces have shattered our Ordinary World, throwing us into a land of deceit and trickery. Shapeshifters abound. No one can be trusted, and true Allies may never be revealed without the light of the Ordinary World. Perhaps only we alone can restore our lives and return the Elixirs of justice and goodness from this world of shadows.

"HOW COULD I HAVE KNOWN THAT MURDER CAN SOMETIMES SMELL LIKE HONEYSUCKLE?"

Beneath every small town lies a shadow. Not a monster, but the dark side of the Ordinary World. Suddenly the Hero's allies are his enemies. Richard Kimble arrives to find his wife murdered, not by a psychopath but by a one-armed man hired by Kimble's best friend.

On a Thriller's darkest journey (common in film noir), the audience vicariously experiences the forbidden seven deadly sins. We are thrilled when the hero is tempted by and even acts out his greed, lust, or murderous intentions. Secretly we hope he'll get away with it. Sometimes he does.

A good Thriller puts the Hero in a topsy-turvy Ordinary World where no one is who we think they are and where moral boundaries are broken. The audience relates to the Hero's fears—that he can no longer rely on anyone and feels he's losing his identity. Once the fearful situation is established, a Thriller must then work to build and sustain the fear throughout the film. The storyteller keeps the audience fearful and at the edge of their seats through the use of surprise and suspense.

With surprise, the event is a moment of shock or terror, a jolt of adrenaline from which we quickly recover. In contrast, suspense builds and is sustained over a scene, a sequence or perhaps an entire Journey. Suspense relies upon the audience knowing more than the characters on screen and thereby fearing the inevitable dangers that the characters will confront. Both surprise and suspense keep the audience unsettled and anxious, excited to see the Journey through.

HOW DO YOU CREATE SUSPENSE?

Suspense builds from an engaging plot with richly defined and identifiable characters. The Thriller plot runs like a roller coaster, with its build, sudden dips and breathers, and mounting anticipation that takes us to the breathtaking conclusion. The construction of this thrill ride entails placing a Hero in great jeopardy that worsens and worsens until we fear that he has no escape. The Hero must be fully developed and grounded in our real world so we can relate to and sympathize with him in this high-stakes Journey of life and death.

Suspense means that the audience knows more than the characters. Using Hitchcock's model, a couple talking at the breakfast table is boring, but if the audience is aware that a bomb is beneath the table (and the poor couple isn't), the scene becomes suspenseful. We, the audience, sit in our seats armed with the knowledge of the stakes involved. Suspense builds because we anticipate the fate that awaits the Hero, yet we don't know what the ultimate outcome will be.

The Chase can be an important tool used throughout the Hero's Journey to heighten suspense. In Thrillers, the storyteller can build suspense by putting two chases on a collision course. For example, while Dr. Kimble races to confront Nichols, the man responsible for his wife's murder, Nichols has ordered the one-armed man to kill Kimble. These two chases collide in a fight on the subway. Kimble survives but a police officer is killed.

Several chases can converge or build upon each other to further heighten suspense. Kimble resumes his chase to confront Nichols, but now the police believe Kimble's the cop killer and will shoot him down. Meanwhile, Marshal Sam Gerard is in a chase to get to Kimble before the cops do. The cops, Gerard and Kimble all converge at the hotel where Gerard is able to stall the police. Gerard's chase can now build on Kimble's finally completing the exhausting journey. Most chases are relentless physical trials, but they don't have to be. One of cinema's most suspenseful cinema chases is a slow descent down a staircase (*Notorious*).

THE TALES OF THE THRILLER

Thriller Stories can be classified several ways. First, in the use of suspense. Second, in the nature of the Hero's Journey. These classifications are not strictly delineated. A story may blend the different story types.

The Use of Suspense:

A. The "who-dun-it." The Audience follows the story in the shoes of the Hero. These are common Journeys for the detective or mystery Thriller (*Chinatown*). The Journey told from the Hero's point of view can effectively fuel paranoia as a Hero seeks some kind of control in his Special World (*The Fugitive, La Femme Nikita*).

B. The Audience is a few steps ahead of our Hero. We can call these tales the "when-is-it-gonna-happen." These tales exploit suspense as we anticipate the powers of the Special World catching up with the Hero (*Notorious, The Fugitive*). For detective and mystery Thrillers, the Audience knows the Villain or Shadow and hopes the detective will stop him before he strikes again.

We can also look at the Thriller from the perspective of the Hero's Journey, specifically how the Hero enters the Special World. The Thriller's two basic Journeys:

A. The Hero is wrongly accused, and pushed into a Special World from where there is no return. He is thrown into a downward spiral of despair. Everything is against him, and he must choose his Allies well, as he tries to save himself (*The Fugitive, Notorious*).
B. The Hero is seduced into the Special World. He leaves logic and morality behind in the Ordinary World, and lets his sinful desires for forbidden love, murder and greed fuel his Journey. The situation becomes out of control because of mistrust and paranoia, and the Hero must eventually suffer the consequences (*Double Indemnity*).

FILM NOIR

The Thriller's darkest tales are told in Film Noir, a French term meaning "dark film." Popular in the 1940s and 1950s, these pessimistic, often nihilistic tales show cynical and disillusioned Heroes and Villains in a world overrun by crime, corruption and betrayal. Still prevalent today, Noir's world is characterized by shadows, rain-drenched streets, tough guys, alluring dames, and smart and sexy dialogue.

THE SPECIAL WORLD IS NOT EASILY ENTERED

Like the Journeys of Horror, the Thriller's Special World is often not willingly entered. The Hero may be pushed through a series of Thresholds until he has no choice but to accept the Special World or face death (*The Fugitive, La Femme Nikita*). The Special World of Film Noir, involving the dark side of love and ambition, may require a sophisticated Call to Adventure or Succession of Calls that stir the Hero on, into deeper, more primal levels. The Shapeshifter femme fatale may need to numb or confuse the Hero's moral judgment, while entreating the Hero's senses with a welcomed glimpse of flesh, or intoxicating scent (*Double Indemnity*).

THE HERO'S SPECIAL POWERS

The powers held by the Hero can make a huge difference when dealing with the rules of the Special World. A man accused of murder, on the run, will have a more limited understanding of the rules and denizens of the Special World than the detective, hired to get them, who inhabits the Special World.

But the innocent Hero on the run will have Special Powers of his own (often intellectual or moral powers) that make him resourceful, and keep him determined to push to the end.

THE ROAD BACK

The Road Back usually puts into question the Hero's commitment to return to the Ordinary World. In tales where the Hero must find justice, or reveal a murderer, the Road Back may be a final clue that will reveal the Shadow or Villain (*Chinatown, The Fugitive*). This signals the Chase that will take us to the climax, and to the final showdown when the Hero reveals the Shadow and ascertains that justice is served.

The Road Back could be a Shadow's effort to end the Hero's Journey. The Hero's chase may be blocked by a Villain (*The Fugitive*). In Noir's darkest tales, the Road Back may flush the Hero out of a Special World of murder, lust and greed (*Double Indemnity*). Or the Road Back may be an Ordeal that pushes the Hero to reject the Special World (*La Femme Nikita*).

THE ELIXIR

The unpredictability of Thrillers can open up lots of possibilities for endings and Elixirs. But this Elixir can be an extremely important message the storyteller conveys to the Audience. Can someone get away with murder? Can the Hero free himself from the web of deceit that has stolen his identity? In Thriller stories where the innocent finds himself on the run, or in need of redemption, justice is served, and he reclaims his place in his Ordinary World (*The Fugitive*). Most detective stories see the murderer revealed and punishment served. Be cautious of open endings in mysteries. The mystery Audience expects some closure. But there can be wonderful twists that support the movie's theme and satisfy the viewer, even if it's with a feeling of unease.

GENRE CHALLENGES: THRILLER

1. Can you relate to Walter Neff or Phyllis Dietrichson? Why or why not? Take a look at *Body Heat, Fatal Attraction,* or *Basic Instinct.* Can you relate to the hero or the femme fatale of the movie? Is it necessary to relate to the femme fatale?
2. What is the importance of the Lola Dietrichson and Nino Zachette subplot in *Double Indemnity*? How does it heighten suspense?
3. In *Notorious,* in what ways are Sebastian and Devlin shadows of one another? How is contrast between Sebastian and Devlin used to accentuate mistrust, heighten suspense and complicate Alicia's Journey?
4. Hitchcock's "MacGuffin" is described in the analysis of *Notorious*. What is the MacGuffin in *The Fugitive*? *Chinatown*?
5. How is suspense heightened in a detective mystery like *Chinatown* in which we are following in Jake Gittes' footsteps?
6. Using the Character Arc breakdown examined in Drama and presented in "The Stages of the Hero's Journey," how would you show Nikita's transformation as a woman? What phases of character growth are present? Are phases of growth repeated? At what point does Nikita become a sympathetic character?
7. In *The Fugitive,* what are Richard Kimble's Special Powers and how does he use them? In what ways does Kimble overcome the various Threshold Guardians that prevent his Journey? How does he use these same Threshold Guardians to block or assist U.S. Marshal Sam Gerard?
8. Choose one of the sample films, or choose a favorite Thriller. What information is known and how does that information build suspense? When is the audience surprised?

DOUBLE INDEMNITY
(U.S., 1944)

"They've committed a murder and it's not like taking a trolley ride together where they can get off at different stops. They're stuck with each other and they've got to ride all the way to the end of the line. And it's a one-way trip, and the last stop is the cemetery."

— Barton Keyes (Edward G. Robinson)

Screenplay by Billy Wilder and Raymond Chandler
From the novel by James M. Cain
Directed by Billy Wilder

An insurance salesman plots with a beautiful housewife to kill her husband and collect on the insurance money.

LANDMARKS OF THE JOURNEY

Double Indemnity shows the classic scheming, shapeshifting femme fatale in all her devious beauty. Many of Film Noir's dark tales show a Hero being lured into the Special World of sin. And *Double Indemnity*'s Walter Neff, a by-the-book insurance salesman, is no match for Phyllis Dietrichson. She uses sex and tales of her wretched marriage to break down her prey's moral fiber and seduce Neff to instigate her dark deeds.

What makes Neff's Journey so powerful and tragic is his relationship with his Mentor, the claims investigator, Barton Keyes, a surrogate father who suddenly becomes a Shadow Mentor that Neff must outwit. Phyllis and Neff will suffocate in a Special World of growing mistrust, and Keyes will solve the murder plot, finally flushing Neff back into the light of the Ordinary World, where he must face his Mentor and accept his punishment.

THE JOURNEY

The Journey's opening moments establish the SPECIAL WORLD of deceit and suspense. The wounded Walter Neff limps into his office (a return to his ORDINARY WORLD) and begins to dictate his "death-bed" confession, the ELIXIR of truth. He didn't get away with murder; he didn't get the girl. And he's going to tell us what happened. His tale takes us back several months, where a SUCCESSION OF CALLS are needed to push Walter Neff into the SPECIAL WORLD of adultery and murder.

Insurance salesman Walter Neff pays a visit to the house of Mr. Dietrichson. Dietrichson's not home, but Neff's welcomed by his wife, Phyllis, clad only in a towel. Disarmed by this physical CALL OF DESIRE, Neff struggles to keep with his initial

OUTER PROBLEM to renew Dietrichson's auto insurance policy. But he's stirred by this smart-mouth beauty. Neff readily shows his SPECIAL POWERS in the world of insurance, and this display doesn't go unnoticed by the SHAPESHIFTER Phyllis. She sizes up this prospective MENTOR, who can't keep his mind off her "honey of an anklet." He pursues this CALL OF DESIRE but Phyllis REFUSES him. She sets an appointment for Neff to return when her husband will be present.

At his office, Neff sees MENTOR Barton Keyes, a claims investigator with a "little man" inside (an INNER MENTOR) capable of sniffing out fraudulent claims. His dealings with Mr. Gorlopis and his false claim show the MENTOR in high form. In Neff's SPECIAL WORLD, Keyes transforms into the MENTOR SHADOW that Neff will have to outwit, and out-think.

Phyllis changes the appointment, and again Walter arrives with no Mr. Dietrichson, only Phyllis. Even the THRESHOLD GUARDIAN maid has the day off. Phyllis assures Neff that her husband will renew, before asking questions about life insurance. Concerned about Dietrichson's risk at his job, Phyllis wants protection for him—without his knowledge. Neff sees through this SHAPESHIFTER'S mask and accuses her of plotting to kill her husband and collect on the insurance, his REFUSAL of her veiled CALL TO ADVENTURE. He leaves her, but this CALL has cracked Neff's ORDINARY WORLD, and even beer and a few lines of bowling won't let him forget it.

Phyllis appears at Neff's apartment that night. The SHAPESHIFTER weaves tales of her wretched ORDINARY WORLD to wear away at Neff's moral code, while her presence works his senses—the scent of honeysuckle, the tight sweater. She offers to leave; faced with this potential CRISIS OF THE HEART, Neff kisses her hard. He finally CROSSES THE THRESHOLD to save Phyllis' pretty neck because he's confident that he's the one who knows how to do it right.

With the stakes at $50,000 and desire for a blonde bombshell, Neff enters the SPECIAL WORLD of murder and insurance fraud. To plot the perfect murder, Neff needs to anticipate every move of his greatest obstacle, his MENTOR, Keyes. Neff tries to wear his MENTOR'S skin and to think with his MENTOR'S brain. This will guide Neff as he and Phyllis enter the TEST PHASE, leading to the murder of Mr. Dietrichson.

They trick Dietrichson into signing a life insurance policy when he signs his auto insurance renewal. Neff wants to collect on a double-indemnity clause, and presses that the "accidental" death must happen on a train. Their plans are delayed when Dietrichson breaks his leg, but this provides the perfect REVERSAL. Dietrichson decides to use a train to attend his college class reunion. With his goal of the money and the girl within reach, Neff REFUSES a promotion from Keyes. This TEST of Neff's greed and morality signals the APPROACH TO THE INMOST CAVE. He is fully committed to this SPECIAL WORLD.

On the night of the murder, Neff executes his meticulously plotted APPROACH. He establishes his alibis, dresses himself in a suit matching Dietrichson's, and hides in the back of the Dietrichsons' car awaiting their trip to the train station.

The ORDEAL happens in three tense stages:

A. With Phyllis driving, Neff murders Dietrichson on the way to the train station.
B. Boarding the train as Dietrichson, Neff goes to the train's observation deck to stage Dietrichson's accidental fall. He can't have witnesses, so he tricks a commuter, Jackson (a THRESHOLD GUARDIAN), to go inside the train so that Neff can jump from the empty observation deck.
C. Phyllis and Neff drag Dietrichson's body to the train tracks and return to their car but the engine won't start, preventing their escape. After tense moments in this "death-like" state, the engine kicks and they drive away (a RESURRECTION).

Neff has crossed a THRESHOLD into a darker SPECIAL WORLD as a murderer. Now Phyllis and Neff have to get away with it, and collect the insurance. But Neff gains an important REWARD that fuels this second half of the Journey. He begins to question Phyllis' trust.

The police do not suspect foul play, leaving it in the hands of the insurance company. Initially, Neff wins an important ALLY, Keyes, who believes the company has to pay the claim, the REWARD. Neff has defeated his MENTOR and prepares to savor the REWARD with Phyllis, but Keyes appears at his apartment unannounced. Neff never anticipated Keyes' INNER MENTOR, his "little man"/intuition that pushes him to suspect Phyllis of murdering her husband. With Phyllis on the way, Neff faces an ORDEAL that threatens to expose the truth to his SHADOW MENTOR. Keyes finally leaves to settle his "little man" with a bicarbonate of soda, and barely misses Phyllis, a RESURRECTION. But Neff tells the DARK REWARD of Keyes' suspicions to Phyllis and suggests they not see each other while Keyes continues his investigation. But Phyllis fears their relationship is changing; this REWARD will fuel her own Journey.

After questioning Jackson, the passenger on the train's observation deck, Keyes tells Neff his solution (Keyes' REWARD), that the murder happened before the train ride, and Phyllis' accomplice impersonated Dietrichson on the train. Now, it's only a matter of time before the accomplice is discovered. As the MENTOR warns, because the murder was committed by two doesn't mean it's twice as safe; rather, "it's ten times twice as dangerous." This discovery initiates the ROAD BACK, setting off the TICKING CLOCK, as Keyes now closes in. Neff and Phyllis draw further apart, their relationship strained by mistrust. At their grocery store rendezvous, Neff wants out but Phyllis threatens him if they don't stay together. After all, he actually plotted the murder; Phyllis only wanted her husband dead. She now blocks his ROAD BACK of escape, but her threat puts the thought of death back into Neff's mind: Phyllis' death. All Neff needs now is the opportunity.

Keyes announces that they've fingered the accomplice, an old boyfriend of Dietrichson's daughter, who had been frequenting the house since the murder. Keyes has dropped Neff's opportunity of escape into his lap, completing the ROAD BACK. Now Neff can kill Phyllis and set up the boyfriend before the police make their arrest (the TICKING CLOCK).

Neff's Journey ends in shadows. He arranges a meeting with Phyllis and arrives at her house unaware that this SHAPESHIFTER has her own dark plans. And her own gun. She doesn't kill Neff with the first shot. Neff invites a second bullet but she can't do it. A CRISIS OF THE HEART resurrects the love that she never realized she felt. But a Journey filled with mistrust will not grant sudden forgiveness. Neff won't buy it. And kills her (Neff's RESURRECTION).

Neff staggers back to his office and we return to the Journey's opening scene, and his confession (the ELIXIR). Keyes has arrived at the office. Neff hopes that Keyes will grant a continued RESURRECTION and let him escape. But Neff collapses in the doorway. Finally, Neff grants his MENTOR the reason Keyes failed to discover him. He was too close, right across the desk. "Closer than that," Keyes assures him (the ELIXIR of deep friendship and the acknowledgement that Neff has disappointed his MENTOR.)

FADE OUT

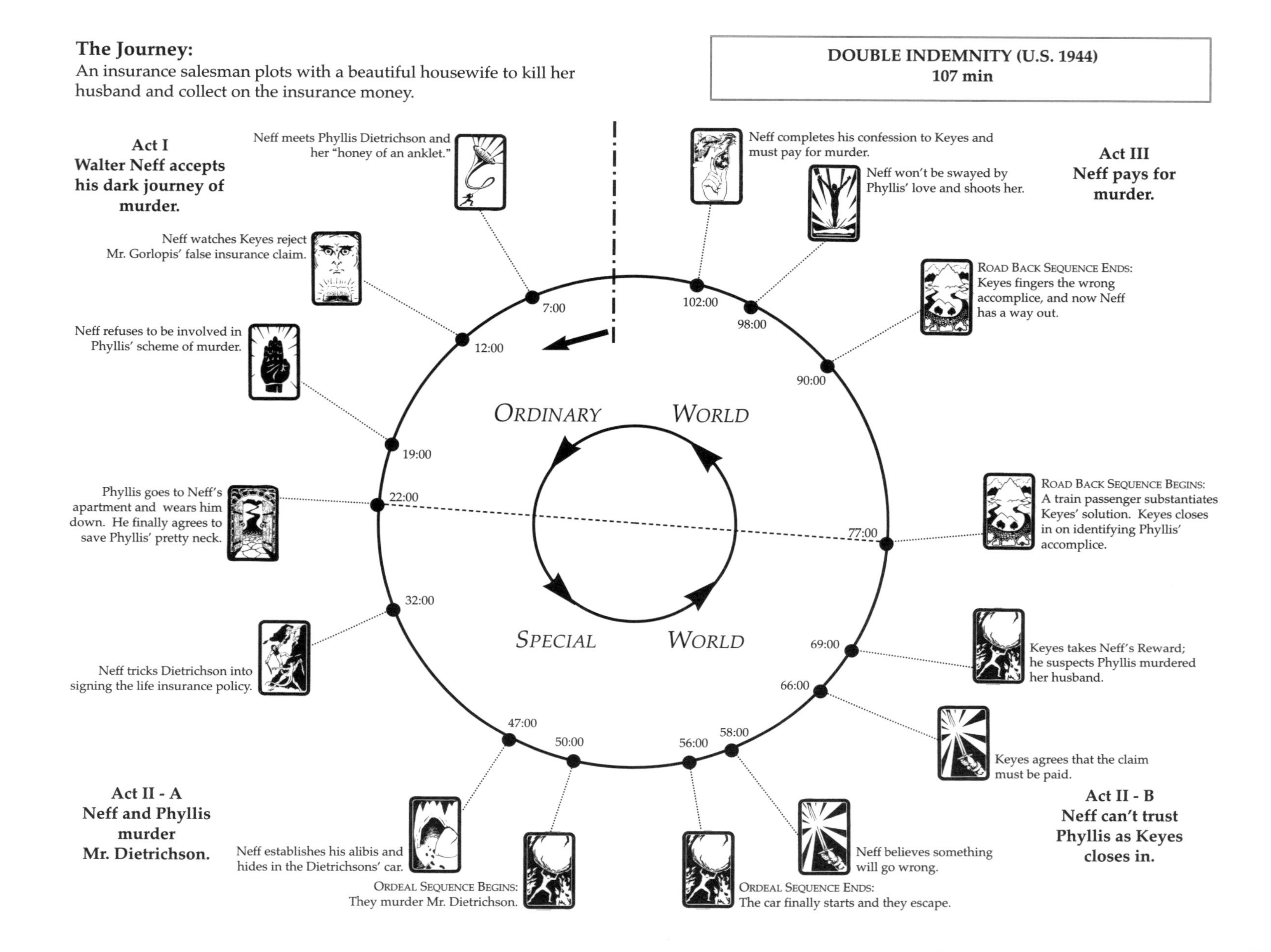

The Journey:
An insurance salesman plots with a beautiful housewife to kill her husband and collect on the insurance money.
DOUBLE INDEMNITY (U.S. 1944)
107 min
Act I
Walter Neff accepts his dark journey of murder.
Neff meets Phyllis Dietrichson and her "honey of an anklet."
7:00
Neff watches Keyes reject Mr. Gorlopis' false insurance claim.
12:00
Neff refuses to be involved in Phyllis' scheme of murder.
19:00
Phyllis goes to Neff's apartment and wears him down. He finally agrees to save Phyllis' pretty neck.
22:00
Neff tricks Dietrichson into signing the life insurance policy.
32:00
Act II - A
Neff and Phyllis murder Mr. Dietrichson.
Neff establishes his alibis and hides in the Dietrichsons' car.
47:00
ORDEAL SEQUENCE BEGINS:
They murder Mr. Dietrichson.
50:00
ORDEAL SEQUENCE ENDS:
The car finally starts and they escape.
56:00
Neff believes something will go wrong.
58:00
Keyes agrees that the claim must be paid.
66:00
Keyes takes Neff's Reward; he suspects Phyllis murdered her husband.
69:00
Act II - B
Neff can't trust Phyllis as Keyes closes in.
ROAD BACK SEQUENCE BEGINS:
A train passenger substantiates Keyes' solution. Keyes closes in on identifying Phyllis' accomplice.
77:00
ROAD BACK SEQUENCE ENDS:
Keyes fingers the wrong accomplice, and now Neff has a way out.
90:00
Neff won't be swayed by Phyllis' love and shoots her.
98:00
Neff completes his confession to Keyes and must pay for murder.
102:00
Act III
Neff pays for murder.
ORDINARY WORLD
SPECIAL WORLD

NOTORIOUS
(U.S., 1946)

"This is a very strange love affair."

"Why?"

"Maybe the fact that you don't love me."

"When I don't love you, I'll let you know."

"You haven't said anything."

"Actions speak louder than words."

— Alicia (Ingrid Bergman) and
Devlin (Cary Grant)

Written by Ben Hecht
Directed by Alfred Hitchcock

To prove her American allegiance, the daughter of a convicted Nazi spy infiltrates a Nazi spy ring in South America and agrees to marry a Nazi conspirator, even though she has fallen in love with her American recruiter.

LANDMARKS OF THE JOURNEY

Alfred Hitchcock used the term "MacGuffin" to mean the key element, the motivation or goal for the characters that directs their action. It doesn't matter what it is—it could be anything as long as it means everything to the story's characters. The uranium ore, a classic MacGuffin in *Notorious*, could just as easily have been microfilm or secret papers, as long as the heroes and villains have a strong motivation to get whatever it is.

THE JOURNEY

Alicia Huberman is the daughter of a convicted Nazi spy to the United States. Disillusioned by her father's deceit, Alicia has become a hard-drinking, self-destructive, "notorious" playgirl. Her ORDINARY WORLD is spent being hounded by reporters and scrutinized by the police. Her OUTER PROBLEM is to escape from the SHADOW of her father's reputation.

Her CALL TO ADVENTURE is presented by a SHAPESHIFTING HERALD, the American secret agent, Devlin. At first, Devlin tries to play according to her ORDINARY WORLD. He drinks with her at her party. He doesn't discourage her obvious flirtations (Alicia's romantic CALL), and agrees to join her for a reckless spin in her sports car. But once she discovers that Devlin's SHAPESHIFTING mask hides the face of a government agent, he presents her CALL, to help the U.S. government by securing secrets from associates of her father in Rio de Janeiro.

Disoriented by the hangover and put off by this HERALD'S underhanded tactics, Alicia REFUSES the CALL and denies her patriotism. But Devlin uses a recording of Alicia declaring her patriotism and denouncing her father's schemes to stir her INNER MENTOR and choose the noble cause.

Alicia's friend, the Commodore, arrives offering her a retreat on a yacht to escape the Press and the police. Faced with these CONFLICTING CALLS, to escape or finally redeem herself, Alicia accepts Devlin's HIGHER CALL.

During their plane trip to Rio (a physical THRESHOLD), Devlin informs Alicia that her father committed suicide in jail. The death of this SHADOW is an emotional THRESHOLD that gives Alicia the opportunity to finally change her ways (her INNER PROBLEM).

Days later in a Rio cafe, Alicia is pleased by her own sobriety, but Devlin REFUSES to accept any long-term transformation. Now wearing the HERALD'S mask, Alicia challenges Devlin to fall in love with her. Devlin REFUSES to accept her as anything other than a tramp. His rejection pushes her back to the bottle; however, Alicia breaks his resistance down, addressing his fear of falling in love with a no-good gal. He kisses her to finally shut her up, and the two CROSS THE THRESHOLD.

Now, as their JOURNEY OF THE HEART blossoms, Alicia's JOURNEY FOR PATRIOTIC REDEMPTION kicks back in. But this noble cause is no longer so noble. Devlin receives Alicia's orders from his MENTOR, Prescott. Alicia must befriend an old admirer and Nazi conspirator, Alexander Sebastian. The U.S. government believes Sebastian's house is a front for Nazi scientific activities. Like Mata Hari, Alicia is quick to observe, she's expected to do what's necessary to get the needed information. Alicia TESTS Devlin, hoping that his commitment to their relationship will prevent this Journey from going any further. He refuses to answer. This denial of their relationship pushes Alicia THROUGH THE THRESHOLD of the noble cause.

Devlin wears the MENTOR'S mask to deny his true feelings and to push Alicia forward on her Journey. He orchestrates her meeting with Sebastian at the Riding Club, forcing her horse to bolt and allowing Sebastian to rescue her. The initial TESTS run smoothly for Alicia. Using the SHAPESHIFTER'S mask, Alicia transforms into an ALLY "allergic to government agents." She flatters her mark and quickly wins Sebastian's feelings. No longer just a THRESHOLD GUARDIAN to the secrets Alicia has been employed to find, Sebastian has become a RIVAL for Alicia's heart.

Sebastian invites her to his home for dinner. MENTORS Prescott and Devlin prepare her for this most difficult TEST, setting her rules for being a spy. She must memorize the guests' names, and not ask questions. At the dinner party, Sebastian's mother greets Alicia. This SHAPESHIFTER and RIVAL for Sebastian's heart questions Alicia's loyalty to her father. Sebastian rescues her from the "interrogation," and welcomes her into his house. Alicia follows his MENTORS' directions and becomes suspicious when a guest, Emil, becomes agitated about one of the wine bottles. He's quickly pacified by other guests before Alicia can know what was wrong.

At the race track, where they meet, Alicia passes this information to Devlin, along with the names of the guests. She also confesses that Sebastian can be added to her list of playmates. Devlin the RIVAL turns bitter and spiteful at this news, unwilling to accept the part that Devlin the MENTOR played to push this dangerous Journey. Sebastian discovers them, and Alicia confesses that Devlin is a rejected RIVAL. But Sebastian wants proof that Devlin means nothing to her.

Alicia arrives unexpectedly at Prescott's office, and announces that Sebastian has proposed to her. She needs the advice of her MENTORS. The news thrills Prescott; his plot is playing out better than expected. The goal is in sight. This APPROACH moment is also an ORDEAL of Alicia's JOURNEY OF THE HEART. Secretly Alicia hopes that the announcement (a CRISIS OF THE HEART) will force Devlin to admit his love and end the Journey. Devlin walks out—washing his hands of the decision. This ORDEAL OF THE HEART dashes all hope of her relationship with Devlin, and forces Alicia to sacrifice herself and enter a darker, more dangerous SPECIAL WORLD.

In her new role as Sebastian's wife, Alicia has free reign of the house. Almost. She discovers the locked wine cellar—the forbidden room—and only Sebastian holds the key.

Upon hearing this news, Devlin devises a way to get into the house to break into the cellar. He suggests that Sebastian throw a party to welcome home his new bride, and that Devlin be invited to see how happily married she is. This scene begins a suspenseful APPROACH TO THE INMOST CAVE. On the night of the party, Alicia steals Sebastian's key and barely survives being discovered. The theft of the key to the wine cellar initiates an unusual TICKING CLOCK. The guests are depleting the champagne bottles faster than anticipated. More bottles will soon need to be retrieved from the wine cellar.

Devlin and Alicia sneak into the wine cellar. Pressured by the TICKING CLOCK, a bottle is broken and the two accidentally discover their goal, uranium ore stored in the wine bottles. Devlin quickly takes a sample of the ore and disguises their accident. The two leave the cellar as Sebastian comes down the stairs with his butler to retrieve more champagne. Devlin quickly kisses Alicia in full view. He allows Sebastian to witness his RIVAL'S indiscretion to place suspicion on Devlin and not Alicia (a RESURRECTION that completes the ORDEAL SEQUENCE), and to prevent Sebastian from discovering the missing key.

Alicia hasn't escaped Sebastian's suspicions. Finally returning to the cellar for champagne, Sebastian realizes his key is gone. When Alicia returns the key during his sleep, Sebastian goes to the cellar and discovers that the plot has been uncovered, a DARK REWARD. He must confess Alicia's disloyalty to his domineering mother (SHADOW).

Sebastian fears his fate if the other spies discover his mistake in trusting Alicia. His mother devises a slow unsuspecting way to get rid of Alicia—they poison her coffee. And she gradually gets sicker and sicker.

At Prescott's office, Alicia receives congratulations for her success in retrieving the uranium ore (the REWARD). Now all they need to know is the location of the ore deposit. Prescott also tells her that Devlin will no longer be her contact. He has requested a transfer to Spain.

Alicia meets with Devlin one last time, but Devlin won't admit that he's leaving the Journey. This CRISIS OF THE HEART, combined with the poison, turns Alicia extremely bitter toward her love. She rejects his concern for her health, blaming her illness on a hangover. MENTORS often leave the HERO'S Journey, forcing the HERO to prove that he or she has acquired the MENTOR'S lessons and can complete the Journey. Devlin's heart can no longer take this Journey, but this glimpse of a "SHADOWY" Alicia makes him reconsider.

Feeling abandoned by her MENTOR and love, Alicia returns to Sebastian's. A member of Sebastian's inner circle, a scientist, observes Alicia's poor health and advises a vacation in the European mountains where he works, inadvertently revealing the location of the uranium ore deposits, a REWARD. When Sebastian and his mother suddenly stop the scientist from accidentally drinking Alicia's poisoned coffee, Alicia realizes their plot to get rid of her. She tries to retreat to her bedroom but the poison has blocked her ROAD BACK, and she collapses.

Her ROAD BACK is placed in the hands of Devlin, who finally becomes suspicious when five days pass without a word from Alicia. His devotion to duty placed her in this situation; now his heart must rescue her. He pays Sebastian a visit. The butler, Joseph, admits that Alicia is terribly ill. Devlin easily passes this THRESHOLD GUARDIAN when Joseph leaves to get Sebastian; Devlin sneaks upstairs and finds Alicia deathly ill in bed. He finally proclaims his love for her (RESURRECTION and ELIXIR). She tells him she's being poisoned. Devlin's emotional RESURRECTION gives Alicia the strength to rise from the bed (a physical RESURRECTION). Devlin helps her to her feet and tries to keep her awake. She reveals the location of the uranium ore deposit (ELIXIR), and warns of the danger they are in—Sebastian's Nazi friends will not let them leave if they are uncovered as spies.

Devlin takes her out of the room, confronting Sebastian at the top of the stairs. Sebastian's not easily swayed by Devlin's threats of Sebastian's life at the hands of the other Nazis; however, Sebastian's mother protects her son's life and helps Devlin and Alicia down the long, suspenseful staircase (a RESURRECTION). The suspicious Nazis wait at the bottom of the staircase, and Sebastian finally senses his fate if his disloyalty is revealed. He insists that they must rush her to the hospital. Sebastian helps Devlin and Alicia outside into the car, but Devlin leaves Sebastian behind, throwing suspicion on his RIVAL and forcing him to return to his house and face the Nazi SHADOW.

FADE OUT

CHINATOWN
(U.S., 1974)

"Why does it bother you to talk about it?"

"It bothers everybody that works there."

"Where?"

"Chinatown, everybody. To me, it was just bad luck."

"Why?"

"You can't always tell what's going on—like with you."

— Evelyn Mulwray (Faye Dunaway) and
Jake Gittes (Jack Nicholson)

Written by Robert Towne
Directed by Roman Polanski

Private Detective Jake Gittes is set up to tail the city's head of Water and Power, and finds himself in a labyrinth of murder, incest, and an L.A. water scandal.

LANDMARKS OF THE JOURNEY

Many Noir tales show a detective uncovering crimes of passion and corruption. J.J. Gittes is our stoic detective, the impeccably dressed knight with a code of honor to serve justice. Gittes uncovers deeper and deeper layers of corruption, trying to understand the meaning of the puzzle pieces, even trying to understand this corruption on his own terms. But Gittes must finally accept the futility of his attempts. This isn't just a dark tale of incest or adultery. Gittes uncovers a corrupt city, a grand arena that gives the Shadow, Noah Cross, power beyond the Hero's control.

Gittes is a Catalyst Hero, a common archetype in detective stories. The Catalyst Hero affects change in others while remaining unchanged. *Chinatown* is a wonderful character study of how Gittes makes his impact in this Special World, especially the various creative, bold and desperate methods he employs to get past the Threshold Guardians and Shapeshifters blocking the truth. But Gittes is a tragic catalyst. His search for truth leads to the death of the one person he is trying to protect. And what is the truth? Ironically, by Journey's end, do we really know? That's why it's called *Chinatown*.

THE JOURNEY

Los Angeles, 1937. Jake Gittes is a private detective specializing in divorce work, "other people's dirty laundry," his ORDINARY WORLD. Made cynical by his ineffectiveness as a cop working Chinatown for the D.A., Gittes now wields his code of justice for the individual desperate for a little help.

Gittes meets Mrs. Mulwray, who wants to hire Gittes to follow her husband. She believes he's having an affair. Gittes turns down this CALL TO ADVENTURE. He tries to convince Mrs. Mulwray "to let sleeping dogs lie," a REFUSAL. But when she mentions that her husband is Hollis Mulwray, the chief engineer of the Department of Water and Power, Gittes realizes the potential money to be earned. He enters the THRESHOLD of the case, to find out if Hollis Mulwray is having an affair.

Although this establishes an OUTER PROBLEM, to solve the case and earn the money, it is not the OUTER PROBLEM and SPECIAL WORLD of the story. That THRESHOLD will be crossed in time. For now, Jake begins his investigation, entering a TEST PHASE where he follows Mulwray and stumbles across a SUCCESSION OF CALLS in disguise. These CALLS also show us the desperate state of drought-stricken Los Angeles. If taken, these CALLS would unveil a larger problem in Jake's and Los Angeles' ORDINARY WORLDS.

- Gittes observes the City Council meeting, where Mulwray adamantly opposes a water bill to build a dam that would bring the city much needed water.
- A farmer interrupts the meeting with his herd of starved sheep. This HERALD accuses Mulwray of being bought off to denounce the water bill.
- Gittes observes Mulwray examining a dry riverbed and speaking briefly with a Mexican boy.
- Gittes follows Mulwray to the beach where water mysteriously flows through the run-off channel.
- Gittes' assistant, Walsh, shows photos of Mulwray in a heated argument with Noah Cross (the SHADOW).

Gittes is unable to see the significance of these CALLS until he is well into the SPECIAL WORLD OF MURDER. For now, he does his job and finally takes the incriminating pictures of Mulwray with a beautiful young girl. The case is closed. Mrs. Mulwray receives the photo proof of her husband's indiscretion. Somehow the photos splash across the front page of the daily paper, creating a major scandal and naming Gittes as the private investigator (a CALL TO ADVENTURE).

Gittes returns to his office where he confronts the real Evelyn Mulwray. Since she never hired Gittes, she threatens him with a lawsuit. Gittes doesn't like to be set up, and his moral code (INNER MENTOR) pushes him through a THRESHOLD to find out who's behind it and why.

He launches a TEST PHASE and goes to Mulwray's office. Mulwray's out, so Gittes slips past the secretary (THRESHOLD GUARDIAN) and snoops around Mulwray's office before Mulwray's chief deputy, Yelburton (THRESHOLD GUARDIAN), escorts him out.

At the elevators, Gittes sees Claude Mulvihill, a RIVAL ex-cop, now working for Yelburton.

Gittes goes to Mulwray's house. Waiting for Mulwray, Gittes observes the groundskeeper replacing dead grass near the fishpond. Again, Gittes isn't deep enough into the SPECIAL WORLD to comprehend the importance of this HERALD'S warning. Gittes spots something in the pond. Before he can retrieve it, he's interrupted by Mrs. Mulwray, who directs Gittes to find her husband at the reservoir.

Gittes uses Yelburton's card to pass the reservoir's security guards (easily tricking these THRESHOLD GUARDIANS), and finds his old partner, Escobar, dredging Mulwray's body from the reservoir, completing the second stage of Gittes' THRESHOLD.

The TEST PHASE is renewed with the further complications of Mulwray's death. Gittes tries to put together the pieces of the mystery and find the truth hidden by a series of SHAPESHIFTERS, THRESHOLD GUARDIANS and SHADOWS.

Gittes rescues SHAPESHIFTER Evelyn from Escobar's interrogation. The police want to know about the mysterious young woman photographed with Mulwray. Evelyn lies, saying that she hired Gittes to get her husband's affair in the open.

The Coroner (ALLY) shows Gittes the corpse of a town derelict who drowned mysteriously in the L.A. River in the middle of the drought. This CALL TO ADVENTURE makes Gittes backtrack, recalling Mulwray's stops while Gittes was tailing him.

Gittes returns to the dry riverbed and questions the Mexican boy. This THRESHOLD GUARDIAN willingly tells Gittes that he would report to Mulwray when the water arrived down the river.

At the reservoir, the scene of Mulwray's death, Gittes almost drowns in a sudden release of fresh water through the run-off pipes. He confronts two THRESHOLD GUARDIANS, Mulvihill and a Man with a Knife. They want Gittes out of this SPECIAL WORLD and slice his nose as a warning. Instead of pushing him away, this TEST pushes a determined Gittes to catch the big boys behind the water scandal.

Back at his office, Gittes receives a call from Ida Sessions, confessing her role as "Mrs. Mulwray"—the imposter who first hired Gittes. The SHAPESHIFTER refuses to reveal those who employed her, but directs Gittes to find "one of those people" in the obituary column.

Gittes has lunch with Evelyn Mulwray. Gittes knows this SHAPESHIFTER is hiding something. He's able to find out that her maiden name is "Cross." Desperate to get her to drop her SHAPESHIFTER mask and reveal her motives and loyalty, Gittes tells her that he suspects her husband was murdered for knowing that thousands of gallons of water were being dumped into the ocean.

Gittes returns to Mulwray's office, and discovers that Noah Cross had co-owned the Water Department with Mulwray. Gittes accuses Yelburton of hiring Ida Sessions. Although offended by the accusations, this THRESHOLD GUARDIAN confesses that water is being diverted to the northwest valley orange groves.

Evelyn Cross officially hires Gittes to find her husband's murderer. She confesses that Cross is her father, and that Cross and Mulwray had a falling out after a dam had collapsed.

Gittes meets Noah Cross for lunch. This SHAPESHIFTER SHADOW hires Gittes to find the mysterious girl in the Mulwray pictures.

At the Hall of Records, Gittes discovers that land lots in the valley have been recently resold, and he "borrows" one of the pages.

Gittes visits an orange grove, and has a run-in with the farmer and his sons. The farmers discount Yelburton's claims. The Water Department has been destroying their water, not supplying it. These THRESHOLD GUARDIANS-turned-ALLIES fetch Evelyn Mulwray to take the wounded Gittes away. Gittes figures out Ida Sessions' clue, a REWARD. He finds a name in the obits that matches his list of new landholders from the Hall of Records. The man died two weeks ago, yet he bought the land only last week. The details of the obituary lead Gittes to a retirement home.

Equipped with the clues accumulated over this TEST PHASE, Gittes APPROACHES THE INMOST CAVE. He and Evelyn trick the retirement home director, allowing them to meet the new land holders, all retirees unaware of the riches they possess. Gittes is soon escorted out, where he confronts Mulvihill, the ORDEAL. Gittes tricks this THRESHOLD GUARDIAN and barely escapes with his life, as Evelyn pulls up to the rescue and drives him away (a RESURRECTION).

Evelyn takes Gittes back to her home, where she cleans his wounds, and they make love, a REWARD. Evelyn uses this moment to find out about Gittes' dark futile past in Chinatown. Granted new insight from his Journey's APPROACH and ORDEAL, Gittes tells her his additional REWARD, he believes Evelyn's father, Noah Cross, is behind her husband's murder. Evelyn leaves abruptly after receiving a mysterious phone call. Even after sharing the REWARD of love, Gittes can't trust this SHAPESHIFTER. He follows her to a mysterious house, where Mulwray's alleged lover is being held captive. Gittes accuses Evelyn of killing her husband. Evelyn denies it, admitting that the girl is her sister.

He goes home alone to get some sleep. He receives a phone call that draws him to Ida Sessions' house, where he discovers her murdered. Escobar and his cops have baited Gittes and they want answers. Gittes explains the water scandal but Escobar refuses to believe this ELIXIR.

Gittes returns to Evelyn's house and finds everything packed up. Again, Gittes sees the gardener struggling with dead grass in the fishpond, and Gittes finally retrieves the object he saw before: a pair of broken glasses. Gittes returns to the mysterious safe house and confronts Evelyn with this REWARD. He holds the proof, Mulwray's glasses, that Evelyn murdered her husband. He calls Escobar giving the police the address to pick up Evelyn. Faced with this TICKING CLOCK, Evelyn finally abandons the SHAPESHIFTER mask and confesses that the mysterious woman, Katherine, is both her sister and daughter, the outcome of her rape by her father. Evelyn's Journey has been driven by her INNER NEED to protect Katherine from the SHADOW, Noah Cross. Gittes sends Evelyn and Katherine to Evelyn's servant's home in Chinatown, while he takes care of Escobar. Before they leave, Gittes shows Evelyn the broken bifocals; they aren't her husband's, she tells him (completing the ROAD BACK).

Gittes keeps Escobar and his men busy, leading them on a wild goose chase. Gittes uses the home of a client, Curly (ALLY), to escape the cops. He enlists Curly to take Evelyn and Katherine to Mexico.

Gittes arranges a meeting with Noah Cross at Mulwray's house. He tricks this SHADOW into admitting that the bifocals are his. The SHADOW presents his devious plan to "bring L.A. to the water," before his THRESHOLD GUARDIAN, Mulvihill, forces Gittes to give up the glasses. At gunpoint, Gittes takes them to Evelyn and Katherine.

Gittes' Journey ends in the land of his greatest fear, Chinatown, a territory that symbolizes his ineffectiveness when he was a cop. He finds his associates in the custody of Escobar and his men. Escobar refuses to accept Gittes' ELIXIR that Noah Cross murdered Mulwray. Evelyn appears with Katherine to make her escape. Cross wants Katherine, and Evelyn shoots him, only wounding the SHADOW. She drives off. Gittes tries to protect this RESURRECTION, but the cops shoot at the car. It stops. The horn blaring. Katherine screams. And they find Evelyn dead.

Stunned, Gittes sees yet again the futility of his efforts in Chinatown. Mirroring his past, Gittes has tried to help someone, and that person is killed. The SHADOW, Noah Cross, gets away with murder, and gets his daughter. Gittes tries to comprehend this DARK ELIXIR. "Forget it, Jake. It's Chinatown."

FADE OUT

LA FEMME NIKITA
(France, Italy, 1990)

"There are two things that have no limit—femininity and the means of taking advantage of it."

— Amande (Jeanne Moreau)

Written and Directed by Luc Besson

A violent young woman and convicted cop-killer is enlisted by an ultra-secret government agency and transformed into a "hit-man."

LANDMARKS OF THE JOURNEY

La Femme Nikita is a beautiful metaphor for a woman's journey of healing and reclamation of the femininity that has been suppressed by her violent Ordinary World. Her male Mentor, Bob, pushes Nikita's Journey to transform her from violent cop-killer to government assassin. He uses a woman Mentor, Amande, to open up Nikita's femininity, to make her a powerful lethal weapon—the kind that can disarm you with her looks before blowing you away with her gun. Bob never anticipated that this brutal, ultra-violent Journey would actually continue Nikita's Resurrection to embrace her feminine nature. She is not reborn a tool for the boys, but a woman. The violence cleanses her, allowing her to move on and let the boys play with their guns.

THE JOURNEY

Nikita lives her ORDINARY WORLD strung out in the street, a member of a violent gang always hunting down their next fix, like a pack of wolves. Nikita's cold unexpressive mask reflects an inflated animus, the masculine element of her psyche. This SHADOW mask denies her inner beauty. Nikita's INNER NEED is to escape, and she resorts to drugs, masculine clothes, and a Walkman. The gang breaks into a pharmacy, but the police arrive and the vicious gun battle leaves all of Nikita's gang members dead, an ORDEAL. A policeman finds Nikita hiding under the table, Walkman blaring in her ears, too strung out to be aware of the bloodshed that surrounds her. Nikita takes a fallen comrade's gun and shoots the policeman.

The Judge (HERALD) sentences Nikita to life imprisonment, a CALL TO ADVENTURE. She lashes out at the courtroom, requiring several officers to contain this violent REFUSAL. They drag her away.

Suddenly, Nikita finds herself being strapped into a chair, as prison officials prepare her lethal injection. Now faced with death, the RELUCTANT and unusually emotional and tearful Nikita pleads for her mother. The injection works quickly and she "dies." This stage of RESURRECTION, usually seen at the end of the Hero's Journey, is a

THRESHOLD into the SPECIAL WORLD. Nikita awakens, her RESURRECTION, in her white "cell." The only vestiges of her past are her grunge clothes. Her SPECIAL WORLD, with its glaring fluorescent lamps and cold floor, is unsettling. She believes she's dead. Bob enters her cell, confirms that she is dead to her ORDINARY WORLD, and shows her the pictures of her funeral.

Bob offers her a new life (an ELIXIR of the RESURRECTION and her CALL TO ADVENTURE), to learn whatever is necessary to serve her country. Her grave awaits her if she refuses. Nikita asks for time to think about it. Bob returns in an hour and is ambushed by Nikita, a REFUSAL. She holds him at gunpoint and uses him to demand her escape. But this MENTOR won't negotiate. No way out, Nikita tries to shoot herself (a REFUSAL), but Bob grabs the gun, and quickly teaches her the first lesson of her training: "First bullet's not for you." He shoots her in the thigh to "clip her wings."

Her MENTOR has given her no choice but to accept the SPECIAL WORLD. But her lingering doubts will weigh on her training throughout the initial TEST PHASE. We can view this as an extended REFUSAL SEQUENCE, as she rebels at any opportunity. She learns computer skills, marksmanship, and martial arts. She's quick to use her skills from her ORDINARY WORLD.

She meets her second MENTOR, Amande, who offers an extremely uncomfortable SPECIAL WORLD. Amande teaches Nikita how to nurture her femininity. She places a wig on Nikita's head, offering her a new mask. But Nikita's SHADOW mask is so firmly ensconced that she has difficulty even smiling (a REFUSAL).

When Bob refuses to grant her leave for her 20th birthday, Nikita sabotages her training. Her violent REFUSAL leaves her MENTORS no choice but to offer her an ultimatum. As Nikita escapes into a movie on television, Bob presents her with a birthday cake and the ultimatum. She has two weeks to prove her commitment to this SPECIAL WORLD. The MENTOR takes her boots and leather coat, the "skin" of her violent ORDINARY WORLD. The television movie ends, and the Journey completes the REFUSAL SEQUENCE and signals her THRESHOLD of acceptance.

She returns to her MENTOR OF FEMININE POWER. She sits before the mirror and finally begins to glimpse what lies beneath her SHADOW mask. Amande allows her to explore the simple pleasure of putting on lipstick, a THRESHOLD of her JOURNEY of HEALING. Her MENTOR uses the lipstick to stimulate Nikita's feelings of pleasure and power as a woman.

The image dissolves to Nikita before the mirror, completing her makeup. She is more secure, maturer, and quite beautiful. In contrast, she is savoring this time. Not two weeks, but three years have passed. And Nikita approaches the THRESHOLD of completing her training. Dressed in sleek black, her transformation into a beautiful woman is complete. Her feminine nature is further aroused when her MENTOR, Bob, grants her the wish she requested three years ago; he takes her out to dinner for her birthday. She anticipates an evening of romance, but at dinner her SHAPESHIFTER MENTOR toasts her future and presents a gift: a gun, and her final TEST to prove she has completed her training. Nikita must assassinate the three people at the neighboring table. Her MENTOR leaves her. She quickly suppresses her feminine side's disbelief at this CALL and does the job. But Bob's escape plan is a dead-end. She must fend for herself and barely escapes through the kitchen and down the laundry chute. She returns to her training facility and beats an explanation out of her MENTOR. He assures her that she just passed her final TEST in training, and will be getting out in the morning, a REWARD that completes her THRESHOLD in becoming an assassin. But before she moves on, she kisses Bob, turning the tables on the MENTOR who had taken advantage of her femininity. She leaves Bob in the hallway, with only the memory of her lips.

Nikita enters a SPECIAL WORLD as a government assassin. The director gives her six months to establish herself (a TICKING CLOCK.) Bob gives Nikita her new identity for this SPECIAL WORLD. Her new name is Marie Clement, a nurse. Her mission code name, Josephine. Entering the unknown of any new world can leave the HERO unsettled. But Bob assures her that the worst is over. Nikita leaps into the TEST PHASE of her new life. She rents a room that's desperate for remodeling. She buys groceries, and finds love at the checkout stand. The clerk, Marco (SHAPESHIFTER), charms Nikita, a CALL FOR ROMANCE. Nikita invites him to her place for dinner, where she boldly crosses the THRESHOLD OF ROMANCE and kisses him.

Six months pass and Nikita has thrived during this TEST PHASE. She now lives with Marco in her redecorated apartment. But this SPECIAL WORLD is a lie; she must keep her past from Marco and makes him agree to not ask questions. The TICKING CLOCK winds down and she gets the phone call announcing her first assignment, a simple TEST of delivering a tray rigged with surveillance equipment to a hotel room. Bob calls her to congratulate her on the job. She tells Bob the success of her new life; she and Marco (a RIVAL to her MENTOR) are engaged. She invites "Uncle Bob" over for dinner, and he presents his engagement present, tickets to Venice.

Nikita and Marco enjoy their Venetian holiday, an APPROACH TO THE INMOST CAVE. Their foreplay is interrupted by a phone call announcing her next assignment. The timing creates a CRISIS OF THE HEART that threatens her relationship with Marco. She locks herself up in the bathroom to complete her assignment, the ORDEAL. Tension mounts as she must build her high-powered rifle, break the glass, and await her target, unable to respond to Marco's professions of unconditional love and his need to know her past. Nikita completes her job and quickly hides the gun as Marco enters the bathroom, rejected that she didn't respond to him. Faced with this ORDEAL, Nikita begins to realize that this world of lies may not hold.

Nikita stands up to her MENTOR, fully aware of his sadistic games, a REWARD. She blames Bob for setting up the ORDEAL that threatened to destroy her relationship. Bob acknowledges his RIVAL by confessing that he misses the time when he had her all to himself. This is his SHAPESHIFTER attempt to confess his love, but he immediately changes gears and presents Nikita her REWARD for the success of her Venice assignment. She must get to an ambassador who will be leaving the country in five months (a TICKING CLOCK). Not simply an assassin, Nikita will take charge of the mission.

As Nikita studies the files and photos of her target at her apartment, Marco interrupts with flowers and champagne, his REWARD for their renewed love.

Nikita uses ALLIES to prepare for her mission, keeping surveillance of the Ambassador, revealing his lust for good art and feminine beauty, defining her ultimate goal. They don't need the Ambassador. They need important data locked in an embassy safe. And only the Ambassador holds the keys. This assignment requires "magic, not havoc."

The months of late nights during this TEST PHASE are making Marco suspicious, threatening their relationship. Nikita tells him tonight will be the last.

She initiates the APPROACH TO THE INMOST CAVE. Using the power of her femininity, Nikita plays an art dealer and seduces the Ambassador into an apartment. She and her associate drug the Ambassador and take his keys. Nikita's ALLY begins to disguise himself as the Ambassador, but the assignment quickly spins into an ORDEAL. Nikita gets a phone call; the Ambassador has changed the password he used with his guards who are waiting in the outside hallway. Nikita and her ALLY are trapped in the room. Against Nikita's protests, the agency sends a "cleaner," Victor, who effectively disposes of the guards. He deposits their bodies in the bathtub, and begins to use sulfuric acid to get rid of the evidence. Before Nikita can warn him, acid burns the still living Ambassador. This horrible ORDEAL sickens Nikita's ALLY. He wants to end the mission but Victor kills him. Nikita wants to call in for orders but Victor threatens to kill her. He doesn't stop missions in progress, the ROAD BACK.

Victor and Nikita (disguised as the Ambassador) pass through the embassy gates. Nikita alone must enter the embassy; Victor waits in the car. She successfully bypasses THRESHOLD GUARDIANS, and gets to the Ambassador's safe. Opening the safe triggers the security camera. Soon THRESHOLD GUARDIANS move in; Nikita flees with the documents. She rushes outside. Victor wants to use his violent powers to "clean up." Nikita pleads that she has had enough, the RESURRECTION of her feminine force to end the violence. Victor won't be swayed. From within the getaway car, Nikita watches Victor shoot a slew of guards before they riddle him with bullets. Still alive, Victor drops into the driver's seat, plows the car through a brick wall and disappears into the night, a RESURRECTION. The car stops. Victor is dead. Nikita emerges from the car and walks away.

Back home, she tries to shower away the night. She joins Marco in bed, seeking the comfort of his arms. Marco confesses that he knows about her secret life, and wants her to leave the job. They kiss, sharing the ELIXIR of their love for each other. She will leave the job and her life with Marco. Nikita must move on and live.

The following morning, Bob arrives. Marco welcomes him. The protector of the ELIXIR of Nikita's freedom, Marco asks Bob for her protection. He hands over the embassy documents. There's no need to track her down now except for the love the two RIVALS share for this woman.

FADE OUT

THE FUGITIVE
(U.S., 1993)

"I didn't kill my wife."

"I don't care."

— Fugitive Richard Kimble (Harrison Ford) and
U.S. Marshal Samuel Gerard (Tommy Lee Jones)

Screenplay by Jeb Stuart and David Twohy
Story by David Twohy
Based on characters created by Roy Huggins
Directed by Andrew Davis

Wrongly convicted of murdering his wife, fugitive Dr. Richard Kimble tries to find out who's responsible as a determined U.S. Marshal hunts him down.

LANDMARKS OF THE JOURNEY

The Fugitive weaves mystery (the who-dun-it) with suspense thriller (the when-is-it-gonna-happen). Fairly early on we know that Richard Kimble is an innocent man; and suspense is heightened as Gerard and his Team close in on him. The mystery is Richard's quest to identify his wife's murderer, the one-armed man. Neither Kimble nor the Audience knows the identities of the one-armed man and the real Shadow that orchestrated Helen's murder. We solve the murder with Kimble (and Gerard) while the pursuit pushes the Journey to its inevitable conclusion.

Two Heroes travel opposing Journeys in *The Fugitive.* Dr. Richard Kimble's initial Journey is to run. When the Justice System, represented by Gerard, will not listen to his plea of innocence, Kimble alone must bring the real killer to justice, and prove his own innocence. At the same time, U.S. Marshal Sam Gerard must track down and capture his fugitive. But seeing Kimble's conviction revealed through unbelievable actions, Gerard tries to enter Kimble's "skin" to find his motive and soon joins Kimble's Journey to seek justice.

THE JOURNEY

The brutal murder of Helen Kimble disrupts Richard Kimble's Ordinary World (the CALL TO ADVENTURE). During his interrogation by the police, Kimble tries to piece together the evening's events (THE ORDINARY WORLD) leading up to her murder. Through these flashbacks we learn that Kimble is a respected vascular surgeon, who places enormous value on saving human life—yet he was unable to save his own wife. Kimble cherished his loving wife, Helen. But Helen's murder is only the first of a

SUCCESSION OF CALLS that will finally push him into the SPECIAL WORLD "on the run." Each CALL TO ADVENTURE raises the stakes. Kimble REFUSES to believe that the detectives (ANTAGONISTS) suspect him, and demands they find the real VILLAIN, the one-armed man. The evidence is too damning, and Helen's 911 phone call is the misinterpreted evidence that convicts Kimble. The Judge (HERALD) sentences Kimble to death (CALL TO ADVENTURE). Kimble is pushed through the FIRST THRESHOLD of his SPECIAL WORLD, an innocent man convicted of his wife's murder.

Convicts try to overtake the prison bus transporting Kimble. The driver is shot and the bus careens off the road. Kimble saves a wounded guard (THRESHOLD GUARDIAN) and escapes before a train obliterates the bus, an ORDEAL as CALL TO ADVENTURE. Kimble rises from the train wreck (a RESURRECTION). A convict, Copeland (a MENTOR of this SPECIAL WORLD), pushes him to accept this CALL, to flee. He unshackles Kimble and gives him the ground rule, "Don't follow me." Kimble flees, CROSSING THE THRESHOLD. He is a fugitive of the law.

The U.S. Marshal's TEAM, led by ANTAGONIST Samuel Gerard, arrives at the crash site. Gerard is the "old dog" of his TEAM, a slick, cohesive band of agents determined to track and bring back fugitives of the law. His persistence is matched by his black-and-white view of the Justice System. Gerard doesn't care about the circumstances of the crime. Conviction is guilt, and Gerard does not bargain. A member of his TEAM finds "leg irons with no legs in them" (CALL TO ADVENTURE), and Gerard launches the manhunt for his fugitive, Dr. Richard Kimble (Gerard's OUTER PROBLEM).

While Gerard initiates standard procedures for his manhunt, his fugitive, Richard Kimble continues his THRESHOLD SEQUENCE. This consists of a series of TESTS and CALLS, pushing Kimble to finally accept his HIGHER CALL TO ADVENTURE. Wounded, Kimble steals a pair of coveralls to sneak into a local hospital. He slips into a treatment room and stitches his wound. Hiding in a patient's room, Kimble shaves off his beard, steals the patients' clothes and breakfast and prepares to leave the hospital. Clean-shaven, and disguised with a doctor's coat, Kimble successfully TESTS his new identity with the passing Sheriff (THRESHOLD GUARDIAN).

Kimble "plays doctor" to make his escape. He assists the paramedics as they wheel in the wounded guard; however, the guard recognizes Kimble. He muffles his accuser with an oxygen mask, yet helps this ENEMY, quickly giving the paramedics (THRESHOLD GUARDIANS) the correct diagnosis, before stealing their ambulance.

Gerard's first TESTS are standard procedures in his ORDINARY WORLD. His CALL TO ADVENTURE is still to come. A blood trail is found at the crash site and Gerard orders a blood match against the prisoners. Kimble's picture is faxed to local hospitals. Gerard orders phone taps, beginning with Kimble's lawyer (perceived as a THRESHOLD GUARDIAN protecting Kimble). The TEAM researches Kimble's past: a respected surgeon with lots of friends. Gerard must "enter the skin" of his fugitive to anticipate his moves; however, he never figured that Kimble would steal an ambulance. He launches a CHASE.

They trap Kimble in a tunnel, but the doctor escapes. And Gerard's dogged pursuit continues in the reservoir's tunnel system, where he finally confronts Kimble. Kimble pleads to this authority of justice (MENTOR), "I didn't kill my wife." Gerard counters with indifference, "I don't care." (Gerard as RELUCTANT HERO). Kimble flees and soon faces the end of the tunnel, the falls and sure death. Gerard traps him at gunpoint. Surrender or jump. Gerard has already given him his answer; surrender to Justice means death. Kimble jumps (an ORDEAL as THRESHOLD).

The jump shatters Gerard's ORDINARY WORLD. Gerard is stunned. His TEAM bickers as they try to reorganize themselves. They assure Gerard that Kimble couldn't have survived. But the "old dog" has seen his fugitive's determination first-hand and won't give up the trail. He wants proof.

Cold, exhausted, Kimble is visited by visions ... making love to his wife ... kissing her ... trying to resuscitate her ... struggling with his ENEMY, the one-armed man. Kimble awakens with his plea to the police, "You find that man!" echoing in his head. These visions are the HERALD of his CALL to a HIGHER JOURNEY. Since Justice (Gerard) has rejected him, the stakes have been raised, completing Kimble's entrance THROUGH THE THRESHOLD. He alone must find the man who killed his wife (his OUTER PROBLEM). His INNER PROBLEM is to get justice.

Gerard's TEAM tracks down Copeland, one of the bus fugitives. When Copeland threatens one of Gerard's men, Gerard shoots the convict. Gerard doesn't bargain. This successful TEST raises the stakes and heightens the suspense in Kimble's search for justice.

Kimble initiates a new TEST PHASE. He returns to Chicago and seeks ALLIES, first calling his lawyer, who reveals himself as a THRESHOLD GUARDIAN pushing Kimble to give himself up. Kimble also needs money in this SPECIAL WORLD and borrows from his best friend and associate (ALLY), Dr. Charles Nichols. Kimble rents a basement flat.

Gerard's TEAM examines the tape of Kimble's conversation with his lawyer. Gerard was right; Kimble survived. Although Kimble's "Peter Pan" dive into the reservoir disrupted Gerard's TEAM, their TEST PHASE brings them back together. Together they deduce that Kimble has returned to Chicago. Gerard has regained his TEAM'S respect, but Kimble's return to Chicago has confused Gerard. Questioning Kimble's motives, he orders his TEAM to re-interview everyone involved in the original murder investigation. This begins Gerard's character arc. This "old dog" is learning a new trick, transforming from unsympathetic SHADOW to Kimble's protector. But suspense is heightened when the Chicago Police launch their own manhunt to track down Kimble, a TICKING CLOCK.

To find his wife's murderer—the one-armed man—Kimble must access the central database in the Prosthetics Lab at Cook County Hospital. He steals a hospital custodian's I.D. (a TEST), and mocks up a fake I.D. Asleep, Kimble relives the struggle with the one-armed man. He sees the specifics of the prosthetic arm. (Kimble's dreams work as his MENTOR.) The vision of Helen awakens him (a HERALD'S warning) as Police arrive; however, they arrest the landlord's son, a drug dealer (SHAPESHIFTER/THRESHOLD GUARDIAN). Kimble flees the flat and uses his fake I.D. to access the hospital computer files to find his suspects. Using the specifics of the prosthetic arm, he narrows his field of potential VILLAINS down to five.

Meanwhile the landlord's son squeals on Kimble (escalating threat). Gerard enters Kimble's flat and finds the remnants of his I.D. fabrication, leading him to the hospital.

Kimble emerges from the lab with his list of names, but he can't escape the hospital. An ER doctor needs this "custodian" to help move patients. Kimble observes that a boy has been misdiagnosed. His INNER CODE to help another in need jeopardizes his JOURNEY. As he wheels the child away, he changes the diagnosis and saves the child. But the doctor stops him and threatens to turn this SHAPESHIFTER over to security. Kimble flees.

Later Gerard questions the ER Doctor. She confirms that Kimble saved the boy's life. This important TEST reveals the goodness of Gerard's fugitive. Gerard and SIDEKICK Cosmo can't figure out why Kimble would hang out in the ward, until they see an amputee patient and follow this HERALD into the Prosthetics Lab. Gerard has finally entered Kimble's mind and understands his motives. He begins his own quest to find the one-armed man.

Both Gerard's and Kimble's JOURNEYS enter the APPROACH TO THE INMOST CAVE. Kimble narrows down his five suspects, while Gerard uses the Prosthetic Lab computers to create his own list of suspects. Both lists lead them to the same ORDEAL.

To find his man, Kimble must enter the Correctional Facility where ENEMIES and THRESHOLD GUARDIANS abound. He sees one of his last two leads, a felon named Driscoll. Gerard and his men arrive to check on the same man (initiating the ORDEAL). Kimble knows at first sight that Driscoll is not his man, and makes a quick escape. But Gerard recognizes him on the staircase and the CHASE begins. Kimble races to the main entrance, briefly tricking the officers into stopping Gerard. Kimble pushes through the security doors but his foot is caught, allowing Gerard to shoot, but the shot can't penetrate the glass door. Kimble escapes, finally eluding Gerard in the middle of a St. Patrick's Day Parade, a RESURRECTION completing the ORDEAL SEQUENCE.

Kimble earns his REWARD from this ORDEAL. Down to his last lead, he breaks into Sykes' apartment. Inside, he finds a spare prosthetic arm, and photos linking Sykes with Lentz and other executives at Devlin-MacGregor Pharmaceuticals.

Kimble wants to give this REWARD to Gerard and calls his pursuer knowing they'll be tapping his phone. Before, Kimble had been trying to elude Gerard, always staying one step ahead. Now he wants them on his trail to find what he finds. He leaves the phone off the hook, leading Gerard and detectives to Sykes' apartment. Kimble's fingerprints lead them to the incriminating photos.

Kimble also shares his REWARD with ALLY Dr. Charles Nichols. The target for murder was Kimble not Helen. Sykes worked for Lentz at Devlin-MacGregor, the company developing a new drug that Kimble had discovered causes liver damage. But Nichols tells Kimble that the perceived SHADOW, Lentz, died last year in a car accident. Kimble won't stop his Journey; he needs to clear himself. Nichols agrees to give Kimble access to the hospital. (Kimble doesn't know that this SHAPESHIFTER agrees in order to keep a close eye on him, and to hire Sykes to finish the job.)

Using ALLIES in the hospital, Kimble examines the liver samples from the study, and discovers that the unhealthy liver samples have been replaced by healthy samples. This REWARD unlocks the final mystery. Lentz died on the same day that samples had been replaced. Someone else, someone with access, manipulated the research. Finally realizing that Nichols was behind everything, Kimble initiates his ROAD BACK to "see a friend." But his SHADOW has other plans. Sykes intercepts Kimble on the subway; Sykes shoots a policeman. But Kimble disarms Sykes, handcuffs him and escapes, completing the ROAD BACK SEQUENCE and initiating a CHASE. Kimble races to a medical convention where Nichols is preparing to make his keynote address.

At this point, Gerard has been following Kimble through each Stage of his Journey revealing the same SHADOW, Dr. Charles Nichols. But the stakes have been raised. Now that Chicago police blame Kimble for the downed subway officer, Gerard needs to beat the police to the medical convention.

Kimble begins his RESURRECTION at the convention. He enters a banquet hall filled with his colleagues and ALLIES from his ORDINARY WORLD, as their MENTOR, Nichols, praises Devlin-MacGregor's new drug on the "cusp of approval." Nichols stammers, seeing Kimble "resurrected" in the audience. Kimble tries to reveal this SHADOW'S deceit in front of their colleagues (an ELIXIR). But Nichols wants to deal with Kimble in private and leads him out. Nichols turns Kimble's showdown of words into a physical fight that takes them onto the hotel rooftop, while Gerard and his TEAM pursue to protect Kimble from the trigger-happy police.

Kimble has his SHADOW vanquished until the two fall through a skylight and land on top of a freight elevator. Nichols stumbles out of the elevator to make his escape, and we fear the worst for Kimble. As the elevator door closes, Kimble emerges in pursuit (a RESURRECTION), taking us to the final cat-and-mouse CHASE through the obstacles of the laundry floor. Gerard tries to flush the two out, announcing Kimble's innocence and

Nichols' guilt (an ELIXIR). Nichols prepares to shoot and silence Gerard, but Kimble strikes his SHADOW down, saving Gerard. Gerard approaches Kimble and lowers his gun, assuring Kimble of his innocence, the RESURRECTION. Their exhausting Journeys are complete.

Gerard escorts Kimble back into his ORDINARY WORLD. He leads Kimble past his ANTAGONISTS, the detectives now tap-dancing in front of the probing media, as their real murderer, Sykes, is placed into custody.

In the Journey's final moment, the "old dog" releases Kimble's handcuffs and reveals the completion of Gerard's character arc. Although Kimble goes through the greatest physical Journey of the movie, it is Gerard who makes the greatest change of character (an ELIXIR). We've watched his transformation from uncaring to caring, but "don't tell anybody, okay?"

FADE OUT

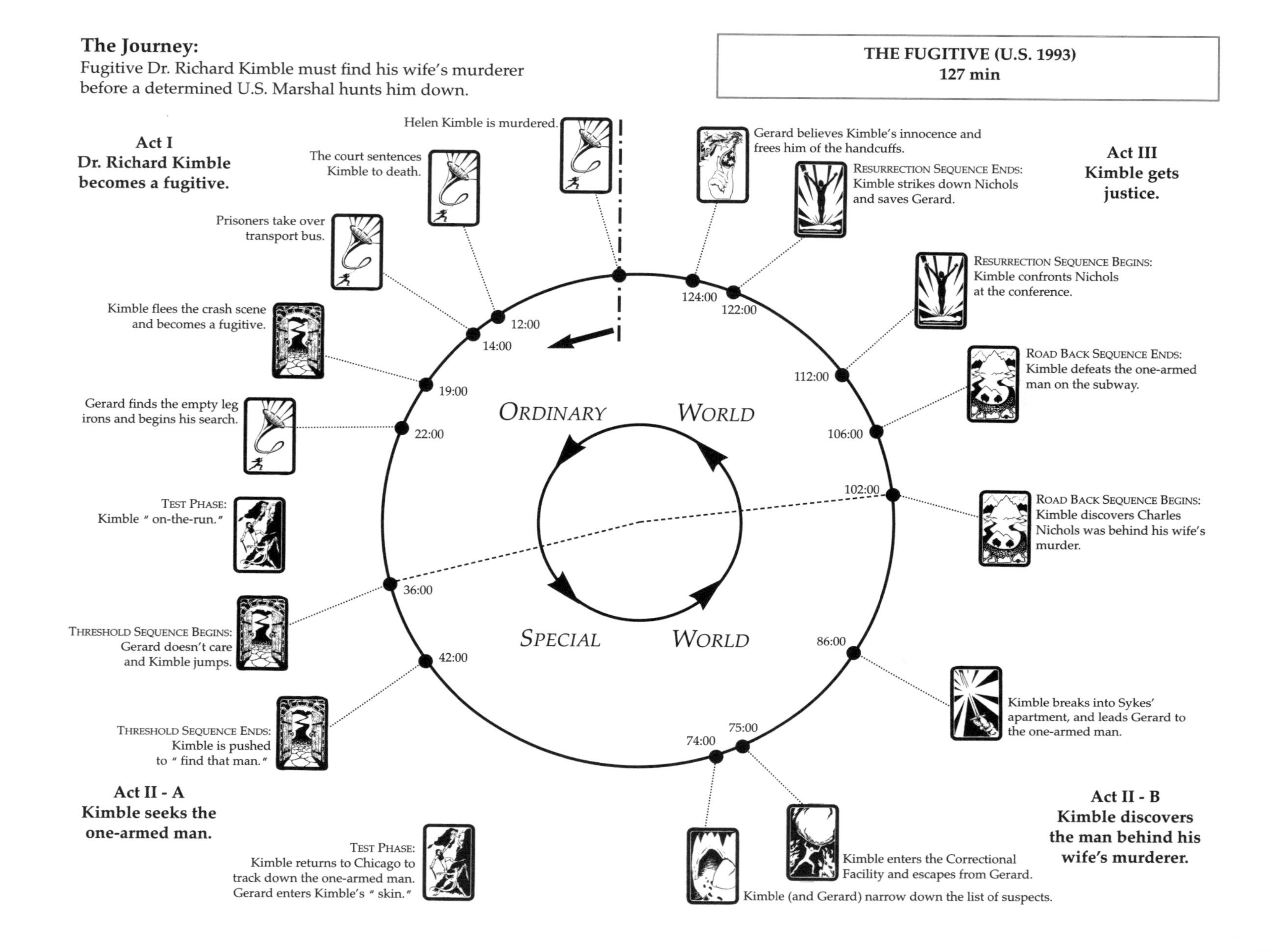
The Journey:
Fugitive Dr. Richard Kimble must find his wife's murderer before a determined U.S. Marshal hunts him down.
THE FUGITIVE (U.S. 1993)
127 min
Act I
Dr. Richard Kimble becomes a fugitive.
Helen Kimble is murdered.
The court sentences Kimble to death.
Prisoners take over transport bus.
Kimble flees the crash scene and becomes a fugitive.
Gerard finds the empty leg irons and begins his search.
TEST PHASE: Kimble " on-the-run."
THRESHOLD SEQUENCE BEGINS: Gerard doesn't care and Kimble jumps.
THRESHOLD SEQUENCE ENDS: Kimble is pushed to " find that man."
Act II - A
Kimble seeks the one-armed man.
TEST PHASE: Kimble returns to Chicago to track down the one-armed man. Gerard enters Kimble's " skin."
12:00
14:00
19:00
22:00
36:00
42:00
74:00
75:00
86:00
102:00
106:00
112:00
122:00
124:00
ORDINARY WORLD
SPECIAL WORLD
Kimble (and Gerard) narrow down the list of suspects.
Kimble enters the Correctional Facility and escapes from Gerard.
Kimble breaks into Sykes' apartment, and leads Gerard to the one-armed man.
Act II - B
Kimble discovers the man behind his wife's murderer.
ROAD BACK SEQUENCE BEGINS: Kimble discovers Charles Nichols was behind his wife's murder.
ROAD BACK SEQUENCE ENDS: Kimble defeats the one-armed man on the subway.
RESURRECTION SEQUENCE BEGINS: Kimble confronts Nichols at the conference.
RESURRECTION SEQUENCE ENDS: Kimble strikes down Nichols and saves Gerard.
Gerard believes Kimble's innocence and frees him of the handcuffs.
Act III
Kimble gets justice.

THE MYTHIC STRUCTURE OF WAR

We accept the Call to Arms and separate from our Ordinary World. Reborn as warriors, we join a new family of brothers, led by our Mentor Father and his lessons of the great battlefield of death. Together we share agony and glory to fight our Enemy; alone we must confront our fears to accept our noble sacrifice for country.

"...WHEN THE MACHINE BREAKS DOWN, WE BREAK DOWN."

Without death there can be no rebirth. From our darkest moments comes the light. This is the essence of the Hero's Journey. Confronting "death," whether literal or figurative, reminds us of our mortality, and may even resurrect us with new awareness and new life goals. We are reborn.

On most journeys our Hero confronts "death-like" experiences at two stages: the Ordeal in Act II, and the Resurrection in Act III. In some genres such as Action Adventure, Horror, and Thriller, the Hero may confront death at many stages. But in War, the Soldier Hero confronts death throughout the Journey. He is surrounded by death, which can strike quickly and viciously without warning. The soldier enters this Journey aware that he may not survive, and part of his Journey may be the search for inner strength to accept his Noble Sacrifice of life for country and his fellow man.

Valor. Fear. Sacrifice. Cowardice. The journeys of War are filled with contradictions of actions, emotions, and morality. A soldier is elated that he was spared the Enemy's gunfire that cut down his comrade, yet that same soldier will willingly throw himself on a grenade to protect his squadron. We embrace our war heroes; we shun war's destruction. Yet the latest war epic promising the gruesome reality of battle feeds an audience's hunger to experience the sacrifices our sons, fathers and grandfathers made on the battlefield.

Personal experiences fuel these tales of war. Throughout the history of the war film, writers, directors, cinematographers and producers have been compelled to tell their personal tales, giving the War genre an immediacy unlike that of any other genre. Whether celebrating war's heroism or revealing war's Hell, the journeys of War have become our most memorable, most gut-wrenching, and most cathartic cinema experiences.

Why do we explore war stories? Why are audiences attracted to tales of valor and sacrifice? Serving in war is our society's rite of passage. Traditionally rites of passage are ceremonies or acts during which a youth (usually male) faces and overcomes death in order to cross the Threshold of manhood. War is an arena where innocence is lost, and manhood achieved.

THE ESSENCE OF WAR: DEHUMANIZATION

Wars are not battles of man versus man, but of "us" against "them." Once the Hero accepts the Call to Arms, War strips him of his Ordinary World and issues a "new skin," his uniform. He is no longer an individual but a part of the War Machine. His importance is as part of a team. The squadron, unit, or platoon becomes his new family (the Hero Team); the platoon leader, his Mentor Father. He must live by the group's rules of conduct, sacrificing his own rules in order to survive.

The soldier is further dehumanized by impersonal titles of "soldier" or "grunt." In the case of *Platoon,* our Hero enters the Special World without an identity, but must prove himself if he is to be accepted into the Hero Team. He's a "cherry" until he has suffered enough to be considered a "grunt."

Each of these levels of dehumanization is necessary for the soldier to be able to kill the Enemy. When the law of dehumanization is broken and we come face to face with our Enemy, seeing the consequences of our violence, we begin to question our motives. The Soldier Hero's connection with the dehumanized war machine begins to crumble; we begin to question war's morality and acknowledge war's waste of human life. Confrontations with a *human* Enemy make powerful moments in anti-war films, whether there's an individual killing (*All Quiet on the Western Front*), the sinking of a ship (*Das Boot*), or the potential massacre of a village (*Platoon*).

THE JOURNEYS OF WAR: THE HEROES AND THE HORRORS

Whether they encompass the epic telling of the D-day invasion, or a platoon's battleground sacrifice, war stories depict the agony and exhilaration of war. Many different stories can be told: search and rescue missions (*Saving Private Ryan*), biographical tales (*Patton*), POW ordeals (*The Bridge on the River Kwai*), or home front perspectives (*The Best Years of Our Lives*).

War films are set against the backdrop of overwhelming powers in conflict. No other Special World portrays greater stakes than war. Epic war films may center on the event and we see the Higher Powers at work (*The Longest Day, They Were Expendable*). Other war stories speak from the infantry's or grunt's point of view; the larger forces are rarely seen save for currents that sweep and churn the soldiers like leaves in a stream (*All Quiet on the Western Front, Platoon*). These latter stories oftentimes show an unpredictable, chaotic Special World of battle. With all stories, the characters are aware that the thin battle line marks the difference between valor and fear, sacrifice and retreat.

THE EVOLUTION OF THE WAR FILM

We can learn much about the story-telling traditions and audience expectations of the war story by looking at its evolution during the Twentieth Century. War films emerged as a major genre after World War I, when society suffered a war unlike any other. The first significant war films were anti-war in nature, depicting the gruesome world of war. The message was simple: War is Hell on Earth and its first casualty is innocence (*All Quiet on the Western Front*). The power of these early films continues to resonate.

During World War II, American war films were used by the military to generate support of home front sacrifices and a Call to Arms against the Nazi and Japanese shadows. The Office of War Information sanctioned Hollywood's scripts and pushed for conventions and structure to fight a propaganda war. These tales softened the horror of war so that even heroic tales of defeat stirred our patriotism and made a powerful Call to Arms (*They Were Expendable*). These combat films stressed the importance of the Hero Team led by the battle-experienced squad leader. There wasn't room for the rugged individual seeking his cause. The stories stirred audience's pride and established conventions that persisted beyond the war and the military's censorship.

Although conventions of the war film were born in Hollywood, they did not always reflect the reality and morality of later wars, notably Vietnam. Conventions can be enforced to meet an audience's expectations and make them more comfortable while watching these harrowing tales. Breaking the conventions can make the audience uneasy and forced to accept the futility of war's sacrifice.

THE MENTOR AS FATHER FIGURE

The Mentor plays a vital role on the Soldier's Journey. Rarely does the Hero's Ordinary World prepare the soldier for the Special World of the battlefield. And while Boot Camp can solidify the Hero Team, it cannot provide the reality of the battlefield. The Team needs its leader, the sergeant or commander. This Patriarch Mentor teaches the Soldier how to use the weapons and other special tools of battle, how to kill the enemy, and how to die for one's country.

SACRIFICE OF THE MENTOR

At some point along the Journey the Mentor may sacrifice himself in order for the Hero Team to move on. Having learned the Mentor's lessons, the soldiers must prove that the Hero Team can incorporate them. His death can also be his greatest lesson: how to sacrifice oneself for one's country and the Team. On the Journey of War no one is protected from death. The death of the Mentor can foreshadow the end of the war, or prepare the hero to accept his own death (*All Quiet on the Western Front*). In *Platoon*, the death of one Mentor actually destroys the platoon. The Hero, Chris Taylor, realizes he must sacrifice the other Mentor to save what is left of his platoon and humanity.

NO TIME FOR APPROACH

Approaching the Inmost Cave can be an important time to re-group the Team and assign duties for the impending attack. However, war's unpredictability can leave little room for preparation. An Enemy's sudden attack can ruin the best preparation and immediately throw the Hero and his Team into a chaotic Ordeal.

THE ELIXIR

The Hero may not receive the Elixir he had hoped to get when he first accepted the Call to Arms. A young man seeking heroism, fame and sacrifice for country may realize that death is a horrible waste (*All Quiet on the Western Front*). In tales of sacrifice and defeat, the Elixir may be intended for the audience. While the films of World War II were used to rally a country to arms (*They Were Expendable*), the tragic war stories of Vietnam helped to heal a nation (*Platoon*).

GENRE CHALLENGES: WAR

1. In *All Quiet on the Western Front*, what is Paul's need in the beginning of his Journey? What does he hope to gain? And how is that different from the Elixir he earns?
2. In what ways do Brickley's and Rusty's journeys in *They Were Expendable* arouse patriotism and support from the audience? How do language, actions, and music help to soften the horror of war and support the cause?
3. In anti-war films, moments that demonstrate the breaking down of dehumanization are important to reveal the destruction of humanity. In stories celebrating the heroism of war (*They Were Expendable*), how is dehumanization a positive Elixir?
4. Do you feel sympathy for Saito's journey in *The Bridge on the River Kwai*? How about Nicholson's Journey? Why or why not?
5. How is the breakdown or solidification of dehumanization used in each of the five sample films? What messages do they convey to the audience?
6. Looking at each of the sample films, what is the role of the Shadow/Enemy with regard to dehumanization? How does that role affect the film's message?
7. Compare and contrast *All Quiet on the Western Front* with *Platoon*. What do their Elixirs stand for and how do they make you feel as an audience member?

ALL QUIET ON THE WESTERN FRONT
(U.S., 1930)

"When it comes to dying for your country, it's better not to die at all."
— Paul (Lew Ayres)

Screenplay by George Abbott
Adaptation & Dialogue by Maxwell Anderson
Adaptation by Del Andrews
Based on the novel by Erich Maria Remarque
Directed by Lewis Milestone

A young man and his classmates fight for their country and are destroyed by war.

LANDMARKS OF THE JOURNEY

In this classic anti-war film, innocence is the first casualty of war. The Call to Arms takes Paul and his classmates onto the great battlefield for their rite of passage. But their dreams of heroic sacrifice are shattered by the sobering reality of death. Each of the Journey's stages is an Ordeal. Each death that Paul faces rewards him with love of life, and the growing realization of war's waste. Tragically, the Ordinary World refuses Paul's Elixir and sends him back to his Special World where he must join his classmates and his Mentor.

THE JOURNEY

A small German town at the dawn of World War I. Townspeople cheer the German soldiers marching off to war, while inside a classroom, Professor Kantorek fervently rallies Paul and his classmates to fight and die for the Fatherland. The global, visual CALL of the parade reinforces this MENTOR/HERALD'S personal CALL. The boys' visions of glory (their INNER PROBLEMS) show little reluctance; however, they do have to convince their classmate, Behm. Soon they march out of the classroom ready to sacrifice themselves for their country, their OUTER PROBLEM.

Their new drill sergeant, Himmelstoss, a merciless THRESHOLD GUARDIAN, blocks their passage to the Front and the battlefield. The meek postal carrier suffers an inflated ego with his RESURRECTION into his new rank and uniform, and delights in drilling his unit through the mud. Soon enough the unit gets its CALL to the Front, and the boys leave their FALSE MENTOR in the mud.

They begin their THRESHOLD SEQUENCE arriving at the Front in the confusion of an enemy attack. They take cover in an abandoned factory where they meet seasoned and cynical veterans. They meet an important MENTOR, the veteran "Kat" Katczinsky, who prepares their THRESHOLD to the battlefield and takes them out on "wiring duty." Unlike Himmelstoss, Kat is a true MENTOR and patriarch figure for these boys, teaching them how to accept their fear and how to survive on the battlefield. They complete their passage THROUGH THE THRESHOLD when they witness the death of their own, the RELUCTANT Behm. This first taste of death initiates Paul into his SPECIAL WORLD of death and destruction. Paul's Journey through this SPECIAL WORLD is a series of three ORDEALS, each bringing death closer to the HERO, and rewarding him with a deeper understanding of war's waste of youth.

1ST ORDEAL: PAUL WITNESSES WAR'S DESTRUCTION

The unit survives days trapped in an underground bunker awaiting the signal to attack (APPROACH THE INMOST CAVE). Kemmerick cannot accept the stifling quarters. He flees and gets shot in the leg. The signal to attack comes, and they suffer trench warfare (ORDEAL). The ferocious seesaw battle between French and Germans yields no change in battle lines, at the cost of thousands of young men's lives. The survivors share wine and bread, and later eat rations for the living and the dead (REWARD). With bloated stomachs, they question the cause of war and blame the French, maintaining a dehumanization of the ENEMY. ("They" are to blame.)

2ND ORDEAL: PAUL WITNESSES HIS FRIEND'S DEATH

Paul visits Kemmerick, who cannot accept the loss of his leg (APPROACH THE INMOST CAVE). Overwhelmed with casualties, the doctors cannot help Kemmerick, and Paul witnesses his friend's death. Paul leaves the ordeal overpowered by an appreciation of life (REWARD).

3RD ORDEAL: PAUL KILLS A SOLDIER

Paul and his unit question their training as they await their next attack. Paul remembers the fallen and realizes that most of his classmates have suffered in this SPECIAL WORLD (APPROACH THE INMOST CAVE). The Germans launch an attack turning a church cemetery into a battlefield. Paul finds refuge in a shell-hole and stabs a French soldier (ORDEAL). Paul suffers the Frenchman's long, painful death. Coming face to face with the enemy, Paul denounces the war and sees his victim no longer as the "enemy" or "them" but as "brother." MENTOR Kat assures Paul that soldiers kill, quickly easing Paul of his uncomfortable REWARD of guilt.

If killing is a part of being a soldier, then Paul has crossed that THRESHOLD of "manhood" and lost innocence. Paul additionally crosses the sexual THRESHOLD of manhood, losing his innocence to a French farm girl, a REWARD. With this celebration of life Paul is equipped for his ROAD BACK, where he faces his own death. A sudden attack leaves Paul wounded. While his friend Albert loses his leg, Paul survives a near-fatal wound and receives temporary leave to go home, the ROAD BACK.

Paul can now return to his ORDINARY WORLD with the ELIXIR of his lessons. But his ELIXIR is repeatedly refused, pushing Paul to return to the SPECIAL WORLD of the battlefield and death. His bedridden mother refuses to believe that her son has returned. He changes into his old clothes and looks at the mounted butterfly collection, a symbol of his boyhood innocence. Later, his father toasts his son as a war hero but his father's friends insult Paul, blaming the soldiers for the sacrifices that must be made at home.

Paul visits his old classroom, where Professor Kantorek continues to push romantic ideals of heroism to rally support to save the Fatherland. He convinces Paul to speak to the students, and Paul tells them the bitter reality of fighting for their Fatherland. He denounces Kantorek's CALL to die for one's country, and the youths reject this coward's ELIXIR with boos and hisses. Paul confesses to Kantorek that he never should have returned; his place remains in the SPECIAL WORLD.

Paul returns to the Front, almost with relief. But few remain in his unit. The dead have been replaced by "green" sixteen-year-olds who only know how to die. Paul finds his true MENTOR and friend, Kat, gathering food for the young recruits. Paul tells of his bitter rejection at home, but Kat cannot ease his pain and tells Paul that they are up against a huge ENEMY. A sudden air attack strikes down the MENTOR. Reciting his MENTOR'S lessons, Paul carries Kat back but his friend is already dead. Perhaps Paul can have hope that the MENTOR'S death signals the end of the war.

During a quiet lull, Paul sits alone in a trench. He sees a butterfly and reaches for it, a RESURRECTION of his boyhood innocence. A sniper gunshot rings out. Paul's hand goes still. Quiet returns to the Front.

We are left with a corpse-strewn hill, and the haunting ghosts of Paul and his classmates marching into eternity, a bitter ELIXIR. Their innocence and their lives are lost forever.

FADE OUT

THEY WERE EXPENDABLE
(U.S., 1945)

"So you're really quitting the squadron, eh Rusty?"

"Can't build a Navy reputation riding in a plywood dream."

"What are you aiming at, building a reputation or playing for the team?"

— Lt. John Brickley (Robert Montgomery) and
Lt. Rusty Ryan (John Wayne)

Screenplay by Frank Wead, Commander U.S.N. (Ret)
Based on the book by William L. White
Directed by John Ford, Captain U.S.N.R.

A PT Squadron battles Navy brass and the Japanese to prove their worth during the U.S. protection of the Philippines.

LANDMARKS OF THE JOURNEY

Heroism and sacrifice can turn our darkest moments of history into inspiring stories of courage and hope. This was the power of the conventions enforced by the War Information Office during World War II.

They Were Expendable shows the classic conventions of the World War II combat tale: the Hero Team standing by their Patriarch Mentor, a young Hero wanting to serve his own needs, and the Mentor pushing the Hero to accept the Higher Cause. In this epic story, the Hero Team isn't simply Brickley's PT Squadron, but the entire U.S. Military effort in the Philippines. Two men desperately want to serve in the heat of battle. Loner Hero Rusty's ambitions are self-serving, while Brickley pushes his own Journey for the benefit of the entire Naval Team. Brickley must prove to his Mentors that his PT squadron can serve the Higher Cause.

The Journey can be divided into two consecutive Journeys. The story's first Journey (and the first half of the film) shows how Brickley and his squadron prove their worthiness in battle. They go from the lowly job of running messages to successfully transporting General MacArthur and his family from the encroaching Japanese Shadow. The Reward of success pushes them into the devastating second half where the ordeals of war break Brickley's squadron apart. But they make their impact, and by Journey's end the High Command orders Brickley and Rusty to return to the Ordinary World to regroup.

THE JOURNEY

Manila Bay. 1941. Lt. John Brickley leads his squadron of PT boats. War threatens their ORDINARY WORLD, and Brickley wants acceptance of his squadron's value in the event of war, the OUTER PROBLEM. Despite being impressed by the maneuverability of PT boats, the Navy Brass REFUSES to see the value of these small boats in the heat of a sea battle. Brickley maintains a stoic wait-and-see attitude but, LONER HERO Lt. Rusty Ryan is tired of taking Brick's fatherly advice. He's had enough of these "high-powered canoes," an INNER STIRRING, and wants to serve on a Destroyer and build a Navy reputation (his INNER PROBLEM). Brick accepts Rusty's request for transfer but not without a warning about being a "one-man band" and sacrificing the HERO TEAM. The Japanese attack on Pearl Harbor interrupts Rusty's plans. He cannot REFUSE this CALL TO ADVENTURE and he willingly returns to his post by his MENTOR'S side.

Brick sees the outbreak of War as a THRESHOLD to prove what his PT boats can do, but the High Command (Brick's MENTORS) keep the untested squad on standby for lowly messenger duty (a REFUSAL).

The Japanese launch an air strike on Manila Bay, giving Brick a chance to prove himself, and send his own CALL to the Navy Brass. His squadron battles the Japanese and downs several of their planes; however, Rusty injures his hand in the skirmish.

Returning to their demolished base, Brick hears of another Japanese fleet of planes and prepares to "knock them out," but the Admiral REFUSES this call. This MENTOR warns that they have to sacrifice Manila to the Japanese. He pushes Brickley to accept his squadron's role in this war: to run messages. Brick, Rusty and the squad accept the sacrifice they must make for the entire Naval TEAM, and soon move their headquarters to Sisiman Cove at Bataan.

They pay their dues as messengers and finally receive the assignment they'd been hoping for—to sink a Japanese Cruiser plaguing the troops at Bataan. Brickley prepares his TEAM for the attack. During this MEETING WITH THE MENTOR, Brick lays out the rules and issues the proper gear. Since only two PT boats are needed for this assignment, some men will be REFUSED from this TEST, but the eagerness of the entire squadron emphasizes that the HERO TEAM together passes through this important THRESHOLD.

Because of Rusty's wounded hand, Brick orders him to the hospital at Corregidor. Rusty has difficulty accepting this REFUSAL. Rusty's individualism threatens the HERO TEAM and he must temporarily leave his TEAM'S Journey to accept a personal Journey of healing—his hand, as well as his heart. His stubbornness is matched by the no-nonsense persistence of his nurse, Lt. Sandy Davyss, a CALL TO ROMANCE.

Meanwhile, the two PT boats approach the minefields off the coast of Bataan. Led by Brick, the 41 Boat makes the BOLD APPROACH and sinks the Japanese Cruiser. They successfully pass THROUGH THE THRESHOLD, but not without casualties—a grim reminder to the entire TEAM that many will be sacrificed so that others will live.

Back at the hospital, Rusty watches Sandy assist in the treatment of the Bataan casualties. A dedicated TEAM member, she works flawlessly by her doctor's side. Afterwards, Sandy asks Rusty to a dance. Although initially REFUSING THE CALL, he shows up anyway, CROSSING THE THRESHOLD of their romance. They take a break and share their memories of home, an APPROACH TO THE INMOST CAVE. Brick interrupts them. He needs Rusty back on the squad, if Sandy believes he's ready. She does. Rusty's side-journey not only gave him back his health, but someone else to think about beside himself.

The Journey's TEST PHASE becomes a series of victories and losses, but the TEAM'S commitment to these battles cannot turn the Japanese SHADOW. Bataan will fall, the Admiral fears. He orders Brickley's TEAM to transport the Admiral and "key personnel" out of danger to Mindanao (and eventual air transport to Australia). But Brickley must SACRIFICE part of his TEAM, leaving behind the "expendable" to support Bataan.

Brick and his TEAM face the ORDEAL of their SPECIAL WORLD, the greatest TEST to prove their worthiness, and it demands a cautious, careful APPROACH. During this APPROACH SEQUENCE Brickley prepares his eager TEAM for the dangerous route they must take. They also take this time to visit their wounded comrades, and pay respect to those who have fallen. Most importantly, Brickley bids farewell to the "expendables." His rallying speech solidifies the HERO'S TEAM, giving them the courage to move on. For Rusty, unfortunately the APPROACH is a CRISIS OF THE HEART. He sacrifices his love for the HIGHER CAUSE and says goodbye to Sandy.

The four PT boats prepare for departure and realize now that they are the personal escorts of General Douglas MacArthur and his family. With pride, they set off on this ORDEAL. Although uneventful in comparison with their battles against the Japanese, this ORDEAL is the turning point for Brickley. With the safe arrival of MacArthur in Mindanao (a RESURRECTION), Brickley and his HERO TEAM have earned the ELIXIR of their worth in the eyes of the General of the Army.

The convoy didn't arrive unscathed, and they have to tow the damaged 34 boat to dry dock. The TEAM works round the clock repairing their boats, too busy with the duties at hand to even acknowledge their receipt of the Silver Star for gallantry. This REWARD pales next to the REWARD of the solidarity of the HERO TEAM and the RESURRECTION of its fleet.

Bataan and Corregidor also face an ORDEAL. General Martin of the Army (a HERALD) announces that U.S. Bombers will arrive in the morning to wipe out the Japanese ships; however, this ELIXIR won't arrive soon enough to prevent a Japanese Cruiser from cutting off the needed supplies going into Corregidor. Brick and Rusty eagerly offer their services to destroy the ENEMY Cruiser, setting a TICKING CLOCK and initiating their ROAD BACK. Since Sandy is still stationed at Corregidor, the decision satisfies both of Rusty's Journey (to serve the HERO TEAM and to save his love).

With his boats still in repair, Brickley decides to use only the 41, with himself at helm. But his squad protests; his entire TEAM eagerly wants this ROAD BACK. They launch the 34 from its dry dock, an exhilarating RESURRECTION. Led by Brickley and Rusty, manned by what remains of the HERO TEAM, the 41 and 34 make their BOLD nighttime APPROACH on the Cruiser. They use every available torpedo to sink the Cruiser, but the two PT boats are separated in battle, each team fearing the other dead.

Rusty and his TEAM outmaneuver an air attack, and find refuge on an island. They barely bring the wounded to shore when the Japanese destroy their boat. Rusty sinks to his knees; all seems lost. This moment initiates an extended "death," as Rusty and his crew face the grim reality of their defeat.

At a church, Rusty officiates at the funeral ceremony for his two dead crewmen. He commends their heroism and dedication to the TEAM. He abruptly breaks away and reopens the bar to drown his sorrows. The ROAD BACK has shattered Rusty's faith in himself and the TEAM. He hears the radio report announcing the fall of Bataan and the Japanese attack on Corregidor. We can see the fear on Rusty's face that Sandy may not have survived. Faced with the destruction of the squadron, the fall of Bataan, and the probable death of his love, Rusty takes command "the way Brick would have wanted it," beginning his RESURRECTION. He must find Brick and send his men to secure themselves until support arrives.

Rusty soon finds his MENTOR relinquishing his last PT boat to the Army, continuing this "death-state." They return to their base, decimated by the ENEMY. But new orders from the High Command quickly RESURRECT the two from the pits of despair. Washington orders their return to rebuild the PT squadron, an ELIXIR and ROAD BACK. Brickley must make sacrifices for this HIGHER CAUSE. The transport planes have limited space; Brick and Rusty will have to abandon their remaining TEAM. The TEAM shows the respect their leader deserves and marches off with pride, the RESURRECTION. Without the PT boats and their MENTOR, the HERO TEAM will continue, an ELIXIR.

As Brick and Rusty board the transport plane, they are told to take back the message that the end is near in the Philippines. The remaining troops—"the expendables"—need the ELIXIR of fuel and men to start taking the islands back. With seats limited, Rusty offers to sacrifice his seat to another soldier. Rusty recognizes his CRISIS OF THE HEART and needs to find Sandy, but Brick pushes him to remember the HIGHER CAUSE. Rusty accepts his NOBLE SACRIFICE, completing his RESURRECTION. He commits to his MENTOR'S Journey, an ELIXIR. As they prepare to take off, Brickley emphasizes that this ROAD BACK will be brief: "We're going home to come back."

As Brickley's TEAM marches down the beach, they look above at the departing transport plane. Their faces are filled with the ELIXIR of pride and hope that MacArthur's words will come true: "We shall return."

FADE OUT

THE BRIDGE ON THE RIVER KWAI
(U.K., 1957)

"Madness! Madness!"

— Major Clipton (James Donald)

Screenplay by Michael Wilson and Carl Foreman
Based on the novel by Pierre Boulle
Directed by David Lean

To save his soldiers' morale, a British Commander builds a bridge for their Japanese captor, while British Intelligence plots to destroy it.

LANDMARKS OF THE JOURNEY

Undying convictions come head-to-head in this stunning character study showing the tragic waste of war. The story is structured by two Journeys. Colonel Saito needs to build the bridge, and his biggest obstacle is Colonel Nicholson's devotion to the Geneva Convention. The British commander is forced through an almost insufferable Threshold / Ordeal from which his Resurrection can be seen as "madness." Although our Mentor remains devoted to maintaining the discipline and sanity of his Hero Team, his own sanity is in question.

The story depicts the depths of dehumanization and how face-to-face contact with the Enemy can destroy this survival technique and make the Journey of War personal. No longer seen as soldiers and officers, Saito treats his prisoners equally, as slaves. And yet he must accept the Special Powers of the British Mentor, Nicholson, who is usurping his Journey. As both colonels endure the Journey's Tests and Ordeals, they begin to see the face of the Enemy and recognize that they are more alike than they care to admit.

The American POW, Shears, becomes the Hero of the story's second Journey. His road is an interesting inversion of the Ordinary and Special worlds. The Loner Antihero Shears must escape the Ordinary World of the POW camp, but once "safe" in his Special World, he's pushed to return in order to destroy Saito's (and Nicholson's) bridge.

THE JOURNEY

A Japanese POW camp. Escape from this "island" in the impenetrable Burmese jungle is impossible. If prisoners work hard, they will be treated well; yet, death by labor, exhaustion and disease is commonplace in this ORDINARY WORLD.

British Colonel Nicholson (MENTOR) marches his company into the Japanese POW camp. Japanese Colonel Saito (SHADOW) greets his new prisoners, who have been chosen to build the bridge across the River Kwai (Saito's OUTER PROBLEM), providing a key link to the Bangkok-Rangoon "death railway." Nicholson reminds Saito of the Geneva Convention (MENTOR) that REFUSES the use of officers for manual labor. Nicholson's OUTER PROBLEM is to lead and protect his men, and to uphold the civilized code in this jungle Hell.

Saito doesn't need to be reminded of the Geneva Convention. A SHADOW MENTOR, Saito refuses to acknowledge the power of Nicholson's MENTOR. He strikes Nicholson and tosses his "coward's code" into the dirt. All are equally slaves, and no longer soldiers. The SHADOW MENTOR demands that officers work alongside their soldiers. Although humiliated in front of his men, MENTOR Nicholson will not bend. He and his officers REFUSE to move.

Saito never anticipates the strength of Nicholson's pride before his HERO TEAM, and brings him into his headquarters. Nicholson's men shout their protests of the ORDEAL they are sure is occurring within. Finally their MENTOR appears, beaten; he is then dragged into a sweatbox. Nicholson's REFUSAL forces Saito to punish Nicholson until he accepts the CALL, initiating an ORDEAL / THRESHOLD SEQUENCE.

Meanwhile, Shears plots his escape from this Hell. ANTIHERO Shears has survived the sinking of his ship; but when captured by the Japanese, he takes the identity of a U.S. naval officer, believing he'll receive preferential treatment. Now a "living slave" in Saito's ORDINARY WORLD, Shears accepts a fellow prisoner's CALL to escape. Only Shears survives the THRESHOLD to freedom.

While Nicholson and his officers languish in their "ovens," Saito's use of the soldiers to build the bridge brings disaster. During this TEST PHASE, design mistakes and accidents push construction far behind schedule. Saito blames sabotage and Nicholson's stubborn REFUSAL. He offers Nicholson British food and stories of his own time spent in London, to show identification with Nicholson's ORDINARY WORLD, and to drop the SHADOW masks revealing how very much alike they are. Nicholson will not accept his SHADOW'S last desperate attempt, and Saito finally crumbles. To save face, Saito honors the anniversary of Japan's 1905 victory over Russia and grants Nicholson the light of day. He gives a day of rest to his soldiers and amnesty to Nicholson's officers. Nicholson readjusts his uniform, and his troops welcome his RESURRECTION with congratulations.

Nicholson allows Saito to continue using the soldiers to build his bridge, and surveys the bridge building with his officers. During this MEETING WITH THE MENTOR, Nicholson observes a failure of morale, and his officers warn that Saito's bridge is poorly designed. Nicholson realizes he needs to rebuild his battalion, and will use Saito's bridge as his means, CROSSING THE THRESHOLD, and completing the THRESHOLD SEQUENCE.

Nicholson takes control of the bridge building. He and his officers meet with Saito and push their changes. Throughout this MEETING OF MENTORS, Saito desperately tries to save face and maintain command of his journey.

With Nicholson's Journey moving into the TEST PHASE of the building of the bridge, the story jumps to Shears' Journey. Recovering in a Ceylonese military hospital, Shears' freedom is disrupted by British Major Warden. This MENTOR from British Intelligence requests Shears' assistance on a secret mission to destroy Saito's bridge. The success of the mission depends upon Shears' first-hand knowledge of the jungle and Saito's camp, but Shears REFUSES to return. He wants his medical leave to go home. But the U.S. Navy knows that Shears is impersonating an officer, and rather than have him face trial, they happily hand him over to British Intelligence. Shears doesn't have a choice. "I might as well volunteer," he says crossing THROUGH THE THRESHOLD.

Nicholson's TEST PHASE impresses Saito with the bridge's progress. But Medical Officer Clipton (MENTOR/ALLY) question's Nicholson's "collaboration with the enemy," and considers his conviction to build a better bridge treasonous. APPROACHING THE INMOST CAVE, Nicholson doesn't see the bridge as treason but as a permanent tribute to the British Soldier.

Back in Ceylon, Warden and Shears initiate their TEST PHASE. They put together the HERO TEAM, choosing a young Canadian, Lt. Joyce. Before they depart, Shears is issued a suicide pill, which RAISES THE STAKES of this Journey. No one can be captured alive. Quickly, the HERO TEAM parachutes into the jungle. They use native women (ALLIES) to lead them through the dense jungle terrain, suffering heat and leech-infested swamps. They receive an important radio transmission telling them to synchronize the demolition with the arrival of a special train carrying Japanese troops and VIPs.

The VIP train arrival sets a simultaneous TICKING CLOCK at Saito's camp. Pressed to complete the bridge on schedule, Nicholson sacrifices the Geneva Convention rights that he so adamantly defended. Obsessed with his crusade, Nicholson uses officers and then the sick to help the construction, an ORDEAL that reveals his "madness." Trusting their commander in war, the sick accept their MENTOR'S orders.

The demolition TEAM continues its arduous TEST PHASE through the jungle. They confront a Japanese patrol, and Warden is seriously injured, the ORDEAL. He tries to push the TEAM ahead with Shears in charge. But Shears stands up to his MENTOR who has pushed this Journey to death and destruction, and forces Warden to see it to its end, a RESURRECTION. At last, they ascend the mountaintop and behold their REWARD, the River Kwai and the completed bridge. Warden can't understand why the bridge is so sturdy, unlike the temporary bridges the ENEMY throws together. Nicholson proudly secures his plaque commemorating his men (his REWARD), as the demolition TEAM watches, unaware of Nicholson's role. Warden prepares for their ROAD BACK and assigns their jobs. The VIP train is expected in the morning; they make their preparations for that night.

Protected by the darkness of night, the HERO TEAM sets the charges on the bridge, the ROAD BACK, as Nicholson's men celebrate their achievement. They have survived with honor and turned defeat into victory, a REWARD. However, having lost face *and* his Journey to Nicholson's cause, Saito prepares for his suicide the next day. Meanwhile, the HERO TEAM sets the plunger. Everything is in place. The ROAD BACK complete. Taking the Journey to its harrowing, and suspenseful conclusion.

Morning rises and the HERO TEAM discovers that the river's water level has dropped, exposing the demolition wires and the explosives. On the bridge the opening ceremonies have begun and the train whistle announces its approach. Nicholson spots something wrong in the river, beginning the RESURRECTION SEQUENCE. He leads Saito to the riverbank to investigate, and they find the exposed wire and follow it to Joyce who waits with the plunger. Joyce kills Saito, and struggles with Nicholson, telling him the TEAM'S plan to blow the bridge. Incredulous, Nicholson must stop the destruction of everything he has created. The Japanese shoot Joyce. The VIP train continues its approach. Shears swims the river after Nicholson and toward the plunger. He too is shot in the confusion of gunfire, but Nicholson recognizes Shears and he finally realizes "What have I done?!" (His RESURRECTION).

Warden fires a mortar to ensure no survivors. Shrapnel hits Nicholson, who staggers toward the plunger. He falls on it (completing his RESURRECTION). He blows the bridge and the VIP train, the ELIXIR. The demolition mission is successful, but at what cost? Medical Officer Clipton's shouts of "madness" rise above the confusion, destruction and death, as Nicholson's dedication plaque disappears down the river.

FADE OUT

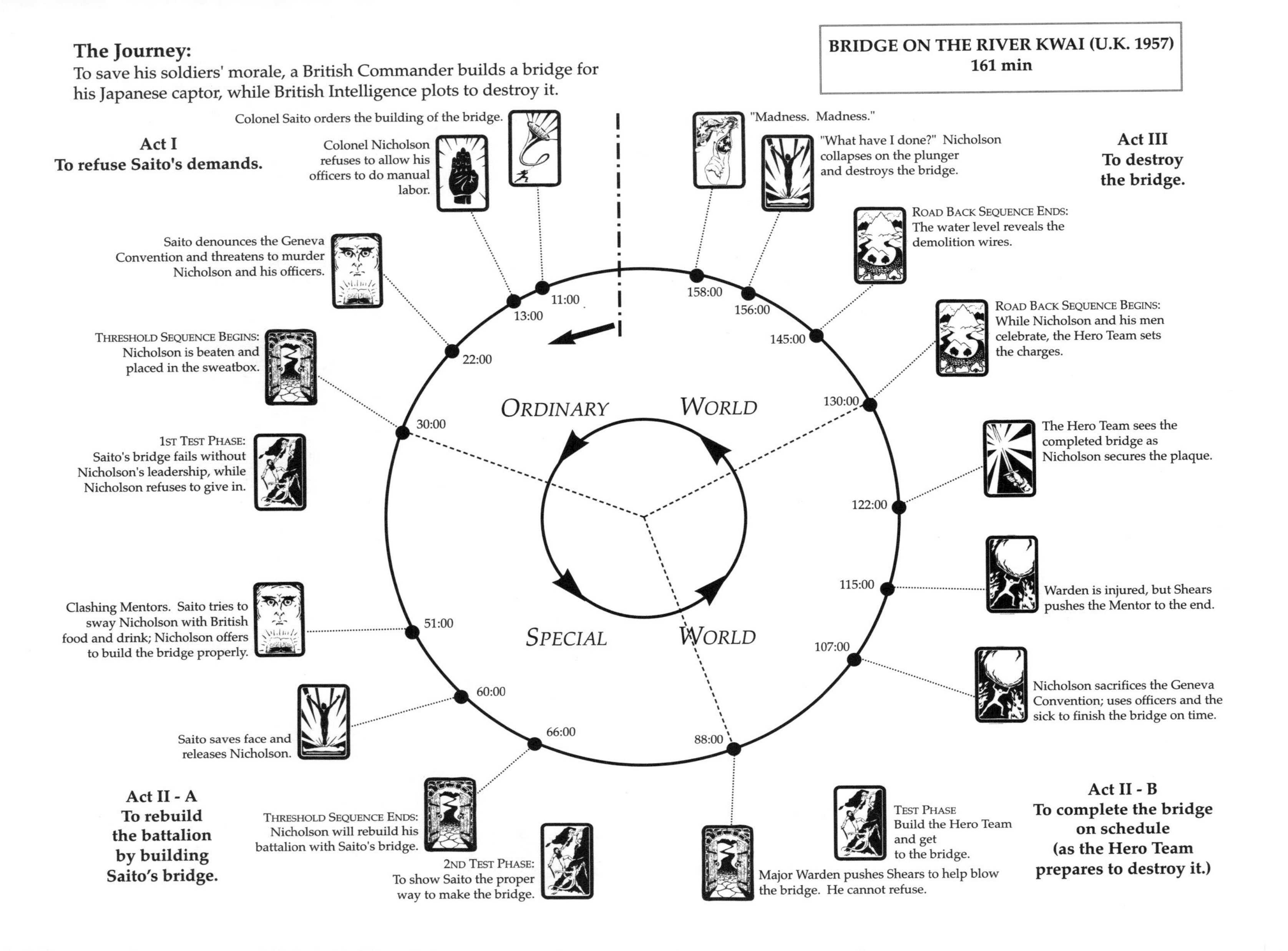

BRIDGE ON THE RIVER KWAI (U.K. 1957)
161 min
The Journey:
To save his soldiers' morale, a British Commander builds a bridge for his Japanese captor, while British Intelligence plots to destroy it.
Act I
To refuse Saito's demands.
Colonel Saito orders the building of the bridge.
Colonel Nicholson refuses to allow his officers to do manual labor.
Saito denounces the Geneva Convention and threatens to murder Nicholson and his officers.
THRESHOLD SEQUENCE BEGINS: Nicholson is beaten and placed in the sweatbox.
1ST TEST PHASE: Saito's bridge fails without Nicholson's leadership, while Nicholson refuses to give in.
Clashing Mentors. Saito tries to sway Nicholson with British food and drink; Nicholson offers to build the bridge properly.
Saito saves face and releases Nicholson.
Act II - A
To rebuild the battalion by building Saito's bridge.
THRESHOLD SEQUENCE ENDS: Nicholson will rebuild his battalion with Saito's bridge.
2ND TEST PHASE: To show Saito the proper way to make the bridge.
Major Warden pushes Shears to help blow the bridge. He cannot refuse.
TEST PHASE
Build the Hero Team and get to the bridge.
Act II - B
To complete the bridge on schedule (as the Hero Team prepares to destroy it.)
Nicholson sacrifices the Geneva Convention; uses officers and the sick to finish the bridge on time.
Warden is injured, but Shears pushes the Mentor to the end.
The Hero Team sees the completed bridge as Nicholson secures the plaque.
ROAD BACK SEQUENCE BEGINS: While Nicholson and his men celebrate, the Hero Team sets the charges.
ROAD BACK SEQUENCE ENDS: The water level reveals the demolition wires.
"What have I done?" Nicholson collapses on the plunger and destroys the bridge.
"Madness. Madness."
Act III
To destroy the bridge.
ORDINARY WORLD
SPECIAL WORLD
11:00
13:00
22:00
30:00
51:00
60:00
66:00
88:00
107:00
115:00
122:00
130:00
145:00
156:00
158:00

DAS BOOT
(Germany, 1981)

"You have to have good men, good men all of them."

— The Captain (Jurgen Prochnow)

Screenplay by Wolfgang Petersen
Based on the novel by Lothar-Gunther Buchheim
Directed by Wolfgang Petersen

A U-boat is crippled during a mission to torpedo Allied shipping in the North Atlantic. The war-weary Captain must keep his crew together and resurrect his ship.

LANDMARKS OF THE JOURNEY

For the Germans who served in World War II, no military duty was more respected or honored than service aboard a U-boat. In reality, U-boat duty was a harrowing, claustrophobic affair, and Wolfgang Petersen's taut war thriller takes us into this stifling Special World.

Lt. Werner, the German war correspondent, is our witness on this Journey. We learn the Special World, its rules, procedures, and dangers through him. And we meet the individuals who are bound by the strongest bonds created under the continual hardships and victories experienced in war.

We have seen the Mentor in previous war films as battle-smart and dedicated to victory. Das Boot's Captain is weary of the war, as are many members of his crew, worn down by repeatedly cheating death in this 10-foot by 150-foot world. They know the odds of survival become slimmer with each mission. The stoic, cynical Captain is quick to criticize the military strategy that has crippled what once was a U-boat stronghold in the North Atlantic. He doubts their future, and his command. He's not perfect, yet he leads his men and maintains their respect. He keeps the Hero Team together and protects his boat as if she were the Journey's Hero.

This analysis uses the theatrically released version of 1982. Despite being a drastically cut version of the six-hour German mini-series, it was both critically (including six Academy Award nominations, an unprecedented achievement for a foreign film) and commercially successful, becoming one of the most successful foreign films released in the United States.

THE JOURNEY

Hitler counted on the U-boat to control the Atlantic and starve out England; however, the British turn the tide and protect their freighters with better equipped Destroyer envoys. Hitler refuses to lose his stronghold and orders more U-boats staffed with younger, untested crews. The grim reality of this ORDINARY WORLD is that, of the 40,000 German sailors serving on U-boats, 30,000 never return.

1941. La Rochelle, France. On the eve of their next mission, the U-boat's crew members drown their fears in schnapps and women (a type of REFUSAL). Tomorrow the HERO TEAM will willingly return to duty (their OUTER PROBLEM). Meanwhile, the Captain introduces Lt. Werner to his officers. A German war correspondent, Lt. Werner's OUTER PROBLEM is to report the true facts of life aboard a U-boat.

Werner's entrance into this SPECIAL WORLD begins early the following morning. Although Werner and the audience are new to this physical world, the Captain and his crew accept this cramped ORDINARY WORLD where there's one shit-house shared by the crew of fifty.

The Captain leads the crew and their ship through a series of standard TESTS. They take the U-boat through a practice dive to TEST the valves and seals, diving a nerve-wracking 160 meters before resurfacing. For the Captain and crew these TESTS are an important phase to prepare them for the demands of the SPECIAL WORLD yet to come. For Werner and the audience, this TEST PHASE effectively presents the rules and limitations of the world. Now that the U-boat has passed, the HERO TEAM members are anxious to seek their prey, in what can be an interminable period of waiting. The Captain will do what's necessary to buoy the crew's morale as he weighs their odds against potential targets and takes in the circumstances of the sea and visibility before finally crossing the THRESHOLD. All the crew can do is wait, pick their noses, complete crossword puzzles, and begin to question their effectiveness.

On their 45th day at sea they confront their prey, a convoy of five ships with no apparent protection. At first RELUCTANT—the full moon could reveal them—the Captain decides it is worth the try. They attack, hitting three ships and crossing THROUGH THE THRESHOLD. Now that they've revealed themselves they must submerge and await the explosions signaling their hits, followed by the groaning of their prey's bulkheads collapsing. Suddenly they endure a grueling counter-attack, a REVERSAL. The hunters quickly become the hunted, pushing them into a TEST PHASE, as Destroyers criss-cross above them dropping depth charges. The U-boat crew must remain silent—a whisper could give them away. They take damage. The crew douses a fire, endures smoke inhalation. They must dive deeper, descending to 200 meters. The seals strain. 220. The rivets burst. The ENEMY'S charges continue. Pushing them deeper, TESTING the crews' nerves in addition to the ship's seals. They take another hit, and the U-boat takes on water. The crew fears they are sinking (an ORDEAL) as we black out ... Werner awakens. Many still sleep. The Captain assures him they outlasted the Destroyer (a RESURRECTION).

They surface to finish their duty, granting one of their victims its death blow, but the horrified Captain watches the human consequences of their attack as crewmen leap from the Allied ship. Why weren't they rescued by their own Destroyers? The Allied survivors swim toward the U-boat. The Captain hears the pitiful cries from his very human ENEMY. Helpless, he must turn his back; a U-boat has no room for prisoners of war. This horrifying ORDEAL of personal death jars them out of the impersonal battles of radar blips they are accustomed to fighting. Soon they hear the metallic groans of the ENEMY ship finally succumbing to its watery grave.

Acknowledging the wear on his crew, the Captain decides to return to port at La Rochelle. And his men look forward to their REWARD of a Christmas leave. However, they receive new orders to go to Italy, a CALL that makes several of the crew wary, for they must face the impossible task of passing Gibraltar.

They arrive in Vigo, Spain, to fuel and load supplies. The disheveled HERO TEAM and its Captain receive a lavish REWARD of tables filled with delicacies, music from a boy's choir, and officers' salutes. Everyone hungry for stories of the TEAM'S sea battles. Uncomfortable with the surrounding opulence, the Captain and his crew move on. They fill every available space on the U-boat with food and supplies, and prepare for the Straight of Gibraltar, a seven-mile passage heavily defended by British patrol boats. With a map, the Captain presents his plan (APPROACH THE INMOST CAVE). Using the cover of darkness, they'll drift on the water's surface past the British forces. His officers welcome his "clever trick."

That very night, they begin the ORDEAL. The Captain and his navigator remain above while the TEAM stays below, anxiously waiting and listening. Quickly they draw an air attack, a tragic REVERSAL that leaves the navigator seriously wounded. The U-boat is crippled but the Captain refuses to let them abandon ship. He steers them toward the North African coastline and orders them to dive. The damaged U-boat sinks, jammed in a dive, her pumps strained. They can only pray that they hit bottom before the pressure crushes the ship. They finally set down on a "shovelful of sand" an unbelievable 280 meters below surface. Miraculously the U-boat is in one piece ... but the crew realize their ORDEAL has only begun. After several tense moments, the ship "blows" from the strain, gaskets split, and the HERO TEAM jumps to action to stop the flooding. Chlorine gas begins to leak. The Captain must keep his TEAM together to fix their crippled ship. He's REWARDED with a levelheaded crew dedicated to working together. Soon the leaks are stopped; however, there's too much water in the hull.

The Chief offers their ROAD BACK, and suggests they use the ballast pump to blast the water out. They'll have only one chance and lots of repairs must be made. With limited oxygen, only four men can work at a time while the rest turn in. The Captain realizes that this is their only way to resurrect the ship and agrees to the Chief's plan.

They suffer fifteen hours in this "death-like" state. The Captain finally admits to Lt. Werner that he doesn't see a RESURRECTION. Fearing death, the Lieutenant denounces his duty for the Fatherland and confesses his loneliness, a DARK REWARD. Although they have lived as a TEAM, each will die alone.

From the darkest depths of despair, the Chief grants them a bit of light, their ROAD BACK. The ship is ready. The Captain praises his HERO TEAM, "good men all." They prepare to blow out the water, an APPROACH before their Journey's RESURRECTION SEQUENCE. Restoring his TEAM'S morale, the Captain promises everyone a half bottle of beer if they make it. And he reminds them of their one advantage; the ENEMY boats will never be expecting their RESURRECTION.

They blow the tanks and purge the excess water. The HERO TEAM and their Captain watch for any movement of the depth gauge. The U-boat groans ... she slowly levels herself ... and rises, her RESURRECTION. Soon they break the surface and start the engines, and quickly race to their port at La Rochelle (a CHASE).

The engines hold and soon the salutes of officers and the cheers of citizens welcome them. But this ELIXIR is short-lived. A massive air strike shells the port, a tragic REVERSAL. Everyone scrambles for cover, and many are killed and wounded. Lt. Werner rushes back to the U-boat and sees the fallen crew members. The Captain watches his U-boat sink to the bottom of the harbor. He collapses, joining his ship in death.

FADE OUT

PLATOON
(U.S., 1986)

"Maybe I finally find it, way down here in the mud. Maybe from down here I can start up again, be something I can be proud of without having to fake it. Be a fake human being. Maybe I can see something I don't yet see, learn something I don't yet know."

— Chris Taylor (Charlie Sheen)

Written and Directed by Oliver Stone

Serving his country in Vietnam, a young soldier faces civil war within his platoon led by two Mentors warring for his soul.

LANDMARKS OF THE JOURNEY

Platoon shows the unpredictability of war, the long tedious periods of boredom interrupted by vicious ordeals. Despite its sudden unexpected twists and turns, *Platoon* tells a simply structured story, with richly layered characters and dialogue.

We have come full circle from *All Quiet on the Western Front* and again see war as Hell fought by the innocent souls of our youth. In contrast, *Platoon* doesn't show a clear line of battle. The Viet Cong, the apparent Enemy, are beyond dehumanized uniforms becoming literal shadows that flit through the jungles. The platoon—the sacred Hero's Team of World War II—is the battlefield. And *we* have become our Enemy.

Also unlike World War II conventions, our Hero is torn between two Mentors. The Ordeals of battle have resurrected these Rival Mentors into Shadows of themselves. The righteous Elias has ascended to Christ-like stature and is ultimately sacrificed by Barnes, the betrayer. The battle-scarred Barnes has bathed in so much blood of the battlefield that he has become a crusader of violence, waging war on his own terms. Both Mentors fight for their grunts' souls. And the battle lines of this civil war are drawn during the Ordeal in a small village.

THE JOURNEY

Chris Taylor's Journey begins a THRESHOLD into a world of war. He steps off the transport and faces a pile of body bags taking his place on the return flight. Chris cannot turn back from this SPECIAL WORLD of death.

September, 1967. Bravo Company. 25th Infantry. Somewhere near the Cambodian Border. Chris is a new member of the company's ORDINARY WORLD. He's a "cherry," an untested recruit and the lowest of the low. The "grunts" won't even acknowledge the "cherries" until they've served (and suffered) their time. Chris enters a TEST PHASE where he must keep up with the rest. He humps through the jungles with a ton of supplies breaking his back, suffering humidity, hacking bamboo, avoiding snakes, always in fear of what lies ahead. His only ALLIES seem to be the other Cherries—tragic lost souls wandering this Hell without guidance.

Chris meets his two MENTORS. The three-year veteran Elias walks without helmet, rifle across his back, silently accepting this Hell. His RIVAL and SHADOW, the career killer Sergeant Barnes, marches in full gear, barking at his grunts. This battle-scarred veteran has risen from so many ordeals that his men believe he cannot be killed.

When Chris dry-heaves from the sight of a rotting corpse, the unsympathetic MENTOR Barnes refuses to help the cherry, whereas MENTOR Elias shows compassion and helps Chris.

Chris settles into the physically and emotionally exhausting ORDINARY WORLD of digging foxholes, getting supplies, and marching endlessly. In a letter to his grandma, he reveals his hatred and fear that he won't be able to complete his tour of duty (a REFUSAL).

The platoon leaders expect an ENEMY ambush that night and prepare their trap (an APPROACH TO THE INMOST CAVE). Elias REFUSES to use his untested cherries for ambush patrol, but Barnes is running this show. Elias prepares his TEAM, stripping them of unnecessary equipment, giving them final assignments, and they march out.

That night, the patrol sets their trap and positions their claymore mines. They take their shifts for ambush watch while the rest sleep. Chris passes his shift on to Junior, and tries to catch some zzz's in the rain and mud.

Chris awakens with a start and sees the shadowy ENEMY approaching the perimeter. Chris freezes. Suddenly gunfire, explosions, chaos. Chris is wounded during this ORDEAL and blamed for the mishap by Junior. Chris tries to defend himself but Barnes and his ALLIES are quick to castigate the cherry. This ORDEAL marks an important THRESHOLD for Chris. He has survived (unlike Gardner, the other cherry) and soon returns from the hospital. Only now the platoon members welcome Chris, even showing interest in knowing more about Chris' ORDINARY WORLD. His baptism of fire has RESURRECTED Chris into a grunt, and he quickly enters a TEST PHASE. He joins Elias and his "pot head" ALLIES who rely on drugs and dance to escape the reality of war, while Barnes and his ALLIES drink and play poker. This clearly defines the two sides of this company. According to the HERO TEAM conventions of the World War II film, a divided platoon must fail. Ordeals can solidify or destroy a team; Chris' platoon faces a tragic CALL that could destroy the TEAM forever.

They find an enemy camp, and tragically realize that they've walked into a trap. The platoon recovers from this failed TEST and finds one of their own strung up with his throat slashed. They cannot ignore this CALL. Together the HERO TEAM descends upon a nearby village they suspect is harboring the ENEMY. The platoon makes the BOLD APPROACH, eager for revenge and led by Barnes—"the eye of rage"—determined to set things right. They overtake the village, and abuse the villagers. Chris discovers a boy and woman hiding. Committed to Barnes' quest for revenge, Chris makes the boy "dance." But one of Barnes' ALLIES, Bunny, jumps in and kills the boy, crushing his skull. The blood spatters Chris' face. The violence and "taste of blood" quells Chris' need for revenge, RESURRECTING his moral reason. But Barnes wages his own war and demands answers from the villagers. They REFUSE him. Barnes shoots an old woman and threatens to kill her daughter; however, Elias arrives in time to stop Barnes and prevent a massacre. Their Lieutenant refuses to recognize the conflict between MENTORS and orders the burning of the village. However this ORDEAL is a THRESHOLD into a deeper SPECIAL WORLD that forces Chris to change, a REWARD, showing allegiance toward the humanist MENTOR, Elias. He discovers several soldiers raping a young villager, and defends the "human being" from these "animals."

Elias wants Barnes court-martialed and Captain Harris promises a full investigation. For now the TEAM must be maintained; he orders the MENTORS to "cease fire." Meeting briefly with his ALLIES, we know that Barnes will wage his own personal war to protect his position on the battlefield.

That night, Chris meets with his MENTOR. As the two watch the stars Elias warns Chris that the ORDEAL of the village was only a beginning. He foreshadows that they will lose this war.

The village ORDEAL has disrupted the HERO TEAM, causing infighting and questioning of right and wrong. Barnes believes in what he's doing and continues to fight the war as he sees it by his rules. A Viet Cong ambush decimates the platoon, catching them in crossfire and causing absolute chaos. Barnes uses this ORDEAL to hunt Elias and gun him down. Although Chris wasn't on the scene he suspects Barnes' guilt. The TEAM scrambles into the helicopter with their wounded. The chopper ascends (their RESURRECTION) and Chris sees Elias fleeing the Viet Cong. They cannot save their MENTOR before he is gunned down, and Chris finally sees Barnes' SHADOW mask. This knowledge is Chris' REWARD.

But Elias' ALLIES are reluctant to accept Chris' REWARD. Yes, Barnes must pay, but they fear Barnes. Perhaps the devil MENTOR was never meant to die. Barnes interrupts their powwow, and justifies Elias' death. Because he was no longer a member of the war machine, he was sacrificed to restore the HERO TEAM. Barnes offers himself to the "pot heads," but they REFUSE to kill him. Finally, Chris jumps this SHADOW MENTOR, who quickly pins Chris. Under these circumstances the HERO cannot defeat the SHADOW.

And while Barnes could get away with murder on the battlefield, he must spare Chris for now. He cuts the HERO'S cheek—a scar from the scarred MENTOR. The MENTOR must wait for the battlefield to deal with this betrayer, initiating the ROAD BACK.

The platoon must return to the valley where Elias was gunned down. The HERO TEAM can sense death awaiting them on this ROAD BACK. One fortunate soul, King, has served his time. He can return to his ORDINARY WORLD. Others aren't so lucky and try devious ways to cheat death. But their leader, MENTOR Barnes, knows the tricks and forces his TEAM to accept their sacrifice: "Everybody's gotta die."

The RESURRECTION SEQUENCE consists of two stages. The first shows Chris as a true SOLDIER HERO: killing the ENEMY, anticipating ENEMY maneuvers, and protecting the members of his HERO TEAM. But the ENEMY forces are too great. Grunts as well as their leaders perish. The remains of the HERO TEAM desperately fight a lost cause while High Command orders an air strike that could sacrifice everyone.

On the battlefield, Barnes is shot but Chris shoots the ENEMY saving the SHADOW MENTOR. But Barnes turns on the young HERO and will kill him as the artillery hits, igniting the battlefield and leaving the audience in a "death-state," wondering what happened.

Chris awakens in a lush, peaceful forest. This physical RESURRECTION feels disorienting. Is this a dream? Perhaps death? He rises and limps into the silent battlefield, which is scarred by artillery, and littered with corpses.

Miraculously Chris has survived, and so has Barnes, who tries to crawl away from the battlefield of death. Barnes asks Chris to kill him. Chris shoots Barnes dead. Killing is essential in this SPECIAL WORLD, as Chris has learned from MENTOR Barnes. He sacrifices the SHADOW MENTOR with the same violence that caused their JOURNEY and killed Elias. One MENTOR is sacrificed for the other, with the hope that some morality and healing will return to the HERO and his TEAM (an ELIXIR).

The new troops move in to bury the dead. The platoon survivors must RESURRECT the HERO TEAM; some members reluctantly step into their MENTOR'S boots. A helicopter lifts the wounded Chris (a RESURRECTION). As he looks down upon the waste, the destruction and the death, he carries the ELIXIR OF HOPE that perhaps we can learn from our tragedies.

FADE OUT

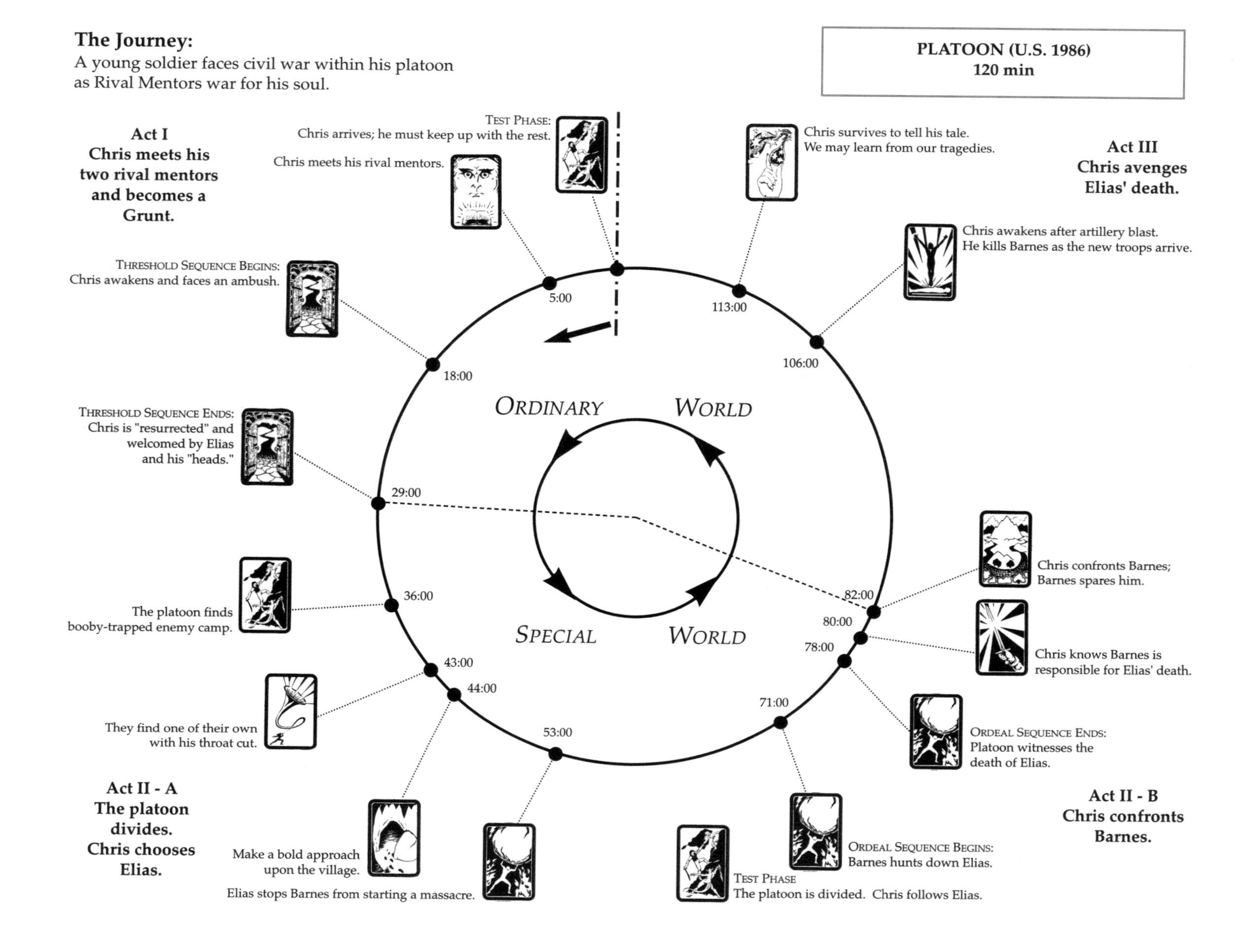

The Journey:
A young soldier faces civil war within his platoon as Rival Mentors war for his soul.
PLATOON (U.S. 1986)
120 min
Act I
Chris meets his two rival mentors and becomes a Grunt.
TEST PHASE:
Chris arrives; he must keep up with the rest.
Chris meets his rival mentors.
THRESHOLD SEQUENCE BEGINS:
Chris awakens and faces an ambush.
THRESHOLD SEQUENCE ENDS:
Chris is "resurrected" and welcomed by Elias and his "heads."
The platoon finds booby-trapped enemy camp.
They find one of their own with his throat cut.
Act II - A
The platoon divides.
Chris chooses Elias.
Make a bold approach upon the village.
Elias stops Barnes from starting a massacre.
TEST PHASE
The platoon is divided. Chris follows Elias.
ORDEAL SEQUENCE BEGINS:
Barnes hunts down Elias.
ORDEAL SEQUENCE ENDS:
Platoon witnesses the death of Elias.
Act II - B
Chris confronts Barnes.
Chris knows Barnes is responsible for Elias' death.
Chris confronts Barnes;
Barnes spares him.
Chris awakens after artillery blast.
He kills Barnes as the new troops arrive.
Chris survives to tell his tale.
We may learn from our tragedies.
Act III
Chris avenges Elias' death.
ORDINARY WORLD
SPECIAL WORLD
5:00
18:00
29:00
36:00
43:00
44:00
53:00
71:00
78:00
80:00
82:00
106:00
113:00

THE MYTHIC STRUCTURE OF DRAMA

Crisis strikes our personal world, throwing us into a Special World of pain and loss. The problem must be solved, but which side should we embrace? Our Mentor can show us the way, but the Shadow's road can be just as appealing. The Elixir of this Journey comes from within. We must accept our greatest fear, the fear of change, even accepting what we rebelled against in our Ordinary World. And perhaps our transformation can provide the Elixir for others to celebrate.

"FASTEN YOUR SEATBELTS, IT'S GOING TO BE A BUMPY NIGHT."

The key to the power of Drama is that it is driven by character. The characters of Drama face journeys not unlike our own—sickness, marital problems, discrimination, unemployment, aging and death. We can easily identify with the character's plight. The character's problem can be our own; his pain can be our pain, making the Journeys of Drama the most difficult to watch. But Drama can also provide our most rewarding Journeys, offering the audience the Elixir of awareness of our personal and societal problems. The Hero's transformation can provide a catharsis that allows us to purge our own insecurities, giving us the strength to face our own fears, and even heal our inner wounds.

THE ESSENCE OF DRAMA: TRANSFORMATION

All Journeys involve transformation. In other genres, the transformation may be secondary or happen as a result of the overriding motivation or Outer Problem the Journey needs to solve. The Journeys of Drama are often the transformation. In *Boyz N the Hood,* Tre transforms from a kid of violence to a young man of non-violence. Conrad Jarrett's transformation is a Journey of healing his broken Ordinary World (*Ordinary People*).

The Journeys of Drama show our greatest transformation of characters—often with the Hero accepting, even embracing, what he or she had shunned in the Hero's Ordinary World (*The Godfather, All About Eve*). Such an extreme transformation cannot happen at once, but occurs in phases throughout the Journey.

THE CHARACTER ARC

The Character Arc is the pathway of growth (or decline) that a character accomplishes during the Journey. The Character Arc requires phases of change; these changes are reflected by the character's actions. The "traditional" Character Arc incorporates twelve phases that correspond to the twelve stages of the Hero's Journey. As an overview, here are the phases of character change (with their associated Journey stages):

1. The Hero has limited awareness of the need to change in the Ordinary World.
2. The Call to Adventure gives the Hero increased awareness.
3. The fear of change makes the Hero Reluctant.
4. A Mentor helps the Hero overcome this Reluctance to change.
5. The Hero makes a commitment to change as he crosses through the Threshold.
6. During the Test Phase, the Hero must experiment with this first change.
7. He Approaches the Inmost Cave, and prepares for the big change.
8. The Hero attempts his big change during the Ordeal.
9. The Hero must accept the consequences of his attempt. These Rewards are the improvements and setbacks from his Ordeal.
10. The Hero rededicates himself to change at the Road Back.
11. The Hero makes his final attempt at the big change during the Resurrection.
12. Now transformed, the Hero can master the problem, the Elixir, that required the change.

This is not a twelve-step program that must be followed in strict order. The phases needed for a particular Journey depend upon the individual character's growth.

THE ISSUES OF DRAMA

While other genres may exist solely to entertain—to take us on an emotional, visceral ride—Drama's Journey may make us think. We use Drama to look at the issues that directly affect our lives (violence, racism, pollution, workers' rights, etc.)

THE DRAMATIC TRIANGLE

Like any good debate, the storyteller may wish to pose both sides of the issue, the Light and the Shadow side. Our Hero is torn between the two sides, creating a Dramatic Triangle similar to the Romantic Triangle where two Rivals fight for the same heart. *Boyz N the Hood* presents the problem of urban violence that has been killing our Black youth. John Singleton presents the two sides of this issue through two characters who try to push the young Hero, Tre Styles, to accept their path. Tre's father, Furious Styles (Mentor and actualized Hero), upholds non-violence. Tre's best friend, Doughboy (Shadow), accepts the need for violence to combat a violent world. Mentor and Shadow are one hundred percent committed to their beliefs, making Tre's Journey extremely difficult and emotional as he searches to accept the right changes and follow the right path.

In *Ordinary People*, the Dramatic Triangle pits Conrad's psychiatrist, Berger, against his mother, Beth. Conrad seeks Berger's help to reclaim his Ordinary World, but this commitment requires that not only Conrad change, but also that his Ordinary World change. But Beth, having recently buried her favorite son, can not change, making her unable to be a part of Conrad's transformed Ordinary World.

WITHOUT CONVICTION THERE IS NO DRAMA

A Hero's strength of conviction determines how easily he can overcome the obstacles along the Journey's path. Threshold Guardians, Enemies, Shadows, and Shapeshifters, whoever tries to sway the Hero from his convictions, create the conflict and crisis in Drama. Great conflict and drama arise when the Hero's conviction is matched by the opposing conviction of the Rival, Enemy or Shadow.

The significance of a Hero's Journey may entail the destruction of one conviction and the acceptance of another. Eve takes over Margo's world of the theatre, forcing Margo to leave (*All About Eve*). Michael Corleone rejects the family business until an attempt on his father's life brings him into the fold (*The Godfather*). Seeing what it takes for a Hero to accept what he adamantly opposes can create our most engrossing dramas.

GENRE CHALLENGES: DRAMA

1. Each of Thompson's interviews in *Citizen Kane* can be seen as a mini-Journey. Choose one of the interviews and analyze the structure using the tools of the Hero's Journey.
2. The analysis of *All About Eve* focuses upon Margo's Journey. How would you see the Journey through Eve Harrington's eyes? What stages of the Hero's Journey are present? Are any stages missing, or shown off-screen? At what point along her Journey do you lose sympathy?
3. Michael Corleone's Journey continues in *The Godfather Part II.* Take a look at the film, and continue Michael's Journey and character transformation. What is the Elixir at the end of *The Godfather Part II*? How does it contrast with *The Godfather*?
4. In what ways do Coppola and Puzo generate sympathy for Don Vito Corleone, the Corleone family, and the business? What actions or events are shown or not shown that promote our sympathy?
5. Conrad's Journey in *Ordinary People* forces changes in other characters in his Ordinary World. Describe the Journey that Conrad's father, Calvin, takes. What stages of the Hero's Journey are shown? Does he show phases of character change?
6. Using the twelve phases of the Character Arc, plot out Tre's transformation in *Boyz N the Hood.* How does he show change through his actions? Now, plot Doughboy's transformation. Do you sympathize with Doughboy? Why or why not?

CITIZEN KANE
(U.S., 1941)

"A toast, Jedediah, to love on my terms. Those are the only terms anybody ever knows—his own."

—Charles Foster Kane (Orson Welles)

Written by Herman J. Mankiewicz and Orson Welles
Directed by Orson Welles

A man uses his power and money to buy love on his own terms and loses everything.

LANDMARKS OF THE JOURNEY

Citizen Kane is framed by the mystery of a man's dying word that presents the story's central dramatic question. Who was Charles Foster Kane? Not the facts of his achievements shown in the "News on the March" newsreel, but the man within. What was the heart of Kane? And that's the key to this Journey's beauty—aside from all the technological achievements in direction, cinematography, editing, acting—all deserving of their accolades. *Citizen Kane* is about a man who, as a boy, was ripped from his mother's love, and raised by a cold guardian who replaced love with wealth. Tragically Kane tries to reclaim love the only way he knows how, through his wealth. He ends up losing everything.

Our guide, the reporter Thompson, tries to unlock the mystery of "Rosebud" by interviewing the people closest to Kane. We experience Kane's tragic quest for love in flashback as each interview takes us closer to Kane's heart. We begin with Thatcher, the one most distant from the real Kane. This Shadow had replaced Kane's mother's love with wealth. The loyal yes-man, Bernstein, shows us the glory days of Kane's ascent to fight for the love of the people using the power of his newspaper. The interview with Kane's closest friend, Jedediah, begins to show how Kane's inability to love destroys others. Each reflection of Charles Kane takes us deeper, beneath the veneer of the "News on the March" newsreel (the Ordinary World), and closer to Kane's heart, until we are finally prepared to hear the painful story of Kane's greatest love, Susan.

As Kane seeks love, he becomes more aware that he can only love on his own terms. But Kane's tragedy is that his terms are determined by the lessons of the man who initiated this Journey, the guardian Thatcher, the same man Kane dedicated his Journey to defy. Ironically, Kane loses everything in his quest for love and becomes his Shadow by Journey's end.

THE JOURNEY

The Opening Image of a "No Trespassing" sign bookends the Journey, and establishes the theme that no matter how hard we try we may never be able to understand the truth of a man.

We begin Kane's Journey at his end. He clutches a snow globe, and gasps "Rosebud." The snow globe drops and this single word ELIXIR shatters with the glass. This ELIXIR is a CALL TO ADVENTURE to the audience. What is the significance of this man's dying word? First, we need to know something about our TRAGIC HERO, Charles Foster Kane. A newsreel "News on the March" shows us the historic facts about Kane, in essence what the ORDINARY WORLD already knows of the man. The newsreel provides our frame of reference upon which we can better understand the emotional pieces of the jigsaw puzzle. We will journey beyond these facts into the SPECIAL WORLD to find the meaning of "Rosebud" and the heart of Charles Foster Kane.

The newsreel producer wants more than the sterile facts of Kane's accomplishments. He wants the essence of the man, and believes the answer lies behind Kane's final word. His reporter, Thompson, accepts his CALL TO ADVENTURE, to question anyone who knew Kane (MENTORS, ALLIES, ENEMIES, SHAPESHIFTERS) and unlock the secret of "Rosebud."

Thompson boldly APPROACHES Kane's second wife, Susan, but she REFUSES his interview. Thompson's Journey will take him to the heart of Kane, but others have to be interviewed before he's ready to get this close to his ELIXIR. For now, Susan serves as a THRESHOLD GUARDIAN barring him as soundly as the "No Trespassing" sign from this intimate part of the SPECIAL WORLD.

Thompson must first consult the person most distant from the real Kane: Thatcher, Kane's legal guardian and bank manager. Thompson enters Thatcher's cavernous reading room and begins reading Thatcher's memoirs. Thatcher's formal handwriting wisps away transporting us THROUGH THE THRESHOLD to a snow scene and young Charles sledding, and the most significant moment in Kane's life: the theft of his innocence and love (the ELIXIR) by his Mother and Thatcher. His mother assures him that this sacrifice is for his own good. But this harsh act of separation is Charles' last example of his Mother's love. He will carry and use this lesson throughout his life as he separates from friends and lovers finally becoming embittered and lonely, the opposite of what his mother and MENTOR promised.

Under Thatcher's guardianship, love is replaced by wealth. And we quickly see Kane's RESURRECTION into the idealistic champion for the people against everything Thatcher represents. Upon his 25th birthday, Charles is given his trust, now the world's sixth largest private fortune. With the power and wealth to do anything, he chooses to run a small newspaper, the *New York Inquirer*, and uses this ELIXIR to defy and battle his

MENTOR/SHADOW (his OUTER PROBLEM). Charles uses his crusade to veil his INNER PROBLEM, to win acceptance and love. As Thatcher's memoir comes to a close, we learn that Kane runs the business into the ground, and finally goes bust during the Depression.

Thompson next interviews Bernstein, Kane's forever faithful ALLY. Bernstein still benefits from Kane's estate and gladly tells of how his HERO and best friend Jedediah turned the *New York Inquirer* into a newspaper empire. Bernstein's interview can be seen as Kane's TEST PHASE showing his rise to power. Kane takes control of his newspaper (CROSSING THE THRESHOLD) and makes it his sword for his readership. He pledges a "Declaration of Principles," offering himself as the HERO/MENTOR for his people. But Kane enters this TEST PHASE armed with the only tool that his MENTOR Thatcher has given him, his wealth. He buys the RIVAL newspaper's Editorial Staff and builds a newspaper empire. Although he loses interest in the newspaper's operation and travels, Kane returns with a wife and aspirations of politics (where the people's love can be shown by votes).

Thompson interviews Jedediah Leland, Kane's best friend. While the first half of the Journey has shown Kane's ascent, Thompson now APPROACHES the real Kane and the beginning of his fall. His newspaper empire flourishes, but Kane's marriage fails. This CRISIS OF THE HEART pushes Kane to seek an answer from his past. On his way to the warehouse that stores all of his childhood belongings, Kane meets Susan and is attracted by her innocence, a CALL TO ROMANCE. Kane has an affair with Susan, his JOURNEY OF THE HEART, as he seeks election as the Governor of New York (Kane's JOURNEY FOR POWER).

On the eve of the gubernatorial election, Kane makes an impassioned speech denouncing his RIVAL, Boss Jim Gettys (APPROACH THE INMOST CAVE). Kane is assured to win the governor's seat, but Gettys exposes Kane's extra-marital affair to Kane's wife and prepares to tell the public if Kane doesn't withdraw from the race, the ORDEAL. Trusting that the voters will stand by Kane, he refuses to be blackmailed. Gettys proves Kane wrong. Kane's RIVAL newspapers splash the affair on the front pages and Kane loses the election. In following his heart, Kane sacrifices his wife and son, and the respect of his friend Jedediah (a MENTOR representing Kane's conscience). Jedediah will later send Kane his "Declaration of Principles," rejecting Kane's broken ideals.

His political future ruined (he has lost the love of his people), Kane marries Susan (a REWARD) and channels all of his energy into fulfilling her dream to be an opera singer ("We're gonna be a great opera star.") He builds her an Opera House in Chicago. Susan's opening night is Kane's REWARD, but his dramatic critic, Jedediah, is too drunk to complete his scathing review of Susan's performance. Kane completes the review true to Jedediah's intent, and fires his best friend.

Thompson is now prepared to interview the one closest to Kane's heart, his second wife, Susan, and the one most devastated by his life (and death). Returning to flashback, Susan recalls her humiliating opening night, an ORDEAL. Susan rebels against Kane's drive to live through her success. She attempts suicide and Kane at last agrees to give up this Journey, the ROAD BACK. But Kane's drive for her career was the only way he could show his love, and now that she has rejected that love, their relationship grows more distant. Charles Kane walks the cavernous halls of Xanadu, built as a monument to his love for Susan. Separated from the love of his people and the friends that he had fought for, Kane spends his old age surrounded by his possessions, including his cynical wife who wastes away with her jigsaw puzzles.

Kane takes Susan on a picnic. "Released" from her prison of Xanadu, Susan stands up to Kane to make him see that he never loved her. Love on his terms meant only that he wanted her love. He had no love to give in return, only wealth.

They return to Xanadu. Susan packs her bags and leaves Kane, beginning the RESURRECTION SEQUENCE. Charles Kane has lost everything he fought for. Facing this deepest moment of despair, this death-state, Kane finally sees the greatest truth about his life.

Thompson finally interviews Kane's Butler, Raymond, perhaps the one who is closest to the man without his vision being clouded by love. We see Raymond's description of Kane's breakdown, his RESURRECTION. Furious, Kane tears Susan's room apart, and finds a snow globe with a small winter scene, and remembers "Rosebud." He stops his tirade. Holding the snow globe he emerges from Susan's room, and walks through a mirrored hallway. The infinite reflections of Kane represent the different views and the different emotional puzzle pieces provided by his ALLIES and ENEMIES. Yet those reflections boil down to one man, and the essence of that man he tucks into his pocket (his ELIXIR). More valuable than the vast accumulation of wealth stored in Xanadu, is the one ELIXIR that can't be bought, Kane's innocence and an unconditional love between a child and parent symbolized by "Rosebud." Tragically, this ELIXIR is lost forever. The word fades with his final breath of life, the snow globe shatters, and his most important possession, "Rosebud," is discarded into the furnace. The smoke dissipates into the night sky.

FADE OUT

The Journey:
A man uses his power and money to buy love on his own terms and loses everything.

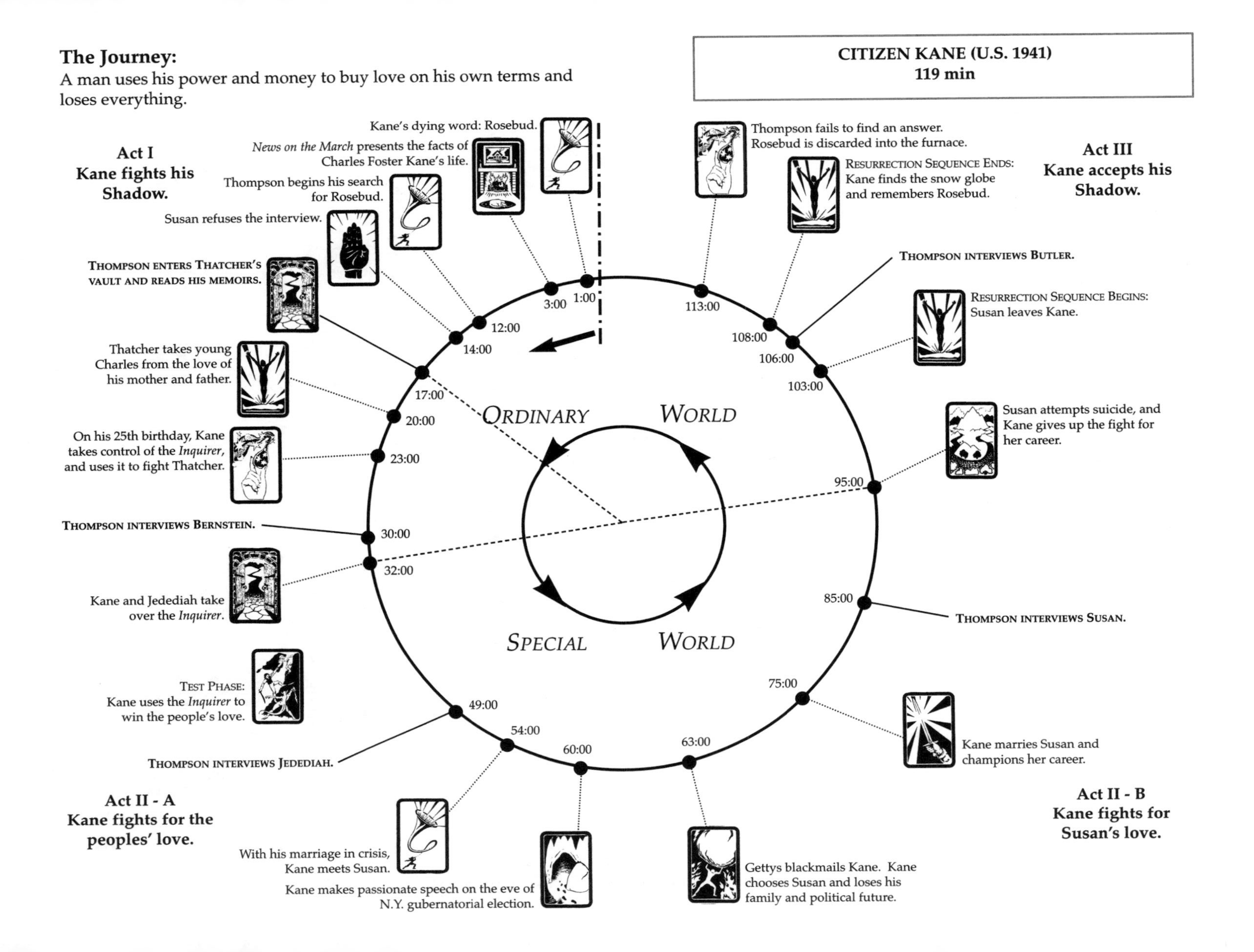

ALL ABOUT EVE
(U.S., 1950)

> *"So many people—know me. I wish I did. I wish someone would tell me about me."*
>
> —Margo Channing (Bette Davis)

Screenplay by Joseph L. Mankiewicz
Based on the story "The Wisdom of Eve" by Mary Orr
Directed by Joseph L. Mankiewicz

A young woman ingratiates herself with a successful actress in order to take her "throne" as the toast of the theatre world.

LANDMARKS OF THE JOURNEY

This witty, cynical, backstage look at the theatre presents a universal theme about the masks we wear to survive and how our most difficult role may be the one without any mask at all. Like the characters, we immediately fall under Eve Harrington's spell. We sympathize with this "lost lamb's" need for a Mentor, and initially dislike the star actress Margo's paranoia-fueled theatrics. But Mankiewicz beautifully turns the tables on our sympathies. We begin to prefer Margo's shoes, and like Margo, see Eve's cutthroat manipulations behind her Shapeshifter's mask. Eve's journey is focused upon the overthrow of Margo's position in the theatre world and everything that comes with it. Eve wants the audience applause ("the waves of love"), the critics' praise, the playwright's coveted roles, all symbolized by the Sarah Siddons Award that frames the Journey. She wants a world that's all about Eve.

What about Margo? Eve's journey forces Margo to face her greatest fears. At the age of 40, Margo sees the end of her acting career. But accepting a new life without acting means relinquishing the many masks of her roles, and most importantly her public persona; and it means agreeing to play her greatest and most challenging role—her self. Even more frightening is the question of how others, especially her director fiancé, accept her in this new "role." Margo's acceptance of this personal journey grants the greatest Elixir of the movie.

Eve accepts her Elixir, the Award, only to forget it in the taxicab. This empty Elixir puts her in the position of her Mentor at the Journey's beginning—with her eyes in the mirror on the look-out for her Rivals "snappin' at her rear end."

THE JOURNEY

The cynical, merciless critic, Addison deWitt, whose "native habitat is the theatre," welcomes us into this Journey of backstage rivalry. As critic and commentator, deWitt's a

SHAPESHIFTER who with the power of his pen can wear the mask of MENTOR, THRESHOLD GUARDIAN, or SHADOW. He can create or destroy a career, yet he's "an essential" of the ORDINARY WORLD of the theatre. He introduces our main characters as Eve Harrington receives the Sarah Siddons Award, the youngest actress ever to receive this distinguished honor. Eve's dream has come true (an ELIXIR), but at what cost? That's the tale to be told.

Karen Richards transports us back several months to the Journey's beginning. The wife of playwright Lloyd Richards and best friend of actress Margo Channing, Karen sets the Journey in motion. She arrives at the theatre after Margo's performance, surprised not to see Eve, a waif who has hung outside the stage door for six nights a week, weeks on end. This CALL TO ADVENTURE stirs Karen. Eve appears from the shadows and charms this THRESHOLD GUARDIAN with her devotion to Margo's work. Karen eagerly invites her backstage to meet her MENTOR face to face. Although at first RELUCTANT to see a star-struck fan, Margo is moved by Eve's tragic tale of her ORDINARY WORLD as a war widow and the solace she found in Margo's performance. Margo invites Eve to accompany her to the airport to see her boyfriend and director, Bill, off to Hollywood.

At the airport, Eve begins to push her way into Margo's ORDINARY WORLD. She graciously offers to check in for Bill. Faced with the CRISIS OF THE HEART of seeing her boyfriend leave for Hollywood for a job, Margo expresses her INNER PROBLEM. She fears Bill will leave her for a younger woman. Bill assures Margo of his love, but Eve interrupts their kiss. This subtle CALL OF ADVENTURE expresses Eve's INNER PROBLEM to take everything Margo has, including Bill. As Bill boards his plane, he tells Eve to take care of Margo. Margo accepts this MENTOR'S advice; she hires Eve as her assistant, CROSSING THE THRESHOLD.

At first Margo enjoys the TEST PHASE of this SPECIAL WORLD. Eve takes care of everything, quickly becoming Margo's closest ALLY. But Margo soon realizes that this ALLY is a RIVAL and SHADOW waiting in the wings. A SUCCESSION OF CALLS raises Margo's suspicion and paranoia:

- Margo discovers Eve holding Margo's costume and practicing her bows to an empty theatre.
- Margo receives Bill's unexpected phone call in the middle of the night. Eve neglected to tell Margo that she had set up the call for Margo to wish him a happy birthday.
- During this phone conversation, Bill mentions his welcome home party that Eve has been planning (again without Margo's knowledge.)
- Margo's oldest companion, Birdie (MENTOR), warns Margo that Eve is studying her every move.

Margo asks Eve about the phone call and Eve confesses that she'd never be forgiven if she had forgotten Bill's birthday (Margo in fact forgot it!). And Eve mentions that she herself sent a personal telegram to Bill. This disclosure is the final warning that pushes Margo THROUGH THE THRESHOLD of a darker SPECIAL WORLD of suspicion and jealousy. Her Journey is now fueled by her need to reveal Eve and reclaim her ORDINARY WORLD. But during Bill's welcome home party, we see that Eve has already effectively worked her powers on the other members of Margo's world, making Margo look jealous and paranoid without foundation. And Eve's CALLS have surfaced Margo's greatest fear, her insecurity with her age. Drunk and morose, Margo loses all sympathy, and begins to destroy her relationships with Bill, Lloyd and Karen.

Bill's party does provide the opportune TEST PHASE for both Margo and Eve to push their Journeys forward. Margo convinces her producer (ALLY), Max Fabian, to give Eve a job in his office; in return she promises to help audition a young actress, Miss Caswell. Meanwhile, Eve gets Karen (ALLY) to ask Max to hire Eve as Margo's new understudy. Although Karen reminds Eve that Margo never misses a performance, she is so taken by Eve that she'll do anything to help her out.

Margo arrives late for Miss Caswell's audition. Critic Addison deWitt stops her before she enters the theatre, lavishing praise of the "fire and music" of Eve's performance as Margo's new understudy. Margo never knew of Eve's new job, but now armed with this knowledge and taking a lesson from her RIVAL, Margo dons a SHAPESHIFTER'S mask to see how Eve's performance has charged playwright Lloyd and director Bill, an APPROACH TO THE INMOST CAVE. But Lloyd sees through Margo's mask, and refuses to let Margo's accusations spoil the ELIXIR of Eve's inspiring performance. Possessed by jealousy, Margo insults Lloyd and finally pushes Bill out of her life, a CRISIS OF THE HEART. Eve has shattered Margo's world, an ORDEAL, forcing Margo to accept her need to move on.

When Karen hears of Margo's ravings, she wants to give Margo the "boot in the rear" she deserves, and calls Eve with a plan (an APPROACH TO THE INMOST CAVE).

Karen and Lloyd spend a weekend with Margo. But on the trip home, Karen ensures that they run out of gas, making Margo miss her performance (the second stage of Margo's ORDEAL). However, Karen never anticipates how easily Margo will accept this ORDEAL, or her revelatory change of heart (a RESURRECTION). Margo apologizes for her bad behavior, and she admits that—as she APPROACHES her need to change, and accept her new role as woman—she fears that she doesn't know the woman beneath the role of Margo Channing. And if she doesn't know her, how can she expect Bill to know her?

Meanwhile, Eve experiences her own ORDEAL and RESURRECTION. Having to fill in for Margo, Eve performs superbly. But Eve had prepared for this ORDEAL, inviting all of the powerful critics, including Addison deWitt. Now that Eve has replaced Margo onstage, she tries to take Margo's place in Bill's heart. But Bill soundly rejects her; he still loves Margo. Now Bill knows that Margo's jealousy was not unfounded, a REWARD.

DeWitt lifts Eve up from her CRISIS OF THE HEART and takes charge of her career, writing a column that makes Eve a star (a REWARD) and damages Margo's career. However, deWitt's "poison pen" brings Bill back to Margo (a REWARD).

Karen and Lloyd are invited out by Margo and Bill to celebrate the RESURRECTION of their relationship. Signaling the ROAD BACK, Bill officially announces their engagement and plans to marry as soon as possible. In the powder room, Eve blackmails Karen into letting her have the part of Cora in Lloyd's new play—a part written for Margo. And if Karen doesn't help her, Eve threatens to reveal Karen's role in making Margo miss her performance. Karen returns to the celebration prepared to end her best friend's acting career. Margo unexpectedly announces her retirement from acting. She is accepting her new role as woman and wife (her commitment to change), a REVERSAL that relieves Karen. However, Eve gets the role of a lifetime and her ROAD BACK.

The play's rehearsal makes Lloyd more vulnerable to Eve's lure. Eve prepares for the play's opening night of its preview run, a performance that is sure to reward her with everything she has wanted for her professional career. Eve has also won over Lloyd, who chooses to ruin his marriage for Eve. But Eve's MENTOR, deWitt, derails this personal Journey. DeWitt knows all of Eve's secrets, the lies of her fabricated ORDINARY WORLD as well as her schemes and manipulations. He rips the SHAPESHIFTER mask from her face and reveals her true scheming self. DeWitt holds the power to make or ruin her career and he's determined to use it. She belongs to no one but her SHADOW MENTOR. In a death-like state, Eve feels lost, unable to perform. But her SHADOW MENTOR demands that she give the performance of her life (her RESURRECTION). And she does, receiving the praise and admiration of the entire theatre world (an ELIXIR).

We return to Eve's acceptance of the Sarah Siddons Award, her ELIXIR. She thanks her friends, Margo, Karen, Bill and Lloyd; but now that we have seen her Journey, we sense her hollow praise and see its acknowledgement on their faces.

Perhaps the ELIXIR of the award is not enough for Eve. She has become a young star, the toast of the theatre world. But at what cost? She has lost everything else, and now must live the life that Margo had—in the role of "Eve Harrington." Eve forgoes the producer's party honoring her victory, favoring the solitude of her apartment (and forgetting her ELIXIR in the cab!) A young fan, Phoebe, is waiting for her. A reflection of Eve at the beginning of the Journey, Phoebe quickly ingratiates herself with the star. DeWitt arrives to deliver Eve's award. He greets Phoebe and assures this aspiring actress that she's in the hands of the right MENTOR, for Eve can tell her everything about getting this award.

We close on Phoebe donning one of Eve's robes. She holds Eve's award (the ELIXIR) and admires herself in a mirror. We see the many reflections of Phoebe. This cycle will not end.

FADE OUT

THE GODFATHER
(U.S., 1972)

"That's my family, Kay. It's not me."

—Michael Corleone (Al Pacino)

Screenplay by Francis Ford Coppola and Mario Puzo
Based upon the novel by Mario Puzo
Directed by Francis Ford Coppola

The violence of his family's business forces a young man to accept his bloody legacy and ascend his father's "throne" as Godfather.

LANDMARKS OF THE JOURNEY

To refer to *The Godfather* only as a crime film does injustice to the power and depth of Coppola and Puzo's script. *The Godfather* is Michael Corleone's rite of passage, and a journey about family, loyalty and trust. Michael rebels against the violence that his family's business represents; yet Michael experiences several "baptisms of blood" that push him to accept his legacy and transform him into the Shadow he soundly denounces in his Ordinary World. The blood of his father initiates his Threshold. He spills blood by his own hand (the Ordeal) when he kills Sollozzo and McCluskey in the Italian restaurant. The brutal slaying of his brother and misfortunate killing of Michael's Italian wife signal Michael's return to New York and his position at his father's side. Finally, the powerful "baptism massacre" completes his Resurrection as Godfather.

Although Ordeals abound along Michael's Journey, the most important stage is the Ordinary World. While crime or mob films may begin with a killing, Coppola and Puzo invite us to a wedding. We enter the Corleones' world and meet the people and relationships during a time of celebration. The traditions of the Sicilian wedding allow us also to see the family business and its patriarch Mentor Don Vito Corleone at work. Most importantly, the Ordinary World is essential for us to accept the Corleones before Michael must. We must be able to relate to Michael. And what better way than to relate to the world he is about to enter?

THE JOURNEY

1945. New York. Don Vito Corleone, Godfather, heads one of five crime families controlling New York City. Corleone is a powerful crime boss and a man of integrity who values family and loyalty above all else. As Michael states: "Don't ever take sides against the family."

The ORDINARY WORLD of the Corleone family is shown in two distinct stages:

1. The power of family, shown at the wedding celebration of Michael's sister, Connie.
2. The power beneath the family, shown by Tom Hagen delivering the Godfather's "offer" to film producer Jack Woltz.

What better event to invite us into the ORDINARY WORLD of the Corleone family than a wedding, symbolizing a THRESHOLD of new beginnings, love, and family commitment. The significance of this event allows the audience to also see the influence and respect of the Godfather, Don Vito Corleone, and the power he holds. As his daughter Connie celebrates her lavish nuptials, Don Vito holds court in his study. No Sicilian can refuse a request on the day of his daughter's wedding. He receives his family ALLIES, accepts their blessings and weighs their requests for revenge.

Michael Corleone arrives with his girlfriend, Kay. A World War II hero and Vito's youngest and favorite son, Michael rebels against the family business, shown even by his choice of a WASP girlfriend. As Michael and Kay watch Luca Brasi practice his blessing to Don Vito, Michael introduces Kay to the traditions of the family business, and the power of his father. Michael also flatly REFUSES his allegiance to this power: "That's not me." Michael's INNER PROBLEM to rebel will be tested as the violence of his family's world strikes close to home, namely his SHADOW and father, Don Vito.

The Second Stage of the ORDINARY WORLD illustrates the violence and power held by Don Vito Corleone and adamantly shunned by Michael. Tom Hagen, representing Don Vito, negotiates with movie producer Jack Woltz to secure a coveted film role for family friend, Johnny Fontane. When Woltz refuses Don Vito's initial offer, he awakens in bed with the head of his prized stud horse.

But the Corleones' ORDINARY WORLD is changing. Don Vito is losing power within the larger structure of the five crime families. A power base supported by unions and gambling may be antiquated; the future is narcotics. Despite the support of Tom Hagen and oldest son, Sonny, Don Vito REFUSES to play a part in the growing narcotics business. The HERALD of this plan, Sollozzo, represents the Tattaglias, a RIVAL crime family. During the meeting with Sollozzo, when Sonny exposes his support of the drug venture, Don Vito anticipates revenge from the Tattaglias to divide the family. Don Vito sends his top hit man, Luca Brasi (ALLY/THRESHOLD GUARDIAN), to spy on Sollozzo and the Tattaglias. Sollozzo sees through the ruse and retaliates. Sollozzo kills Brasi and kidnaps Tom Hagen. Finally, Don Vito is shot down in front of a fruit stand. Sollozzo muscles Tom to convince Corleone's sons to accept the drug deal. But with Don Vito in the hospital at the brink of death, Sonny wants war.

Michael sees the headlines of his father's assassination attempt. This SUCCESSION OF CALLS initiates Michael's entrance into the SPECIAL WORLD of the family business that he REFUSED with such conviction. Michael abruptly ends dinner with Kay to go see his father in the hospital. He pushes Kay to return to New Hampshire; the ORDEAL suffered by his father makes Michael choose the HIGHER CAUSE of family over his rebellion and his life with Kay.

Michael CROSSES THE THRESHOLD when he finds the hospital oddly abandoned, and his father vulnerable to another mob hit. Michael saves his father, wheeling his bed into another room. Alone, he tells Don Vito, "I'm with you," assuring his former SHADOW, now father MENTOR, that he is committed to the protection of his family and all that it represents. He shows his commitment on the steps of the hospital. He enlists Enzo the baker (ALLY), and the two wear the "skin" of THRESHOLD GUARDIANS to trick a carload of hit men.

The police arrive, but this ORDEAL as THRESHOLD has given Michael the insight (a REWARD) to reveal the treachery beneath the SHAPESHIFTER mask worn by Police Captain McCluskey. Michael accuses him of working for Sollozzo. The Captain strikes Michael down, but Hagen's men arrive to protect Don Vito and take Michael home.

This THRESHOLD and his confrontation with McCluskey push Michael to accept an ORDEAL: he will be the HERALD of violence. Sollozzo wants to meet with Michael to negotiate a truce. Michael agrees, intending to use this meeting to murder Sollozzo and McCluskey. Sonny chides Michael's need for personal revenge; he wants to protect Michael from this world. But Michael's conviction is set; this isn't personal, it's strictly business.

The APPROACH must be made with great security. Sonny won't leave Michael's fate to chance. They use their network of informants (ALLIES) to find out the location for the "public" meeting and plant Michael's murder weapon in the restaurant's bathroom. During the fated dinner, Michael excuses himself to the men's room and retrieves the gun. He nervously smoothes his hair into place (the only show of fear, a type of REFUSAL), returns and coldly shoots Sollozzo and McCluskey. Michael remembers the lessons of MENTOR Clemenza, dropping the gun and walking out of the restaurant, a RESURRECTION that completes this ORDEAL.

Michael's action is a CALL that ushers further gang violence. But Michael's ORDEAL gives the Corleones the REWARD of Don Vito's safe return from the hospital. This TEST PHASE forces Michael to seek exile in Sicily until his safe return can be assured. Protected by bodyguards, Michael sets off on a pilgrimage to Corleone, his father's birthplace. He reclaims his Italian heritage and symbolically reconciles with his father, REWARDS. He also seizes the REWARD of love, marrying Apollonia.

Meanwhile, back in New York, Sonny humiliates Connie's husband, Carlo. Carlo retaliates. Working for family RIVAL Barzini, Carlo sets up Sonny's horrible death at a toll station.

Anxious to return home with his new bride, Michael receives word of his brother's death. But his ENEMIES at home finally reach Michael. He's double-crossed by a bodyguard (a SHAPESHIFTER working for the ENEMY). Apollonia dies in an explosion meant for Michael. This ORDEAL is Michael's FIRST ROAD BACK, pushing him out of exile and back to America.

With the death of heir apparent Sonny, and exile of Michael, Don Vito arranges a meeting of the crime families to stop the mob wars and ensure Michael's safe return. Don Vito agrees to allow drug trafficking, but warns revenge if Michael is harmed. Wearing his SHAPESHIFTER mask, Don Vito figures out that Barzini was behind Sonny's murder.

Michael returns to New York and sees Kay. Showing how far he has transformed, Michael confesses that he's working for his father now (a REVERSAL of who he was at the wedding). She can't understand why he now works for his SHADOW. But he insists that his family's methods of business have changed. Unlike at Connie's wedding, Michael is protecting the family business from her. He asks Kay to marry him. She REFUSES, but he sways her with his need for children—their children.

Michael takes over as head of the family for his father, but he must pass a series of TESTS to prove himself worthy of replacing Don Vito. During this TEST PHASE, Michael shows how much he has become like his father as he prepares for his final RESURRECTION. Michael plans to expand the gambling operations in Las Vegas, but casino owner Moe Greene refuses Michael's offer to buy out his share. Moe will soon regret his decision just as Jack Woltz did. Michael reprimands his brother, Fredo, for siding with Moe Greene. Don Vito served a similar warning to Sonny after their meeting with Sollozzo.

Impressed by Michael's commitment to his new role, Don Vito meets with his son. This important MEETING WITH HIS MENTOR prepares Michael for his SECOND ROAD BACK. The Don as HERALD / MENTOR twice warns Michael that a man "you absolutely trust" will guarantee safety at a meeting with Barzini. That man will be the traitor. The meeting will be Michael's assassination.

Don Vito dies of a heart attack. Michael must now run the family on his own. His father's warning comes to fruition at his funeral. Sal Tessio sets up a meeting between Michael and Barzini. Michael now knows that Tessio is the family traitor. Michael's SECOND ROAD BACK is set; he can now settle all family business, and be prepared to leave a road strewn with the bodies of his ENEMIES.

Michael's Journey ends in the powerful, cathartic baptism massacre. Brilliantly mirroring the wedding celebration of the ORDINARY WORLD, a family ceremony celebrates new beginnings, this time the baptism of Connie's son. But now Michael holds his father's strings of power, and uses this ceremony to take his father's throne. While the Church ordains Michael godfather of his nephew, Michael's ALLIES deliver his bloody revenge against his RIVALS. In striking contrast to his ORDEAL when he murdered

Sollozzo, Michael's bloodshed occurs by commandment alone. His baptism of blood continues after the ceremony, striking down the traitors to the family (his true SHADOWS): Tessio, and Connie's husband, Carlo.

In the final scene, we see how far Michael has transformed on his Journey. Michael lies to Connie about the circumstances of Carlo's death, but Kay demands the truth. Again, Michael denies the ELIXIR she seeks (the truth about his business). Assured for now, Kay watches as he's welcomed as Godfather, his RESURRECTION complete. He has taken his SHADOW'S title. Don Michael Corleone accepts this ELIXIR of power and family legacy, as the doors to his study close on Kay and the audience.

FADE OUT

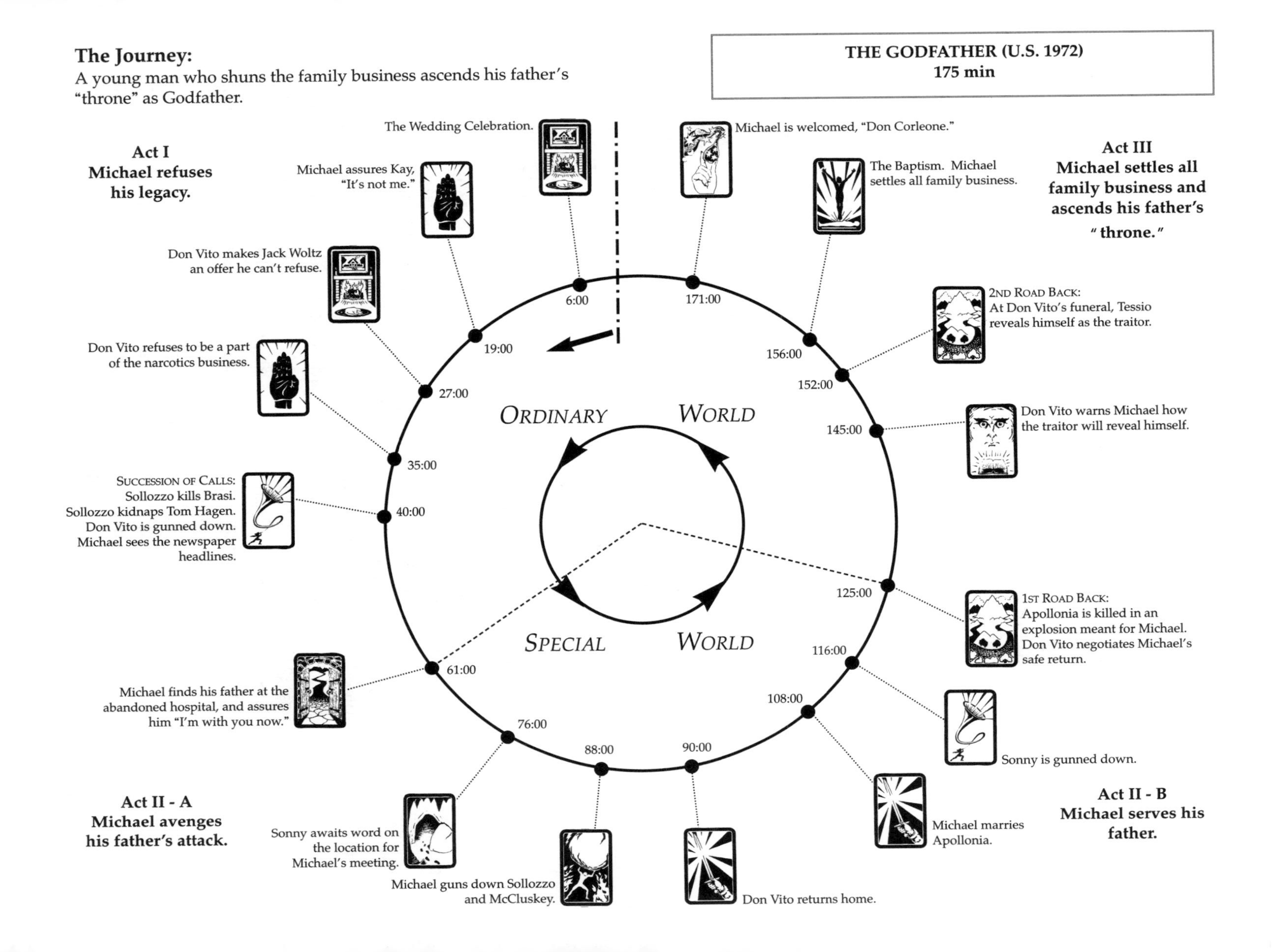

THE GODFATHER (U.S. 1972)
175 min
The Journey:
A young man who shuns the family business ascends his father's "throne" as Godfather.
Act I
Michael refuses his legacy.
The Wedding Celebration.
6:00
Michael assures Kay, "It's not me."
19:00
Don Vito makes Jack Woltz an offer he can't refuse.
27:00
Don Vito refuses to be a part of the narcotics business.
35:00
SUCCESSION OF CALLS: Sollozzo kills Brasi. Sollozzo kidnaps Tom Hagen. Don Vito is gunned down. Michael sees the newspaper headlines.
40:00
Michael finds his father at the abandoned hospital, and assures him "I'm with you now."
61:00
Act II - A
Michael avenges his father's attack.
Sonny awaits word on the location for Michael's meeting.
76:00
Michael guns down Sollozzo and McCluskey.
88:00
Don Vito returns home.
90:00
Michael marries Apollonia.
108:00
Sonny is gunned down.
116:00
Act II - B
Michael serves his father.
1ST ROAD BACK: Apollonia is killed in an explosion meant for Michael. Don Vito negotiates Michael's safe return.
125:00
Don Vito warns Michael how the traitor will reveal himself.
145:00
2ND ROAD BACK: At Don Vito's funeral, Tessio reveals himself as the traitor.
152:00
The Baptism. Michael settles all family business.
156:00
Michael is welcomed, "Don Corleone."
171:00
Act III
Michael settles all family business and ascends his father's "throne."
ORDINARY WORLD
SPECIAL WORLD

ORDINARY PEOPLE
(U.S., 1980)

"A little advice about feeling, kiddo. Don't expect it always to tickle."
—Berger (Judd Hirsch)

Screenplay by Alvin Sargent
Based on the novel by Judith Guest
Directed by Robert Redford

A guilt-ridden teen seeks guidance from a psychiatrist to help him learn to love and live.

LANDMARKS OF THE JOURNEY

The Jarretts have suffered the loss of their oldest son in a boating accident. Buck's death wounds the family as well as each member, but individual wounds must be acknowledged and healed before the family as a whole can heal. When the surviving son, Conrad, attempts suicide to escape his pain and guilt, his parents believe that his wounds alone prevent the family from healing. Beth and Calvin initially deny their wounds and responsibility in the healing process. No longer able to fit into this broken Ordinary World, Conrad accepts his Special World of therapy. But Conrad will never be able to create change and heal his wounds unless his Ordinary World can change as well. This establishes the beauty of Conrad's Journey, and our essential Dramatic Triangle. Conrad seeks a psychiatrist to help him transform and reclaim his Ordinary World. His mother, Beth, represents the Shadow refusing any more change in her life. Finally, Calvin serves as intermediary. He sees the rift between wife and son and must decide whether the responsibility of the family's survival lies solely in Conrad's hands.

The importance of the Test Phase stands out on Conrad's Journey. Many Journeys show the Hero separating from his Ordinary World for an extended period during which wounds can be healed and transformation made. By the Road Back, the Hero can finally recommit to change and return to the Ordinary World. In contrast, Conrad can separate from his troubled Ordinary World only during his two hours per week of therapy. Each session with his Mentor, Berger, challenges Conrad, releasing deeper emotions that Conrad immediately brings back to his Ordinary World. As Conrad attempts to change during the Test Phase, so must his Ordinary World deal with these changes, either embracing them or refusing them, creating obstacles that further Test Conrad's commitment to heal. Also note that the Mentor doesn't follow Conrad back into the Ordinary World except through his lessons and guidance; however, Berger's always there when Conrad needs him, especially at Conrad's Road Back when he learns of Karen's death. Now with a choice between suicide and Berger—Conrad is strong enough to turn away from his old ways and seek his Mentor's help for the final commitment to change.

THE JOURNEY

Conrad Jarrett survived a boating accident that killed his older brother, Buck. The weight of guilt pushes Conrad to slit his wrists. He survives the suicide attempt and spends several months in a psychiatric hospital. Now back with his parents, Conrad has made a pact with his father, Calvin, to seek the help of a psychiatrist if he continues to have problems. The month's up and the problems won't subside. Conrad can't fit back into his ORDINARY WORLD (his OUTER PROBLEM). He's plagued with nightmares of the boat accident; he can't sleep, has no appetite, and can't focus on classes. Conrad chooses to lock up his feelings rather than accept the pain that his ORDINARY WORLD causes (a REFUSAL of his INNER PROBLEM). He avoids his and Buck's old friends and teammates on the swim team. But a REFUSAL of his feelings also restricts his ability to love. Conrad is attracted to Jeannine, but will not act on his feelings.

Conrad's INNER STIRRING finally pushes him to call Dr. Berger. This MEETING WITH THE MENTOR is an uncomfortable time for Conrad that surfaces his fear of change (a REFUSAL). Conrad discusses the circumstances of his suicide attempt and confesses his need to get control (OUTER PROBLEM) but balks when Berger suggests they'll need to meet twice a week. This will eat into Conrad's swim practice (a REFUSAL). If Conrad wants to change, then he's going to have to show commitment, and his ORDINARY WORLD will have to wait for Conrad to heal. Conrad accepts Berger's terms but he needs the approval of several potential THRESHOLD GUARDIANS at home and school. Proud of Conrad's decision, Calvin pushes him to accept the Journey, while Beth shows her reserve. Conrad's unsympathetic Swim Coach demeans Conrad but lets him miss practice for therapy. Conrad finally passes THROUGH THE THRESHOLD into the SPECIAL WORLD of healing.

His greatest obstacle, a SHADOW in many ways, is his mother. Beth Jarrett fights to keep what remains of the ORDINARY WORLD intact. Buck was her favorite son, and her love was buried with Buck. Now she can't express love toward Conrad, let alone communicate with him. She denies that Conrad needs any outside help, and she'd never admit his therapy to anyone beyond the immediate family. Beth's uncompromising REFUSAL for any change in her world will be her downfall.

Having accepted his Journey, Conrad enters an important TEST PHASE structured by his therapy sessions with his MENTOR. Berger encourages Conrad to express feelings and emotions. These TESTS will promote phases of growth (REWARDS) that Conrad must bring back to his ORDINARY WORLD, where he (and his world) can enjoy/suffer the improvements/setbacks. As Conrad brings these changes into his ORDINARY WORLD, that world must accept his growth. The world may realize that it too needs to change (as demonstrated by Calvin's Journey). Or THRESHOLD GUARDIANS barring any change may be forced to leave (Conrad's swim coach, and finally Beth). Likewise the

TESTS of the ORDINARY WORLD can surface issues that are brought back into the therapy sessions.

During his first therapy session, Conrad's discomfort with his ORDINARY WORLD pushes him to consider quitting the swim team altogether; however, he fears how it will look to his friends and his mother (a type of REFUSAL). Berger wants Conrad to accept that he's a different person than last year. He also challenges Conrad to talk to people again. Talking with his friends is too painful, so Conrad chooses Karen, a fellow patient from the safer world of the hospital. Karen makes Conrad feel uncomfortable about his Journey of seeking therapy. But Conrad can see this THRESHOLD GUARDIAN'S REFUSAL to accept her own need to get better. Later, Conrad makes a stronger effort to communicate with his mother (a TEST). He brings up memories of Buck and the pigeon, but she won't enter that world. He's desperate to connect, but she refuses to open to him.

Conrad brings this frustration with his mother to his next therapy session, but he REFUSES to express his feelings. Berger encourages him to not hold back. With this "nudge" from his MENTOR, Conrad has the strength to quit the swim team (a TEST). He stands up to his coach, who tries to bully him with words. Conrad even defends his decision to best friend Lazenby, but Lazenby's inability to understand makes Conrad RELUCTANT to face the pain of telling his parents.

Berger now tries to push Conrad to APPROACH THE INMOST CAVE. Perhaps there's a connection between Conrad's need for control and his lack of feelings. Conrad tries to REFUSE this lesson, but the MENTOR prods Conrad until he finally explodes in anger. It's better to let the anger go than to keep it locked up. He brings this lesson back home. Conrad gets angry during the family's Thanksgiving photo session, shocking his ORDINARY WORLD.

Perhaps feeling doesn't always tickle, as his MENTOR suggests, but the ability to express anger opens up other feelings as well. Conrad follows the feelings of his heart and musters the courage to ask Jeannine out on a date. Crossing this THRESHOLD OF THE HEART, Conrad begins to feel good about himself.

Conrad's choice to protect his family from some of the changes he's made blows up in his face. While he and Calvin decorate the Christmas tree, Beth comes home upset and embarrassed that she heard Conrad had quit the swim team. Seeing her son's action as a personal attack, Beth matches Conrad's anger. He escapes upstairs to his room. Calvin has seen the changes in his son and now witnesses this ORDEAL. Against his wife's demands, he goes upstairs to satisfy his OUTER NEED to understand what is going on. His son insists that Beth hates him, but Calvin can't see this ELIXIR. This ORDEAL makes Calvin question the usefulness of Berger, but Conrad defends his MENTOR.

In his session with Berger, Conrad tries to repair his ORDINARY WORLD, defending Beth's hatred as a lack of forgiveness for the mess he made with his suicide attempt.

However, Conrad realizes that he's the one who can't forgive Beth for the limitations of her love. But Berger quickly checks Conrad's efforts to revert to his "ordinary self." Instead of blaming himself for being unlovable, Conrad must accept his need to forgive himself. The session ends and the MENTOR leaves the WOUNDED HERO in limbo. Forgive himself for what? The REWARD is within grasp.

Conrad's Journey begins to heal his ORDINARY WORLD (a REWARD). Calvin decides to meet with his son's MENTOR. He had hoped to satisfy his OUTER PROBLEM to help his family, but the MEETING surfaces an INNER NEED to talk about himself. He realizes that perhaps he needs to accept some change as well (a REWARD). He returns home hoping to share this MEETING with Beth, and begins to see the THRESHOLD GUARDIAN that prevents his son from growing and his family from healing. He wants the family to meet with Berger, but Beth REFUSES to be changed. Instead, she wants to take Calvin to Houston to enjoy New Year's Eve with her brother. This SHAPESHIFTER pushes to take her husband and herself away from Conrad's SPECIAL WORLD and his MENTOR'S influence.

Without the pressure of Beth's presence, Conrad can now face his most daring TESTS. Three events cause setbacks that finally push Conrad to accept his ROAD BACK of change.

During his date with Jeannine, he talks about the suicide for the first time. But when his moment of winning some understanding is shattered by a gang of intrusive boys, Conrad closes off his feelings and abandons his JOURNEY OF THE HEART.

After a swim meet, Conrad beats up a RIVAL for Jeannine. Lazenby pulls him from the fight. He wants to help Conrad, but Conrad closes off his friend. It hurts too much.

Returning home, Conrad calls Karen, but is shocked to learn of her suicide, initiating the ROAD BACK. Conrad rushes to his bathroom. This ORDEAL unleashes his memory of the boating accident, and the guilt, and the thoughts of suicide. But Conrad is much stronger than he was in his ORDINARY WORLD. He chooses life and rushes off into the night desperate to see his MENTOR.

Berger ushers him into his office. This MENTOR tries to catch up with the memories (a psychological CHASE). He sees Conrad reliving the accident and, using transference, Berger plays Buck, pushing Conrad to accept his RESURRECTION. Conrad forgives himself for having the strength to hang on to the boat—and for his anger toward his brother for not having that same strength. Conrad survives this ROAD BACK, guided by a good MENTOR and friend.

Conrad quickly shares the ELIXIR of his growth with Jeannine. He apologizes for the way he treated her on the date, and accepts her invitation to breakfast (a RESURRECTION of their relationship). His appetite for companionship and food has returned.

But he must bring this ELIXIR back to his parents. Beth and Calvin return from an emotional Houston trip. Conrad wishes them good night and hugs Beth. She cannot reciprocate. Calvin sees her reject the ELIXIR of their son's transformation. Perhaps she doesn't hate Conrad, as his son believed, but she cannot return his love.

Late that night, Beth finds Calvin weeping at the dining table. He realizes that the Beth who loved him was buried with their son. And now he's afraid that he doesn't love her anymore. Beth cannot respond to his RESURRECTION. Alone in her bedroom, Beth finally breaks down and cries. She must accept the pain and destruction of her ORDINARY WORLD and has no choice but to leave.

Beth's taxi awakens Conrad. He sees his father and immediately blames himself for his mother's departure, but Calvin REFUSES to hear it. Conrad welcomes this strong MENTOR, and the two share the RESURRECTION of father and son, and the ELIXIR of their love.

FADE OUT

BOYZ N THE HOOD
(U.S., 1991)

"You may think I'm being hard on you right now, but I'm not. What I'm doing is I'm trying to teach you responsibility. Like you know your friends across the street. They don't have anybody to show them how to do that. They don't. And you'll see how they end up, too."

—Furious Styles (Larry Fishburne)

Written and Directed by John Singleton

A young black man moves in with his father to learn how to survive in the violent world of South Central L.A.

LANDMARKS OF THE JOURNEY

Our parents are our most important Mentors. Furious Styles, the father of our Hero, Tre, is an actualized Hero. He's traveled the road of the young Black male, lured by Calls of violence, drugs, and crime. Yet Furious dedicates himself to earn the respect of his son. And now that his son is reaching the Threshold of manhood, Furious must prepare him for the violent world of Black urban America, where one in 21 black American males die, many at the hands of other young Black men. Mentors of these young men have fallen, and their sons suffer. One young man, Doughboy, lives the violent Shadow of Furious' lessons. Volatile and hotheaded, Doughboy has chosen the road of drugs and booze that has landed him in and out of jail. An important Elixir of Tre's transformation is that he can share his father's lessons with his friends by the example of his behavior, dress, language and actions in the Special World. Tre serves as a Mentor for Doughboy, but he is not above the seductions of Doughboy's violent code. In the end, Tre heeds his Mentor's lessons and rejects the violent path. Unfortunately, the stubborn Doughboy learns his lesson too late.

THE JOURNEY

Tre Styles' Journey begins in 1984. South Central L.A. An ORDINARY WORLD of gangs and drugs. Gunshots, police sirens, helicopters fill the night. This violent ORDINARY WORLD extends beyond the bullet-riddled and bloodstained alleys, into Tre's elementary school, where it is reflected in the children's drawings and Tre's interactions with other kids. When Tre is sent home after fighting with another boy (a CALL TO ADVENTURE), his mother, a single parent, realizes that Tre is approaching the THRESHOLD of manhood. He needs the guidance that his father can provide to overcome his violent ways and prepare for that SPECIAL WORLD.

His father, Furious Styles, welcomes his "prince." And Tre is eager to revisit with his old friends, especially Doughboy and Ricky, half-brothers living across the street. But Tre must also accept his MENTOR'S strict rules that will prepare him for his SPECIAL WORLD of manhood. Tre may grimace at the chores (a REFUSAL to change) and prefer to play with his friends, but he accepts this new path of learning responsibility. And his MENTOR assures Tre that he has the advantage of a father who can teach him. His friends don't. Furious warns Tre that he will see the difference at Journey's end.

One night, Furious teaches Tre the power of non-violence. He scares a house intruder away and cautions Tre not to contribute to the killing of a brother, a REFUSAL to the CALL OF VIOLENCE. Furious also stands up to a pair of cops (THRESHOLD GUARDIANS), apathetic to the war of survival being fought in the neighborhood.

While this series of MEETINGS WITH HIS MENTOR prepares Tre for the Journey of non-violence and respect, Ricky and Doughboy seek different roads to deal with their world. Ricky sees his future in football. Doughboy slacks off, refusing to see anything beyond his violent world.

During a father and son fishing trip, Furious reveals his own experiences as a young man CROSSING THE THRESHOLD of manhood and how he REFUSED the DARK CALLS of crime and booze, and accepted his Journey of responsibility for his future son. They return home from this important MEETING WITH THE MENTOR, and see the police hauling Doughboy away. Furious places a hand on his son's shoulder and leads him into the house. Equipped with the lessons of his MENTOR and this sight of his friend suffering for his acceptance of the SHADOW OF VIOLENCE, Tre CROSSES THE THRESHOLD, completing his preparations for being a young Black man.

Seven years pass and we see how the THRESHOLD has affected Tre and his friends. Tre has grown into a polite, respectful and well-groomed young man. Having mastered some of his father's lessons, Tre has assumed the role of MENTOR to his peers. At a barbecue welcoming Doughboy back from yet another stint in jail, Doughboy's mother asks Tre to help keep her son from his violent ways. But passing the THRESHOLD doesn't guarantee Tre's transformation will hold. He must continue to apply his MENTOR'S lessons as he confronts the TESTS, ALLIES AND ENEMIES of the SPECIAL WORLD. He saves a toddler, neglected by her crack-addict mother. He stands up to a carload of his "brothers" threatening him with a shotgun. Tre passes this TEST, but these ENEMIES will resurface later with a greater ORDEAL.

His JOURNEY OF LOVE presents his most difficult TEST. His sexual urges conflict with his greatest fear of being a responsible father. Tre pressures Brandi for a physical relationship but he tries to respect her desire to wait.

The TEST PHASE also shows how Tre, Doughboy and Ricky deal with their violent SPECIAL WORLDS. Tre feels the growing pressure of his violent world, the gunfire and helicopters outside as well as his parents' phone argument inside. He must leave this world (INNER PROBLEM), or shut it out. Doughboy turns to violence to combat violence. Ricky focuses on football as his ticket out, and he has everything going for him—except a football scholarship at USC. He needs a 700 on his SATs, his OUTER PROBLEM. Both Ricky and Tre accept this TEST as their way to get into college and move on. Doughboy won't even deal with it.

After taking the SATs, Tre takes Ricky to his father who shows them the poorer neighborhood. He shows them how Blacks are being pushed into their world of violence and destruction. This MENTOR encourages them to focus on responsibility and take command of their futures, APPROACH THE INMOST CAVE.

Hanging out that night with their friends, Tre and Ricky meet up with Doughboy. Ricky is bumped by another Black youth, Rock, and the two exchange words, an ORDEAL. Doughboy defends his brother, waving his handgun, forcing the ENEMIES to back off. Rock responds to Doughboy's display of violence by unloading his automatic rifle into the air, dispersing the crowd. Ricky and Tre flee the scene but they can't escape the ORDEAL. A pair of cops stops them and threatens Tre with a gun before finally letting them go. This ORDEAL is too much for Tre. He sees Brandi and at last the pressure blows and he lets out his hostility and frustration, his INNER SHADOW of violence. His outburst shocks Brandi. At last purged of the violence within (a RESURRECTION of his ORDEAL), Tre clutches his love. Soon the two make love, the REWARD.

Rock and his gang scout out Doughboy and Ricky's home. Doughboy stands defiant and the ENEMY speeds off—for now. They wait for Ricky to take a trip to the grocery store and gun him down in an ally. This ORDEAL as ROAD BACK will finally question the strength of Tre's transformation. Having witnessed the merciless slaying of his friend, will Tre hang on to the values of non-violence taught by his father or succumb to the SHADOW of violence and revenge?

Tre and Doughboy take Ricky's body back home. The sight of the pain inflicted upon Ricky's mother, girlfriend and his little boy, resurrects Tre's SHADOW of violence. He will now follow Doughboy's ROAD BACK to get revenge.

Furious returns home as Tre is loading his gun. The MENTOR of non-violence tries to derail this SHADOW'S Journey that has overcome Tre. Tre finally gives up the gun, a RESURRECTION, and goes to his room. Furious believes that the RESURRECTION is complete, and that Tre has finally mastered the MENTOR'S lessons. But Tre sneaks off and jumps into Doughboy's car and they speed off. His MENTOR of non-violence can only wait and worry for his son's life.

Tre rides along as Doughboy and his gang make their APPROACH, loading their guns, preparing for violence. The sight of the weapons and conviction for revenge make Tre realize he doesn't belong here; his MENTOR'S lessons have defeated his SHADOW. He demands to be let out. He allows Doughboy and his ALLIES to follow their road of violence; Tre goes home, his RESURRECTION.

Doughboy and his gang get their violent revenge, but we can see that the bloodbath leaves a bitter taste in Doughboy's mouth. The following morning, Doughboy sees Tre. The act of revenge has made Doughboy aware of why Tre rejected the Journey of Violence, a RESURRECTION. Doughboy confesses his hope that he might have time to make the same transformation, but he fears someday he'll be "smoked." Unfortunately, Doughboy's RESURRECTION comes too late. We learn in the Epilogue that he is soon murdered. Tre has been RESURRECTED from this SPECIAL WORLD of violence, and he moves on to college, enjoying the ELIXIR of a future with his girlfriend.

FADE OUT

THE MYTHIC STRUCTURE OF ROMANCE

A chance encounter awakens our heart with a passion that crumbles mountains and brings countries to war. Although many obstacles will keep us from this Journey, refusing its Call can leave us broken and embittered. Love's Elixir can heal us with love's desire, or purify us with a greater understanding of our life's purpose—preparing us for the greatest act of love, to make the Noble Sacrifice and set our love free for the sake of a Higher Cause.

"KISS ME. KISS ME AS IF IT WERE THE LAST TIME."

Romance transcends all genres; yet, the grand passion of love fuels our most memorable films, making Romance deserving of its own genre. These Journeys explore the forces of the heart that sweep our Heroes into a Special World with a power that surmounts obstacles of time, culture, class, and even death. Although we may find *some* comedy in this section, we will explore Romantic Comedy in its own chapter. Here, we explore the serious, and oftentimes tragic, side of Romance.

The most enduring and affecting love stories end with the lovers apart, defying the Hollywood happy ending. Romeo doesn't live happily ever after with Juliet. And what about Rhett and Scarlett? Even the great Kong sacrifices himself for his beauty. The most beloved American movie ends with Bogie making the ultimate sacrifice and sending Bergman on the plane with her husband.

The Romances explored here are not necessarily Boy meets Girl, Boy loses Girl, Boy wins Girl back; however, like its comedic cousin, Romance is rooted in the battle of the sexes. Love blossoms out of hostility, a wonderful paradox illustrating Romance's defiance of logic and reason. In Romantic Comedy, lovers' conflicts makes us laugh. In Romance, they may break our heart.

THE ROOT OF ROMANCE: FORBIDDEN LOVE

Rick and Ilsa find their perfect love in Paris. Although married, Ilsa believes her husband has been killed in a concentration camp. Upon news that he is still alive, she abandons Rick. But their paths cross again in Casablanca.

A Prince is cursed and transformed into a hideous Beast. He must learn to love and earn love in return. But who could ever love a Beast? Certainly not the most beautiful girl in the land.

To earn back her piano, a mute woman makes a deal that opens the doors to her passion. Will she explore these passions, or honor her husband and a marriage that suffocates her?

This is forbidden love, dangerous love, and the foundation of many of our most memorable romances. Forbidden love arises from differences between the lovers, including conflicts of class and culture (*Titanic*), race (*Jungle Fever*), gender (*The Crying Game*). An unmarried man has an affair with a married woman (*Casablanca, The Piano*). A beautiful girl falls in love with a hideous beast (*Beauty and the Beast*).

Forbidden love involves great risks, conquering enormous obstacles, and yet even when this love goes against the grain of our morality, as in the case of adultery, we identify with and long for its consummation. This forbidden love could be the greatest love of the Heroes' lives (*Casablanca*). Or it could actually be the purest of all loves, the only Elixir that can break a curse (*Beauty and the Beast*) or heal a wounded Hero (*La Strada, The Piano*).

THE JOURNEYS OF THE HEART

The Romance can be broken down into three basic story patterns:

1. Two people love each other and neither realizes it (*Beauty and the Beast*). On many of these journeys, love is not the goal but the Reward for overcoming physical Tests and Ordeals along their Journey together (*The African Queen*).
2. Two people are in love and one doesn't realize it. Their Journey may focus on warming one's cold, unresponsive heart with love's fire (*The Piano*). We may see a Tragic Hero who never acknowledges love until it is too late (*La Strada*).
3. Two people realize their love, but their passion is denied by some great obstacle such as a Rival (*Titanic*), a Higher Cause of patriotism (*Casablanca*), world events (*Doctor Zhivago*), or even death (*Ghost*).

THE ROMANCE TRIANGLE

The Rival proves an effective obstacle in many romances. The Rival's presence creates a Romance Triangle where two vow for the same heart, thus opening the arena of personal conflict. Within this Triangle, lovers and rivals can become Shapeshifters to deceive, betray and hide their heart's true path. A spurned Rival will seek revenge. And in the end the Hero must confront the Rival and rescue his or her true love.

The Rival may not be a person but a Higher Cause that pulls the Hero away from the Journey of the Heart, and forces the Hero to make the Noble Sacrifice choosing between the Cause and Love. The Higher Cause can be patriotism (*The African Queen, Casablanca*), self-discovery and wholeness (*The Piano*), redemption (*Casablanca*), or the safety of a loved one (*Beauty and the Beast*). The Higher Cause could be love itself or the ability to show love (*La Strada*).

THE NOBLE SACRIFICE

In *Casablanca,* Rick Blaine must choose between love and patriotic duty; there is no middle ground. He must make the Noble Sacrifice, and ensure that Ilsa boards that plane with her husband. His sacrifice is the greatest act of love, representing a love so powerful and intense that it cannot be fulfilled except in their memories of Paris.

A Hero or Antihero makes this sacrifice to resurrect or purify himself to heroic status. And the Romance Audience relishes the catharsis erupting from this selfless act. Seeing Rick become a Noble Hero, and find the strength to sacrifice his love for country, makes us more fulfilled.

This Noble Sacrifice may in fact bring our lovers together in the end. Following the Higher Cause may yield the Elixir of pure love (*The African Queen*), or the Higher Cause may be love itself (*Beauty and the Beast*). In *The Piano,* the Elixir of love heals Ada, giving her the strength to sacrifice the piano that had previously been her only means of speaking her passions. These Journeys of the Heart yield a happy ending, but the tale can quickly turn tragic if the Hero cannot make the sacrifice or refuses to recognize the Higher Cause of Love (*La Strada*).

ORDEALS, THRESHOLDS AND THE CRISIS OF THE HEART

Romance stories generally weave two journeys: (a) the Journey of the Heart, and (b) the Journey of the Higher Cause. How these two journeys weave and interplay can be important in the overall structure of the Romance story. The Ordeal of one Journey can be the Threshold of the second. Facing the Ordeal of the Journey of the Higher Cause can make the lovers realize their love for each other, the Crisis of the Heart, consequently forcing them through the Threshold of their Journey of the Heart. As examples, let's look at three films:

1) *Casablanca.* Rick and Ilsa's love is the Journey of the Heart. The Journey of the Higher Cause is Ilsa and Laszlo's need to obtain exit visas so Laszlo can continue his work for the Resistance. Ilsa begs Rick for the exit visas and finally threatens to kill him, the Ordeal. But she can't. This Crisis of the Heart forces her to admit her undying love for Rick, pushing them through the Threshold of the Heart.

2) *The African Queen.* Rose and Charlie's Journey to sink the Louisa (the Higher Cause) propels the story. Surviving the series of Ordeals, especially the final rapids (the Crisis of the Heart) resurrects their love and pushes them through the Threshold of their Journey of the Heart.
3) *The Piano.* The Journey of the Higher Cause (to earn back the piano) transforms into Ada and Baine's Journey of the Heart. Baines calls off the bargain and returns the piano, forcing Ada to realize that she is in love with him (the Crisis of the Heart), committing herself to their Journey of the Heart.

THE IMPORTANCE OF THE SHAPESHIFTER

The Shapeshifter is a key archetype encountered along the Journey of the Heart. It's human nature to veil one's desires, to protect oneself or the object of love from the pain of rejection. A Romantic Hero may don the Shapeshifter's mask early in the Journey, especially to refuse the temptation of Forbidden Love. A Shapeshifter's hideous looks and beastly behavior may push away any potential suitor (*Beauty and the Beast, La Strada*). The Shapeshifter may be more subtle. Ada allows her husband to take her hand, sending a message of Refusal to Baines and his Call of Forbidden Love (*The Piano*).

But the Shapeshifter's mask can be worn for only so long. The Hero must finally cast aside the mask and confess his or her love. This could occur spontaneously after cheating death (*The African Queen*). Or the mask may fall when faced with the loss of the loved one (*Beauty and the Beast, Casablanca, La Strada*). The Romantic Hero may boldly cast aside the Shapeshifter's mask when the Journey at hand conflicts with the longings of the heart (*The Piano*).

THE SHADOW OF ROMANCE

Like Shapeshifters, Shadows can be elusive, shifting masks that veil hidden agendas and locked passions. Many characters can wear the Shadow's mask: the spurned lover, the challenged Rival, the wounded Hero. In the Romance Triangle, the Shadow's mask can quickly shift or slip from one character to the next as hidden passions come to light (*Casablanca, The Piano*).

Since much of Romance depends upon character contrast to fuel conflict and love, the Heroes of Romance may be Shadows of one another. An example is the beautiful positive Belle and the hideous hopeless Beast of *Beauty and the Beast.* The audience welcomes this "Journey of Opposites" in anticipation that, by Journey's end, the lovers will accept their unyielding love for one another.

GENRE CHALLENGES: ROMANCE

1. *La Strada* has been analyzed as Gelsomina's Journey. Look at the story through the eyes of Zampano. What stages of the Hero's Journey are present during his Journey? Who is his Mentor? Who is his Shadow? In what ways do we identify with Zampano?
2. Who is the Shadow in *Beauty and the Beast*? Are there multiple Shadows? Does the Shadow shift from one character to another? When do these exchanges of the mask occur?
3. As a movie of interweaving journeys, *Casablanca* ultimately is Rick's Journey. At which key moments or stages do we see Rick playing a Reactive rather than Active Hero? Is there another Hero who takes control of the Journey at these moments? How do these moments reveal character and enrich Rick's Journey?
4. Looking at the Journeys of the three main characters in *The Piano*'s Romance Triangle (Ada, Stewart and Baines), what Noble Sacrifices are made? What do the characters gain or lose from these sacrifices?
5. How are the contrasting Ordinary Worlds of Rose and Charlie revealed in *The African Queen*? How do these contrasts create obstacles and promote conflict? How does opposition force Rose and Charlie to change?
6. In Romantic Comedy a best friend usually acts as a counselor or Mentor of Love who helps, sometimes actually pushing the Hero onto the Journey of the Heart. Looking at the Romance movies analyzed in this chapter, is there a similar Mentor of Love?
7. Select a movie with a strong love story from one of the other genres in this text. Using the Hero's Journey paradigm, analyze the Romantic Journey of your chosen film. What is the Call? The Threshold? The Approach? The Ordeal? Is there a Higher Cause? A Noble Sacrifice? A Crisis of the Heart? Suggested films: *The Fly* (Horror), *Die Hard* (Adventure), *High Noon* (Western), *Some Like It Hot* (Comedy), *The Empire Strikes Back* (Science Fiction/Fantasy), *They Were Expendable* (War), *Ordinary People* (Drama).

CASABLANCA
(U.S., 1942)

"Ilsa, I'm no good at being noble, but it doesn't take much to see that the problems of three little people don't amount to a hill of beans in this crazy world."
—Rick Blaine (Humphrey Bogart)

Directed by Michael Curtiz
Screenplay by Julius Epstein, Philip G. Epstein, and Howard Koch
Adapted from the play *Everybody Comes to Rick's* by Murray Burnett and Joan Alison

The painful past catches up with a cynical saloon-owner forcing him to choose between love and patriotic duty.

LANDMARKS OF THE JOURNEY

In *Casablanca* the Rival is both a person and a Higher Cause. Two "pasts" come back to haunt the Hero, Rick: a love relationship with Ilsa, and a life as a freedom fighter. It isn't enough that Ilsa is married. The fact that her husband is a legendary Hero who serves the Resistance against the Nazi Shadow fuels the conflict and enriches the Romance Triangle. Ilsa's arrival stirs Rick's heart; Laszlo's arrival rekindles Rick's freedom-fighting blood and Inner Need for redemption. Rick's Resurrection of heroism grants him the awareness that his former-Rival-now-Mentor, Laszlo, cannot continue his work without Ilsa at his side. Unlike many Romance Triangles where Rivals duke-it-out for a woman's heart, Rick sacrifices his love to follow his Rival's heroic path.

THE JOURNEY

1941. The Second World War. Casablanca has become a sanctuary for the influx of refugees fleeing the oppressive Nazi SHADOW overtaking Europe. The fortunate ones may use whatever means possible to obtain exit visas granting freedom to the New World. The remaining must wait out this unstable ORDINARY WORLD in Casablanca ... and wait and wait ...

A teletype report announces the murder of two German couriers and the theft of two letters of transit. This CALL disrupts the ORDINARY WORLD. Local police, led by Captain Louis Renault, "round up the usual suspects." The investigation proves fruitful, and Renault plans to honor the arrival of German Gestapo leader Major Strasser (SHADOW) with the arrest of the murderer at Rick's Cafe.

Run by world-weary Richard Blaine, Rick's Cafe Americain is one of Casablanca's favorite haunts, a physical THRESHOLD frequented by SHAPESHIFTERS and THRESHOLD GUARDIANS promising freedom. Rick's tough, cynical shell protects a broken heart, his INNER PROBLEM. An ex-patriate, this disillusioned ANTIHERO adamantly keeps neutral ground. Rick will stick his neck out for nobody. Yet he allows Ugarte, the murderer and black market agent (THRESHOLD GUARDIAN), to slip him the stolen visas for safekeeping, a CALL TO ADVENTURE.

Later, Renault prepares Rick for Ugarte's arrest and the arrival of Czechoslovakian Resistance leader, Victor Laszlo. This MENTOR of the Law warns Rick not to get involved in either man's plight (a REFUSAL).

Meanwhile, Victor Laszlo enters the cafe with his beautiful wife, Ilsa Lund. On the run from the Nazis, Laszlo has slipped into Rick's for sanctuary and to secure exit visas, his OUTER PROBLEM.

A SUCCESSION OF CALLS occurs, affecting the film's two major journeys:

1) A Resistance operative tells Laszlo that Ugarte has been arrested and the visas have disappeared (The Journey of the Higher Cause).
2) Ilsa discovers that the saloon-owner Rick is her former lover from Paris (The Journey of the Heart).

Ilsa asks the piano player, Sam, about Rick and pressures him to play "As Time Goes By." This HERALD reluctantly plays this Romance's most significant and memorable CALL TO ADVENTURE. The love song resurrects a wellspring of passion and memory in Ilsa and brings an angry Rick to the piano. The former lovers meet in stunned silence. Renault interrupts them and, to his surprise, Rick joins Ilsa and Laszlo for a drink. The stoic Rick compliments the freedom fighting work of HERO/MENTOR Laszlo while silently taking in the relationship of Laszlo and Ilsa. He REFUSES to show that he has been affected by Ilsa's arrival; however, we see the impact of this CALL later that night.

Rick confronts his GREATEST FEAR, that his past has caught up with him, and drinks in his darkened cafe. Although Sam tries to get him to REFUSE this THRESHOLD, Rick believes in his wounded heart that Ilsa will show up to see him. He tries to comprehend why she has walked back into his life and, most important, why she walked out of his heart in Paris, his INNER PROBLEM.

In flashback, Rick relives the ORDEAL/RESURRECTION of his Paris romance with Ilsa. Both had found the loves of their lives, but the outer forces of war interfered. Rick and Ilsa had planned their escape from the Germans, but she abandoned him at the train station. Rick's REWARD from this CRISIS OF THE HEART is his RESURRECTION into a cynical pacifist.

As Rick anticipated, Ilsa appears at the cafe. But painful memories and the alcohol unleash feelings of betrayal by this Shapeshifting Lover. Ilsa offers him an explanation for Paris. However, Rick turns caustic and REFUSES this ELIXIR that could heal his wounded heart.

Ilsa's arrival and Ugarte's stolen visas force Rick through a painful THRESHOLD, but he has not clearly committed to any Journey. He TESTS the SPECIAL WORLD to decide what Journey he will take. He wears a SHAPESHIFTER mask to veil his intentions, yet this mask will not protect him from the forces of a SPECIAL WORLD that gradually resurrect him from wounded ANTIHERO to redeemed PURE HERO.

Rick sees RIVAL saloon-owner Ferrari and discovers how valuable the visas are. Later, Rick apologizes to Ilsa, but she refuses to speak with the SHAPESHIFTER that showed such hatred the previous night. Rick invites her to his apartment, warning that one day she will lie to Laszlo as she did to Rick. But Ilsa REFUSES Rick's CALL, finally confessing that Laszlo is her husband, and was so when they were in Paris. She leaves Rick stunned with this unexpected news (an ELIXIR).

Laszlo and Ilsa see Ferrari with the hopes of obtaining exit visas. Ferrari suggests that they see Rick, whom he suspects possesses Ugarte's stolen visas.

Strasser as well suspects that Rick holds the visas, but Renault's thorough search of Rick's Cafe yields nothing. With the SHADOW'S pressure and a new understanding of his FORBIDDEN LOVE with Ilsa, Rick begins his RESURRECTION.

Rick helps a young couple buy visas from Renault, thwarting the Captain's offer to the young bride of sex for freedom. Rick is moved by the bride's willingness to accept her sexual sacrifice for the sake of pure love; her pleas for understanding awaken Rick's Anima, his feminine side. Now Rick begins to understand Ilsa's Journey and the NOBLE SACRIFICE she had made in Paris. Passing this TEST, Rick allows the bride's husband to win at roulette, to the shock of Renault. Rick is making his transformation, foreshadowing his decision at the film's climax.

Laszlo makes the bold APPROACH TO THE INMOST CAVE and offers to buy the visas from Rick. When Rick REFUSES to sell them, this HERO/MENTOR uses Rick's past record as a freedom fighter to win his understanding. Rick REFUSES to be swayed.

While the MENTOR'S words fail, his actions surprise this ANTIHERO who forbids the display of politics in his cafe. As German soldiers sing "Wacht am Rhine," Rick allows Laszlo to rouse the cafe into an emotional singing of the French anthem, drowning out the Germans. The HERO Laszlo has humiliated SHADOW Strasser, who orders the closing of the cafe. Laszlo's actions have also awakened Ilsa's pride in her husband's patriotic work, the HIGHER CAUSE.

The Journey's APPROACH continues later that night. Laszlo prepares to attend a secret meeting of the Resistance and tells Ilsa that Rick will not give up the visas. Sensing the Paris romance, Laszlo forgives her for her past transgressions. Ilsa prepares to take matters into her own hands and asks forgiveness for her future actions. Her husband cuts her off and confirms his faith in her.

Ilsa now dons the HERO'S mask. She begs Rick for the exit visas, imploring his sense of duty for the HIGHER CAUSE. Without Rick's help, Laszlo will die in Casablanca. Rick will not be swayed and Ilsa threatens to shoot him, the Journey's ORDEAL. Rick prefers death, and Ilsa can't pull the trigger, melting into sobbing confessions of her love for him, the RESURRECTION. Ilsa's CRISIS OF THE HEART destroys the defenses that have prevented her from acknowledging the true love of her life. Her confession opens the THRESHOLD of their love, the REWARD. Rick can now finally listen to her reason for abandoning him in Paris, his ELIXIR.

Ilsa has sacrificed herself to Rick, and REFUSES to abandon him again. In a final poignant moment of the REWARD, Ilsa realizes that her heart guides her now, that she has lost her masculine power of reasoning, her Animus. She passes that responsibility and the HERO'S mask to Rick. Rick takes control, finally committing to complete his Journey. What his Journey will be keeps us in suspense until the end.

A disturbance in the cafe interrupts them. Rick's headwaiter, Carl, arrives with Laszlo, wounded during a police raid of the Resistance meeting. Rick detains Laszlo, allowing ALLY Carl to sneak Ilsa away. RIVALS for the same woman, Laszlo asks Rick to use the letters of transit to take Ilsa away. Rick is impressed by Laszlo's NOBLE SACRIFICE. But before he can accept, French officers burst in and arrest Laszlo. The ROAD BACK begins.

Rick tries to convince Captain Renault to release Laszlo. Rick admits he possesses the letters of transit (the ELIXIR), and bargains to set up Laszlo in return for Rick and Ilsa's freedom.

Rick meets with Ilsa and Laszlo, who believes Rick has helped them escape. But as the letters of transit are passed into Laszlo's hands, Captain Renault appears and arrests Laszlo. Rick sees Ilsa go to her husband's side, a RESURRECTION. Now fully aware of her soul's desire, Rick knows what he must do. He threatens Renault and demands that Ilsa and Laszlo receive safe passage to the airport (Rick grants RESURRECTION to his MENTOR).

With the airplane in the background, symbolizing the ELIXIR OF FREEDOM, Rick makes the NOBLE SACRIFICE and sends his love away with her husband. Rick assures Ilsa that because of this Journey "they will always have Paris," the ELIXIR OF LOVE. But both must face their HIGHER CALLS. Rick has other work to do of which she can't be a part. And Ilsa must stand by her husband and his CAUSE against the evil Nazis.

Major Strasser tries to stop the plane, forcing Rick to kill the SHADOW. Captain Renault eyes the body of Strasser and looks hard at Rick, whose life now depends on the Captain's decision. "Round up the usual suspects," he pronounces, granting Rick's freedom (completing the RESURRECTION SEQUENCE).

Rick has been redeemed. His sacrifice completes his RESURRECTION into a HERO with a HIGHER CALL, the ELIXIR OF PATRIOTISM. Following in the footsteps of MENTOR Laszlo, Rick joins the French Resistance. He walks off into the distance, passing through this THRESHOLD with an additional ELIXIR, his new alliance with Renault.

FADE OUT

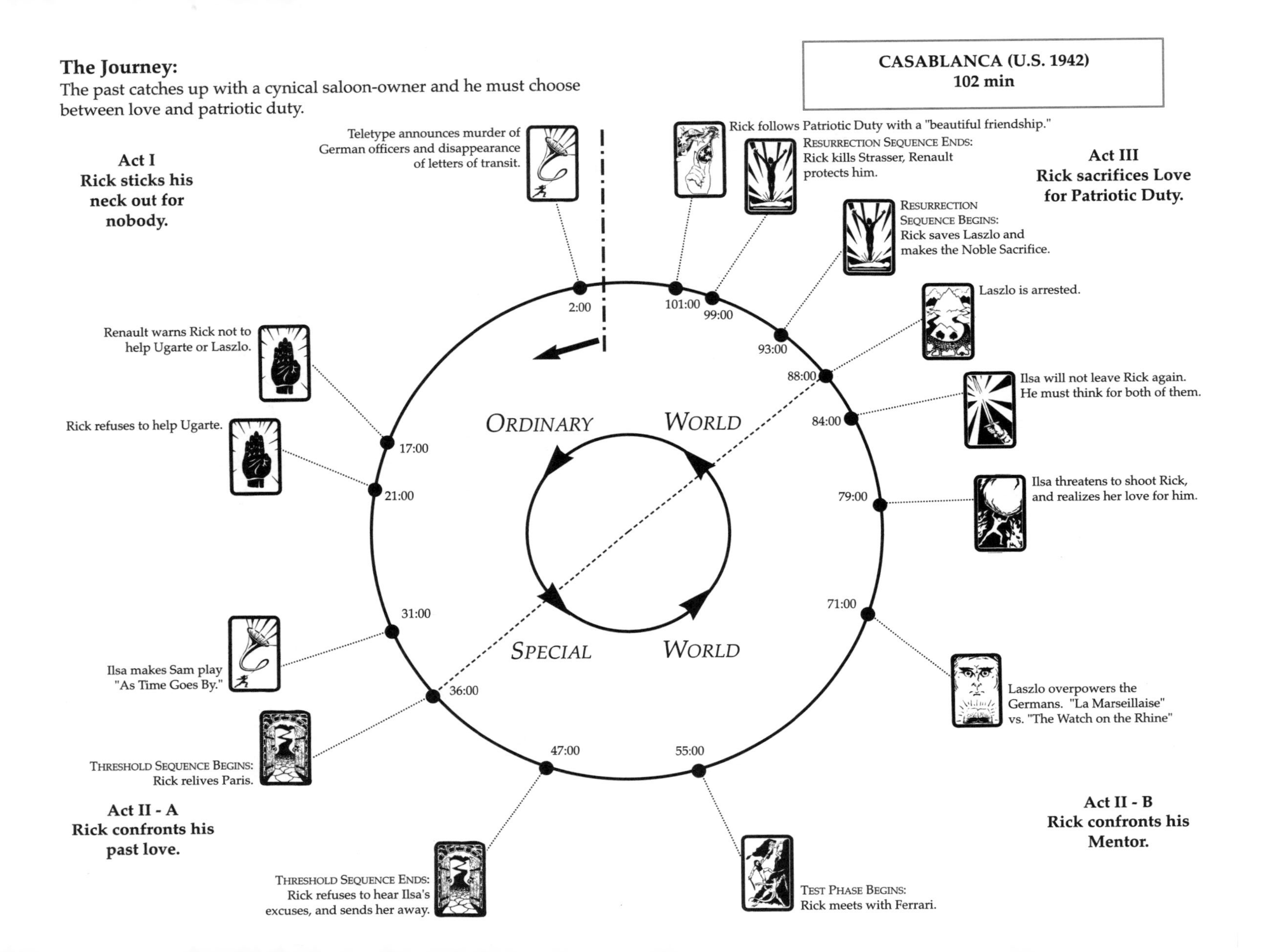

The Journey:
The past catches up with a cynical saloon-owner and he must choose between love and patriotic duty.
CASABLANCA (U.S. 1942)
102 min
Act I
Rick sticks his neck out for nobody.
Teletype announces murder of German officers and disappearance of letters of transit.
Renault warns Rick not to help Ugarte or Laszlo.
Rick refuses to help Ugarte.
Ilsa makes Sam play "As Time Goes By."
Threshold Sequence Begins: Rick relives Paris.
Act II - A
Rick confronts his past love.
Threshold Sequence Ends: Rick refuses to hear Ilsa's excuses, and sends her away.
Test Phase Begins: Rick meets with Ferrari.
Act II - B
Rick confronts his Mentor.
Laszlo overpowers the Germans. "La Marseillaise" vs. "The Watch on the Rhine"
Ilsa threatens to shoot Rick, and realizes her love for him.
Ilsa will not leave Rick again. He must think for both of them.
Laszlo is arrested.
Resurrection Sequence Begins: Rick saves Laszlo and makes the Noble Sacrifice.
Resurrection Sequence Ends: Rick kills Strasser, Renault protects him.
Rick follows Patriotic Duty with a "beautiful friendship."
Act III
Rick sacrifices Love for Patriotic Duty.
Ordinary World
Special World
2:00
17:00
21:00
31:00
36:00
47:00
55:00
71:00
79:00
84:00
88:00
93:00
99:00
101:00

THE AFRICAN QUEEN
(U.S., 1951)

"Don't be worried, Mr. Allnut."

"Oh, I ain't worried, Miss. Gave myself up for dead back where we started."

—Rose (Katharine Hepburn) and
Charlie (Humphrey Bogart)

Screenplay by James Agee and John Huston
Based on the novel by C.S. Forester
Directed by John Huston

A mismatched couple finds love as they journey an African river aboard a ramshackle launch, intent on sinking a German warship.

LANDMARKS OF THE JOURNEY

Outside forces caused by the approaching Great War throw Rose and Charlie onto their Journey aboard the *African Queen.* But Rose's need for vengeance and patriotic duty pushes them into their Special World, to sink the German warship *Louisa.* The Tests and Ordeals of this Higher Cause bring this mismatched couple closer together until they can no longer refuse their love for each other. Only together, committed to both their hearts and the Higher Cause, are they able to defeat the Germans and sink the warship.

THE JOURNEY

German East Africa. 1914. Reverend Samuel Sayer and his prim, spinster sister, Rose, are missionaries determined to bring civilization and religion to an African village, a conflicting ORDINARY WORLD. Their futile attempts to rouse the natives into hymn are disrupted by the arrival of the *African Queen* and its captain, Charlie Allnut. Charlie is a gin-swilling, foul-mannered mechanic who lives his ORDINARY WORLD traveling the African rivers to deliver mail and supplies aboard his derelict launch. The *African Queen* is all he's got and nobody but Allnut can "get up a good head of steam on the old *African Queen.*" Charlie's arrival is the first of a SUCCESSION OF CALLS that eventually destroy Rose's ORDINARY WORLD, and place Charlie and Rose together aboard the *Queen.*

First, to effectively set up Rose and Charlie's conflict in the SPECIAL WORLD, their contrasting ORDINARY WORLDS must be established. In a humorous and touching scene, Allnut agonizes during tea with the Reverend and Rose, struggling to remember good manners and placate his growling stomach.

Later, Charlie tells them he won't be delivering mail for awhile on account of the war. This HERALD warns them of the larger forces threatening their jungle peace. Sure enough, these forces strike with a deadly CALL. A German platoon takes over the village and strikes down the defiant Reverend who stares in disbelief at the destruction of his church. Broken, the Reverend loses his mind and soon dies.

Charlie helps Rose bury her brother, and takes her away on board the *African Queen*, a physical THRESHOLD. Charlie is content to keep a low profile in the backwaters until he can take Rose safely to civilization, his OUTER PROBLEM. But Rose wants revenge and pushes Charlie to take them down the river to sink the German warship, *Louisa*. (Both fail to realize their INNER PROBLEMS: to find companionship.) Charlie REFUSES her ridiculous CALL; so Rose appeals to the MENTOR in Charlie. As Captain and Mechanic, he agrees that the *African Queen* could be transformed into a torpedo to sink the *Louisa*, but he remains unconvinced. The river has too many dangers. Rose dons her own MENTOR'S mask and appeals to Charlie's patriotic duty until he reluctantly agrees to take her. Although Rose has committed to the Journey, entering the FIRST THRESHOLD, Charlie remains a disgruntled RELUCTANT HERO. The initial trials will TEST their respective convictions of commitment and reluctance.

Charlie teaches her how to steer the rudder and read the river. They tolerate their differences in these awkward living conditions; Charlie swigs gin, Rose sips tea. They take baths on opposite sides of the *Queen*. Charlie seeks shelter during a nighttime downpour; Rose misinterprets his intentions, and sends him back in the rain. Quickly realizing her mistake, she invites him back, showing compassion for the man.

They face the ENEMY, the river, and brave its rapids. Charlie hopes this MENTOR'S TEST will scare Rose, swaying the HERO away from her foolish intents. However, the rapids exhilarate Rose, making her more understanding of Charlie's world and steadfast in her commitment to sink the *Louisa*.

Finally, Charlie swigs enough "courage" to speak his mind. Revealing his mask as THRESHOLD GUARDIAN, he insults Rose and breaks his promise (a REFUSAL) to take her to the Louisa. The next morning, a hung-over Charlie awakens to witness Rose dumping the last of his gin into the river. She forces him to change his ways, raising the stakes.

Poised at the THRESHOLD, each tries to push the other past stubborn RELUCTANCE. Charlie willingly makes small sacrifices, trying to cater to Rose's neat and proper ORDINARY WORLD. He shaves and cleans himself, and scrubs down the *Queen*. He even attempts polite conversation, but Rose gives him the silent treatment. Charlie pleads for her to say something. Rose finally speaks her objection to his broken promise. Charlie tries to make one last stand, but she REFUSES to budge. Worn down, Charlie finally passes through the THRESHOLD. But two ORDEALS will push them into a deeper, emotional SPECIAL WORLD not anticipated by these mismatched HEROES.

In the first ORDEAL, the two must pass the armed German fort at Shona. With Charlie's ingenuity and quick hands, as well as the fortune of the sun (a hint that someone is looking out for our couple), they survive—and head at breakneck speed into the rapids. When Charlie and Rose miraculously survive this second ORDEAL, they shout triumphantly, embrace and kiss. Awkwardly the two fall in love, the THRESHOLD of their relationship.

They gently TEST the bounds of their feelings, and confirm that their love is mutual. Having entered this SPECIAL WORLD of Romance, Rose reconsiders her crazy plan; however, Charlie pushes her on, wearing the mask of the WILLING HERO to hide his own RELUCTANCE. His strength renews Rose's commitment to continue the Journey of the HIGHER CAUSE. They have overcome too much to let their Journey go to waste and now APPROACH THE INMOST CAVE. Before they can continue they must fix the *Queen*'s propeller. Together, they pass this IMPOSSIBLE TEST.

With their deep love and renewed hope, Rose and Charlie willingly resume their Journey and face their greatest challenge, the Journey's ORDEAL. The channel narrows and the *Queen* becomes stuck, forcing Charlie to physically pull her to deeper waters. Charlie and Rose suffer the humidity, the mud and the leeches, but fail to free the *Queen*, which is dead in the water. They are truly at the furthest point from their goal. They resign themselves to their deaths, but never regret their attempt. Charlie has failed in his use of his physical power to get them through the ORDEAL. He sleeps, exhausted, giving Rose the chance to use her "gifts." Before she follows him in sleep, Rose prays for God to open the doors of Heaven for the two of them.

In answer to her prayers, rain pours from the heavens, raising the river level and RESURRECTING the *African Queen*, Rose, and Charlie from their muddy grave. Their REWARDS are life and a deep, committed love for one another. Their ROAD BACK appears in a similarly serendipitous fashion: they are only yards away from the lake, and the *Louisa* is in sight.

They plan to take the *African Queen* out that night when the *Louisa* makes its return. Charlie transforms his launch into a torpedo, and they make the *Queen* look her best for her NOBLE SACRIFICE. Rose and Charlie have their "first quarrel" about who should man the mission, but finally agree that they will complete the Journey as they began it: together. The ROAD BACK of their Relationship is assured.

Together, Rose and Charlie steer the *African Queen* toward the warship, beginning the RESURRECTION SEQUENCE. A sudden storm capsizes the *Queen* and separates Charlie and Rose. Their mission has failed.

The Germans capture Charlie, and bring him on board the *Louisa*. He REFUSES to discuss his adventure and is convicted of being a British spy. He awaits hanging, just as Rose is brought aboard. Rose stands by her man, but first she must tell the Germans the truth of their heroics, a tale the Germans refuse to believe. As a last request, Rose asks that she and Charlie be hanged together. As they are escorted on deck to their awaiting nooses, Charlie asks the German Captain to marry them, the RESURRECTION of their Love. The Captain begrudgingly grants his last request. The quick ceremony celebrating their love is all the time the HEROES need. As the nooses tighten around the newlyweds' necks, an explosion rocks the *Louisa*. The capsized *African Queen* has resurfaced (the *Queen*'s RESURRECTION) and collided with the *Louisa*, detonating Charlie's torpedoes.

Treading water and surrounded by the burning remains of the *Louisa*, Rose shows Charlie a piece of wreckage with the name of the *African Queen*. Triumphant, Mr. and Mrs. Allnut swim away with the ELIXIRS of their transformation into HEROES, and the commitment of their love.

FADE OUT

LA STRADA
(Italy, 1954)

"I don't know what purpose this pebble serves, but it must serve some purpose. Because if it is useless, then everything is useless."

—The Fool (Richard Basehart)

Screenplay by Federico Fellini and Tullio Pinelli, with the collaboration of Ennio Flaiano
From a story by Federico Fellini and Tullio Pinelli
Dialogue by Tullio Pinelli
Directed by Federico Fellini

An innocent seeks her purpose in life on the Italian back roads with a carnival strongman.

LANDMARKS OF THE JOURNEY

La Strada's story plays with mythic structure, almost a tragic flirtation, as the innocent Gelsomina finds her purpose and commitment along "la strada." Our Hero walks a fine line (like the Fool's tightrope) between Zampano's earthy, brutal world and the ethereal, playful world represented by the angelic Fool. She wanders between these two Special Worlds, torn between embracing and rejecting their Calls. Although Zampano throws Gelsomina into his Special World, she must ultimately pass the Threshold of commitment on her own. Indeed, she makes this noble and tragic sacrifice with the help of two important Mentor/Threshold Guardians, the Fool and the Nun. Both push her toward her Higher Cause: to love Zampano.

THE JOURNEY

Children beckon Gelsomina from her seaside ORDINARY WORLD, initiating her CALL TO ADVENTURE. Her widow mother tells her that Gelsomina has been bought by Zampano, a traveling carnival strongman. Zampano had purchased Gelsomina's sister Rosa, who has died mysteriously, and now he silently sizes up his latest assistant. The impoverished widow pushes Gelsomina into this SPECIAL WORLD. Her family needs Zampano's money. And she promises Gelsomina that Zampano will treat her well and teach her a trade. Although the widow's tears reveal her fear for her daughter (REFUSAL), Gelsomina welcomes this THRESHOLD into the world of a circus performer. But not without a bit of RELUCTANCE. Riding in the back of Zampano's caravan, she watches with a touch of sadness as her ORDINARY WORLD disappears.

Seen by others as strange and queer, Gelsomina dwells in an ORDINARY WORLD of innocence. She knows nothing of the world beyond her seashore, and experiences everything with childlike awe. Gelsomina possesses a strange affinity for communicating with children and animals, which makes her a tragic fit into Zampano's brutish ORDINARY WORLD.

Strongman Zampano wanders the Italian back roads aboard his ramshackle caravan, his ORDINARY WORLD. His life consists of performing one circus act (breaking a chain with his chest) and seducing women. Unable to communicate his feelings, Zampano relies upon strength and muscle to get what he wants.

Zampano pushes Gelsomina into the first TEST PHASE. Zampano needs her for his act and teaches her the ropes, MEETING THE MENTOR. He fits her with her costume; she wears her new hat with childlike glee. She must accompany his act, but he refuses the trumpet, forcing her to play the drums. He whips her with a switch until she strikes the beats perfectly. Traveling this SPECIAL WORLD involves pain. When she REFUSES to sleep with him, he forces her into the back of the caravan. While Zampano sleeps, she watches him with love and fondness. His brutish actions have stirred an INNER CALL for Romance.

The TESTS continue on this deeper level as Gelsomina tries to fathom Zampano's mixed messages. During dinner at a cafe, Zampano introduces Gelsomina as his wife, yet overtly flirts with a redhead and drives off with her, leaving Gelsomina to wait all night in the gutter. The following morning, she finds Zampano passed out and wanders away (a REFUSAL), yet she can't wander far. Zampano awakens to find Gelsomina planting tomatoes at their camp, symbolizing an INNER STIRRING for home and hearth. The eternal vagabond quickly rejects her CALL and they return to the road.

Zampano and Gelsomina perform at a wedding celebration. Now, Gelsomina must face Zampano's overt seduction of a widow in exchange for her dead husband's clothes. Later in a barn, as Zampano tries on his new clothes, Gelsomina asks if he can teach her how to play "the song" (Gelsomina's theme.) Zampano ignores her request, a REFUSAL. Gelsomina cannot communicate her frustration and falls into a hole, where she sleeps for the night. She resurfaces later and speaks her mind while Zampano sleeps. She finally leaves, REFUSING his SPECIAL WORLD.

Gelsomina doesn't want to return to her ORDINARY WORLD. She loves the SPECIAL WORLD of the artist; she just doesn't like Zampano. She sits by the roadside when three musicians (HERALDS) pass her by. She follows this CALL into town, and is swept into a religious procession that leaves her at an open-air performance. Gelsomina watches in awe as the Fool performs his high wire act (a CALL).

Wearing angel wings, this HERALD will become an important MENTOR on Gelsomina's Journey. After his performance, Gelsomina tries to meet him but the TRICKSTER mocks her looks and drives away, REJECTING her from his SPECIAL WORLD.

Zampano finds Gelsomina wandering the street. She REFUSES to go with him, and Zampano beats her, forcing her back onto the caravan THROUGH THE THRESHOLD of his world.

Gelsomina awakens at Giraffa's Circus, where Zampano secures a job. She hears the Fool playing her song on his violin, but Zampano pulls her away, a REFUSAL of the Fool's CALL. This RIVAL MENTOR mocks Zampano, ridiculing his strongman act. Zampano threatens him, but the TRICKSTER Fool will not be intimidated and interrupts Zampano's act during a performance. Zampano chases him down but the Fool escapes.

The Fool allows Gelsomina to assist him in his act, an APPROACH TO THE INMOST CAVE of the Fool's SPECIAL WORLD. Zampano disrupts the lesson and threatens the Fool with a knife. Zampano is arrested, the ORDEAL.

While Zampano languishes in jail (a CRISIS OF THE HEART), the lonely Gelsomina hears the Fool's violin and finally MEETS HER MENTOR. Gelsomina questions her purpose in life (INNER STIRRING). The Fool uses the parable of the pebble as encouragement—that perhaps her HIGHER CAUSE is to love Zampano, and that Zampano's abusive actions are signs of his love for her. The Fool nudges her back into Zampano's SPECIAL WORLD, giving her renewed strength (a REWARD and an emotional RESURRECTION of purpose) to willingly pass THROUGH THE THRESHOLD.

Zampano emerges from jail and with few words drives off with Gelsomina (his physical RESURRECTION and the emotional RESURRECTION of their relationship.) They stop briefly at the seashore. Zampano just wants to soak his feet, but Gelsomina interprets his entrance into her ORDINARY WORLD as a sign of commitment to their relationship, a REWARD. She observes that her home is now with Zampano, but the strongman belittles their relationship, in his abrupt, cruel fashion.

The two give a Nun a ride to her convent. Another important MENTOR keeping Gelsomina committed to Zampano, the Nun notes the similarities of Gelsomina's Journey with her own Journey as the bride of Christ. This moment of counseling is an APPROACH TO THE INMOST CAVE. Gelsomina's commitment is again TESTED that night when Zampano tries to steal the Convent's silver hearts, and thrashes Gelsomina for refusing to help him, the ORDEAL. The following morning, the Nun senses Gelsomina's sadness and offers a place for her to stay. Gelsomina refuses. She has been resurrected from the ORDEAL of the silver hearts with the acceptance of her fate, no matter how painful it will be.

Fate takes them back onto the Fool's path, the Journey's ROAD BACK. They find the Fool fixing his flat tire. The Fool believes Zampano has come to help, but Zampano lashes out at the TRICKSTER and slams his head against his car. The Fool collapses and dies. Gelsomina mourns his death, but Zampano acts quickly, leaving his body and dumping his car.

This ROAD BACK takes a more desolate, snow-covered path, not the pastoral scenes we've seen earlier on this Journey. Distraught, Gelsomina can no longer assist Zampano's performances without mumbling about the Fool's death. Her strength of purpose has been destroyed by the death of her MENTOR, and with it, Zampano's ability to make a living.

One morning, Zampano makes a campfire along the road. Gelsomina emerges from his caravan apparently well, but she quickly remembers the poor Fool. Frustrated by this FALSE RESURRECTION, Zampano offers to return her to her ORDINARY WORLD, but Gelsomina voices her commitment to take care of him, a commitment that is ruining Zampano's ability to "earn his life." Gelsomina falls asleep. In a TRAGIC SACRIFICE, Zampano chooses his "living" over companionship. He abandons her on the road, initiating the RESURRECTION SEQUENCE.

Sometime later, Zampano performs at a circus. He's earning his living again, but as a shell of what he was. Broken, depressed, Zampano takes a walk. He hears a woman singing Gelsomina's song (Gelsomina's RESURRECTION). This HERALD tells him about the strange woman who taught her the song, but is now dead. Her memory awakens Zampano's conscience (his TRAGIC RESURRECTION).

Zampano tries to numb his inner pain with drink. He's thrown out of the bar and into the street where he shouts in defiance of his need for anybody. Zampano staggers toward the seashore, the symbol of Gelsomina's ORDINARY WORLD. He looks up at the stars and realizes his loneliness in a world without Gelsomina, the ELIXIR. Overcome by emotion, Zampano clutches the sand and weeps.

FADE OUT

BEAUTY AND THE BEAST
(U.S., 1991)

"...for who could ever learn to love a beast?"

—Narrator

Screenplay by Linda Woolverton
Based upon the fairy tale as penned by Jeanne-Marie Leprince de Beaumont
Lyrics by Howard Ashman
Music by Alan Menken
Directed by Gary Trousdale and Kirk Wise

A prince who is cursed and turned into a hideous beast must learn to love the town's most beautiful girl and earn her love in return.

LANDMARKS OF THE JOURNEY

The Noble Sacrifice does not need to occur at the Journey's Resurrection. Sacrifices can occur at the Thresholds of the Hero's Journey, pushing the Hero into or out of the Special World. The noble act could be the impetus that brings the lovers together (or separates them.) In *Beauty and the Beast,* a story that weaves together two journeys, Belle sacrifices herself in order to free her father. This Noble Sacrifice forces her through the Threshold into the Beast's Special World. The Beast's sacrifice happens at the end of the Second Act; he sets Belle free (again to save her father), knowing that by letting Belle return to her Ordinary World, he sacrifices any hope of lifting the curse. Beautifully balanced, this sacrifice happens on the Road Back, the turning point or Threshold into the Third Act. Through sacrifice both heroes learn that a Forbidden Love may hide the purest of all loves, the most powerful Elixir that can grant life and lift spells.

THE JOURNEY

The Opening Prologue tells the tale of the Beast's curse, his DARK RESURRECTION creating the story's SPECIAL WORLD. Depicted in stained glass representing the timelessness of the legend, it portrays the Beast's failed Journey thus far... An old beggar woman approaches the spoiled Prince offering a beautiful rose in return for shelter. Repulsed by her ugliness, the Prince turns her away (a REFUSAL). But this HERALD warns the Prince not to be deceived by outward appearances. Beauty is found within. Again, he rejects her. The SHAPESHIFTER/MENTOR reveals herself as a beautiful enchantress, and transforms the Prince into a hideous Beast, a DARK ORDEAL/RESURRECTION. Ashamed of his looks, the Beast secludes himself in his cursed castle. A magic hand-mirror, a MENTOR'S GIFT, is his only window to the outside world. The Enchantress also gives him the rose that will bloom until his 21st birthday, a TICKING CLOCK. If before the last rose petal falls the

Beast can learn to love another, and earn her love in return, his spell will be broken (the ROAD BACK and the Beast's OUTER PROBLEM). As his 21st birthday approaches, the Beast has given up hope. He locks himself up in his castle, rejecting his ROAD BACK to his ORDINARY WORLD.

Belle's opening song establishes her ORDINARY WORLD and her INNER STIRRING, as well as the polar opposites of the hopeless Beast and the hopeful Belle. Although Belle is the most beautiful girl in this French town, the townsfolk consider her strange with "her head in the clouds" and her nose in a book. Belle lives with her eccentric inventor father, Maurice. Fueled by the romanticism of her favorite books, Belle dreams of something more than her provincial life—to find love and a prince in disguise, her INNER PROBLEM.

Gaston (the RIVAL) sees Belle as the perfect match. After all, the most beautiful girl belongs to the most handsome man. While her father is away, Gaston proposes to Belle, but Belle rebuffs Gaston's advances, REFUSING his CALL.

Maurice's horse emerges from the forest alone, and without hesitation Belle answers this CALL and sets off in search of her father. She APPROACHES the Beast's castle, and although the dark fortress looks dangerous and foreboding, Belle enters this SPECIAL WORLD. She must bypass THRESHOLD GUARDIANS, the Enchanted Objects of the Beast's castle. She finds her father locked in the dungeon cell. Before she can rescue him, she confronts the Beast hidden in shadows. At this SHADOW'S mercy, Belle offers herself in place of her dying father. Beast accepts her CALL, and finally reveals himself in the light. At first repulsed by his beastly appearance (a REFUSAL), she swallows her fear and stands by her NOBLE SACRIFICE, passing THROUGH THE THRESHOLD.

This THRESHOLD into the SPECIAL WORLD is extremely disorienting. The Beast has Maurice whisked out of the castle without allowing Belle a chance to say good-bye. Beast escorts her to her room, and tells her she can go anywhere in the castle except through the mysterious door in the forbidden wing. (We know that in time Belle's curiosity cannot REFUSE this DARK CALL.)

Beast locks Belle in her room. She rejects Beast's offer for dinner, even after he tries to ask kindly (with coaching from the Enchanted Objects as MENTORS). Belle's Enchanted Dresser tries to make her feel more comfortable in this SPECIAL WORLD. Located everywhere, these Enchanted Objects share the Beast's curse and hope that Belle is the one who can ultimately break the spell. Stakes are high for these MENTORS to make sure that Belle and the Beast stay together. Belle finally leaves her room in the middle of the night and receives dinner from the Enchanted Objects. They warmly welcome Belle with the song "Be Our Guest."

Curiosity peaked, Belle tricks her new ALLIES and sneaks into the forbidden room, APPROACHING THE INMOST CAVE. She discovers the torn portrait of the Prince, but cannot make out its significance. The Beast finds her and banishes her from his castle, beginning the ORDEAL SEQUENCE. Belle flees into the dark, dangerous woods. Wolves attack her (the ORDEAL continues). The Beast arrives in time to save her; however, the wolves ambush the Beast and strike him down. Indebted to the Beast for his act of heroism, Belle nurses Beast back to health, his RESURRECTION.

This CRISIS OF THE HEART opens the door to their friendship and their love (the REWARD). Beast gives Belle his library. And soon the two prepare for the ULTIMATE BOON, a romantic dinner and waltz in the grand ballroom. The Beast has earned his REWARD for saving Belle. Belle has looked beyond the beast's monstrous looks, her REWARD.

Belle longs to see her father, and the Beast shows her the magic mirror, the window to the outside world. She sees her father in danger, beginning the ROAD BACK. With time running out and the last rose petal threatening to fall, the Beast makes his NOBLE SACRIFICE. He sets Belle free to save her father, and gives her the Magic Mirror, the MENTOR'S GIFT. As the Enchanted Objects observe, the Beast has learned to love but his SACRIFICE barricades his own ROAD BACK.

To save her father, and foil Gaston's plot to lock Maurice up in an asylum, Belle reveals the Beast to the townsfolk, the second stage of the ROAD BACK. The sight of the fierce looking Beast pushes Gaston (the new SHADOW) to rally the townspeople to attack the Beast's castle. They lock up Belle and Maurice, beginning the RESURRECTION SEQUENCE. Young Chip, the teacup, saves Belle and Maurice by using one of Maurice's inventions (a MENTOR'S gift).

Meanwhile, the Enchanted Objects defend the castle from the townspeople's siege. Gaston tries to kill the Beast, but the Beast overpowers the SHADOW. Beast spares Gaston; however, Gaston proves that he doesn't deserve his RESURRECTION. Gaston stabs the Beast before plummeting to his death.

As the Beast lies dying, the Enchanted Objects watch the last rose petal fall, the TICKING CLOCK has run out. When all appears lost, Belle confesses her love (her RESURRECTION). She kisses the Beast. The Beast has earned returned love and redemption for his past mistakes. Magically, Belle's ELIXIR OF LOVE resurrects the Beast into the handsome Prince. His RESURRECTION and redemption also bring an ELIXIR to his castle and his people, restoring all to their Ordinary selves.

FADE OUT

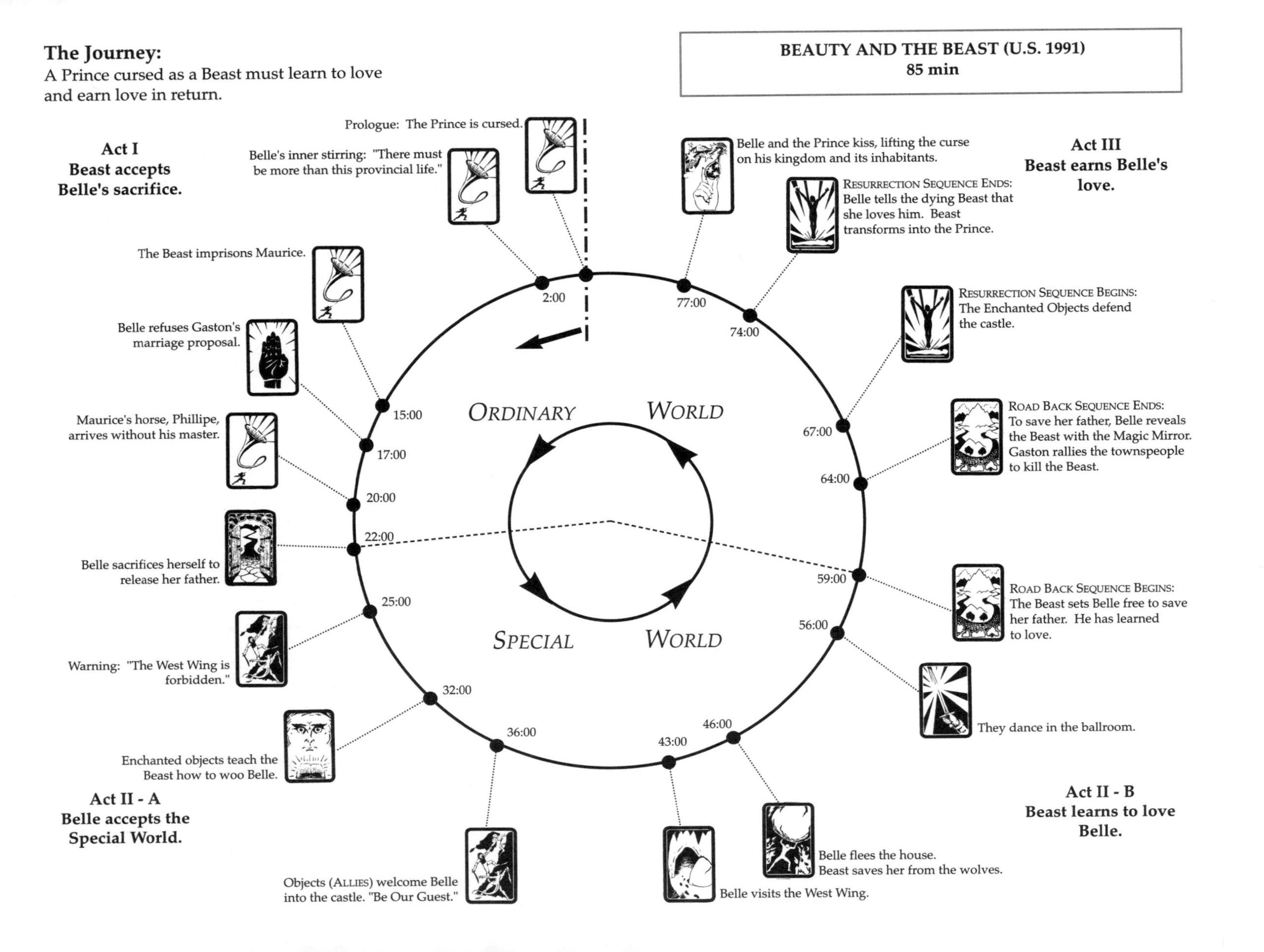
BEAUTY AND THE BEAST (U.S. 1991)
85 min
The Journey:
A Prince cursed as a Beast must learn to love and earn love in return.
Act I
Beast accepts Belle's sacrifice.
Prologue: The Prince is cursed.
Belle's inner stirring: "There must be more than this provincial life."
2:00
The Beast imprisons Maurice.
15:00
Belle refuses Gaston's marriage proposal.
17:00
Maurice's horse, Phillipe, arrives without his master.
20:00
Belle sacrifices herself to release her father.
22:00
Warning: "The West Wing is forbidden."
25:00
Enchanted objects teach the Beast how to woo Belle.
32:00
Objects (ALLIES) welcome Belle into the castle. "Be Our Guest."
36:00
Act II - A
Belle accepts the Special World.
Belle visits the West Wing.
43:00
Belle flees the house.
Beast saves her from the wolves.
46:00
Act II - B
Beast learns to love Belle.
They dance in the ballroom.
56:00
ROAD BACK SEQUENCE BEGINS:
The Beast sets Belle free to save her father. He has learned to love.
59:00
ROAD BACK SEQUENCE ENDS:
To save her father, Belle reveals the Beast with the Magic Mirror. Gaston rallies the townspeople to kill the Beast.
64:00
RESURRECTION SEQUENCE BEGINS:
The Enchanted Objects defend the castle.
67:00
RESURRECTION SEQUENCE ENDS:
Belle tells the dying Beast that she loves him. Beast transforms into the Prince.
74:00
Belle and the Prince kiss, lifting the curse on his kingdom and its inhabitants.
77:00
Act III
Beast earns Belle's love.
ORDINARY WORLD
SPECIAL WORLD

THE PIANO
(Australia, France, 1993)

"Were good he had God's patience, for silence affects everyone in the end. The strange thing is I don't think myself silent, that is, because of my piano."
—Ada (Holly Hunter)

Written and Directed by Jane Campion

A mute woman's bargain to earn her piano takes her into a forbidden world of passion and eroticism where she learns to find herself.

LANDMARKS OF THE JOURNEY

The Hero's Journey of the Heart can bring great pain, yet in the end the courageous one may rise as a better person. She may even achieve power she had never anticipated. Ada's is a Journey of passion, and in director and screenwriter Campion's world, passion cannot be refused. Ada relies upon her piano to speak, yet her new husband refuses to acknowledge this need (his Tragic Flaw). His denial pushes her through the Threshold of Forbidden Love with the lone workman, Baines. Indeed, Baines has heard her "speak." He brings back the piano to hear her music, and to unlock a passion that doesn't need a piano.

THE JOURNEY

A young mute woman, Ada, cannot be separated from her piano, her only means of expressing her passion. She is a Lacking Hero who relies upon her music for wholeness. Ada lives with her daughter, Flora, in Scotland. But her father disrupts her civilized, cultured ORDINARY WORLD when he arranges Ada's marriage to a man in New Zealand, the CALL TO ADVENTURE. The story quickly transports Ada, Flora and the piano through a THRESHOLD into the bleak landscape of New Zealand, an almost dreamlike SPECIAL WORLD with harsh beaches, lush forests, and impenetrable mud.

They have to make the best of their new world, taking shelter beneath a petticoat. Soon Ada's fiancé, Alisdair Stewart, arrives with the native Maoris, led by Baines. Stewart decides they must leave the piano. He is just as unsettled by this THRESHOLD. His new wife speaks only in sign and written messages, and she's smaller than expected. Fiercely independent, she refuses to leave the piano behind. Stewart gives her no choice.

The party travels the "difficult journey" to Stewart's hut. Ada crosses a physical as well as an emotional THRESHOLD as she becomes Stewart's wife. After their wedding picture is taken in the pouring rain, Ada rips her wedding dress off and stares out the window at the downpour. She REFUSES to settle into Stewart's SPECIAL WORLD without her piano. When Stewart leaves Ada to examine some land, Ada asks Baines to take her to her piano (CALL TO ADVENTURE). At first he REFUSES, but eventually her stubbornness sways him.

Baines leads Ada and Flora to the beach. Ada plays her piano with uninhibited emotion, as young Flora dances in the sand. The music stirs Baines, CALL TO ADVENTURE. He can see the piano's power; he can feel Ada's passion. Ada's music has lured Baines from his solitary world.

Baines makes a deal with Stewart. He trades 80 acres of land for Ada's piano. And he suggests that Ada teach him to play as part of the bargain. Ada adamantly REFUSES to give up the piano. As her new husband and MENTOR OF AUTHORITY, Stewart demands that Ada make the sacrifice.

A RELUCTANT Ada arrives at Baines' hut, but her new student REFUSES to play the piano, requesting to listen to his MENTOR. He offers Ada another Journey. If Ada will do as he asks, she can earn her piano back, one white key for every visit. Ada bargains him down to the black keys (a type of REFUSAL), passing THROUGH THE THRESHOLD into this SPECIAL WORLD of earning back her piano.

Ada's TESTS become more challenging with each "lesson," as Baines' requests become more erotic ... lifting her skirt, undoing her bodice. This SHADOW representing her repressed physical passion tries pushing her into a deeper Journey, and Ada is unwilling to pass that THRESHOLD OF FORBIDDEN LOVE, changing her music to shatter his amorous mood. At the performance of *Bluebeard*, Ada shows her disapproval of Baines. She allows Stewart to take her hand as a sign to Baines of her commitment to her marriage.

At their next lesson, Baines takes the BOLD APPROACH and reveals himself naked. He bargains for Ada to lie naked with him. TRICKSTER Flora spies on them and confesses to Stewart about Baines' strange lessons. Before Stewart can investigate these lessons on his own, Baines ends the deal and gives the piano back to Ada, APPROACHING THE INMOST CAVE.

Baines refuses to go any further with a bargain that is turning Ada into a whore. He confesses his true feelings for her, but realizes she is unable to reciprocate. This SHADOW severs the bargain, releasing her from the SPECIAL WORLD. But Ada can no longer play the piano without Baines. She returns to Baines' hut to confront her SHADOW (the ORDEAL and CRISIS OF THE HEART). Baines demands that she leave if she has no feeling for him. Frustrated by her feelings, she slaps him, but Ada cannot deny her love and finally kisses him. This ORDEAL takes them through the THRESHOLD into their SPECIAL WORLD of the Heart, their REWARD. Stewart spies on the lovers, mesmerized by the bodies entwined in the aftermath of their lovemaking. During their lovemaking Baines receives the additional REWARD of hearing her whisper.

Awakened by his wife's eroticism, Stewart boards Ada up in his hut to keep her for himself. He can physically bar Ada from her lover, but he can't lock out her fantasies of Baines. One night, Stewart awakens to find her caressing him in her sleep. Quickly he realizes that he has become a sexual object to fulfill her dreams of Baines. Although Stewart gives up and removes the planks from the windows, he makes her agree never to see Baines.

Ada defies her SHADOW husband and prepares a piano key with the message, "You have my heart" (The ROAD BACK). She entrusts the message with her daughter, Flora. However, the SHAPESHIFTER HERALD spites Ada and delivers the key to the SHADOW, Stewart.

Enraged by the message, Stewart chops a finger from Ada's hand, and has Flora deliver it to Baines, initiating the RESURRECTION SEQUENCE. Stewart had hoped to "clip the wing" of his "love bird," preventing her from playing the piano and expressing her passion. Stewart tries to make love to her, but she stares defiant, stunning Stewart.

Later that night, Stewart storms Baines' hut. Stewart confesses that Ada put words into his head, wishing she would wake up from the dream, and asking Stewart to let her go, and allow Baines to "try to save me."

Stewart releases her (a NOBLE SACRIFICE). Baines takes Ada, Flora and the piano away, but during the voyage, Ada wants the piano dumped into the sea. Prompted by the crew, Baines has them release the "coffin" into the watery grave. Making this SACRIFICE is difficult and Ada allows the piano to pull her down into the ocean depths. Facing death, Ada realizes she no longer needs the piano and releases herself, completing her RESURRECTION.

Healed by Baines' love, Ada has become a whole woman, her ELIXIR. She now teaches piano. Baines has fashioned a metal fingertip, so that she can play again. And now she is even learning to speak.

Ada dreams of the piano in its watery grave, and sees herself in the dream floating above it. This is her lullaby that comforts her to sleep. After all, it is now only a dream.

FADE OUT

THE MYTHIC STRUCTURE OF ROMANTIC COMEDY

It takes the greatest courage to romance the heart. We make the leap of faith and give ourselves whole-heartedly to this Special World; or we prefer deception to mask our fears and insecurities. The Special World only seems to get more complicated when it's shared by two, but in the end somehow love triumphs, untangling all the misunderstandings and granting us the sweetest, most rewarding Elixir of all.

"I NEED HIM LIKE THE AX NEEDS TURKEY"

With its trademark characteristics of Screwball, the Hollywood Ending, the battle-of-the-sexes, and the oft-used formula boy-meets-girl-loses-girl-love-triumphs-in-the-end, Romantic Comedy has earned its respected place as one of Hollywood's distinctive genres. While the Journey of Romance often shows us the sacrifice of the heart, Romantic Comedy celebrates our Hero's quest for the Elixir of Love. Romantic Comedy is fraught with complications as two people try to share the same Special World exchanging witty dialogue, pratfalls, or simply a beautiful kiss. As the Special World becomes more complicated, the audience wonders how the lovers could possibly get together. But the comic side of love should not be taken lightly; it takes great commitment and courage to pursue love. The greatest obstacles we face will be our own fear of rejection and our insecurities, which is why the Hero may need plenty of coaxing and support, and a trusty Shapeshifter's mask as protection, before committing to this Journey.

Romantic Comedy borrows from similar elements of her serious cousin, Romance, as well as Comedy. We may discover Forbidden Love, Romantic Triangles and Rivals, Shapeshifters and Shadows. We even see similar story types. Like Comedy, Romantic Comedy's Journeys use surprise and suspense. Comedy of romance rises from the pain of dealing with the rituals of romance: asking someone out, the first kiss, preparing the romantic dinner, the morning after.

THE ESSENCE OF ROMANTIC COMEDY: OPPOSITES ATTRACT

The primary source of conflict in Romantic Comedy arises from the contrast of the lovers. The greater the contrast between lovers, the greater opportunity for conflict. Contrast may come from class (*Bringing Up Baby*), politics, physical distance (*Sleepless in*

Seattle), or even death (*Dona Flor and Her Two Husbands*). Conflict also arises when the goals of the lovers are in conflict. A professional career may require a sacrifice of the heart (*Annie Hall*).

The ultimate battle-of-the-sexes, Screwball Comedy, sets in opposition a woman and man from different social standings. Usually the woman comes from wealth and high society and the man is from the working or professional world. Somehow they meet and battle it out until they fall exhausted into each other's arms and hearts.

LOVE'S GREATEST FEAR

The greatest obstacle in the pursuit of love is the fear of rejection. Taking the plunge, throwing oneself into the Special World of love is extremely dangerous and requires a final leap of faith. Potential lovers may hold interior barriers, fears and insecurities, which threaten the Journey. Sacrificing oneself for love often requires more courage than walking through a snake pit.

MANY GOALS, ONE HEART

Heroes in other genres commonly have a specific Outer or Inner problem that complicates the journey, and provides identification with the Hero. The Romantic Comedy Hero often has several problems to overcome.

Multiple problems create conflict by getting in the way of love. The problems must be solved or cast aside for love to triumph. In Romance Triangles, the Rival must be dealt with before the Elixir of true, destined love can be enjoyed (*Singin' in the Rain*). If a Romantic Comedy Hero sacrifices love in favor of a conflicting goal (a professional obligation or Rival), by Journey's end he will realize that love is the Elixir he desires after all, and try to fix his mistake (*Annie Hall, Sleepless in Seattle*). A good old-fashioned Crisis of the Heart—the threat of the loss of a lover or relationship—can make the Hero throw aside everything in favor of love (*Bringing Up Baby, Dona Flor and Her Two Husbands*).

FIND UNUSUAL WAYS TO PUT THEM TOGETHER

One of the exciting moments in the Romantic Comedy happens when the two lovers are placed together on their Journey of the Heart. In their Ordinary World it's likely these people would never even meet. So, how a storyteller introduces the lovers and presents the first Call of the Heart can be approached with much creativity. Individual needs, outside powers, fate can all bring the potential lovers together. The lovers could fight over a golf ball (*Bringing Up Baby*). A mob may force the hero into the lover's car (*Singin' in the Rain*). A widower's radio testimony of perfect love may be enough to stir the Journey of the Heart (*Sleepless in Seattle*).

A SHARING OF ORDINARY WORLDS

Complications may arise from the way a Romantic Comedy Hero uses his Ordinary World. He may veil his Ordinary World with a Shapeshifter's mask. The Hero will become someone he feels is more to the intended lover's image of true love. Struggling to conform to the lover's intended Ordinary World offers ample opportunity for comedy, especially when there's a strong contrast between the lovers' respective Ordinary Worlds.

A neurotic lover stuck in his Ordinary World will instead force his Ordinary World onto his lover (*Annie Hall*). Moments of pushing one's tastes on the other, or experiencing the "oil and water" clash of Ordinary Worlds provide wonderful comic moments (e.g., the family dinner scene in *Annie Hall*).

In the world of Screwball Comedy, the Trickster Lover (usually the smart-mouth woman) will manipulate and destroy her intended heart's Ordinary World until he has nowhere to go but into the arms of his determined lover (*Bringing Up Baby*).

THE MANY MENTORS OF ROMANTIC COMEDY

Mentors are anyone or anything that serve to guide the Hero on the Journey. More importantly, Mentors help the Hero overcome the fear of the unknown. The Mentors of Romantic Comedy come in many forms, including Sidekicks, beliefs and ideals of love, past experiences, and romantic movies and novels.

The Hero may have a Sidekick Mentor, a best friend who pushes the Journey of the Heart. In other genres, the Mentor is an Actualized Hero who succeeded in the Journey and uses his experience to prepare the Hero for the Special World. Yet in Romantic Comedy, rarely is the Sidekick Mentor an Actualized Hero of love. Instead, they've failed and willingly tell their war stories of failed romances, but they push the Hero to find pure, romantic love as if to vicariously experience the Elixir.

A Mentor can guide the Romantic Hero from within. This Inner Mentor can be a belief system of ideal love built upon past experience or observations of other successful couples. Popular culture can contribute to this Inner Mentor with romantic movies, novels and songs.

Past relationships may not be the most reliable Mentors. A Hero repeatedly unlucky in the quest for love, or wounded by love, may shy away from this Journey altogether. A Wounded Hero who has achieved the perfect love (an Actualized Hero of Love), only to have it taken away, will be reluctant to re-enter the Journey (*Sleepless in Seattle*).

TAKING THE WRONG ROAD BACK

The Romantic Hero will likely face two choices at the Journey's Road Back: to commit to the romance, or reject it. The choice to commit (or recommit) to love pushes a Chase to win that special love (Jonah's Journey in *Sleepless in Seattle, The Graduate*). On the other hand, a Romantic Hero rejecting the special love may travel an uncomfortable Road Back along which he realizes his mistake. Faced with this Crisis of the Heart he makes a last-ditch effort to resurrect the Special Love and claim the Elixir (*Sleepless in Seattle, Dona Flor and Her Two Husbands, Annie Hall*).

The Road Back can be the moment when the Hero chooses between Rivals, or when the Rival threatens to ruin the Hero's relationship with his perfect love (*Singin' in the Rain*).

The Romantic Comedy Hero may need a push from a Mentor to pass through the Road Back Threshold. Not that the Hero will heed the Mentor's advice. But this Meeting with the Mentor will again make the Hero and the audience aware of the fears, insecurities and stakes involved with the special love. In *Sleepless in Seattle,* three different Mentors try to push three Heroes onto their Roads Back. Annie's best friend encourages Annie to trust destiny and meet "Sleepless in Seattle" on the top of the Empire State Building. Sam's sister pushes Sam to take the same romantic path. Jonah's girlfriend buys Jonah his plane ticket to ensure that he meets destiny on the top of the Empire State Building. Only Jonah accepts his Mentor's advice. Annie and Sam choose safer paths, sacrificing the Higher Cause of perfect love. However, by Journey's end our hope is renewed. They realize their mistake, and destiny brings them together.

GENRE CHALLENGES: ROMANTIC COMEDY

1. Using *Bringing Up Baby* as an example of Screwball Comedy, are there elements of Screwball in today's romantic comedies? Why does, or doesn't it work for a contemporary audience?
2. In *Singin' in the Rain,* how do Don's and Kathy's respective Ordinary Worlds help transform each other?
3. What are the Threshold Guardians in *Annie Hall*? How do they appear? What actions do they force? How do Annie and Alvy overcome these Threshold Guardians?
4. In *Dona Flor and Her Two Husbands,* do you want Vadinho and Flor to reclaim their love? Why or why not? Are Vadinho and Flor sympathetic heroes? Are they identifiable?
5. What are destiny's Calls in *Sleepless in Seattle* and how do the characters react to each? Are other Mentors involved when these Calls occur to help the Journey, or are there Threshold Guardians that weaken or hinder destiny's Calls?

BRINGING UP BABY
(U.S., 1938)

"Now it isn't that I don't like you, Susan, because after all, in moments of quiet, I'm strangely drawn toward you, but—well, there haven't been any quiet moments."

—Dr. David Huxley (Cary Grant)

Screenplay by Dudley Nichols and Hagar Wilde
Story by Hagar Wilde
Directed by Howard Hawks

An absent-minded paleontologist gets mixed up with an eccentric heiress and her pet leopard as he seeks a rare dinosaur bone.

LANDMARKS OF THE JOURNEY

Initially a box-office failure, *Bringing Up Baby* has become the classic in screwball comedy. Like the baseball pitch, Screwball throws the unexpected curve and presents a topsy-turvy world in which the woman of words and guile (and usually upper class) has control over the man. Here, heiress Susan Vance pulls ordinary paleontologist David Huxley into her world in which he progressively loses control of everything that defines his Ordinary World: his profession, gender, identity, and sanity. At the mercy of Susan's Trickster manipulations, David becomes the lunatic in her madcap world.

David initially juggles three Journeys:

- To retrieve the rare intercostal clavicle bone needed to complete his brontosaurus skeleton.
- To win a million dollar grant for the museum.
- To marry his fiancée, Alice.

With Susan's sight on love, once she discovers David's Journeys, she throws herself onto David's pathway to derail his impending marriage. Susan commits with the best intents and purposes to help him win his grant and find the bone, but this is Screwball. What should be a simple Journey turns into a madcap adventure of mounting complications. Trickster Susan effectively strips David of everything that was his Ordinary World, landing him in a jail cell. But from this vantage in the depth of his Screwball world, David finds out the true Elixir he was after and brings it back home.

THE JOURNEY

Dr. David Huxley, a museum paleontologist for the Stuyvesant Museum of Natural History, receives a telegram announcing that the final bone to his brontosaurus has been located. This ELIXIR will complete four years of hard work (his OUTER PROBLEM). Ironically the bone will arrive on the next day, the day of his marriage to Alice. As David's assistant, Alice insists upon a marriage dedicated to David's profession, even if it means sacrificing a honeymoon and any domestic "entanglements." This distresses David, revealing his INNER PROBLEM of finding a fulfilling relationship.

David has the additional OUTER PROBLEM of trying to secure a museum grant donated by Mrs. Carlton Random. He plays golf with her lawyer, Peabody, a THRESHOLD GUARDIAN that evaluates potential causes for her money, but Peabody REFUSES to discuss finances during golf. They'll have to discuss it over lunch. But the entrance of eccentric heiress Susan Vance and a series of madcap encounters, CALLS TO ADVENTURE, derail David's Journeys.

David fetches his hooked shot and discovers Susan Vance mistakenly playing his golf ball. This first encounter, their CALL TO ROMANCE, shows how comedy can build from the simplest misunderstanding being blown into a life-or-death situation. Both will defend their possession of the golf ball to the death. The battle of golf balls builds to mistaken cars, pulling David further from Peabody, climaxing with Susan driving David away on the running board of his car.

They meet again at the Ritz Plaza Hotel. Intent on meeting Peabody, David takes a pratfall on one of Susan's martini olives. He's learned from their experience at the golf course and quickly leaves her, but two encounters set a pattern in Susan's mind. She seeks the advice from a psychiatrist dining at a table. This MENTOR suggests that David has a fixation on Susan.

David REFUSES Susan's MENTOR'S advice. But their encounters of CALLS and REFUSALS quickly become more "intimate" and more destructive. Susan accidentally tears David's tuxedo, and David mistakenly rips off the back of her dress. Soon gentleman David protects Susan's dignity and swiftly escorts her past the befuddled Peabody and out the door.

As Susan fixes David's tuxedo, she learns of David's OUTER PROBLEMS. Peabody's an old friend of Susan's family and she gladly offers to use her SPECIAL POWER and drive him to Peabody's house. But David needs to meet fiancée Alice at Carnegie Hall (a REFUSAL). Pushing her Journey to win David's heart (her INNER PROBLEM), she insists that Alice can wait until he sees Peabody. Susan's help only makes David's relationship with Peabody even worse. When she fails to arouse Peabody with a handful of pebbles against his window, she tries something bigger and strikes him with a rock. David's had enough of this TRICKSTER SHAPESHIFTER. Although he admits to being attracted to her, he's getting married to Alice. He gives Susan his firm, dignified good-bye (REFUSAL), and falls flat on his face.

The morning of his wedding, David receives the intercostal clavicle and arranges to meet Alice at the museum with this ELIXIR. He's interrupted by a phone call from Susan asking if he needs a leopard that she just received from her brother in Brazil. He REFUSES anything further to do with her, but Susan tricks David into believing that the leopard is attacking her. Convinced by her screams for help (a CRISIS OF THE HEART), David rushes to the rescue and discovers her trickery—and comes face to face with the leopard, Baby. Susan assures David that Baby's as gentle as a kitten. Baby even likes dogs and music, particularly the song "I Can't Give You Anything but Love, Baby." Baby takes an immediate liking to David, which will make things easier on their trip to Connecticut to take the leopard to her Aunt Elizabeth's farm. David has only two things on his mind: finish his brontosaurus and get married. He REFUSES to go with her, but Baby won't have it any other way, finally pushing him through the THRESHOLD—into Susan's car on the road to Connecticut.

Thrown into Susan's SPECIAL WORLD (to keep David from the marriage), David faces a TEST PHASE where he loses control of his ORDINARY WORLD and finds himself going deeper and deeper into a zany world from which there is no return.

- Susan rear-ends a truck with a load of chickens, and David has to pay for Baby's "meal." Later David has to buy 30 pounds of sirloin steak at a meat market.
- Finally arriving at Aunt Elizabeth's farmhouse, with Baby safe in a horse stall, David prepares to return to New York.
- David takes a shower and TRICKSTER Susan steals his clothes.
- Forced to wear a woman's dressing gown, David has a breakdown in front of Aunt Elizabeth and storms off in search of clothes.

Faced with her own CRISIS OF THE HEART, Susan pursues her love and finds him struggling with clothes much too small, but he's determined to escape this SPECIAL WORLD and fix the damage Susan has caused to his ORDINARY WORLD. Susan confesses to David that her aunt is his answer. She's actually Mrs. Carlton Random, the keeper of his grant. Having embarrassed himself in front of her, David now must make a swift exit without Aunt Elizabeth knowing who he really is. But George the Terrier steals his dinosaur bone, blocking his return to the ORDINARY WORLD. David's TEST PHASE shifts to finding the lost bone. He trusts Susan's SPECIAL POWER to convince the dog to unearth the bone and ends up with a bunch of holes, a pile of buried shoes, and no intercostal clavicle.

Aunt Elizabeth questions Susan's JOURNEY OF LOVE with this strange man, but Susan insists they are to be married (although he doesn't know it yet.) To protect David, she fabricates his new identity as a big game hunter, Mr. Bone.

Susan never tells David about his new identity and the complications escalate as the TEST PHASE barrels along.

- Susan and David spend dinner with Aunt Elizabeth and Major Applegate, also a big game hunter (a professional RIVAL). David spends the entire dinner stalking George the Terrier.
- A drunken farm hand, Mr. Gogarty, mistakenly releases Baby from her stall.
- Susan needs to find Baby and threatens to reveal David's disguise if he doesn't help her.
- David calls the zoo to hunt down the leopard, but Susan discovers that her brother had sent it for Aunt Elizabeth. David can't call off the zoo's hunt (a TICKING CLOCK).

Searching through the woods, Susan and David fall down an embankment. They hear the sounds of Baby and George "playing" and see the animals across the creek, APPROACH THE INMOST CAVE. They try to cross the creek and fall in. Later, drying their wet clothes, David no longer sees any chance of repairing his ruined world. And how can he when this TRICKSTER Susan is fabricating his identity in this world without telling him. Dashing all of David's hopes, Susan tells him that Peabody is on his way to visit Aunt Elizabeth. Since Peabody believes David conked him with the rock, his arrival is a TICKING CLOCK that will soon reveal David's true identity.

Meanwhile, a ferocious leopard is being transported to its demise. When the truck pulls over to get directions, David and Susan mistake it for the zoo truck—and the leopard for Baby. They release the ferocious leopard and it runs away.

Later, David breaks his glasses in another spill, and he finally hits his limit, the ORDEAL. What more can happen to him? He sends Susan away. Faced with this CRISIS OF THE HEART, Susan leaves and trips over a log. David rushes to her side. Susan breaks down in tears, distraught that she ruined everything for David. David consoles her (a RESURRECTION of the ORDEAL). She acknowledges that she's manipulated him all along, but now faced with this ORDEAL she's run out of tricks. She begs him to let her rejoin his JOURNEY. The two are on the THRESHOLD of kissing but David avoids this REWARD and resumes the search. They hear Baby on a neighbor's rooftop and try to serenade their REWARD down with "I Can't Give You Anything but Love, Baby." They awaken the neighbor, Dr. Lehman, Susan's psychiatrist MENTOR from the dining room of the Ritz Hotel. Dr. Lehman can't see any leopard and soon David and Susan end up in jail—David for being a Peeping Tom and Susan for being crazy.

Their ROAD BACK begins in jail. David and Susan must convince Constable Slocum of their story. Their "CHASE of words" to reveal the truth faces the roadblock of a worthy Screwball THRESHOLD GUARDIAN; the constable refuses to believe their story about a leopard. The suspects pile up as Gogarty, Aunt Elizabeth, and Applegate can't convince

Slocum and wind up in their own jail cells. But Susan uses her SPECIAL POWERS to talk her way out of jail. She plays Slocum's game and gives him the conspiracy that he's looking for. Pretending that she's "Swingin' Door Suzie," she uses her tale of the famed "Leopard Gang" to escape. The police give chase as Peabody and Alice arrive. These members, direct from the ORDINARY WORLD, are the voices of reason that finally make Constable Slocum listen. But David is too deeply into this Journey. The lies and deceptions of his SPECIAL WORLD catch up. His relationship with Alice is now in question, and Peabody and Aunt Elizabeth refuse the museum's grant.

When the circus officials show up, followed by Baby and George, David realizes that Susan's out chasing down the wrong leopard. He needs to answer this CRISIS OF THE HEART, and sure enough he gets his chance. Susan drags in her dangerous catch, and David saves her (the RESURRECTION). Susan's HERO promptly faints in her arms.

Back in David's ORDINARY WORLD, David accepts the break-up of his engagement to Alice, and returns to his unfinished brontosaurus. Susan arrives with the lost bone and the assurance of Aunt Elizabeth's million-dollar grant; but now that David has returned to his ORDINARY WORLD, these ELIXIRS don't seem so valuable. Susan insists upon delivering her ELIXIR and climbs up the ladder to meet him at the top of the brontosaurus.

Now at this perilous height, David sees his ELIXIR. He realizes that his day of misadventures with Susan was actually the best day he'd ever had. He admits his love for Susan. Giddy with this ELIXIR, Susan begins to sway; but before the ladder collapses, she leaps atop the brontosaurus. The skeleton gives way. David grabs Susan (a physical RESURRECTION), and the fruits of his four years of hard work crumble into a pile of bones. This woman has destroyed his entire ORDINARY WORLD. David gives up and accepts the ELIXIR of their love.

FADE OUT

SINGIN' IN THE RAIN
(U.S., 1952)

"Kathy, I love you."

(He kisses her)

"Don—"

"Kathy, I can't wait until this picture's finished. No more secrecy. I'm going to let Lina know. I'm going to let everyone know."

"Your fans will be bitterly disappointed."

"From now on there's only one fan I'm worried about."

Don Lockwood (Gene Kelly) and
Kathy Selden (Debbie Reynolds)

Story and screenplay by Adolph Green and Betty Comden
Suggested by the song, "Singin' in the Rain"
Directed by Gene Kelly and Stanley Donen

As Hollywood enters the sound era, silent screen star Don Lockwood finds love and a new career as a song-and-dance man.

LANDMARKS OF THE JOURNEY

The obstacles keeping our romantic pair apart don't always arise from the differences between the lovers. Don Lockwood and Kathy Selden are more alike than they initially believe, and soon cross the Threshold of the Heart. However, a shrewd, nasally Rival turns the tables on the lovers. Pushing her way into this Romantic Triangle, Lina Lamont will do whatever is necessary to keep Don for herself, and save her own career.

Song has always been the perfect vehicle to express love. The brilliance of *Singin' in the Rain* is the integration of the songs into the story's structure so that they erupt freely from the inner needs and turmoil of the characters. Many times in *Singin' in the Rain,* the songs mark the Stages of the Hero's Journey. "Make 'Em Laugh" is a Meeting with the Trickster Mentor. The Resurrection of the Ordeal dawns with the new day and our trio's glowing "Good Mornin'." And Don celebrates his Reward of Kathy's love with the unforgettable title song.

THE JOURNEY

Hollywood in the late 1920s, on the THRESHOLD of the talkies. The careers of Monumental Pictures' leading silent screen stars, Don Lockwood and Lina Lamont, flourish (their ORDINARY WORLD.) Their audiences adore them, and the publicity machine stokes the fire of their fame with stories of their real-life romantic linking.

Don and Lina celebrate their curtain call at the opening night of yet another successful romantic swashbuckler. But Don refuses to let Lina speak, and we soon hear why. Her nasal, unrefined speech would kill a speaking career, but Lina is self-centered and hopelessly unaware of her verbal deficiency. Backstage, we also learn that the stories of Don and Lina's pairing are all fabrication for publicity—a deception Lina fights to maintain but Don REFUSES. Don confides in his best friend, Cosmo Brown (a TRICKSTER ALLY/MENTOR), that he wishes he could get Lina out of his hair (INNER PROBLEM).

Outside the theatre, Cosmo's car gets a flat and Don has to escape a mob of screaming fans. He leaps onto a trolley, from which he jumps into the passing car of Kathy Selden. Not recognizing Don Lockwood, Kathy pulls over to turn her intruder over to the police. This MENTOR OF THE LAW sets Kathy straight about her famous passenger, and she offers Don a ride. When Don sees Kathy's concern about his ripped clothes, he begins to make his moves, playing up the lonely life of the Hollywood star. Kathy sees beneath his SHAPESHIFTER'S mask and uses verbal barbs to demean his acting and his movies. This REFUSAL strikes a nerve, making Don question his acting abilities (an INNER STIRRING). In contrast, Kathy strives for a dignified career as a great stage actress, her OUTER PROBLEM. Kathy lets him off and Don heartily accepts "Ethel Barrymore's" REFUSAL, but humiliates himself getting his tuxedo tail caught in her door.

At the post-premier party, producer R.F. Simpson shows his cast and crew a test film demonstrating the new talking picture technology (an industry CALL TO ADVENTURE). Everyone REFUSES this "vulgar toy" and Simpson predicts Warner Bros. will lose their shirts with *The Jazz Singer.*

Don gets his just desserts at the party when Kathy leaps from the cake. "Ethel Barrymore" is a dancing girl. Insulted, Kathy tries to get the last word by throwing a pie at Don, but hits Lina by mistake. Kathy makes a quick exit, but Don's clearly taken by this CALL FOR ROMANCE.

Don feels responsible that she lost her job, but now he can't find her. He arrives at the studio to begin shooting their next feature, *The Dueling Cavalier.* Cosmo echoes Kathy's observation of yet another Lamont and Lockwood romance, "If you've seen one, you've seen them all," re-awakening Don's insecurity with his acting and his career, INNER PROBLEM. But his best friend/MENTOR cheers him up, pushing him forward on his current Journey to make the picture. After all, "the show must go on." He sings "Make 'Em Laugh," a MEETING WITH THE SIDEKICK MENTOR.

During filming Lina gleefully confesses to Don that she was the one who had Kathy fired. Now Don is more committed than ever to find Kathy and fix what this RIVAL has done. Simpson suddenly halts filming. The success of *The Jazz Singer* forces Simpson to turn *The Dueling Cavalier* into a talkie. But CROSSING THIS THRESHOLD poses one serious obstacle, Lina's voice. We are transported through a colorful THRESHOLD SEQUENCE, the "Beautiful Girl" montage, representing the motion picture industry's THRESHOLD into the glorious SPECIAL WORLD of sound. As the SEQUENCE closes, Cosmo watches a dance rehearsal and spots Kathy in the chorus. He quickly grabs Don, who makes amends with Kathy, getting her a small film part.

Don's not about to let Kathy go without letting her know how he really feels. But he needs the right atmosphere. Using a sound stage, the magic of lights and a wind machine, he declares his love, "You Were Meant for Me." They've CROSSED THE THRESHOLD of romance.

Now that the lovers are together, the TEST PHASE focuses on the filming of *The Dueling Cavalier*, and the obstacles presented by the introduction of sound. Now that voices must be heard, Don and Lina work with diction coaches (MENTORS). Lina falters, incapable of improvement; Don breezes through his lessons. The production must cope with the new technology, a TEST played to hilarious effect as cast and crew must learn to work with the microphone.

At last they are prepared to show *The Dueling Cavalier* to a preview audience. Don and Kathy arrive for the premiere, an APPROACH TO THE INMOST CAVE, but they mustn't let Lina see them together. Kathy sits with the rest of the audience, while Don nervously watches with Simpson, Cosmo and Lina. Technical problems and Lina's voice turn the preview into a disaster, a humiliating ORDEAL.

Later that night, Don, Cosmo and Kathy face the ramifications of this ORDEAL. Don fears his career is over. But Cosmo and Kathy offer hope suggesting they use Don's SPECIAL POWERS as a song-and-dance man and turn *The Dueling Cavalier* into a musical. This TEAM celebrates their ingenious solution with "Good Mornin'," but this RESURRECTION is short-lived. Don reminds them that Lina would have to sing also. But MENTOR Cosmo comes up with another brilliant solution: dub Lina's voice with Kathy's. Don objects that Kathy would be sacrificing her career for Lina's. But Kathy willingly makes this NOBLE SACRIFICE to save this one picture and Don's career.

Don takes Kathy home. They kiss goodnight. It's raining but Don sees nothing but sunshine as he enters the downpour. He walks home, but his joy and love erupt into "Singin' in the Rain," an almost rapturous celebration of his REWARDS. He has been RESURRECTED from the ORDEAL with his love for Kathy and a new career on the horizon as a song-and-dance man.

Don and Cosmo convince Simpson to turn *The Dueling Cavalier* into *The Dancing Cavalier.* Quickly they rework the film and dub Kathy's voice. Pleased with her work, Simpson promises a big build-up for Kathy's career, a REWARD.

Kathy completes the final dubbing and the film will soon be released. Initiating the ROAD BACK, Don affirms his love for Kathy, and promises to tell everyone and sacrifice the publicity of his intended nuptials with Lina. However, RIVAL Lina discovers them and vows retaliation.

Determined to save her career, Lina launches a publicity blitz that falsely quotes Simpson praising Lina's "singing pipes and dancing stems." Wielding her studio contract, Lina threatens to sue Monumental Pictures if it doesn't force Kathy to dub Lina's voice for the rest of her career.

The premiere of *The Dancing Cavalier* receives an overwhelming reception. Lockwood and Lamont's career has been RESURRECTED, but Don learns of Lina's plot to ruin Kathy's career. Egotistical Lina wants to savor the ELIXIR of her film's success, and insists upon taking her own curtain call. Don's happy to let her. The audience can't believe this shrill-voiced Lina is the same one on the film; they demand a song. This opens the door for Don and Cosmo to get revenge on the RIVAL and expose the truth. Don sacrifices his relationship with Kathy and demands that she hide behind the curtain and sing for Lina. During Lina's curtain call, the men pull the curtains and reveal the deceit—humiliating both Lina and Kathy. Kathy makes a quick exit, but Don saves her, demanding the audience recognize the real star behind Lina's performance.

Don uses the song "You Are My Lucky Star" to bring Kathy back onstage, a RESURRECTION of her career and their love. Soon they sing and embrace, sharing the ELIXIR of their love. The audience welcomes this new star (an ELIXIR); Don and Kathy become Monumental Pictures' new romantic pair.

FADE OUT

ANNIE HALL
(U.S., 1977)

"A relationship, I think, is like a shark. You know, it has to constantly move forward or it dies, and I think what we got on our hands is a dead shark."
—Alvy Singer (Woody Allen)

Written by Woody Allen and Marshall Brickman
Directed by Woody Allen

Two neurotic New Yorkers fall in love, break up, fall in love and finally break up.

LANDMARKS OF THE JOURNEY

Alvy Singer's childhood beneath a Coney Island roller coaster is as much a reason for his neurosis as it is a fitting image for the Journey he takes us on. Romance can be a roller coaster. We both fear and anticipate its thrills. It moves too quickly; yet we can recall the highs and the lows. And when it's over, we're ready to get back in line to take the ride again.

Originally titled *Anhedonia,* meaning the inability to enjoy anything, describing Alvy Singer's neurosis, *Annie Hall* takes us onto a quest of understanding why a relationship failed. Allen and Brickman ease us onto the roller coaster of memories as Alvy's hyperactive imagination sifts through the emotional puzzle pieces, jumping between fantasy and reality, confronting childhood crises with adult rationale, suffering his defeats and celebrating his triumphs. This unpredictable style gives *Annie Hall* its distinctive comic voice that lets us identify with Alvy as we laugh at his pain.

But *Annie Hall* is not without structure. Alvy's quest is in recollection, freely flashing back to pivotal moments that mark his relationship with Annie. Not coincidentally, these key moments can also be seen as key stages of the Hero's Journey. Alvy Singer faces two journeys:

- Alvy's search for understanding about his break-up with Annie Hall. This is the initial quest that is told in real time.
- Alvy seeks a relationship with Annie Hall. This Journey is told in flashbacks.

Alvy's quest for understanding begins at a Resurrection as he tries to find some Elixir or meaning of why his relationship failed. One can see his entire Journey as one long Resurrection. He remembers the past in order to grow, learn and gain some Elixir that will guide him into his next relationship. This Special World of finding understanding takes us into the heart of the second Journey, the Special World of his relationship with Annie Hall.

THE JOURNEY

Alvy Singer begins his Journey in crisis. He needs to find meaning from his recent break-up with Annie Hall. Where did he screw up? This OUTER PROBLEM fuels the Journey's central dramatic question. We know the relationship will fail; we (along with Alvy) want to know how it failed. Since this is his Journey into his mind and his recollections, it's important to know his view on life and his relationships with women. And Alvy's not afraid to present his ORDINARY WORLD to us through direct conversation and flash-back to his childhood, where his mother, his elementary school teacher and classmates lend some perspective on Alvy's ORDINARY WORLD. A comedian/comedy writer, Alvy Singer distrusts the world. He's paranoid, obsessed with suffering and death and he balks at any change in his life. Instead he forces everything to conform to his way of life (a TRAGIC FLAW).

Alvy also needs to ease us into the problem of his relationship and introduces us to Annie, showing glimpses of the bad and the good times. He begins as they APPROACH their relationship's break-up. Annie and Alvy are having sexual problems that Alvy refuses to accept as mutual.

But Alvy's relationship with Annie is not all disaster. We need to hope, like Alvy, that the two were meant for each other. He lets us enjoy their struggle to cook a lobster feast (a TEST). Later, walking on the beach, Alvy and Annie relive their failed romances and marriages. These perspectives of their pasts complete the ORDINARY WORLDS. We better understand Alvy and Annie, preparing us to see how their relationship began.

Alvy and Annie first meet during a tennis date, a CALL TO ADVENTURE. In her inimitably roundabout manner, Annie acts on this meeting and offers Alvy a ride and eventually invites him up to her apartment. The two begin to learn about each other. Alvy learns about Annie's ORDINARY WORLD from the books and family photos in her apartment. Soon, they share wine on the balcony. As the film uses subtitles to reveal subtext, each character considers a potential relationship and reveals fears and insecurities. Annie fears he's a shmuck like her other boyfriends, a REFUSAL, and prepares to send him away, but Alvy asks her out. She accepts this CALL TO ADVENTURE, agreeing to let him hear her sing at the nightclub.

Approaching the THRESHOLD of romantic commitment can cause great anxiety and anticipation. Following Annie's singing engagement (a THRESHOLD of her singing career), they head to dinner, Alvy asks for a kiss to relieve the anxiety and let them enjoy dinner. Later that night, they make love. The THRESHOLD has given Alvy a great sexual experience, while Annie smokes a joint to help her deal with her insecurity in this new SPECIAL WORLD.

Alvy takes control of the TEST PHASE. He forces himself as a MENTOR to turn Annie into what he wants her to be, and change her to fit into his rigid ORDINARY WORLD.

The rules are simply what she needs to know about Alvy if they want to date. He buys her books on death and dying, his obsession, and a reflection of his pessimistic view on life.

They walk together on the docks, and Annie wants to move the TEST PHASE into the APPROACH of commitment. Although they admit their love with words, Annie questions Alvy's heart. He's willing to show his love with a kiss but Annie wants more and pushes for them to move in together. Faced with this major TEST, Alvy reveals his fear of change. He wants this "life raft" of her apartment to show that they aren't married, not realizing that marriage may be what she desires (her INNER PROBLEM). His reluctance resurfaces Annie's insecurities. She fears she's not smart enough for Alvy, which is why he's been pushing her to take college courses.

The TESTS of the relationship also reveal Alvy's fears and insecurities. Annie's reliance upon grass to relax her for sex makes Alvy question his sexual prowess. Dinner with Annie's family proves an impossible task filled with suicidal brothers and Jew-hating Grammies (THRESHOLD GUARDIANS).

Although the TEST PHASE brings out their insecurities, pushing them to question this relationship, it also heightens their need for each other. Now Alvy's need to push his ORDINARY WORLD onto Annie blows up in his face. He becomes jealous that Annie may be having an affair with one of her professors, and follows her, APPROACH THE INMOST CAVE. Annie catches Alvy and reminds him that his inability to make a commitment doomed their relationship. Annie leaves him, the ORDEAL. Alvy still can't understand why. He wants answers and seeks a REWARD from various passers-by. One person offers that "love fades," which Alvy doesn't want to accept. He blames his inability to choose the right person, continuing to deny that a relationship requires change from both partners.

His friend Rob (SIDEKICK MENTOR) tries to push him on to new relationships, setting him up with Pam, a reporter for *Rolling Stone.* But their lovemaking is interrupted by a call from Annie. He rushes over to kill a spider, an ORDEAL, but Annie tearfully admits she called him because she misses him. Soon they make love, a RESURRECTION of their break-up, and recommit to their relationship, a REWARD. For her birthday, Alvy and Rob take Annie back to their old neighborhood in Brooklyn. She enjoys seeing this part of Alvy (his ORDINARY WORLD). And it looks like their relationship is back on course as Annie sings "Seems Like Old Times" during her nightclub act. Annie receives praise from Los Angeles record producer, Tony Lacey. His invitation to a party arouses Alvy's jealousy, and he makes an excuse to prevent Annie from taking Lacey's Journey. Alvy takes away the REWARD that would further her singing career. His decision forces each to seriously question the relationship with their respective therapists (a MEETING WITH THE MENTOR).

Alvy and Annie accept their ROAD BACK in Los Angeles. They visit Rob, now a star on a hit television series, and end up coincidentally at a party thrown by Tony Lacey. And again, Tony, a RIVAL for Annie's heart, offers her a place to stay while she cuts a record. On the flight back, Alvy and Annie mutually decide that their relationship is a "dead shark," completing the ROAD BACK.

They split up. Annie moves to Los Angeles for Tony and her singing career. Missing Annie, Alvy again seeks advice from passers-by. He returns to dating and tries to push the SPECIAL WORLD of the relationship he had with Annie on these dates. He fails miserably to resurrect what he had with Annie.

Alvy finally gathers the courage to call Annie and confess his love. He flies out to Los Angeles to bring her back, a CHASE. He suggests they get married, but Annie has moved on.

Annie is satisfied with the ELIXIR of their friendship, grateful to Alvy for giving her this new life—a new career, a stronger outlook. Alvy must accept the death of their romantic relationship, the RESURRECTION. After taking out his frustration on his rental car and landing in jail, Alvy returns to New York.

He now rehearses a play based on his relationship with Annie Hall. The ending's different—they make up and she comes back with him to New York. His perfect stage world is his way to cope with the pain of the reality of life, and to vicariously live the RESURRECTION and ELIXIR he had sought. He's seen Annie since the break-up and they've kicked around old times. He can finally look back at the good times the two had and finally acknowledge the ELIXIR. Relationships are irrational, crazy, and painful, but we keep going through them because we need the good times.

FADE OUT

DONA FLOR AND HER TWO HUSBANDS
(Brazil, 1978)

"That's exactly how I feel. Outside, a serious lady. Inside, a bad girl dreaming of naughty things."

"You're a woman. That's normal."

—Flor (Sonia Braga) and
Rozilda (Dinorah Brillanti)

Written by Bruno Barreto
Based on the novel by Jorge Amado
Directed by Bruno Barreto

A woman is torn between her proper new husband and the spirit of her erotic, yet unfaithful, dead husband.

LANDMARKS OF THE JOURNEY

The death of her husband, Vadinho, throws Dona Flor into a state of mourning. In this Special World, her mother pushes her to move on with her life. After all, Vadinho was an unfaithful scoundrel who used Dona Flor for her money. Eventually time heals and Dona Flor remarries. But Vadinho's death makes Flor long for the Elixir of her Ordinary World. Flor's new husband fulfills her need for devotion and stability, yet he fails to fulfill the sensual needs that had been awakened by Flor's dead husband. A woman deserves both worlds. And a ghost answers her prayers. But in Barreto's magical romance, a ghost too can learn the true Elixir of life and redeem himself with the Elixir of his "undying" devotion to Dona Flor.

THE JOURNEY

A small Brazilian town celebrates the magical time of Carnival in 1943. A group of men enjoy the morning with costumed revelry. A woman dancer appears in the street and one of the men, Vadinho, answers her overtly sexual CALL. He dances with her and drops dead. Vadinho's wife, Dona Flor, rushes to his side. No matter how hard she REFUSES to accept this CALL, Vadinho is dead. And with him, Flor is thrown into a death state, an extended ORDEAL of mourning.

During the wake, we learn about Dona Flor's ORDINARY WORLD with Vadinho through the reactions of the villagers. The men show deep sorrow at the loss of their respected "brother" (their HERO). For the women, the gambling gigolo (a SHADOW) had it coming. Dona Flor mourns the loss of her love. She's transported by the memory of the senses, recalling his favorite dish, crabmeat casserole. This remembrance takes us back to the Journey of their marriage...

On their wedding night, Vadinho seduces Flor and they consummate their marriage, CROSSING THE THRESHOLD. But when she awakens, she is immediately thrown into the TEST PHASE determining Vadinho's faithfulness to her. She finds her wedding bed empty; her new husband is off gambling. Vadinho is restless. Despite his declarations of love and devotion to Flor, SHAPESHIFTER Vadinho seduces her students while she conducts her cooking class, and carouses with his girlfriends at the casinos. Flor longs for a normal relationship where, at the end of the day, they can wear pajamas and listen to the radio. And she wants children (INNER NEED). But Vadinho sees plenty of time left for that. He loses a church loan at an all-night party and comes home drunk. Yet, Flor forgives him and takes him in. Vadinho takes advantage of her APPROACH TO THE INMOST CAVE. He beats her and takes her money, the ORDEAL. Vadinho wins at roulette and comes home drunk. He serenades Dona Flor, presenting her with a necklace bought from his winnings (the REWARD). But Vadinho returns to his cheating ways. He disappears for several days, and Flor's mother suggests that she leave him. But Flor remains by her man. Vadinho returns home drunk, and collapses in the street. Dona Flor accepts him yet again, and perhaps her devotion has transformed Vadinho. He finally agrees to take her to the Casino for her birthday. During their romantic evening, he excuses himself for gambling and whores. Dona Flor hoped that Vadinho was on the ROAD BACK to change and recommitment to her, but his death cut that short.

Back in the present, and still dressed in black, Flor confronts a woman who gives Flor a bouquet of flowers. This mystical MENTOR warns Flor not to untie the ribbon binding the flowers until she gets to the tomb, so that the soul of "this son of a devil" will rest. At his tomb, Flor finally lets Vadinho go and unties the ribbon.

But Flor suffers an INNER STIRRING. She longs for the sexually satisfying life he provided, pushing her to accept her RESURRECTION from the ORDEAL of mourning. She discards her black clothes for a new dress and quickly receives a love letter from the pharmacist. Although Flor feels it's still too soon to consider a new relationship (a REFUSAL), her mother pushes her to move on with her life. This MEETING WITH THE MENTOR helps her accept the pharmacist's CALL TO ADVENTURE, and soon he asks Flor to marry him.

Again, Dona Flor passes the THRESHOLD OF MARRIAGE. But her formal, gentle pharmacist husband is the complete opposite of her unfaithful, extremely erotic dead husband. The two are SHADOW RIVALS. Showing their contrast, on the wedding night, Dona Flor now must seduce her new pajama-clad husband. She soon discovers that sex in this SPECIAL WORLD is not as satisfying as what Vadinho gave her in her ORDINARY WORLD. At church she confesses her depression and acknowledges her "evil nature." Flor prays for the satisfaction of her desires, APPROACH THE INMOST CAVE.

At their anniversary party, everyone praises how perfect a couple they make. Dona Flor finds her new life boring and retires to her bedroom. She finds Vadinho naked in bed, the answer to her prayers, an ORDEAL. But Flor is a married woman and refuses this REWARD before the temptation becomes too great. Vadinho insists that he can't be seen by anyone except Flor, and that there's room for both him and his RIVAL. She still won't be swayed, and finally gets Vadinho to leave for the price of one kiss.

He appears again and tries to coax her into bed. Seducing her with kisses, reawakening the senses that had died with him. Vadinho admits that he misses Flor, the REWARD granted to him by the ORDEAL of death. Flor needs to remain faithful to her new husband, but Vadinho's temptation to satisfy her desires becomes too great. Flor seeks a MENTOR'S magic to rid her of Vadinho's spirit, the ROAD BACK.

As the MENTOR dances the spell to banish the spirit (TICKING CLOCK), Vadinho again visits Dona Flor. She can no longer resist his temptation. Flor prepares to claim her ELIXIR. Vadinho vanishes! The MENTOR'S magic has worked. Flor screams. Having tasted the ELIXIR, she can't believe she turned it away. She wants Vadinho back and the RESURRECTION of her desires breaks the MENTOR'S spell. Vadinho returns and they make love.

Vadinho was right. There is room for the three of them. Flor needs the ELIXIR that both husbands provide to satisfy her desires and her need for faithfulness and stability. Her Journey closes as Flor walks happily with her two husbands arm in arm. She has been healed with the ELIXIR of devotion from both of her husbands, one in life and the other in death.

FADE OUT

SLEEPLESS IN SEATTLE
(U.S., 1993)

"I was just taking her hand to help her out of a car. And I knew. It was like magic."

—Sam (Tom Hanks)

Screenplay by Nora Ephron and David S. Ward and Jeff Arch
Story by Jeff Arch
Directed by Nora Ephron

A recently engaged woman and a widower search for their perfect match.

LANDMARKS OF THE JOURNEY

The Mentors of Sam and Annie's Journey come in many forms: best friends, siblings, Sam's son, a radio therapist, memories of perfect love, and even the Hollywood tear-jerker *An Affair to Remember.* But perhaps the most mysterious and powerful is destiny. Destiny serves a Succession of Calls that require a lover to believe that this force is presenting its fateful path. Accepting this guide requires an incredible leap of faith, especially for Annie who doesn't believe in signs or fate. Without belief, one easily rationalizes destiny's Calls as coincidental or ludicrous. But with the hand of destiny in one's pocket, a lover will do anything to find his or her true love.

Interestingly, rational and safe Annie eventually follows destiny, and yet Sam denies the magic of fate's hand. Sam is an actualized Hero, albeit a tragic one because of his loss, but he had found his perfect love. And for Sam, that magical Journey of love happens only once in a life. He just needs a little help from his son to find it a second time.

THE JOURNEY

Both Sam and Annie live unsettling ORDINARY WORLDS. Sam's has been disrupted by the sudden death of his wife and one true love, Maggie. Sam and his son Jonah must accept this tragic CALL TO ADVENTURE, but the void of wife and mother must be filled (their INNER PROBLEM). Sam tries to help his son understand Maggie's death, a MEETING WITH THE MENTOR, but Sam needs a MENTOR'S assurance as well. He cannot focus at home or at the office and finally realizes he needs to move to a different city. Perhaps a new locale will help him heal his heart. But Sam must overcome a strong INNER MENTOR built upon his memories of his love with Maggie.

Annie's ORDINARY WORLD is filled with anticipation of her impending marriage to Walter. A feature writer for a Baltimore newspaper, Annie doesn't believe in signs, destiny or fate, and yet she begins to question whether Walter is her destined love (her

INNER PROBLEM). Annie tries on her mother's wedding dress. During this MEETING WITH THE MENTOR, Annie's mother reminds her of her love for Annie's father—and the "magic" she felt just when they held hands. Moved by this tale of true love, Annie accidentally tears her wedding dress and recognizes this "sign," a CALL that further fuels her INNER STIRRING and trust in the MENTOR of destiny.

Later that Christmas Eve, Annie drives alone to Walter's folks. She tunes in Dr. Marcia Fieldstone's radio phone-in show. Her show devoted to Christmas wishes, Dr. Fieldstone answers young Jonah's telephone wish for a new wife for Sam (Jonah's OUTER PROBLEM). To help Jonah, the radio MENTOR convinces Jonah to put Sam on the phone. Which he does, and Sam reluctantly tells his story. Eighteen months since Maggie's death and now living in Seattle, Sam's ORDINARY WORLD is without sleep, without love and companionship (except with his son). During this MEETING WITH THE MENTOR, Dr. Fieldstone tries to push Sam to accept his INNER PROBLEM to find someone. Sam REFUSES to believe he can find another love like Maggie's. Sam describes the "magic," and Annie anticipates his words with a synchronicity that makes the audience sense that these two are destined for one another.

Sam's testament to true love stirs the female listening audience, and moves Annie to tears. Thousands of phone calls tie up the Chicago radio station's phone lines with women desperate for "Sleepless in Seattle's" address. Becky, Annie's editor and friend, sees how the phone call has affected Annie. This SIDEKICK MENTOR initially tries to push Annie to REFUSE a Journey in pursuit of a possible psycho. But Becky also isn't too excited about Walter.

New Year's Eve, Walter asks Annie to rendezvous in New York City on Valentine's Day. He suggests they could register, a sign of commitment and an APPROACH TO THE INMOST CAVE that makes Annie think. Valentine's Day becomes a TICKING CLOCK that will soon propel Annie's as well as Sam's Journey.

The impact of Dr. Fieldstone's radio show slowly crumbles Sam's and Annie's reluctance to commit to the SPECIAL WORLD. First, Sam receives hundreds of letters from Dr. Fieldstone's listeners. Although Jonah eagerly dives through this THRESHOLD, Sam REFUSES to get a date this way. Sam will CROSS THIS THRESHOLD into the SPECIAL WORLD of dating, but only by heeding his rules—he wants to meet someone face to face. But Sam has doubts (a REFUSAL). Do his old rules still apply? Jonah begins to set him straight about dating, a MEETING WITH THE MENTOR. Later, Sam gets dating pointers from his best friend, Jay. This SIDEKICK MENTOR of the dating life encourages Sam to ask out Victoria, a business acquaintance. Sam returns home and, seeing his son with a new girlfriend, Jessica, summons the courage to get "back in the saddle again." He calls Victoria, but Sam isn't prepared for how much his rules have changed. Victoria upgrades Sam's drink date to dinner, and sets all the arrangements for him. CROSSING THIS THRESHOLD leaves Sam exhausted.

In the middle of the night, Annie listens to "The Best of Marcia Fieldstone" highlighting "Sleepless in Seattle," a repeat performance provided by the MENTOR of destiny. Again, Sam's testament moves Annie to tears. Led by her heart, Annie CROSSES THE THRESHOLD to find "Sleepless in Seattle" (her OUTER PROBLEM). She doesn't want to regret having avoided this Journey to find "magic," but her rational self is telling her how crazy the Journey is. She tries to let her brother talk her out of the Journey; however, her heart's will (and faith in destiny) proves a stronger MENTOR. Annie tries to write a letter to "Sleepless in Seattle" with the help of SIDEKICK MENTOR Becky and the inspiration of Hollywood MENTOR *An Affair to Remember.* The romance film gives Annie and Becky the ideal Hollywood world of romance to aspire to, and offers Annie a way to make her letter stand out. She writes an invitation to meet at the top of the Empire State Building on Valentine's Day. Remembering her date with Walter in New York on Valentine's day, Annie quickly discards the letter. But she hasn't abandoned her Journey. She will take precautions during this initial TEST PHASE, and uses her newspaper contacts to do a background check on "Sleepless in Seattle" (AKA Sam Baldwin).

Meanwhile, Sam prepares for his date with Victoria. Jonah receives Annie's letter (which we learn was dispatched by her SIDEKICK MENTOR), and likes what he reads. But Sam won't consider dating someone clear on the other side of the country (REFUSING the CALL).

Sam has already chosen his SPECIAL WORLD and his TEST PHASE is in full swing. He dates Victoria. However, Sam faces an important THRESHOLD GUARDIAN, his son. In search of a new mother (INNER PROBLEM) and with his sights on Annie, Jonah isn't afraid to show his displeasure with Victoria. When he spies his father and Victoria getting too close, Jonah becomes desperate to stop this APPROACH before Sam goes too far. He needs a MENTOR'S help and calls Dr. Marcia Fieldstone. Broadcast on the radio, Jonah's ORDEAL is heard by Annie. Dr. Fieldstone can't provide any immediate solution except to push Jonah to express his feelings. The young TRICKSTER screams bloody murder to break up the couple's kiss.

This ORDEAL determines the APPROACH TO THE INMOST CAVE that must be taken. First, Jonah (writing as Sam) responds to Annie's letter. Second, Annie commits to pursuing Sam, a THRESHOLD into a deeper SPECIAL WORLD. With her SIDEKICK MENTOR'S support, Annie lies to Walter, and flies out to Seattle to meet Sam face to face.

Destiny strikes its CALL at the airport as Sam's and Annie's paths cross. While Sam's voice has pushed Annie on her Journey without Sam's knowledge, Sam now sees Annie without her awareness. Smitten by her vision, he tries to follow her but quickly loses her in the crowd. Even though they are now in the same city, fate plays a devilish set of TESTS to keep them apart—and flirt with their hearts.

Annie tries to see Sam, and keeps missing him. She finally decides to make the bold APPROACH. But mistaking Sam's sister for a new lover, Annie is stunned in her tracks. Sam recognizes her from the airport and greets her from across the road. Before they can meet, a taxi almost hits her. Humiliated by this ORDEAL, Annie quickly returns to Baltimore. Annie believes that she has earned the REWARD of greater awareness to end this ill-fated Journey.

Prepared to pull the plug on fate, *An Affair to Remember,* and her fantasy of "Sleepless of Seattle," she receives Jonah's letter. Its juvenile tone is the final sign. Against her SIDEKICK MENTOR'S advice to continue her pursuit and meet "Sleepless" on the Empire State Building, Annie accepts her ROAD BACK. Her misinterpretation of Sam's world and Jonah's deception forces her to recommit to Walter.

MENTORS play valuable roles to determine Sam's and Jonah's ROAD BACK. Sam's sister encourages Sam to meet Annie on the top of the Empire State Building. But Sam rejects the "weepy tears" of Hollywood romance. As Valentine's Day approaches (TICKING CLOCK), Jonah's friend Jessica pushes him onto his ROAD BACK. This precocious young MENTOR purchases his airline ticket to New York.

Jonah gives Sam one last chance to commit to Annie. Sam refuses, closing the door on Jonah and Annie's letter. Sam prepares to leave for his weekend away with Victoria and finds that Jonah has taken off for New York, Sam's ROAD BACK. Sam races after him, a CHASE. Jonah arrives in New York and camps out at the top of the Empire State Building in search of Annie.

Meanwhile, in New York City, Annie tries to fit back into her ORDINARY WORLD with Walter, but her pursuit of "Sleepless in Seattle" has made this return uncomfortable. During Valentine's dinner with the view of the Empire State Building a constant reminder of her desire for true love, Annie finally confesses her needs to Walter. They amicably break off their engagement. The lights of the Empire State Building illuminate a huge red heart; destiny pushes Annie to race to the building.

But at the top, Jonah has given up all hope of meeting Annie. Sam arrives and reunites with his son, a RESURRECTION. They board their elevator as Annie makes her ascent. She arrives on an empty observation deck, dashing all hopes of love's ELIXIR. But destiny (and RESURRECTION) now arrives in the form of Jonah's backpack and teddy bear. And soon with it, Sam and Jonah. At last Sam and Annie meet. He invites her to join them and holds out his hand. She takes it—and the three leave with the "magic" ELIXIR of true love.

FADE OUT

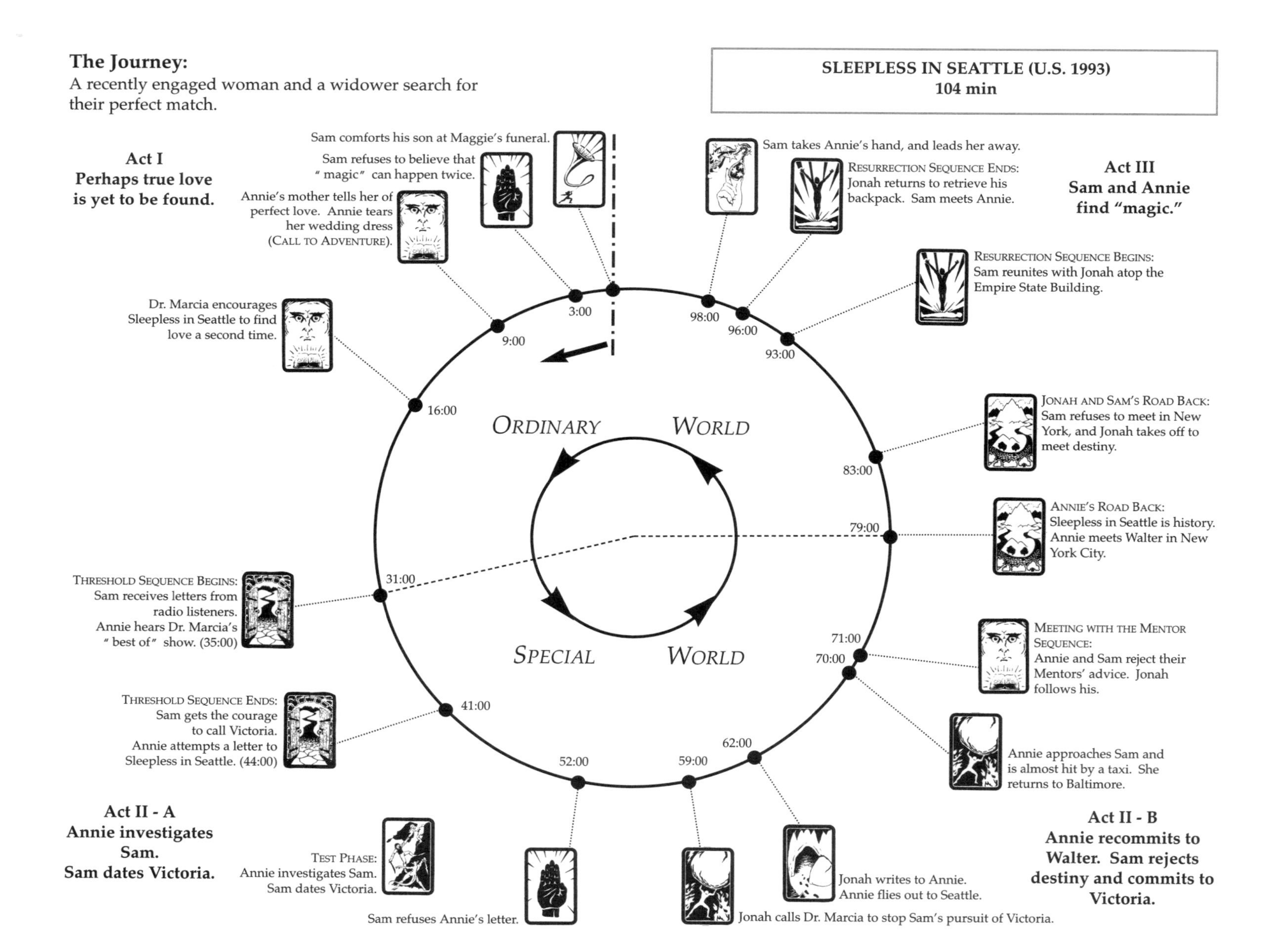

The Journey:
A recently engaged woman and a widower search for their perfect match.
SLEEPLESS IN SEATTLE (U.S. 1993)
104 min
Act I
Perhaps true love is yet to be found.
Sam comforts his son at Maggie's funeral.
Sam refuses to believe that "magic" can happen twice.
Annie's mother tells her of perfect love. Annie tears her wedding dress (CALL TO ADVENTURE).
Dr. Marcia encourages Sleepless in Seattle to find love a second time.
3:00
9:00
16:00
ORDINARY
WORLD
SPECIAL
WORLD
31:00
THRESHOLD SEQUENCE BEGINS:
Sam receives letters from radio listeners.
Annie hears Dr. Marcia's "best of" show. (35:00)
41:00
THRESHOLD SEQUENCE ENDS:
Sam gets the courage to call Victoria.
Annie attempts a letter to Sleepless in Seattle. (44:00)
Act II - A
Annie investigates Sam.
Sam dates Victoria.
TEST PHASE:
Annie investigates Sam.
Sam dates Victoria.
52:00
Sam refuses Annie's letter.
59:00
Jonah calls Dr. Marcia to stop Sam's pursuit of Victoria.
62:00
Jonah writes to Annie.
Annie flies out to Seattle.
Act II - B
Annie recommits to Walter. Sam rejects destiny and commits to Victoria.
70:00
Annie approaches Sam and is almost hit by a taxi. She returns to Baltimore.
71:00
MEETING WITH THE MENTOR SEQUENCE:
Annie and Sam reject their Mentors' advice. Jonah follows his.
79:00
ANNIE'S ROAD BACK:
Sleepless in Seattle is history. Annie meets Walter in New York City.
83:00
JONAH AND SAM'S ROAD BACK:
Sam refuses to meet in New York, and Jonah takes off to meet destiny.
93:00
RESURRECTION SEQUENCE BEGINS:
Sam reunites with Jonah atop the Empire State Building.
96:00
RESURRECTION SEQUENCE ENDS:
Jonah returns to retrieve his backpack. Sam meets Annie.
98:00
Sam takes Annie's hand, and leads her away.
Act III
Sam and Annie find "magic."

THE MYTHIC STRUCTURE OF COMEDY

To solve our problem we take command of a Special World of deception. Our success offers new Thresholds of opportunity. These Journeys may threaten our Trickster world, but the Temptation is too great, and soon our Special World spins out of control. Complications mount. Our perfect deception falls apart. We must sacrifice all to escape this world. We make one last mad chase and claim an Elixir even greater than anticipated.

"I'M IN PAIN AND I'M WET AND I'M STILL HYSTERICAL."

Approaching a theory of comedy can be as daunting as unlocking the mystery of the Sphinx. Many believe Comedy can't be analyzed, relying on one litmus test. We know comedy works when we hear the laughter. The Journeys of Comedy look at ourselves, our foibles and our follies, our pities and our pains, in a humorous way. The more laughter we can share, the greater the Elixir, which is why successful comedies offer identifiable Heroes with "life-or-death" problems to which we can easily relate. But Comedy is an extremely personal Journey, again compounding the mystery of its success. One man's guffaw can easily be a woman's groan.

Name your favorite comedy. Is it the slapstick antics of Chaplin, or Inspector Clouseau? The verbal sparring of Preston Sturges, or the ribald Marx Brothers? How about the darker comedic *Heathers* or *Dr. Strangelove*? You might prefer the taboo-crossing wicked "say no more" Monty Python. Or perhaps you relish the fish-out-of-water complications of *Big* and *Trading Places*, or the outlandish spoofs of Mel Brooks. Even considering the incredible diversity of these successful comedic styles, the Hero's Journey can be used to understand why they make us laugh.

THE COMEDY OF SURPRISE AND SUSPENSE

Effective comedy uses the same techniques as Thrillers: surprise and suspense. While Thrillers use surprise to shock, and suspense to keep the audience glued to their seats, Comedies use surprise for laughs, and comic suspense to build to bigger laughs that will leave the audience rolling in the aisles.

Surprise can provide some of our most hilarious movie moments. Surprise can be the solution to a problem that visually smacks our funny bone, like Joe and Jerry's first appearance in drag at the train station (*Some Like It Hot*). Surprise can be a sudden reversal of fortune. In *The Wrong Trousers*, Gromit eludes capture by the Evil Penguin with the disguise of a "Meatabix" dog food box. Surprise can also be the unexpected, inappropriate, off-the-wall verbal or physical response to something (Osgood's acceptance of Jerry in the closing moments of *Some Like It Hot*).

Suspense helps build the anticipation of greater payoffs and laughs to come. The Surprise moment when we see Joe and Jerry in drag sets up our anticipation that someone at some point will discover they are actually men. In *The Graduate*, Ben's affair with Mrs. Robinson will eventually be revealed.

THE HIGH STAKES OF COMEDY

The Comic Hero is thrust onto his Journey by a problem that must be solved: to flee from the mob (*Some Like It Hot*), to survive being home alone (*Home Alone*), to find a future that is "different" (*The Graduate*). To solve the problem, the Comic Hero often resorts to an extreme, drastic solution that sends him Through the Threshold into an outlandish Special World of deception. But the circumstances have been set such that we believe the Hero's drastic solution is the *only* solution available to him. Joe and Jerry dress in drag to join an all-girl band. Kevin must not let anyone believe that he's home alone, especially a pair of bungling burglars (*Home Alone*). In rebellion, Ben has a secret affair with Mrs. Robinson (*The Graduate*).

CONFLICTING GOALS AND GROWING COMPLICATIONS

Once the Comic Hero crosses the Threshold, committing to the Special World, he takes command of his Special World with a successful series of Tests. Joe and Jerry are accepted by the girls' band (*Some Like It Hot*). Kevin overcomes his fears of being alone and begins to take care of himself (*Home Alone*). But the boost of confidence from this success opens the Hero to the temptation of a Conflicting Call. If pursued, this Conflicting Journey or Complication would jeopardize his Initial Journey, and reveal his deception. Often this Complication is a Journey of the Heart (*Some Like It Hot, The Graduate*).

Ironically, the complication offers an important Elixir that the Hero never realized he needed until he was immersed into the Special World. In *The Graduate*, Ben enters the Special World of his affair with Mrs. Robinson, which brings him to Elaine with whom he falls in love. This love becomes the Elixir he fights for during the remainder of his Journey. But Ben would never have found this Elixir had he remained in his Ordinary World.

THE COMIC HERO'S SACRIFICE

As the Hero juggles the conflicting Calls, complications mount, threatening to destroy his Initial Journey. The proverbial shit hits the fan, and the Hero stands to lose everything. He must make a sacrifice that signals the Road Back. The mobster arrives forcing Joe and Jerry to abandon Sugar Kane and Osgood, and flee the Special World with their lives (*Some Like It Hot*). The Road Back may signal a Hero's recommitment to defeat the Enemy (*Home Alone, Women on the Verge of a Nervous Breakdown, The Wrong Trousers*). Or he may damn the consequences and finally pursue the important Elixir to be claimed (*The Graduate*).

CUT TO THE CHASE: COMEDY'S MAGIC FLIGHT

Often in fairy tales and myth, the Hero needs the help of a Magic Flight to flee the Special World with the Elixir. Along this flight, objects may be sacrificed to delay the Shadow. When the Chase seems lost, an unlikely Ally may step in to further frustrate the Shadow's pursuit, or retrieve the Elixir and resume the flight.

Using deception, surprise and suspense for comic effect, the Magic Flight provides one of Comedy's classic characteristics: the desperate, often madcap Chase to the finish. The Chase can be an endless shapeshifting of disguises as the Heroes try to flee the mob (*Some Like It Hot*). It could be a breakneck pursuit to foil the Enemy's evil plan (*Women on the Verge of a Nervous Breakdown, The Wrong Trousers*), or desperate flight to stop a wedding (*The Graduate*). The Slapstick Chase could be the gauntlet that the Villains must overcome (*Home Alone*). During the Magic Comic Flight, sacrifices may still need to be made and danger may push an Ally to give up the Chase (the bleached-blond Cabby in *Women on the Verge of a Nervous Breakdown*). Or the Chase provides an unlikely Hero's fortunate entrance (*The Wrong Trouser*'s Techno-Trousers, and old man Marley in *Home Alone*).

THE ELIXIR GAINED IS MUCH BIGGER THAN ANTICIPATED

Through all the suffering and rising complications and the mad dash of escape, miraculously the Comic Hero is resurrected. Whether through sacrifice or discovery, the Hero finally strips away the disguise that protected his Special World. His revelation is also an offering of his true unmasked self. Accepted back into his Ordinary World, the Comic Hero's sacrifice opens the door to a boon of Elixirs—more than ever anticipated. Our boys escape the mob and get the girl (*Some Like It Hot*). Gromit reclaims his room and pays all the bills (*The Wrong Trousers*).

GENRE CHALLENGES: COMEDY

1. Comic Surprise can be an unexpected, inappropriate or off-the-wall response to an action. How are unexpected responses used to elicit laughter in *Home Alone*?
2. Who do you identify with in *The Graduate*? Does your identification or sympathy shift during the course of Ben's Journey?
3. Who is the Mentor in a buddy comedy like *Some Like It Hot* or *The Wrong Trousers*? Does the Mentor's mask shift during the course of the Journey? What Journey does the Mentor push? Does that Journey complicate or solve the problem at hand?
4. Choose the final Chase sequence in one of the analyzed films. How are tools of comedy (including Surprise, Suspense, Reversal, Deception, Conflicting Journeys) used for comic effect?
5. How do character eccentricities, characteristics and flaws become Threshold Guardians, Enemies or Allies during Pepa's Journey in *Women on the Verge of a Nervous Breakdown*?
6. Who and what Threshold Guardians does Kevin confront on his Journey in *Home Alone*? How does he overcome them for comic effect?
7. Choose a dark comedy such as *Dr. Strangelove, Heathers,* or *War of the Roses.* What is the Elixir the Hero gains in the end?

SOME LIKE IT HOT
(U.S., 1959)

"Well—nobody's perfect."

—Osgood Fielding III (Joe E. Brown)

Screenplay by Billy Wilder and I.A.L. Diamond
Suggested by a story by R. Thoeren and M. Logan
Directed by Billy Wilder

Two struggling musicians witness the St. Valentine's Day massacre and must escape the mob by joining an all-girl band heading for Miami.

LANDMARKS OF THE JOURNEY

Packed with disguises, complications and chases, *Some Like It Hot* presents classic comedy. The Journey is one long Chase leading to the inevitable—the mob will discover the Trickster Heroes' disguise. But the disguises work too well, drawing Joe and Jerry deeper and deeper into their Special World. Joe falls for the voluptuous Sugar Kane, and uses his disguise as "Josephine" to set up his seduction. Meanwhile, poor Jerry/Daphne rebuffs the advances of an eccentric multi-marriage millionaire. Eventually as the complications rise, the deceptions have to give. The screws tighten. The center cannot hold. Joe and Jerry have to flee their Special World, and receive an Elixir they never anticipated—an ongoing theme in cross-dressing comedies—what it's like to be the opposite sex.

THE JOURNEY

Prohibition Chicago, 1929. This crime-ridden, violent ORDINARY WORLD will follow Joe and Jerry to Miami, and so time is taken to establish the stakes that push our TRICKSTER HEROES to Miami in women's clothes.

Chicago police are trying to crack down on bootlegging. And Police Chief Mulligan wants to nail gangster Spats Columbo. Toothpick Charlie informs on Spats giving the police the opportunity to raid Spats' speakeasy, "Mozzarella's Funeral Parlor." Once this TICKING CLOCK is set in motion, we get to meet our HEROES, saxophonist/cad Joe and bass player/pessimist Jerry, playing in the band backing up the raucous floorshow inside. They've endured months of bad luck, and finally get a playing gig. Tonight's paycheck will help pay off the back rent and other debts. They spot Mulligan slipping on his badge, a CALL TO ADVENTURE, and make a quick exit, avoiding a police raid that shuts down Spats' joint.

Joe and Jerry need a paying job (OUTER PROBLEM). Poliakoff, their agent, has a three-week gig open but he needs women, a CALL TO ADVENTURE. Jerry thinks they should consider dressing up as women and taking the Florida job, but Joe nixes the idea, a REFUSAL. Instead, they take a one-night stand playing at a St. Valentine's dance. They pick up the secretary's car at a Chicago garage and accidentally witness Spats getting his revenge on Toothpick Charlie, the St. Valentine's Day massacre, the CALL TO ADVENTURE. They flee with only a few gunshots in the bass fiddle, but Spats and his men know their faces. Police sirens approach, and Spats vows to take care of the musicians later.

Joe and Jerry are pushed into a SPECIAL WORLD, on the run from Spats and his mob. They have to flee Chicago, and Jerry calls Poliakoff. With a woman's voice, he accepts the Florida job.

They arrive at the train station, in dresses and high heels, the THRESHOLD. Jerry stumbles in his high heels and questions how women can do this. They see the line of women checking in with the bandleader, Sweet Sue, and the manager, Bienstock (THRESHOLD GUARDIANS). Jerry doubts they can pull it off, especially after being mesmerized by Sugar Kane's "Jell-O on springs" assets. It's a whole 'nother sex, a REFUSAL. But Joe tries to push him to the THRESHOLD; they need the disguise long enough to get safely out of Chicago. Jerry's had enough of this SIDEKICK MENTOR'S schemes. Newspaper headlines remind them of the stakes if they refuse this Journey. They cross the THRESHOLD. These "real ladies" charm Sweet Sue and Bienstock. And the entire band quickly accepts "Daphne" and "Josephine."

Passing this THRESHOLD, Jerry willingly accepts this dizzying new SPECIAL WORLD filled with beautiful, available musicians. It's an answer to his dream of being locked in a pastry shop (his INNER PROBLEM), but Joe lays down the rules: they are on a diet. They must be girls. But their TEST PHASE is filled with temptation that could threaten their Journey "on the run." The two run into their strongest CONFLICTING CALL: Sugar Kane. During band practice, Sugar drops her liquor flask and Jerry/"Daphne" takes the rap. Sweet Sue (a THRESHOLD GUARDIAN) sets down the laws: no liquor and no men! Jerry has seized the opportunity to become Sugar's ALLY and complicates the Journey of escape. Sweet Sue becomes suspicious of Daphne and Josephine, and Bienstock promises to keep his eye on them, raising the stakes of discovery. Jerry soon faces an impossible task that night. A scantily clad Sugar jumps into "Daphne's" berth and offers her gratitude. Jerry can no longer deny this CONFLICTING CALL. "She" suggests that they share a good stiff drink and celebrate a "surprise" party, an APPROACH. But his dream of an intimate affair quickly gets out of control and turns into a party with the entire band crammed into Daphne's berth (an ORDEAL). Josephine tries to stop it before they all get fired, but Sugar pulls her into the bathroom to help with the ice.

Unaware of Joe's disguise, Sugar confesses her painful ORDINARY WORLD escaping the temptation of boys' bands. Her uncontrollable desire for saxophone players always gets her into trouble. This "female" sax player finds this CONFLICTING CALL irresistible—but Joe must approach with caution and guile—and he may have to clean up his act (an

INNER CALL of transformation). Sugar's been running from cads who have been using her money for gambling and then dumping her for the next gullible woman—not unlike Joe. Now she sees Sweet Sue's band as a way to solve her OUTER PROBLEM. She's looking for marriage to a Florida millionaire and paints a picture for Josephine of her ideal bespectacled, gentle millionaire, presenting the seeds of Joe's APPROACH.

Meanwhile, Daphne's ORDEAL escalates when the women discover "she's" ticklish. He yanks the emergency break (a RESURRECTION), and the women scamper to their berths before they're discovered by Sweet Sue.

They arrive in Florida, and the Seminole-Ritz Hotel, crossing a THRESHOLD into a deeper SPECIAL WORLD. Jerry and Joe's disguise has passed the TEST PHASE with the women. Now they must face the abuse of the opposite sex. Peering over their *Wall Street Journals*, a string of retired millionaires behold the arrival of romance. Osgood Fielding III eyes Daphne and wastes no time, offering assistance with her shoe. With seven or eight marriages under his belt (Mama's keeping score), the SHAPESHIFTER wants Daphne for his next conquest. He carries her bags and takes advantage of her in the elevator, receiving an expedient slap of REFUSAL for his efforts.

Jerry's had enough of this SPECIAL WORLD. Now that they've safely arrived in Florida, he wants to be a boy again. But Joe's quest for Sugar pushes them to remain. Sugar invites the two to join them at the beach: Daphne jumps at the chance of swimming with the girls and rubbing suntan lotion over everyone. Joe uses their departure to prepare for his CALL TO ROMANCE. He disguises himself in Bienstock's missing clothes and glasses, and camps out on the beach. Soon enough, Sugar fetches a beach ball and Joe trips her. His deception as Shell Oil Junior caters perfectly to Sugar's dream millionaire, but Sugar also uses a SHAPESHIFTER'S deception to present herself as the "society" girl she believes Junior prefers. Daphne arrives and immediately sees through Junior's disguise. Sugar wants to share her good fortune with Josephine, and Daphne rushes her back to the hotel room, a CHASE that threatens to ruin Joe's disguise.

Anticipation of discovery turns to surprise; miraculously they find Josephine taking a bath. Sugar leaves and a soaked Joe threatens Jerry. A phone call from Osgood saves Jerry and presents Joe with his APPROACH. Osgood invites Daphne to join him after the show on his yacht. Joe pushes Jerry to accept the CALL, but Jerry/Daphne will keep Osgood occupied on shore while Joe/Junior uses the yacht to seduce Sugar. Joe uses Osgood throughout the APPROACH SEQUENCE, giving Sugar flowers Osgood intended for Daphne. Finally the girls finish the show, and anticipation of the romance ahead sends everybody to their rendezvous.

Junior takes Sugar aboard the yacht, the ORDEAL. She's concerned because she's never been alone on a yacht with a man before, and certain men would take advantage of a woman. Since the audience knows Joe, we anticipate that he will soon reveal himself as that "certain man" Sugar fears. But the TRICKSTER turns the tables, throwing us into one of the sexiest, most ingenious seductions in cinema. Junior presents himself as a WOUNDED HERO, his heart shattered by past love, making him completely "harmless." He's tried everything from French maids to hot baths. Nothing will warm his heart, but he would immediately marry the woman who could. Sugar wants her millionaire. She meets and crushes his challenge, the RESURRECTION of the ORDEAL. Meanwhile, the ORDEAL continues on the dance floor. Osgood and Daphne tango through the night.

As dawn breaks, Junior brings Sugar back to the hotel. They enjoy the last kisses of their REWARD. Sugar leaves and Joe climbs back into his room, where he finds a euphoric Jerry celebrating his engagement to Osgood, his REWARD. Joe bursts his bubble, reminding Jerry that he's a boy. Soon, Sugar joins them, sharing with her girlfriends the aftermath of her own ORDEAL, and dreams of marriage to Junior.

With Joe's successful seduction of Sugar, he's ready to leave the SPECIAL WORLD. He's prepared to break Sugar's heart and pushes Jerry to call off the engagement with Osgood. But things get worse, the ROAD BACK. They spot Spats in the lobby, attending the "Friends of the Italian Opera" convention (yet another disguise, this time for a mob meeting). They pack their bags and Joe calls Sugar to end their romance. In moments, Sugar enters to drown her broken heart, and Joe can see first-hand the devastation he has caused. She leaves, the two flee out the window to avoid Spats, and they climb down onto Spats' terrace.

The CHASE begins, a "magic flight" where Joe and Jerry use a string of disguises to flee the mob. Trapped in the "Friends of the Italian Opera" dining room, Joe and Jerry hide beneath Spats' table until they can slip away. But the mob leader, Little Bonapart, has other plans for this convention. An ALLY of Toothpick Charlie, Little Bonaparte makes Spats pay for the St. Valentine's Day massacre and guns him down. Once again, our HEROES are in the wrong place at the wrong time. Our HEROES are witnesses, and they flee Bonaparte's men. The magic flight continues and soon "Daphne" and "Josephine" prepare to leave. They overhear that all accesses—including railway, road and airports are blocked—except water. Osgood's yacht will provide their RESURRECTION. "Daphne" sets up the rendezvous with Osgood at the dock while Jerry hears Sugar and Sweet Sue's band playing "I'm Through with Love." Hearing her song resurrects his love for Sugar, and responsibility for the pain he caused. Her song ends and "Josephine" kisses her, offering the ELIXIR that no guy is worth the pain. The kiss is enough for Sugar to realize that Josephine / Junior are the same. Joe is already racing out the door, chased by Bonaparte's men, Sweet Sue and Bienstock, and now Sugar Kane won't let her love go.

The final CHASE takes Joe and Jerry to Osgood's motor boat, with Sugar right behind, the RESURRECTION. As Osgood takes them to the salvation of his yacht, all disguises are removed, and everyone accepted despite their foibles, the ELIXIR. After all "Nobody's perfect."

FADE OUT

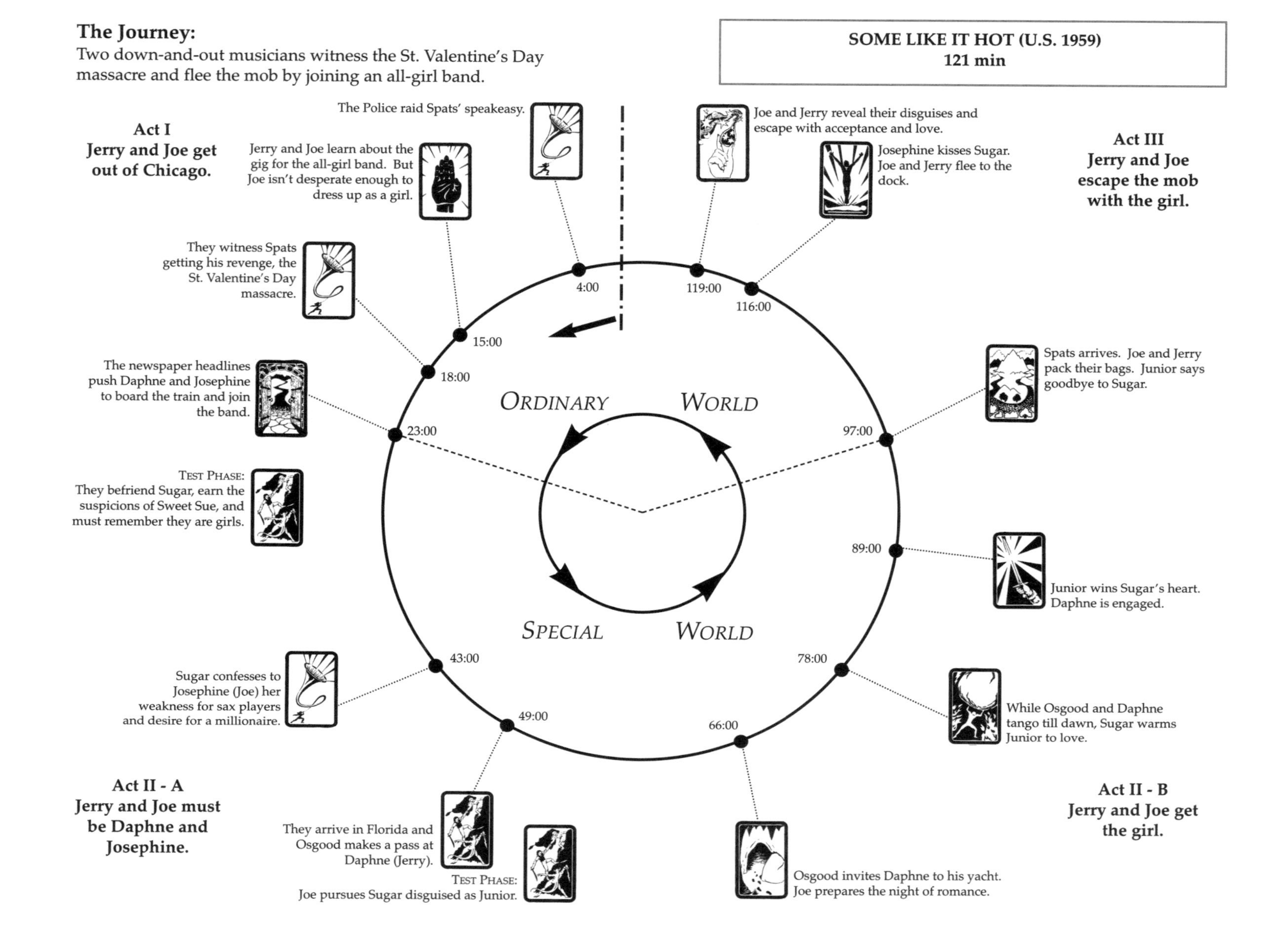

The Journey:
Two down-and-out musicians witness the St. Valentine's Day massacre and flee the mob by joining an all-girl band.
SOME LIKE IT HOT (U.S. 1959)
121 min
Act I
Jerry and Joe get out of Chicago.
The Police raid Spats' speakeasy.
4:00
Jerry and Joe learn about the gig for the all-girl band. But Joe isn't desperate enough to dress up as a girl.
15:00
They witness Spats getting his revenge, the St. Valentine's Day massacre.
18:00
The newspaper headlines push Daphne and Josephine to board the train and join the band.
23:00
Test Phase:
They befriend Sugar, earn the suspicions of Sweet Sue, and must remember they are girls.
Sugar confesses to Josephine (Joe) her weakness for sax players and desire for a millionaire.
43:00
They arrive in Florida and Osgood makes a pass at Daphne (Jerry).
49:00
Test Phase:
Joe pursues Sugar disguised as Junior.
Act II - A
Jerry and Joe must be Daphne and Josephine.
Ordinary
World
Special
World
Osgood invites Daphne to his yacht. Joe prepares the night of romance.
66:00
While Osgood and Daphne tango till dawn, Sugar warms Junior to love.
78:00
Junior wins Sugar's heart. Daphne is engaged.
89:00
Spats arrives. Joe and Jerry pack their bags. Junior says goodbye to Sugar.
97:00
Josephine kisses Sugar. Joe and Jerry flee to the dock.
116:00
Joe and Jerry reveal their disguises and escape with acceptance and love.
119:00
Act II - B
Jerry and Joe get the girl.
Act III
Jerry and Joe escape the mob with the girl.

THE GRADUATE
(U.S., 1967)

"Mrs. Robinson, you're trying to seduce me ... aren't you?"
—Benjamin Braddock (Dustin Hoffman)

Screenplay by Calder Willingham and Buck Henry
Based on the novel by Charles Webb
Directed by Mike Nichols

Seeking a future that is "different," a college graduate is seduced by his father's partner's wife and falls in love with her daughter.

LANDMARKS OF THE JOURNEY

In this social satire, college graduate Benjamin Braddock's need for a future that is "different" takes him on a multi-Journey quest. This succession of Journeys transforms Benjamin from idleness to action as Ben finally fights for something he believes in.

Ben initially embarks on a Journey of Rebellion against his parents' affluent Ordinary World. He accepts the seductions of Shapeshifter Mrs. Robinson and wastes away his summer. It's a matter of time before the secret of the affair becomes known; but Ben accepts this Special World—that is, until the worst possible thing happens. He falls in love with Mrs. Robinson's daughter, Elaine. This new Journey of the Heart takes him into a dangerous Special World that is finally destroyed by Mrs. Robinson. But Ben surfaces with his love for Elaine and begins his Road Back. Ironically, Ben must re-enter the college world to reclaim his love and find his future. The Hero takes control of this Special World with at least the hope that Elaine will accept his proposal. And again, his affair with Mrs. Robinson shatters his world. Ben launches a final, desperate Chase to pick up the pieces and fight for his future.

THE JOURNEY

College graduate Ben Braddock returns home to his parents' upscale, materialistic world. An award-winning scholar and a track star, Ben faces the real world worried about his future. He wants it to be different, his INNER PROBLEM. After four years of college, Ben has been resurrected as a LONER HERO who's RELUCTANT to enter society—the "society" defined by his parents and their friends. His parents throw a party in honor of their graduate and invite all the family friends. Ben makes his presence but soon finds himself drowning in the ELIXIR of praise for his accomplishments and suggestions about his future. He quickly returns to the solitude of his room, shutting the door on the praise of his past.

Mrs. Robinson "stumbles" into his room looking for the bathroom and asks him to take her home, a CALL. At her house, this SHAPESHIFTER presents a succession of deceptive CALLS OF SEDUCTION. She toys with his nervous REFUSALS, finally making a blatant, naked CALL for sex. Mrs. Robinson traps Ben in her daughter Elaine's room and offers her availability at any time, the CALL TO ADVENTURE. Ben hears the arrival of Mr. Robinson and bolts, a REFUSAL. Ben runs into Mr. Robinson, a formidable THRESHOLD GUARDIAN. Now wearing a MENTOR'S mask, Mr. Robinson encourages Ben to take advantage of his youth and sow his wild oats. He also encourages him to call Elaine when she returns from Berkeley.

After a humiliating 21st birthday party, again with his parents' friends, Ben rebels in his own ultra-naïve way. He invites Mrs. Robinson to the Taft Hotel for a drink. Ben approaches a challenging THRESHOLD that requires a push from Mrs. Robinson (SHAPESHIFTER MENTOR). Ben secures a room from a suspicious front desk clerk (THRESHOLD GUARDIAN).

Finally in the room with Mrs. Robinson, his fears resurface, and his MENTOR continues to lead him into the seduction. Again, he REFUSES, fearing that his parents will discover the affair. But Mrs. Robinson suggests the real source of Ben's insecurity is his fear of inadequacy. This must be his first time. She strikes a nerve. Ben boldly accepts her challenge and dives into this affair, CROSSING THE THRESHOLD.

Ben's TEST PHASE explores his physical affair with Mrs. Robinson while he relaxes the summer away, closing himself off from his parents and concerns of his future. Fed up, Ben's father wants him to take stock in himself and get off his ass. His mother takes a more gentle approach. Neither succeeds. Ben won't give them a straight answer about his nighttime whereabouts.

But Ben wants to turn his relationship with Mrs. Robinson into more than just sex, an APPROACH TO THE INMOST CAVE. He tries conversation that spirals them into an ORDEAL. He pries into her relationship with her husband, and she reveals her painfully lonely ORDINARY WORLD without love. When Elaine is mentioned, Mrs. Robinson forces Ben to promise that he'll never take her daughter out. She will bar that journey because he's not good enough. Offended, Ben threatens to leave. But he admits that their affair is the one thing he looks forward to. He accepts her Rules of this Special World: no Elaine and no talking. But complications force Ben to break his promise in order to protect their affair. His parents encourage Ben to call Elaine. And his mother won't let him refuse. She threatens to invite all the Robinsons over, pushing Ben to ask Elaine out.

Ben purposefully makes his date with Elaine a wretched, humiliating ORDEAL in a strip club. He sees the pain he's putting her through as she flees in tears. He CHASES her down and apologizes for the way he treated her. He kisses her, CROSSING THE THRESHOLD. They soon share burgers—and unlike his relationship with Mrs.

Robinson, Ben and Elaine are talking. Elaine suggests they share a drink at the Taft Hotel. The bellhops and clerks recognize Ben, making Elaine suspicious that he's having an affair. Ben confesses his attraction to Elaine. He also admits he had an affair with a married woman, but it's over. Elaine is glad.

They plan to meet the following day but Mrs. Robinson derails the Journey. She jumps in Ben's car and threatens to tell everyone about their affair. Ben races to the Robinsons' house to see Elaine. With Mrs. Robinson on his heels, Ben confesses the horrible truth: the married woman is Elaine's mother. Elaine sends him away, and Mrs. Robinson, in tears, says goodbye, the ORDEAL.

During the affair with Mrs. Robinson, Ben wasted away in inactivity. Now his love for Elaine pushes Ben to action (REWARD), even if it is irrational. He tells his folks that he's going to marry Elaine Robinson. She doesn't know it yet, but he's off to Berkeley to tell her, Ben's FIRST ROAD BACK.

Ben has committed himself to another SPECIAL WORLD that he hopes will lead to his desired future with Elaine. He must face TESTS and overcome physical and personal THRESHOLD GUARDIANS to re-enter the collegiate world. He gets a room with a paranoid landlord. He tries to watch Elaine from a distance but he's soon discovered. He pursues her on a bus, and follows her to the zoo, where he meets her new boyfriend, Carl. Ben tries to disrupt this meeting with the RIVAL, but Carl pushes ahead with Elaine in his arms.

Elaine goes to Ben's room and demands to know why he's at Berkeley. He confesses his love. And Elaine tells him her mother's SHAPESHIFTING tale of how Ben raped her, the ORDEAL. Ben tries to deny it, but Elaine refuses to hear his explanation. She screams, disrupting the entire house. The landlord forces Ben to move out. Elaine apologizes and finally accepts Ben's truth. Ben packs his bags, but Elaine doesn't want him to leave, offering him the REWARD OF HOPE. She wants him to have a definite plan before he goes anywhere. So he proposes to her, but Elaine's reluctant to accept. But she continues to give him hope.

Ben buys an engagement ring, preparing his final ROAD BACK. But he's blocked by Mr. Robinson. This SHADOW MENTOR takes Ben's affair with his wife as a personal insult. Ben tries to confess his love for Elaine, but Mr. Robinson has hidden his daughter where Ben will never find her, initiating Ben's SECOND ROAD BACK. Ben begins a desperate and painful CHASE to win back Elaine.

Ben drives back to Los Angeles, and breaks into the Robinsons' house. Elaine isn't there, but Mrs. Robinson is packing her bags for her daughter's impending nuptials. Offering no further details, she calls the police and Ben flees. Ben drives back to Berkeley and learns from Carl's buddies that the wedding's taking place in Santa Barbara. He finally arrives in Santa Barbara and stops at a filling station to locate the church. Impatient to resume his ROAD BACK before it's too late, he drives off without filling his tank. And he runs out of gas. Ben runs the rest of the way, arriving at the church as the ceremony concludes. He looks down from the balcony window, and pounds on the glass in anguish. Elaine is torn between her new husband and her true heart, Ben. Seeing her family's anger towards Ben, she chooses his rebellious path, granting his RESURRECTION.

Ben runs off with Elaine, and they board a bus. Initially, the two are pleased with the ELIXIR of this freedom. But as it sinks in, they reluctantly accept an uncertain future.

FADE OUT

WOMEN ON THE VERGE OF A NERVOUS BREAKDOWN
(Spain, 1988)

"Pardon the mess. My life's been hectic lately."

—Pepa (Carmen Maura)

Written and Directed by Pedro Almodóvar

A woman copes with the breakup of her relationship with her womanizing lover and learns to move on with her life.

LANDMARKS OF THE JOURNEY

Trying to keep her sanity after the bitter breakup with her lover, Pepa enters Almodóvar's matchless comedic frontier. Eccentric characters fill Pepa's Special World—Allies, Enemies, Threshold Guardians, many desperately pushing their own journeys and complicating poor Pepa's seemingly simple quest to speak with Ivan. As Pepa's Journey becomes more complicated, she actually becomes more grounded, purged of her growing insanity. Pepa becomes the sanest in an insane world.

The beauty of Almodóvar's story is how he uses coincidence as an essential comedic characteristic of the Special World. If a movie has one or two coincidences, they stand out as plot holes. But if a storyteller skillfully layers coincidence throughout the journey—three, twelve, twenty-seven times—the audience accepts it as a characteristic and finds the humor of this Special World.

THE JOURNEY

Pepa has just broken up with her lover, Ivan, a CRISIS OF THE HEART. After living with him for several months, she knew it was coming. The philandering boyfriend finally admits that he doesn't love Pepa any longer, and moves out. Both work as actors, specializing in voice-over and dubbing, and Ivan's departure spins her ORDINARY WORLD into agonizing turmoil. Memories of Ivan fill her home, and his voice fills her head at work. Pepa needs to speak with Ivan (her OUTER PROBLEM) and resurrect their relationship, but she will soon abandon this INNER PROBLEM. We learn by Journey's end that Pepa also deals with the INNER PROBLEM of being pregnant with Ivan's baby. This is the life-or-death motivation that pushes Pepa throughout her Journey of survival.

Her lifeline of sanity is her phone, symbolizing the hope that Ivan will call to apologize and resurrect the relationship. She continues to check her messages with still no word from Ivan, a SUCCESSION OF CALLS that pushes Pepa to consider suicide. But she refuses this answer, dumping the barbiturates into her fresh batch of gazpacho, a RESURRECTION that initiates her THRESHOLD to survive. Purging herself of the relationship, she packs Ivan's suitcase, and (accidentally) lights their bed on fire. Calmly, she puts it out with a garden hose, completing the THRESHOLD SEQUENCE.

Now that she has entered the SPECIAL WORLD of surviving the break-up, Pepa finds herself TESTED by a more complicated, crazy world. Ivan's insane wife, Lucia, presents the first complication. She sees Pepa as a RIVAL, who blocks her from making Ivan pay for her insanity. Pepa's girlfriend, Candela, presents the second complication. But Pepa doesn't have time to answer her desperate calls. The third complication is the coincidental arrival of Ivan's son, Carlos.

Returning home, again Pepa checks her messages. She ignores Candela's pleas for help. Again, no message from Ivan. Pepa rips the phone from the wall. Having failed to contact Pepa by phone, Candela drops by, but Pepa is too focused on her own problems to acknowledge her desperation.

Soon Carlos and his fiancée show up to rent the penthouse. Initially amazed by the coincidence of their arrival, Pepa uses Carlos to find out about Ivan. She figures out that Ivan is leaving the country with another woman. Her growing awareness of his cheating ways is a REWARD. But Candela finally gets desperate enough to make everyone listen to her. She tries to jump from the terrace. She fails her suicide attempt and Carlos pulls her to safety.

Pepa can no longer ignore Candela's CALL, and listens to her terrible tale of an affair with a Shiite terrorist who was recently arrested. Since she gave them a place to stay, she believes she's wanted by the police.

Depressed by Carlos' sudden attention to Candela, his fiancée, Marisa, finds solace in Pepa's laced gazpacho. She's knocked out by the barbiturates. Pepa lets Marisa sleep it off, and offers to help Candela by talking to famed feminist lawyer, Paulina Morales. Paulina will understand Candela's lovelorn side of the story. With Pepa gone, Candela confesses the Shiites' plan to hijack the 10 p.m. Stockholm flight; Carlos offers his help and phones the police with a quick, anonymous tip.

While waiting to see Paulina at her office, Pepa prepares to make a phone call. She notices a pair of airplane tickets to Stockholm and answers an incoming call. It's Ivan. He quickly hangs up at the sound of her voice. The coincidences begin to make Pepa question her own sanity. Nothing's making sense any longer, even Paulina Morales refuses to sympathize with Candela's plight. In frustration, Pepa strikes this SHAPESHIFTER, making Pepa feel much, much better.

Pepa returns to her apartment building and finds Ivan's packed bag downstairs with the manager. She drags it back upstairs, insisting that Ivan will have to get it himself.

Pepa convinces Candela that the two of them should take a vacation away from Madrid. As they make preparations (APPROACH THE INMOST CAVE), Pepa receives a phone call from Lucia, Ivan's mad wife. She insists upon meeting with Pepa, but Pepa refuses this complication. Carlos asks Pepa to be more understanding with his deranged mother. Realizing that Lucia represents a painful Journey taken if one becomes obsessed with Ivan, Pepa decides to end this Journey and move on (a REWARD). She also acknowledges that goodness can come from Ivan—his son. Through with her obsession, she drags Ivan's suitcase back downstairs and dumps it into the garbage, an APPROACH TO THE INMOST CAVE.

Pepa finally seems in control of her world (a REWARD) when the complications converge, barely avoiding collision outside her apartment building, an APPROACH TO THE INMOST CAVE. Ivan arrives to pick up his bag, shocked to find it missing from the manager's office. His new lover, Paulina Morales, waiting in the car, sees Pepa dump the suitcase. Ivan makes a quick phone call, leaving a message for Pepa. He spots Lucia's determined approach. Meanwhile, Pepa returns to her penthouse and hears Carlos and Candela listening to records. The music resurrects Pepa's feelings for Ivan, the ORDEAL. She flings a record out the window and it coincidentally hits Paulina in the head. Pepa listens to Ivan's phone message. Reading the truth behind his SHAPESHIFTING testimony of love, Pepa rips the phone yet again from the wall and tosses it off the terrace. It smashes onto the hood of Paulina's car. Ivan and Paulina quickly escape the apparent wrath of Pepa.

But the ORDEAL isn't over. The complications finally collide in the Penthouse with the arrival of Lucia and the police. The police are investigating the anonymous phone call Carlos had made. Pepa protects her SPECIAL WORLD and denies that any phone call has been made. But the police find the mounting coincidences difficult to believe. Pepa offers her story. And to assist her RESURRECTION of this ORDEAL she serves everyone the laced gazpacho. Pepa bares her soul to explain everything from the ripped out phone to the charred bed to the comatose Marisa. During the tale, she figures out that Ivan is leaving on the ill-fated Stockholm flight with SHAPESHIFTER Paulina Morales (the REWARD).

By her tale's end, everyone has passed out except Pepa and SHADOW Lucia. Lucia grabs one of the cop's guns and threatens Pepa, the ROAD BACK. Pepa tries to convince Lucia to forget Ivan, but Lucia won't be able to forget him until she kills him. Lucia throws gazpacho in Pepa's eyes and flees. Their CHASE ends at the airport.

Before Lucia can shoot Ivan, Pepa knocks her down with a luggage cart, the RESURRECTION. Lucia's gun goes off; Pepa promptly faints and Ivan rushes to her side. Pepa soon awakens unharmed, and is finally facing her former lover. But having survived this physical RESURRECTION, Pepa confesses that she no longer wants anything to do with Ivan. She just wanted to stop Lucia; now that that's over, she leaves Ivan for good, the ELIXIR.

Pepa returns home at last. The place is a mess, with everyone passed out. Except Marisa, who rises as if reborn. The two share their intimate secrets on the terrace, a celebration of their ELIXIRS. Marisa remembers an erotic dream so vivid that she questions her virginity. Pepa confesses for the first time that she is carrying Ivan's baby, which she will happily keep from Ivan's world of lies.

FADE OUT

HOME ALONE
(U.S., 1990)

"This house is so full of people, it makes me sick. When I grow up and get married, I'm living alone."

—Kevin McCallister (Macaulay Culkin)

Written by John Hughes
Directed by Chris Columbus

A precocious eight-year-old is left home during the Christmas holidays and single-handedly defends the house against a pair of bungling burglars.

LANDMARKS OF THE JOURNEY

Home Alone addresses one of our greatest, universal fears: the fear of being left alone. But *Home Alone* also delivers one of the greatest fantasies held by a kid of any age: the ability to single-handedly defend the homestead from the bad guys. Although Kevin is considered incompetent in his Ordinary World, he rises to the needs of this Special World. He gains confidence and uses his Special Powers as a kid to befuddle, torture and humiliate his nemesis.

But perhaps the key to *Home Alone*'s incredible success can be attributed to young Kevin's Inner Journey of healing. Although he wished his family would disappear, the Journey of surviving alone and protecting the house makes him realize that he misses his family (and his family misses him). Kind of like *It's a Wonderful Life* through a kid's eyes.

THE JOURNEY

Christmastime. On the eve of their flight to France, the McCallisters madly pack their bags (their OUTER PROBLEM). In the middle of this chaotic ORDINARY WORLD, we meet a SHAPESHIFTING ENEMY and our young HERO. Disguised as an officer, Harry (one of our bungling burglars) scouts out the neighborhood for his next heist, and drops by the McCallisters' house in the middle of madness. Harry's future foe, our eight-year-old HERO, Kevin, is a devious, creative, smart-mouthed pain in the butt. Kevin needs attention, and the circumstances are making this INNER PROBLEM very difficult to solve. He's sent off to pack his bag, but he doesn't know how. And no one will help him, instead making him the brunt of jokes and insults. Older brother Buzz torments Kevin with scary tales of their hermit neighbor, Old Man Marley. Buzz delivers the last straw, consuming Kevin's requisite cheese pizza. Frustrated by this over-crowded ORDINARY WORLD, Kevin attacks Buzz, causing a huge mess (and his plane ticket to be inadvertently dumped into the trash). Everyone's quick to blame Kevin and his mom, Kate, swiftly marches the defiant LONER HERO upstairs. Unable to state his case, Kevin stands up to this SHADOW MENTOR and voices his INNER PROBLEM: he wishes he'd never see any of them ever again. Kate warns him not to wish for what he really doesn't want. Set on his goal, Kevin wishes it again. Kate expels him from the ORDINARY WORLD to sleep alone in the attic, where again he wishes his entire family would disappear.

Kevin's CALL TO ADVENTURE arrives with a storm. The power goes off and the McCallisters oversleep. They pile into the waiting shuttles, race to the airport, board their plane, and take off, leaving Kevin home alone. He emerges from his attic cell to face an empty house. But Kevin is RELUCTANT to accept this SPECIAL WORLD. Seeing the cars still in the garage, Kevin believes that he made his family disappear. Replaying the previous night's insults and hatred, he celebrates that his disappearance act worked. He's initiated his THRESHOLD of acceptance, but needs to TEST the reality of this SPECIAL WORLD. He dares his missing family to catch him breaking the rules of the ORDINARY WORLD: eating popcorn in his parents' bed; rummaging through Buzz's private stuff; eating junk food; and watching bad movies. But he forgets these rules are important. The bad movies scare him. He calls out for his mom. He's alone in this SPECIAL WORLD and he's afraid, completing his THRESHOLD SEQUENCE of acceptance.

Kevin's Journey becomes more complicated and more threatening with the arrival of Harry and Marv, the burglars. Harry's previous disguise works like a charm. With vacations in full swing, Harry has every empty house scouted down to the minute the automatic timers go off. They'll begin with the crown jewel: the McCallister home.

Kevin awakens, hearing the ENEMIES' approach, and turns on the basement lights to scare them away. Kevin hides under his parents' bed. He never anticipated the real dangers in this SPECIAL WORLD, but Kevin tries to overcome his fear. He stands outside his front door and proclaims that he's not afraid. But the sight of Old Man Marley sends him scurrying back indoors, to the safety of his parents' covers. Some fears take time to overcome.

Kevin's TEST PHASE continues as he does his best to take care of himself and the house. He showers, takes Buzz's money (collapsing the bookshelf and setting Buzz's pet tarantula loose). He tries to buy a toothbrush and runs into Marley. Kevin flees in fright with the toothbrush unpaid for. Again, Kevin's fear makes him fail this TEST.

Walking home, he's almost run over by Marv and Harry's van. Harry cautions the boy to be more careful and flashes a "golden" smile. The young HERO recognizes Harry's gold tooth from the SHAPESHIFTER'S visit to the McCallisters' living room, and walks away. Harry believes he recognizes Kevin as well. He and Marv follow Kevin, but the boy loses them by hiding in a church Nativity scene (TEST). The ENEMIES leave. Kevin must answer their CALL. He rushes home and prepares for their return.

Kevin's GREATEST FEAR is that the ENEMY will discover he's home alone. That night, the burglars arrive and find the house alive with a Christmas party, an elaborate deception provided by a child's ingenious use of ropes, pulleys, toys and mannequins. Kevin watches the burglars leave. He's beaten his ENEMY.

The TESTS of the SPECIAL WORLD begin to wear down Kevin's commitment. Alone in bed, Kevin realizes life without family is pretty lonely (INNER PROBLEM). He promises that he'll never be a pain in the butt if they come back, and kisses the family picture. His gradual transformation is a REWARD. Kevin also becomes more responsible. He goes grocery shopping, washes clothes, and even overcomes his fear of the furnace, a REWARD. But the persistent burglars reappear, disrupting Kevin's mastery of his solitary world. And soon Kevin faces his GREATEST FEAR. Harry and Marv discover they've been scammed by an eight-year-old who's home alone. They watch through the window as Kevin decorates his Christmas Tree. Kevin sees his ENEMIES' reflection in the light bulb, the ORDEAL. He tries to dupe them, calling out to his parents elsewhere in the house. But the ENEMY won't fall for his tricks. He overhears their plot to strike that night at nine, a TICKING CLOCK.

Kevin is very afraid, and very much alone. He calls out for his mother, but that isn't enough to bring her back. At the pit of his SPECIAL WORLD, Kevin seeks other help. He asks a Santa's helper for the magic of a Christmas wish to break his original wish and deliver his family. Finally, Kevin enters a church seeking an even greater power to break his wish. Inside, he finds Old Man Marley, who welcomes the boy and offers a seat. Kevin overcomes his fear of his neighbor (a RESURRECTION of the ORDEAL) and begins to see him as a loving LONER HERO distraught by his separation from his son and granddaughter. Both act as MENTORS to help each other overcome the pain of failure, and rise above fears to face the ROAD BACK. Kevin helps Marley find the strength to call his son. The MEETING WITH THE MENTOR also helps Kevin gain the strength to confront his own fears. Kevin races home, a physical RESURRECTION of his ORDEAL. He enters his domain, confident that he will defend it from the ENEMY.

Kevin's ROAD BACK is set. He unfurls his map, laying out an elaborate battle plan of booby-traps devised by the devious vision of an eight-year-old Rube Goldberg. He sets his plan in motion, an APPROACH TO THE INMOST CAVE. He prepares his final meal, says grace, and starts to eat when the clock strikes 9 p.m. Armed with his BB gun, Kevin is ready for battle.

The burglars arrive for a showdown that rivals the grand shoot-outs and sword duels of Westerns and High Adventures. However, this showdown uses extensive Slapstick for comic effect—a bit painful at times, but Slapstick nonetheless. Kevin initially takes command, leading these gullible baddies into every trap. He flees from the house, but Harry finally anticipates Kevin's next move. This ENEMY has suffered so much punishment from this kid that he's finally thinking like him. Harry and Marv trap Kevin in the neighbor's house and prepare to take their revenge. But Marley arrives to rescue Kevin, the FIRST RESURRECTION. He clobbers the burglars with his snow shovel. And soon the police arrive to take the burglars away. Kevin watches them and smiles, confident that he has protected his home (ELIXIR of success). But Kevin must face Christmas Eve alone. He hangs the family stockings, sets out milk and cookies, an APPROACH to welcome the arrival of his one true wish.

Christmas morning arrives with a blanket of fresh snow and a boy's hope. Kevin races downstairs calling for his mom. But his hopes are immediately dashed. He faces an empty house. Kevin doesn't suffer this heartbreak for too long. Mother and child reunite with the RESURRECTION of apologies and forgiveness. But the RESURRECTION wouldn't be complete without the rest of the family. They burst through the door, amazed by the ELIXIR. Kevin took care of himself and the house still stands.

Kevin looks out the window and sees that Marley, too, celebrates the ELIXIR of overcoming fear. He has reunited with his son and his family.

Kevin's ELIXIR is not without some ramifications. Buzz discovers his room in shambles and calls out for Kevin...

FADE OUT

THE WRONG TROUSERS
(U.K., 1993)

"It's the wrong trousers, Gromit! And they've gone wrong!"

—Wallace

Written by Nick Park and Bob Baker
With additional contributions by Brian Sibley
Based upon characters created by Nick Park
Directed by Nick Park

A mysterious lodger forces Gromit out of the house in order to use Wallace and a pair of Techno-Trousers for a diamond heist.

LANDMARKS OF THE JOURNEY

The Hero's Journey comes in all lengths, from three-hour romantic epics to shorts and cartoons. Inspired by Hitchcock's Thrillers and Hollywood slapstick, *The Wrong Trousers* offers a fiendish deadpan penguin, technology run amok, and an endearing buddy team rivaling Laurel and Hardy. *The Wrong Trousers* shows how effective comedy arises from suspense and surprise, climaxing in one of the greatest film chases ever. Note that the Comedy's Special World of deception doesn't have to be created by the Hero. Even penguins have their mischievous plans.

THE JOURNEY

Our buddy HEROES are a cheese-loving inventor, Wallace, and his always-faithful dog, Gromit. Wallace uses his inventions to live in the most efficient of modern lifestyle (his ORDINARY WORLD). Inventions fill their house, including his latest—a wake-up "drop" that ejects Wallace from bed, depositing him through a pair of trousers and into his breakfast chair. It's Gromit's birthday, and Wallace presents his independent dog with a dog collar, leash and a pair of automated Techno-Trousers, perfect for Gromit to wear on his "walkies."

He sends Gromit off and focuses on their OUTER PROBLEM, a stack of bills arriving in the morning post. Wallace responds to this CALL TO ADVENTURE by renting out their spare room. Gromit returns from his walkie as Wallace displays the "room to let" sign. They get an expedient reply from a mysterious penguin, Feathers McGraw. Gromit and this beady-eyed SHAPESHIFTER silently size each other up, causing the dog to be concerned (an INNER STIRRING). Feathers eagerly takes Gromit's room, leaving the cold spare for Gromit.

Wallace tries to ease Gromit into this SPECIAL WORLD of having a lodger, and helps him paper and paint the spare. Gromit rigs the Techno-Trousers with a pair of braces so he can hang from the ceiling and paint. Feathers sees this ingenious tool and initiates his plot, an orchestrated SUCCESSION OF CALLS to usurp Gromit's place in the ORDINARY WORLD. He blares baseball organ music on the radio all night, forcing Gromit to the doghouse. He "hogs" the bathroom, and fetches Wallace's slippers and newspaper. This RIVAL even bows to Wallace's obligatory pat on the head. Driven outside by this "paying guest," Gromit watches Wallace and Feathers sharing wine and cheese. Faced with this final CALL and CRISIS OF THE HEART, Gromit packs his knapsack and leaves, CROSSING THE THRESHOLD. The penguin watches the departure of his RIVAL, and rubs his wings fiendishly. With Gromit's electronics book and power drill, the SHADOW approaches the Techno-Trousers.

But Gromit's separation from the ORDINARY WORLD gives him a better perspective to see the dangers at hand. He tries to find a place to stay, but the TEST PHASE so far has yielded an uncomfortable garbage can.

Meanwhile, Wallace awakens and immediately "drops" into the rewired Techno-Trousers, controlled now by the Evil Penguin. Wallace is stuck in the wrong trousers, and there's nothing he can do about it. Feathers sends Wallace and the Trousers on a TEST rampage through the streets.

Gromit scans the postings for rooms and sees a "Wanted" poster offering a REWARD for the capture of a chicken—a chicken that looks oddly familiar. This CALL TO ADVENTURE is made clear in moments by Wallace's cries for help and the sight of Feathers controlling the errant Techno-Trousers. Gromit commits to finding out the Penguin's plot (the OUTER PROBLEM), crossing a second THRESHOLD.

Worn out by the Penguin's wild ride, Wallace (still locked in the Techno-Trousers) falls into bed fast asleep.

Gromit enters his TEST PHASE in pursuit of Feathers, and tails the SHADOW to the City Museum. He watches the Penguin scout the Museum, and risks discovery, but his disguise as a Meatabix Dog Food box allays the SHADOW'S suspicion. Gromit quickly returns home to sneak into the Penguin's room, APPROACH THE INMOST CAVE. He uncovers the SHADOW'S plan to steal the Blue Diamond from the City Museum. But Feathers returns home (Gromit's ORDEAL), and Gromit hides underneath Wallace's covers (with Wallace still sleeping). The SHADOW is making his final preparations, APPROACH TO THE INMOST CAVE. Gromit spies the Penguin fit a rubber glove on his head, becoming the "wanted" chicken thief. Gromit's suspicions are confirmed, a REWARD. The SHADOW launches the Techno-Trousers, with a still-sleeping Wallace. Off they go, depositing Gromit down the "drop" into a face full of strawberry jam, completing his ORDEAL.

The Penguin uses the Techno-Trousers to break the sleeping Wallace into the City Museum, scale the ceiling, and bypass the alarm system (electronic THRESHOLD GUARDIANS).

The Penguin uses a special helmet strapped to Wallace's head to retrieve the Blue Diamond, but a ceiling panel gives way. The alarm awakens a panicked, disoriented Wallace, the ORDEAL. Gromit can't answer Wallace's shouts for help, but the Penguin needs the diamond (his REWARD) and swiftly steers Wallace's RESURRECTION from the ORDEAL. The Penguin soon rides Wallace and the Techno-Trousers down the building, escaping into the night.

The Penguin returns Wallace and the trousers to the house and prepares his escape. He finally pulls off his disguise, and Wallace now discovers the deception of his "paying guest" (a REWARD). The Penguin locks Wallace in a wardrobe and makes his escape. Gromit blocks the door with rolling pin in hand. The SHADOW counters with a revolver and locks Gromit up with Wallace and the trousers. Ingenious and determined, Gromit hot-wires the trousers, the ROAD BACK. They break out of the wardrobe (a RESURRECTION) and race after Feathers. A wild, reckless CHASE ensues on Wallace's toy train.

Several times, escape seems certain for Feathers; but each time, Gromit and bumbling Wallace foil his plans. The Penguin finally disconnects the train cars and sends the two HEROES toward a dead end. Gromit pulls them from the face of doom, quickly laying out their RESURRECTION with a box of train track pieces. He reroutes them across the Penguin's track. Together the HERO TEAM contributes to the SHADOW'S capture. Wallace snatches the Penguin's engine. The Techno-Trousers trip up Feathers, who flies into Gromit's empty milk bottle. The HERO TEAM delivers Feathers McGraw to the authorities. Soon the SHADOW is thrown behind bars of the local zoo, the ELIXIR of his capture.

Back at home, Gromit has earned the ELIXIR of return, winning his place back in his ORDINARY WORLD. Wallace and Gromit also enjoy the ELIXIR of the reward money to pay the bills and then some. Wallace has learned not to rent out the room. This ELIXIR relieves Gromit, who has dumped the Techno-Trousers into the trash. As he fetches some cheese for Wallace, the Techno-Trousers short-circuit and begin to march off into the sunset.

FADE OUT

THE MYTHIC STRUCTURE OF SCIENCE FICTION AND FANTASY

A wondrous Special World awaits us, bounded by our most fantastic hopes and terrifying nightmares. We trek across new frontiers, experience unworldly powers, and combat our own technology gone wrong. A Mentor's help may be needed to understand the powers of this world, and reveal the Elixir within us to defeat a Shadow and save a galaxy.

"WHAT A WORLD, WHAT A WORLD. WHO WHOULD HAVE THOUGHT A GOOD LITTLE GIRL LIKE YOU COULD DESTROY MY BEAUTIFUL WICKEDNESS."

Whether rooted in scientific speculation or inspired by imagination's fancy, Science Fiction and Fantasy allow us to go where we've never been, see what we could never see, and behold what we dare to imagine. They transport us into ancient worlds of gods, wizards and magic, or future societies of space treks, laser battles, and errant computers. These journeys can resurrect childlike wonder, or foretell our most dreadful nightmares. The only boundaries are the storyteller's imagination (and the technical wizardry of special effects).

Science Fiction and Fantasy are our New Mythology, and provide an important canvas that allows us to explore society's issues. The Journeys may propose the dangers we could face if an "evil" continues—e.g., nuclear power, genetic engineering, and technology. These Journeys may represent our society's phobias in a given era (the Cold War, nuclear proliferation, or prejudice); but they may also present our hopes of a utopian world in which we have overcome a contemporary issue, or simply celebrate our humanity.

THE MAGIC "WHAT IF?"

No genre relies upon imagination and prognostication more than Science Fiction and Fantasy. And the key to the magic of this genre lies in two words: "What if?"—the two most empowering words for a writer. With these two words a storyteller can visit Mars, use a wardrobe to travel through time, battle an army of the dead, visit lost civilizations ruled by dinosaurs, or live life as a toy. Simply ask "What if?" What if a lonely boy befriends an abandoned extra-terrestrial? What if we could genetically engineer dinosaurs? What if a killer cyborg arrived from the future to change the past? What if...

THE STORIES OF SCIENCE FICTION AND FANTASY

Although Science Fiction and Fantasy easily blends with other genres—such as Adventure, Romance, War, Horror, and the rest, offering a huge palette of storytelling possibilities—the stories can be categorized as follows:

1) An ordinary Hero enters a fantastic world. The Hero can enter an imaginary or fabled world (*The Wizard of Oz, Alice in Wonderland, The NeverEnding Story*). A lost civilization based on earthly reality could be discovered (*The Lost World, Mysterious Island, Journey to the Center of the Earth*). The Hero could stumble across a portal or create a time machine (*The Time Machine, Back to the Future, Time Bandits*).
2) A fantastic being enters the Hero's Ordinary World. This creature may be stuck in the Hero's world, and the Journey involves finding a way back (*E.T. The Extra-Terrestrial*). The creature arrives to accomplish an intended quest (*Terminator 2: Judgment Day, War of the Worlds, Godzilla*), or pull the Hero into its Special World (*Invasion of the Body Snatchers, Close Encounters of the Third Kind*).
3) The Hero exists within a fantastic Ordinary World armed with awareness of its science and mythology. He must solve a problem, embarking on a quest that leads to greater wonders (*The Star Wars Trilogy, Blade Runner*). These Quest Journeys often show a Hero seemingly manipulated by greater powers of fate, gods or magic (*Jason and the Argonauts*, the many tales of Sinbad). These stories also include space travel adventures (*2001: A Space Odyssey, Star Trek*).

THE ORDINARY WORLD VERSUS THE SPECIAL WORLD

The entire Journey can be considered a Special World to the audience. The storyteller must consider how much the audience needs to know to understand the Ordinary and Special worlds of the Journey.

A prologue can present important backstory quickly and directly (*Terminator 2: Judgment Day, The Star Wars Trilogy, The Road Warrior*). But the storyteller doesn't have to worry about giving the audience all the details. The storyteller may wish to throw the audience into the middle of the Chase, or into the depth of an Ordeal, and let them catch up (*The Star Wars Trilogy*). Or if the Hero himself is thrown into the unknown world, the audience can learn with him as he meets Allies, confronts Enemies, and seeks Mentors.

THE MENTOR'S IMPORTANT ROLE

Because of the extraordinary worlds and powers depicted in Science Fiction and Fantasy, the Hero (and the audience) may need lots of guidance. The Mentor plays an essential role in presenting the powers and rules of the Special World. Symbolizing our inner need for guidance from parent, teacher, or even friend, the bond of Mentor and Hero can be our richest, most rewarding relationship. The archetype surfaces again and again in

Journeys where a young Hero may have lost a parent or guardian, and need this special bond of guidance (*E.T. The Extra-Terrestrial, Terminator 2: Judgment Day, The Star Wars Trilogy*).

The Mentor cannot guide the Hero forever. The time comes when the Hero must prove he has assimilated his Mentor's lessons and can move on alone. The separation of the Mentor from the Journey can be powerful. Obi Wan's sacrifice allows Luke Skywalker and his friends to escape, and pushes the young Hero to accept the last legs of his journey in *Star Wars.* The Mentor may need to move aside for another Mentor to continue the Hero's training. Obi Wan initiates Luke's training, preparing him for the greater, more wizened Mentor, Master Yoda.

THE HERO AND SPECIAL POWERS

The Hero may hold Special Powers that become essential tools when entering the Special World. If so, these powers may need to be established in the Ordinary World. John Connor's talent to crack ATM machines becomes an essential power for *T2*'s Hero Team to succeed. A young, naïve Hero may have hidden Special Powers awaiting a Mentor's guidance to release them. This particular Hero's Journey may involve the Hero learning to access, nurture and eventually master these powers, as Luke Skywalker does in *The Star Wars Trilogy*.

Ordinary objects that hold little magical power in the light of the Ordinary World may become powerful forces and Elixirs in the Special World. Dorothy saves her friend the Scarecrow with a bucket of water, not realizing that this ordinary liquid can also vanquish her Shadow, the Wicked Witch. E.T. builds an interstellar phone using ordinary toys and tools from around Elliott's house.

TECHNOLOGY AS THE SHADOW

A recurring theme in Science Fiction shows humanity threatened, if not falling to the Shadow, due to our growing technology. These stories feed our fear of humans enslaved by their mechanical and computerized creations. Fritz Lang's *Metropolis* set the stage for this thematic tradition that continues to resonate in our futuristic tales (*2001: A Space Odyssey, Star Wars, Terminator* and *Terminator 2: Judgment Day*). Since dehumanization is such a universal primal fear, this theme can present bleak tales with some terrifying Shadows (*Blade Runner*'s tragic replicant; *Alien*'s Shapeshifting android; *Star Trek*'s Borg civilization). Since humanity consistently becomes the Elixir needed to overcome these mechanized Special Worlds, our Heroes usually complete their Journeys as better humans. And, borrowing *T2*'s Elixir of Hope, perhaps by Journey's end, the audience too can learn to value human life.

GENRE CHALLENGES: SCIENCE FICTION AND FANTASY

1. Using the Romance Chapter as a guide, how are the mythic elements of Romance used to structure the friendship of E.T. and Elliott? What is the Higher Cause? When do the two Heroes share the Higher Cause? Is there a Crisis of the Heart? What is the Noble Sacrifice?
2. How are Shapeshifters used in *Terminator 2: Judgment Day* to promote suspense (the audience anticipates what is likely to happen) and surprise (the audience was kept in the dark and surprised by what happens)?
3. Although the *Star Wars Trilogy* focuses on Luke's Journey to master the Force and redeem his "dark side," the three episodes weave various Journeys experienced by other characters. Choose one of the characters (Princess Leia, Han Solo, See-Threepio, Lando Calrissian) and track his or her Hero's Journey through the trilogy's three installments.
4. Take one of the analyzed films and show how the rules of the Special World are presented to the audience. Are there times when the audience is allowed to figure out the rules on their own?
5. What elements of the other genres in this book are present in the *Star Wars Trilogy*?

E.T. THE EXTRA-TERRESTRIAL
(U.S., 1982)

"You could be happy here. I could take care of you. I wouldn't let anybody hurt you. We could grow up together, E.T."

"Home. Home."

—Elliott (Henry Thomas)
and E.T.

Screenplay by Melissa Mathison
Directed by Steven Spielberg

An extra-terrestrial is abandoned on Earth and befriends a lonely young boy who helps him return home.

LANDMARKS OF THE JOURNEY

An extra-terrestrial needs to return home. A lonely young boy needs a friend. These conflicting Journeys intersect physically and emotionally, creating a bond—indeed a mystical bond. The Threshold Sequence becomes an essential and beautiful moment showing the growing bond between E.T. and Elliott. At first the two face the initial awkward stages when two potential friends meet. Communication becomes a major obstacle, and each must serve as a Mentor, using Elliott's toys and other common objects to teach one another about their Ordinary Worlds. But they must pass through this Threshold of Trust and Friendship before E.T. can finally present Elliott with his Call to Adventure, to help him return home.

Childhood friendship can be one of the strongest relationships experienced by humans. And like the great cinema Romances, E.T. and Elliott must learn to make the Noble Sacrifice of love for the Higher Cause of home and family.

THE JOURNEY

E.T.'s ORDINARY WORLD has been aboard a horticultural spaceship with his extra-terrestrial family. They land on Earth to collect botanical specimens, but a group of Earthly scientists, led by Keys (SHADOW), discover their ship and unwittingly trap E.T. The extra-terrestrials must leave E.T. behind and avoid any unwilling close encounters. This THRESHOLD is swift and frightening, and E.T. is thrown into a SPECIAL WORLD of loneliness. E.T. needs an ALLY to escape Keys and his men and find a way back home, E.T.'s OUTER PROBLEM. The lights of the suburbs welcome E.T. with the same warm glow of his spaceship. He follows this CALL and soon finds refuge in the garden shed of Elliott and his family.

Ten-year-old Elliott comes from a broken home. His dad ran off to Mexico with his girlfriend, leaving Elliott's mom, Mary, to raise the three children. Elliott needs a friend (his INNER PROBLEM). His smart-mouthed sister, Gertie (a TRICKSTER), is too young. And his older brother, Michael, and his friends won't accept Elliott into their inner circle. Elliott lives in an ORDINARY WORLD as lonely as the SPECIAL WORLD that E.T. now faces.

Elliott retrieves the boys' pizza delivery and hears noises in the garden shed. He responds to this CALL TO ADVENTURE by tossing a ball into the shed. "Something" tosses it back, and Elliott runs screaming into the house (a REFUSAL). Mary and the boys (THRESHOLD GUARDIANS) investigate and find only "coyote" tracks (a REFUSAL), but later that night, Elliott again hears noises. He willingly investigates and comes face-to-face with E.T. The sudden encounter terrifies boy and extra-terrestrial, a quick REFUSAL. At dinner, Elliott's family mocks his belief in the strange creature. But these attempts to REFUSE the Journey push Elliott to investigate on his own. He uses a trail of candy to lure E.T. back to his house.

Asleep at his post in his backyard, Elliott is startled awake by the answer to his CALL TO ADVENTURE. E.T. gives the boy back a handful of candy, initiating the THRESHOLD SEQUENCE. Elliott uses the candy to coax E.T. up to his bedroom, where the two continue their awkward encounter. E.T. mimics Elliott's gestures, beginning the empathic connection between boy and extra-terrestrial. But sleep quickly overcomes them.

The THRESHOLD SEQUENCE continues with a TEST PHASE that begins bright and early the next day. Elliott feigns sickness to convince Mary, a THRESHOLD GUARDIAN and perceived ENEMY, to let him stay home from school. After Mary leaves, Elliott tries to communicate with E.T. This MENTOR of young boy's culture introduces E.T. to his ORDINARY WORLD of toys, goldfish, and Pez candy. This lesson makes them mutually hungry; their mystical bond continues to solidify. While Elliott gathers food in the kitchen, back upstairs an umbrella frightens the curious alien, startling Elliott. He feels E.T.'s fear, an INNER STIRRING.

Elliott cannot keep his secret friend to himself and trusts his ALLIES, Michael and Gertie. He shows them E.T. but not before making them swear secrecy. After Elliott shows E.T. a globe and the location of the boy's home, the extra-terrestrial now becomes the MENTOR and uses his SPECIAL POWERS to levitate some balls and show the amazed children that he comes from a planet very far from Earth. The "planets" fall suddenly. Elliott feels something "scary" (an INNER STIRRING). The demonstration makes E.T. realize how far away from home he really is. E.T. joins Elliott at the window. Together they look up at the sky, their mystical bond complete. The two have crossed an emotional THRESHOLD OF FRIENDSHIP.

The TEST PHASE of their friendship continues on a deeper, empathic level. Elliott must go to school and risk leaving E.T. home alone. But Elliott also begins to "experience"

E.T.'s explorations at home, and risks revealing the bond he shares with the extra-terrestrial. While E.T. raids the home refrigerator, Elliott prepares to dissect frogs in his science class. E.T. drinks beer; Elliott becomes inebriated. When E.T. uses the television (a MENTOR) to learn about the SPECIAL WORLD, Elliott's INNER STIRRINGS finally transform into a defined CALL TO ADVENTURE, to "save him." In response, he disrupts the class and sets the frogs free.

Meanwhile, back at home, Gertie (a TRICKSTER MENTOR) teaches E.T. to speak with a little help from the Sesame Street gang. Elliott has been dismissed from school, and sees the result of E.T.'s lessons from television, the newspaper and Gertie. E.T. tells Elliott he needs to "phone home," the CALL TO ADVENTURE. Elliott has become the unlikely HERO to help E.T's return home, the HIGHER CAUSE.

Accepting this Journey, Elliott must now help E.T. build an interstellar phone to communicate with his planet. This extra-terrestrial MENTOR is able to use common objects from Elliott's ORDINARY WORLD to magically build this special tool. This second TEST PHASE establishes two TICKING CLOCKS. We see the mysterious Keys and his men's surveillance closing in on Elliott's home, re-establishing the SHADOW'S threat. Additionally, Michael is concerned that E.T. isn't looking too well. Elliott denies any problems, but the boy, too, isn't acting right. Finally, E.T. and Elliott APPROACH THE INMOST CAVE on Halloween night—the perfect night, for the boys can disguise E.T. in Gertie's costume. The APPROACH sequence takes Elliott and E.T. to the forest grove (the forest's "bald spot"). The "bald spot" becomes an almost enchanted borderland, a physical THRESHOLD between E.T.'s home and Elliott's ORDINARY suburbia. E.T. uses his magic to fly the two on Elliott's bicycle to the "bald spot." They TEST the interstellar phone, and it works.

Meanwhile, Elliott's mom, Mary, leaves the house allowing the SHADOW Keys and his men to make their own APPROACH and search for signs that E.T. is harbored there.

With E.T.'s phone working, Elliott acknowledges a CRISIS OF THE HEART. E.T. could soon separate from the boy's world. Afraid to see the loss of his new friend, Elliott offers the extra-terrestrial a home on Earth. Even though E.T. doesn't receive any response from his "phone call," he has already accepted the "break" of friendship. What Elliott doesn't realize is that E.T. must leave, or die.

The following morning, Elliott awakens at the "bald spot," all alone (initiating the ORDEAL SEQUENCE). He shows up at home and accepts the wrath of his worried mother. He can't tell this THRESHOLD GUARDIAN why he disappeared. Sick with a fever and unable to seek E.T., Elliott tells Michael that E.T. has disappeared. On bicycle, Michael evades Keys' men and finds E.T., collapsed in a stream and at death's door.

Michael must trust that Mary will actually become an ALLY to help Elliott and E.T. He shows her the two in the bathroom, both near-death. Mary sees the strange creature as a

SHADOW and tears Elliott away, leaving E.T. all alone. Government agents, clad in space suits, overtake the house.

The ORDEAL SEQUENCE continues. The government agents hook Elliott and E.T. to medical monitors to perform their scientific tests. Keys convinces Elliott to explain the importance of E.T.'s transmitter that continues to operate at the "bald spot." Keys reveals himself not as a SHADOW but as a HERALD / ALLY, an older "Elliott" who's thankful that E.T. found the childlike and accepting young boy first. But it's too late. E.T. accepts his own death and "releases" his friend. Elliott hugs his mother, who begins to understand this important bond that has been severed. The scientists fail to resurrect E.T. and we find ourselves as lost as Elliott, for we have lost a dear friend.

Keys allows Elliott to say good-bye to his only friend. Alone, Elliott confesses his love, an ELIXIR. Elliott closes the casket lid unaware that E.T.'s heart begins to glow. He finally recognizes his friend's RESURRECTION when he sees the flowers' RESURRECTION. E.T. has been reborn from his friend's love. E.T. announces to Elliott that his phone worked; his family is coming, the REWARD. But now Elliott needs to rescue E.T. from the scientists.

Elliott and Michael steal E.T. away in one of the government vans, the ROAD BACK. With the authorities on their tail, Elliott and Michael rendezvous at the park with Michael's friends. The boys stare in wonder as E.T. appears from the back of the van—fully resurrected. Faced with this awesome sight, they resume THE CHASE on bicycles.

Just when their escape appears assured, the authorities pounce on the bikers. Police set their roadblock with guns ready; the HERO TEAM accepts their "death," but E.T.'s magic resurrects them, physically lifting them above the law. The authorities cannot believe the sight of this RESURRECTION. Soon, the HERO TEAM lands at the forest grove, just as E.T.'s spaceship arrives.

E.T. says his good-byes to his new friends, Gertie and Michael. Initially, Elliott refuses to sacrifice his friendship and makes one last request for the extra-terrestrial to stay. E.T. also finds the friendship difficult to break and wants Elliott to go with him. While the ORDEAL SEQUENCE showed E.T. making the sacrifice that granted the boy life, Elliott must now find the strength to let E.T. go. E.T. offers the ELIXIR OF FRIENDSHIP, an ELIXIR residing in their hearts that will always keep them connected even though millions of miles may separate them. They say their final good-byes and E.T. leaves with a plant, a symbol of both his adventure on Earth and his friendship with Elliott, Michael and Gertie. The spaceship leaves.

E.T. is now safe again with his family. His JOURNEY has given him a new friend only a heartbeat away, the ELIXIR. Elliott accepts his ELIXIR as well. He's not as lonely as he was. And his relationship with E.T. has brought his family together, stronger than ever.

FADE OUT

TERMINATOR 2: JUDGMENT DAY
(U.S., 1991)

"The unknown future rolls toward us. I face it for the first time with a sense of hope, because if a machine, a terminator, can learn the value of human life, maybe we can too."

—Sarah Connor (Linda Hamilton)

Written by James Cameron and William Wisher
Directed by James Cameron

Ten years after Sarah Connor defeated the first Terminator, a second is sent from the future to terminate her son. Again, a protector is sent back to save young John Connor and prevent Judgment Day.

LANDMARKS OF THE JOURNEY

Cameron and Wisher present a non-stop chase, a race against time, to destroy a technology that will turn against humanity. James Cameron consistently pushes special effects to the limit and integrates "wow" moments into engrossing stories with memorable characters. Beneath the pyrotechnics, morphing, and heart-pounding stunts, *T2* is about a boy finding a father figure and accepting his destiny as a future leader.

T2's Journey forges a Hero Team. Initially each member (John Connor, Sarah Connor and the Terminator)—all Wounded or Lacking Heroes—faces personal goals that may conflict with those of other members of the Team. But through the physical Ordeals of the Journey, each learns to confront emotional and psychological problems, allowing them to overcome fears and commit to the Higher Cause. A woman warrior learns to be a nurturing mother; a future leader transforms a machine into a surrogate father; and a Terminator learns how to be a protector of humanity. For each, integrity and self-respect will be won. And sacrifice must be learned.

A time-travel adventure, *T2* deals with various perspectives and levels of physical and emotional Special Worlds. Special Worlds must be entered (and avoided!) The Terminator and the more advanced T-1000 enter the Special World of contemporary L.A. to pursue John Connor. John Connor must accept his Special World "on-the-run." But the most important Special World must be avoided at all cost, a future where humanity meets certain destruction at the mechanical hands of the technology it has created.

THE JOURNEY

The Opening Image establishes the horrifying apocalypse on Judgment Day when machines overthrow humans. Quickly establishing the stakes to be faced if John Connor is killed, the prologue sets the stage for the Journey's CALL TO ADVENTURE: the arrival of two travelers. One, a Terminator, is programmed to destroy mankind's future leader. The second has been sent to protect him. But who will reach John Connor first?

Schwarzenegger's Terminator is the first to arrive, and audiences familiar with the first film of the series immediately place a SHADOW mask on its cyborg face. We know the trouble it has caused in the past, and its initial antics at a truck stop fit the methodology of the first film's mechanical SHADOW. Its arrival sets up great tension (and a satisfying REVERSAL when it's revealed to be John Connor's protector.)

The smaller stature of the second traveler makes him more identifiable as the human protector. While Schwarzenegger takes on the renegade outfit of a biker, the second takes on the "protector's" uniform of a cop. Both have CROSSED THE THRESHOLD into their past, and face their big TEST: to find John Connor.

Now that the TICKING CLOCK has been set in motion, Cameron and Wisher introduce the ORDINARY WORLD of young John Connor, the future leader of the Human Resistance against machines. His mother, Sarah, has tried to prepare him for his future, raising him as a commando. But when Sarah was arrested and declared a psycho, John's reality was shattered. He never knew his father, and refuses to respect his foster parents. He needs a father figure, his INNER PROBLEM. John Connor survives the only way he knows how, by using his SPECIAL POWERS to hack ATM machines and escape into video game nirvana.

The third essential member of the HERO TEAM, Sarah Connor, lives her ORDINARY WORLD under Maximum Security at the Pescadero State Hospital. Her psychologist, Dr. Silberman, has diagnosed this HERALD'S doomsday warnings as delusions. This THRESHOLD GUARDIAN prevents Sarah from Minimal Security that would allow her access to her son. Sarah needs a way out so she can protect her son (her OUTER PROBLEM).

The final important piece of the ORDINARY WORLD is established... Kept in the high security vault at Cyberdyne Systems are a mysterious computer chip and a metal hand and forearm—all that remain of Sarah's first Terminator. Dyson and his team at Cyberdyne perceive an ELIXIR that will advance artificial intelligence, not realizing that these DARK ELIXIRS will destroy humanity.

Meanwhile, the "Cop" is breezing through his TEST PHASE to track down John. John Connor's foster parents (THRESHOLD GUARDIANS) direct him to find John at the Mall, also mentioning that the "biker" has already been by. (Stakes and Tension are raised; the Terminator has the lead.)

The Cop and Biker finally converge on the Mall, but they must overcome John's ALLIES to locate the boy. John flees the Cop, a perceived ENEMY representing authority, only to run into the shotgun-toting Biker. In a service hallway, the young HERO is sandwiched between two apparent SHADOWS. In one of cinema's most memorable REVERSALS, the Biker Terminator reveals itself as the boy's protector and HERO, and tries to shoot the true SHADOW, a SHAPESHIFTING polyalloy T-1000. This confrontation has thrown the young HERO through the THRESHOLD into a disorienting SPECIAL WORLD on the run, with no time for explanations.

The CHASE races through the Los Angeles aqueducts as the T-1000 relentlessly tries to run the boy down. The Terminator HERO, riding its motorcycle, snatches John from death. The two survive this THRESHOLD and watch the T-1000 crash and burn. They ride away, but the T-1000 rises from the flames. No charred endoskeleton, this indestructible SHADOW reforms itself into the 'cop,' revealing its perfect SPECIAL POWERS of liquid metal mimicry.

John has witnessed incredible forces at work during the THRESHOLD and demands that the Terminator stop to give him some answers. This MEETING OF THE MENTOR pushes John to accept that his mother was right about the future, and that he himself sent this "protector" Terminator from 35 years in the future. In this SPECIAL WORLD, John fears for his foster parents, but the Terminator uses its SPECIAL POWERS to mimic John's voice and reveal the T-1000's disguise, confirming that his foster parents are already dead, a TEST. The MENTOR also takes this time to teach John the rules and SPECIAL POWERS of the more advanced T-1000.

Realizing that everything his mother had taught him was true, John demands that the Terminator help him rescue Sarah (OUTER PROBLEM). The scene shifts into a second MEETING OF THE MENTOR, only John becomes the MENTOR. John delights in the discovery that the Terminator must follow his instructions; but when he TESTS his SPECIAL POWERS on two men, the Terminator readily prepares to blow them away. John stops it and tries to teach it his rules: you can't kill people. This MEETING establishes John Connor's moral fiber, and is a CALL TO ADVENTURE, launching the Terminator's INNER JOURNEY to become human.

Meanwhile, Sarah breaks out of her cell. She uses the BOLD APPROACH to get past the guards (THRESHOLD GUARDIANS) and threatens Silberman with a syringe of drain cleaner. But her escape to the elevator is blocked by the arrival of the Terminator, initiating an ORDEAL sequence. The experience of her previous Journey with this apparent SHADOW makes her frantic, unable to hear her son's shouts. As the guards move in, the Terminator disposes of the THRESHOLD GUARDIANS. It has proved its allegiance and offers its hand if she wants to live. She takes the HERO'S cyborg hand just in time. Her real SHADOW, the T-1000, attacks, initiating another CHASE during which the HERO TEAM barely overcomes the SHADOW'S extensive and impressive SHAPESHIFTING powers.

The HERO TEAM escapes in a police car, giving a moment's pause for Sarah to discourage John's help. He mustn't risk himself for her. Sarah defines herself as a LONER HERO in conflict with the HERO TEAM. Hurt by his mother's rejection, John begins to cry. This display of human emotion intrigues the Terminator.

They take a needed break to recover from the exhausting CHASE of their Journey's TEST PHASE. Both human and cyborg injuries must be attended to. They hotwire a station wagon and drive south. The individual members use the time to focus on their personal Journeys. John learns that he can teach human values to the Terminator, and turn it into a friend (and surrogate father). Wearing a SHAPESHIFTING mask to hide her personal Journey, Sarah uses the Terminator's extensive files to gather information about her perceived ENEMIES, Dyson and Cyberdyne. The Terminator continues its personal Journey to understand humanity.

After an apocalyptic vision of mankind's destruction, Sarah leaves the HERO TEAM. She's determined to stop the future her own way. Her previous Journey has transformed her into a "terminator." Using a lesson from her cyborg SHADOW, she takes the BOLD APPROACH, breaks into Dyson's home, and threatens to kill him. Faced with the power to end a human life, an ORDEAL, Sarah's humanity wins out, a RESURRECTION. She spares Dyson, as her son and the Terminator arrive. She accepts her son and confesses her love for him, a REWARD. This ORDEAL now allows John to end the destructive future in his own non-violent way. He orders the Terminator to rip away its forearm skin, which reveals a duplicate of the machine hand locked in Dyson's vault. Dyson accepts this glimpse of the future and offers to destroy everything in his lab. This yields an important REWARD. The HERO TEAM has been forged with one mutual goal (the OUTER PROBLEM): to destroy the computer chip and Terminator arm.

The TEAM breaks into Cyberdyne. But their BOLD APPROACH trips the silent alarm, and Dyson's security access fails to open the vault. John Connor uses his SPECIAL POWERS to crack the computerized security system. Relying on the Terminator's firepower, the TEAM penetrates the research lab. Meanwhile, the T-1000 learns of the HERO'S TEAM'S plot and races to Cyberdyne, as the police surround the building.

The HERO TEAM secures the chip and the machine arm, the REWARD, but a helicopter HERALDS a seemingly insurmountable force blockading their ROAD BACK. The Terminator holds off the police, while the HERO TEAM prepares to destroy the research lab. The police break in and shoot Dyson, who holds the detonator. He knows he cannot survive this ORDEAL and willingly sacrifices himself so the others can escape. But Sarah, too, is trapped; the Terminator breaks through the wall and pulls her out (a RESURRECTION) as Dyson releases the detonator, blowing the research lab.

Led by the Terminator (using its MENTOR'S lessons of limiting the body count) and with the REWARD of the chip and the metal hand, the HERO TEAM escapes in a SWAT van, the ROAD BACK. The T-1000 arrives and gives chase in a police helicopter.

The Magic Flight, a common motif seen in fairy tales and myths, shows the HERO fleeing the SPECIAL WORLD with the ELIXIR. During the flight, objects may be sacrificed to delay the SHADOW. Or perhaps when the CHASE seems lost, an unlikely ALLY retrieves the ELIXIR and resumes the flight with renewed energy. We see a similar CHASE here, but vehicles are the objects that are manned and sacrificed by both HERO and SHADOW. The flight culminates with the T-1000's liquid nitrogen tanker pushing the HERO'S TEAM pickup through the gates into a steel mill plant. The Terminator leaps aboard the tanker and forces the juggernaut down like a bull-rider. The tanker splits open, unleashing liquid nitrogen. The T-1000 tries to rise from the wreckage, but the liquid nitrogen freezes the metal SHADOW. The Terminator shoots, shattering the SHADOW into hundreds of shards of frozen metal, a FALSE RESURRECTION.

But the heat from the steel works liquefies the T-1000's shards. Droplets fuse, and soon the SHADOW is RESURRECTED, a REVERSAL. The HERO TEAM'S job is not over. Their flight resumes on foot. The Terminator loads his last grenade cartridge and leads John and Sarah into the guts of the steel mill. The Terminator makes its SACRIFICE along this magic flight, pushing John and Sarah ahead so that it can confront the T-1000. The T-1000 easily entraps the Terminator in the metal works and moves on to its prey.

Now Sarah confronts the T-1000 to ensure that her son escapes. The T-1000 threatens to kill Sarah if she doesn't call her son back. Having extricated itself from the metal works, the Terminator arrives to resume the battle. But the journey has been too much for this member of the HERO TEAM, and the T-1000 easily defeats the Terminator. It cuts its power source, finally killing the Protector. Sarah must resume the role as her son's protector. But the Terminator reroutes its power source and frees itself. It grabs the shotgun, completing its RESURRECTION.

John hears his mother's calls for help and finally sees his wounded mother. But the real Sarah Connor appears revealing the T-1000's disguise, a RESURRECTION. She unloads her shotgun into the T-1000, forcing the SHADOW to the very edge of the vat of molten steel. But she runs out of rounds. Just when all seems lost for the HERO TEAM, the Terminator rises up the conveyor and blows up the T-1000 with the last grenade cartridge, a RESURRECTION. The SHADOW falls and perishes in the molten steel.

With the destruction of his "terminator," John Connor must destroy the DARK ELIXIR. He drops the machine arm and the chip into the vat. But the Terminator must also be destroyed, since it holds the same DARK ELIXIR that would doom mankind. Yet, it cannot self-terminate. And John won't sacrifice his new MENTOR and friend. The Terminator sees the boy's tears and acknowledges their purpose, as well as the realization that he can never be that human, an ELIXIR. Sarah provides the strength needed to complete the Journey. She offers her hand and lowers the cyborg to its death.

The Journey continues on the road, and we hear Sarah Connor. She can now face an unknown future for the first time with the ELIXIR OF HOPE. Perhaps we, like the Terminator, can learn the value of human life.

FADE OUT

THE STAR WARS TRILOGY

"A long time ago in a galaxy far, far away..."

The Myth of Luke Skywalker has been ingrained in our popular culture with hundreds of spin-offs, as well as novels, comic books, computer games and action toys. Now with the cultural event of the eagerly awaited *Episode One: The Phantom Menace,* we cannot deny, nor should we ignore, the impact of *Star Wars.* Truly our modern myth, *Star Wars* presents a unique vision rooted in identifiable themes and issues that struck a chord in 1977 and continue to reverberate today.

George Lucas draws from a rich wellspring of storytelling traditions steeped in mythology (an orphan's quest for his father's legacy, a wise sage's invaluable guidance, Chivalric honor, and an impenetrable fortress) and Hollywood iconography (Western saloons, dogfights, chases, and High Adventure duels). Freely juxtaposing the fantastic with science fiction, Lucas created a timeless world. But *Star Wars* would not be a vision without its soul. In this epic battle of Good versus Evil, the human spirit rises above the shadow of technology. And an individual finds the heroic power within him to make the ultimate sacrifice, save a galaxy and redeem his father.

Luke's spiritual quest encompasses three episodes, each an individual Journey or cycle with stages that hold larger significance upon Luke's overall transformation. To explore the mythic power of *The Star Wars Trilogy,* let's first look at the structure of the individual episodes. We'll then look at how they influence the Journey of Luke Skywalker.

Special Note: Because of the re-release of *The Star Wars Trilogy* and its ready availability on video, I've charted the Journeys using the enhanced Special Editions. Also, to remain consistent with all of the Journey Charts, Luke's Spiritual Quest uses the *complete* run-times of the three episodes, including credits.

STAR WARS EPISODE IV: A NEW HOPE
(U.S., 1977)

"I want to learn the ways of the Force and become a Jedi like my father."
—Luke Skywalker (Mark Hamill)

Screenplay by George Lucas
Directed by George Lucas

A farm boy joins the quest to save a princess and destroy the evil Galactic Empire's doomsday machine, while following in his father's footsteps to become a Jedi Knight.

LANDMARKS OF THE JOURNEY

This Space Opera as High Adventure throws us into the middle of a Chase. A Hero Princess' race home with the Elixir that will restore peace to the Galaxy is cut short by the ultimate Shadow force. Darth Vader locks Princess Leia in an extended Ordeal, unaware that fate and a droid will place the adventure into the unsuspecting hands of an orphan farm boy. With the help of a Mentor, Luke Skywalker chooses his Heroic Journey. Obi-Wan Kenobi plays the classic Mentor. He helps Luke overcome fear so that the boy can accept his Journey. More importantly, Obi-Wan introduces Luke (and the audience) to the Force, the mystical power that binds the galaxy and delineates Good and Evil. During the Hero's Journey, the Mentor must push the Hero on alone to prove that he can utilize the Mentor's lessons and complete the Journey. Obi-Wan's shocking departure initiates the pivotal Road Back. His heroic sacrifice allows Luke and his "awakened" Princess to escape the Death Star, and resume Leia's flight with the plans that will defeat the Shadow.

THE JOURNEY

The ORDINARY WORLD is in a period of civil war. An evil Galactic Empire tries to crush the spreading Rebellion. With their first major victory against the Empire, Rebel spies have stolen secret plans to the Empire's doomsday weapon, the Death Star, an armored space station capable of destroying a planet.

The Journey opens in the middle of a CHASE, as HERO Princess Leia Organa races home on her ROAD BACK, to deliver the plans of the Death Star. Galactic forces, led by the SHADOW Darth Vader, overtake the ship and capture Leia. But she slips a message and the plans to her droid, Artoo-Detoo (a HERALD). Leia's abduction is a galactic CALL TO ADVENTURE that sets the ORDINARY WORLD in imbalance. This CALL will reverberate to the desert planet of Tatooine, where fate places the princess's mechanical HERALD into the hands of an unlikely young HERO.

An orphaned farm boy, Luke Skywalker, lives with his Uncle Owen and Aunt Beru. Impatient with this desolate ORDINARY WORLD, Luke dreams of joining the Academy and fighting space wars (his OUTER PROBLEM). Instead, he's stuck helping his uncle with the crops. Aunt Beru warns Uncle Owen of Luke's INNER STIRRING; the young boy has too much of his father in him (an INNER PROBLEM). Both Beru and Owen are THRESHOLD GUARDIANS who have hidden Luke's heritage.

As Luke cleans Artoo, the droid accidentally projects a portion of Princess Leia's plea for Obi-Wan Kenobi's help. Smitten by the vision, Luke wants to see more, but Artoo (a THRESHOLD GUARDIAN) refuses, insisting that the message must be delivered to Obi-Wan Kenobi, who Luke believes is the old hermit, Ben Kenobi.

The HERALD Artoo braves Tatooine alone to find Obi-Wan and deliver his message. Luke takes off after the droid with C-3PO. Sand People (THRESHOLD GUARDIANS) ambush them, but a mysterious cloaked figure rescues them. He reveals himself as Old Ben (Obi-Wan) Kenobi, a Jedi Knight who has chosen to live in seclusion.

At Obi-Wan's dwelling, this elder MENTOR introduces Luke to the Force and the truth about his father, a Jedi Knight who had been murdered by Darth Vader. He presents Luke with his father's lightsaber, the Jedi Knight's weapon (a MENTOR'S GIFT). Obi-Wan has Artoo play Princess Leia's entire message begging Obi-Wan to bring Artoo—and the Death Star plans locked in its memory system—to her father on Alderaan (the CALL TO ADVENTURE). The MENTOR asks Luke to join in the quest. But Luke's obligation to Uncle Owen's crops forces him to REFUSE.

Luke returns to his home and discovers that Imperial stormtroopers have burned the homestead and killed his uncle and aunt, initiating his THRESHOLD SEQUENCE. Luke has run out of options. The Empire's direct, violent CALL has destroyed Luke's ORDINARY WORLD, and pushes Luke to accept his Journey: to go with Obi-Wan, learn the ways of the Force (his OUTER PROBLEM) and follow in his father's footsteps (his INNER PROBLEM).

Obi-Wan and Luke seek passage to Alderaan. Their arrival in Mos Eisley initiates the TEST PHASE, during which Luke begins to learn the rules of this SPECIAL WORLD, make ALLIES and ENEMIES, and see the powers of the Force. They enter the Cantina, a watering hole for rogues, pirates and other THRESHOLD GUARDIANS. They hire smuggler, Han Solo, and his Wookiee first mate, Chewbacca. These ALLIES take our HERO TEAM aboard the famed *Millennium Falcon.* They escape the pursuing stormtroopers and jump into hyperspace.

Now safely en route to Alderaan, Luke can begin to learn the ways of the Force, under Obi-Wan's guidance. As the boy practices using his lightsaber with a "seeker" robot, Obi-Wan falters. This HERALD feels a great disturbance in the Force and warns of something terrible (not realizing that the Empire has destroyed Alderaan). Luke continues his lessons. Luke learns to trust his instinct to block the "seeker's" laser blasts, taking his first step into the larger world of the Force.

Han takes the *Falcon* out of hyperspace. Obi-Wan's premonition comes true as they are thrown into a middle of a meteor shower formerly known as the planet Alderaan. The Death Star looms in the distance. Han can't turn back; the Death Star locks the *Falcon* in its tractor beam and pulls it into the docking port. The HERO TEAM tricks the Imperial Forces by hiding in smuggling compartments. APPROACHING THE INMOST CAVE, Obi-Wan separates from the HERO TEAM to disable the tractor beam. As soon as the MENTOR leaves, the TEAM splinters into arguments. Artoo interrupts them. Accessing the computer network, the droid has discovered the location of Princess Leia. Luke uses the lure of monetary REWARDS to convince Han to help him save the Princess.

Outfitted as stormtroopers ("wearing the skins" of THRESHOLD GUARDIANS), Luke and Han escort their "prisoner" Chewbacca and overtake the Detention Center. This pushes the TEAM through a SERIES OF ORDEALS that move them deeper into the bowels of the Death Star. Luke locates Princess Leia while Han holds off the attack. Trapped like rats (the FIRST ORDEAL), Leia blows a hole in the wall and the TEAM escapes down a chute into the garbage room.

In the garbage room, a tentacled monster pulls Luke under the sewage. Witnessing this "death" of our HERO, we feel as lost as the HERO TEAM. Luke finally surfaces (a RESURRECTION of this SECOND ORDEAL), the monster disappears, and the entire TEAM faces death as the garbage room walls close in. Using the comlink, the droids witness the death of the TEAM; however, the comlink also provides the lifeline to their RESURRECTION from this THIRD ORDEAL. Artoo shuts down the trash masher. The sounds of death erupt into joy, and our TEAM is miraculously restored. Having "tasted" death in this SERIES OF ORDEALS, the members of the HERO TEAM begin to transform into self-sacrificing HEROES. Han chases down a squad of stormtroopers; Luke swings Princess Leia across a precipice. But a MENTOR'S sacrifice must be made to forge the HERO TEAM and allow their escape from the Death Star.

Obi-Wan successfully disengages the tractor beam, but encounters Darth Vader in a lightsaber duel. Obi-Wan sees the HERO TEAM returning to the Falcon, and his sacrifice to the SHADOW initiates their ROAD BACK. Luke witnesses his MENTOR'S sacrifice, but Obi-Wan's death is questionable. His body mysteriously vanishes, and his mystical voice pushes Luke and the HERO TEAM to flee this SPECIAL WORLD. Their REWARDS are Leia's safety and the stolen Death Star schematics. During their CHASE, Han and Luke defeat a squadron of Imperial TIE fighters; however, Leia suspects that the Empire is tracking them. Their ROAD BACK seems too easy. The TEAM'S arrival at the Rebel Base completes the ROAD BACK SEQUENCE. Armed with the plans, the Rebellion can prepare an attack on the Death Star; but the Empire now knows their location and prepares for their destruction, a TICKING CLOCK.

The Rebellion faces a seemingly impossible task: shooting one photon charge into the Death Star's two-meter-wide thermal exhaust. But Luke brings his SPECIAL POWER of experience from his ORDINARY WORLD which make him believe that the task can be done. ("I used to bull's-eye womp rats in my T-sixteen back home.") During the Rebellion's grand sacrifice, Luke rises above his fallen ALLIES to complete the heroic task.

With Darth Vader on his tail, Luke hears the assurance of his MENTOR Obi-Wan to trust the Force. Since reliance upon technology and machinery failed Luke's ALLIES, Luke takes heed of his MENTOR'S advice to trust human intuition and turns off his targeting computer. Luke's trust in the Force also makes his power known to Vader. The SHADOW locks in on Luke's X-wing. The HERO'S death seems likely, but an ALLY provides his RESURRECTION. The selfish Han Solo joins this HIGHER CAUSE, arriving like the cavalry to send Darth Vader spinning into space, letting Luke make the one-in-a-million shot and destroy the Death Star, completing the RESURRECTION.

Luke has earned the ELIXIR of his trust in the Force. He returns to the Rebel Base, and reunites with his HERO TEAM. They share the ELIXIR of success; and are soon honored as Heroes. The SHADOW has been defeated and the ELIXIR of peace restored to the galaxy, at least for the time being.

FADE OUT

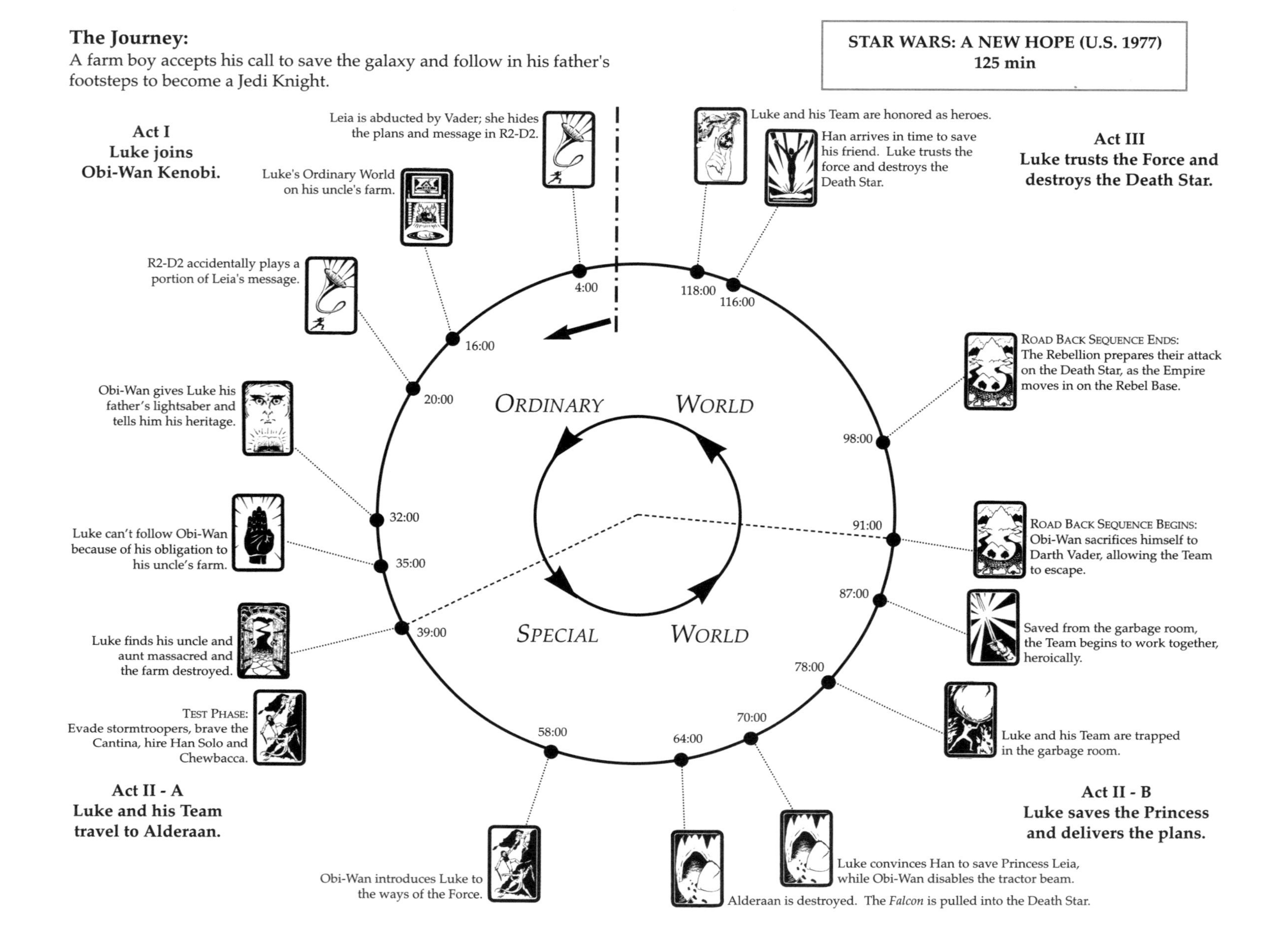
STAR WARS: A NEW HOPE (U.S. 1977)
125 min
The Journey:
A farm boy accepts his call to save the galaxy and follow in his father's footsteps to become a Jedi Knight.
Act I
Luke joins Obi-Wan Kenobi.
Leia is abducted by Vader; she hides the plans and message in R2-D2.
Luke's Ordinary World on his uncle's farm.
R2-D2 accidentally plays a portion of Leia's message.
Obi-Wan gives Luke his father's lightsaber and tells him his heritage.
Luke can't follow Obi-Wan because of his obligation to his uncle's farm.
Luke finds his uncle and aunt massacred and the farm destroyed.
Test Phase: Evade stormtroopers, brave the Cantina, hire Han Solo and Chewbacca.
Act II - A
Luke and his Team travel to Alderaan.
Obi-Wan introduces Luke to the ways of the Force.
Alderaan is destroyed. The Falcon is pulled into the Death Star.
Luke convinces Han to save Princess Leia, while Obi-Wan disables the tractor beam.
Act II - B
Luke saves the Princess and delivers the plans.
Luke and his Team are trapped in the garbage room.
Saved from the garbage room, the Team begins to work together, heroically.
Road Back Sequence Begins: Obi-Wan sacrifices himself to Darth Vader, allowing the Team to escape.
Road Back Sequence Ends: The Rebellion prepares their attack on the Death Star, as the Empire moves in on the Rebel Base.
Luke and his Team are honored as heroes.
Han arrives in time to save his friend. Luke trusts the force and destroys the Death Star.
Act III
Luke trusts the Force and destroys the Death Star.
Ordinary World
Special World
4:00
16:00
20:00
32:00
35:00
39:00
58:00
64:00
70:00
78:00
87:00
91:00
98:00
116:00
118:00

EPISODE V: THE EMPIRE STRIKES BACK
(U.S., 1980)

"I'm not afraid."

"You will be. You will be."

—Luke Skywalker (Mark Hamill)
and Yoda

Screenplay by Leigh Brackett and Lawrence Kasdan
Story by George Lucas
Directed by Irvin Kershner

Luke Skywalker severs his Jedi training with mystical mentor Yoda to save his friends and confront the evil Darth Vader.

LANDMARKS OF THE JOURNEY

Now that the characters have been established in *Star Wars*, we can settle down and enjoy them, test their mettle, and find their deepest longings. Although the darkest of the three episodes, *The Empire Strikes Back* offers the richest Journey because of its focus on personal quest and sacrifice. *Empire* weaves two Journeys: Luke's training as a Jedi, and Han and Leia's Journey of the Heart. Both Journeys separate at the Threshold Sequence. But the overriding Journey of Darth Vader to capture young Skywalker forces the two Hero Journeys to dovetail at the Road Back Sequence, when the Heroes make their greatest sacrifices. Han Solo risks his life to save his love, Leia. Luke jeopardizes his training, and abandons his Mentors, to save his friends. The Journey ends with Han in frozen death, while Luke suffers a spiritual death as he must now accept the Dark Side of his legacy.

THE JOURNEY

Answering the destruction of the Death Star, the Emperor's troops have scattered the rebel forces in an effort to expel all signs of the Rebellion. Freedom fighters, led by Luke Skywalker, have a new secret base on the remote ice world of Hoth. Now that the evil lord, Darth Vader, has sensed the Force in young Skywalker, he has launched a personal quest for Luke's capture, deploying thousands of probe droids.

The HERO TEAM lives in an ORDINARY WORLD of caution and preparation for the next stage of rebellion. Luke and Leia have committed to the Rebellion's cause to defeat the evil Empire (OUTER PROBLEM); however, Han Solo must move on to personal matters, to deal with the bounty placed on his head by Jabba the Hutt (Han's OUTER PROBLEM). Han uses the threat of departure (an impending CRISIS OF THE HEART) to make

Leia admit her feelings for him, pushing their JOURNEY OF THE HEART (INNER PROBLEM). Leia denies her romantic feelings (REFUSAL).

Two CALLS OF ADVENTURE establish the two central Journeys:

1) Luke trains with Yoda to become a Jedi Knight.
2) Han and Leia flee Darth Vader and discover their love.

Having escaped the ORDEAL of the Wampa and now alone on the icy wasteland, Luke sees the vision of Obi-Wan Kenobi, a HERALD. His MENTOR instructs him that he must go to Dagobah to learn the ways of the Force from the Jedi Master, Yoda. Han Solo replaces this vision and provides Luke's physical RESURRECTION to follow the CALL TO ADVENTURE.

Later, Han and Chewie cause an Imperial probe droid to self-destruct, warning the Rebellion that the Empire has found their camp. There's no time to refuse this CALL TO ADVENTURE. The Rebellion must evacuate Hoth as the Empire launches its massive attack, CROSSING THE THRESHOLD, shattering the ORDINARY WORLD and dividing the HERO TEAM into unsettling SPECIAL WORLDS. Han and Leia complete their THRESHOLD of escape from Hoth; but unfortunately they have the Empire on their tail, and the *Millennium Falcon*'s hyperdrive won't operate. Meanwhile, Luke crosses his THRESHOLD as well, and sets course for Dagobah.

HAN AND LEIA'S JOURNEY OF ESCAPE AND THE HEART

On the run from the relentless Imperial fleet, Han and Leia enter a TEST PHASE filled with ORDEALS, shadowy ENEMIES and shapeshifting ALLIES that will finally push Leia and Han to accept their love. Han outmaneuvers a squadron of TIE fighters through an asteroid field and finds refuge on a large asteroid. In the *Falcon*'s closed quarters, Han and Leia face the unsettling issue of their love. They finally kiss, but C-3PO ruins this moment of APPROACH TO THE INMOST CAVE OF THE HEART. The TEAM'S refuge on the asteroid is short-lived. They discover they've actually been in the belly of a space slug, but their flight from this ORDEAL throws them back into the heat of the Imperial CHASE. Desperate, Han makes a direct assault on a Star Destroyer and suddenly disappears. Have they disintegrated? But this ORDEAL is Han's ruse to trick the Star Destroyer's sensors. With the *Falcon* clinging to the side of the Destroyer, Han awaits the starship's standard waste disposal before it enters light speed. Han takes the time to determine their next move (an APPROACH), to go to Cloud City and find sanctuary in the hands of SHAPESHIFTER ALLY Lando Calrissian. Their RESURRECTION of the ORDEAL arrives, and they float away with the rest of the starship's garbage. But bounty hunter Boba Fett (Han Solo's SHADOW) anticipates Han's moves and follows the *Falcon* to Cloud City. Lando grants Han asylum, but he can't be trusted. Pressured by the Empire, Lando surrenders the HERO TEAM to Darth Vader to use as a lure to get Luke Skywalker.

LUKE'S JOURNEY TO TRAIN WITH YODA

Luke's acceptance of his HERALD'S CALL is only the beginning of his THRESHOLD. A WILLING HERO may not realize that his MENTOR must still accept him into the SPECIAL WORLD. Importantly, Luke's THRESHOLD SEQUENCE, the arrival in Dagobah and search for Yoda, surfaces his weaknesses as a HERO. His recklessness and impatience will threaten his MEETING WITH THE MENTOR and put into question his ability to complete his Journey to become a Jedi Knight.

Additionally, Luke's THRESHOLD creates a disturbance in the Force. The SHADOW Emperor fears Luke's Journey, but Vader sees Luke's training as an opportunity to push Luke to the Dark Side. The inevitability of the meeting between Vader and Luke establishes a TICKING CLOCK.

Luke has entered the murky, swampy almost dreamlike SPECIAL WORLD of Dagobah—his X-Wing at the bottom of a swamp, and his hopes dashed (a REFUSAL). Luke meets a strange TRICKSTER THRESHOLD GUARDIAN, who toys with Luke's impatience but promises to take him to Yoda. Luke's impatience prevents him from seeing the power behind this TRICKSTER'S mask. Yoda finally reveals himself, and Luke begs to be accepted by this MENTOR. This MEETING OF THE MENTOR questions Luke's commitment: Will he complete the Journey that he begins? He insists that he isn't afraid, but this MENTOR warns him that fear is necessary for this Journey. With his MENTOR'S acceptance, Luke enters the THRESHOLD into the SPECIAL WORLD of advanced training as a Jedi Knight.

The TEST PHASE begins in earnest as Yoda trains Luke both physically and mentally to be a Jedi. The master chastises Luke for his recklessness. He also prepares him for the ORDEAL, warning him of the seductive Dark Side of the Force. Yoda presents the Tree Cave, a domain of the Dark Side that must be entered by Luke. Inside, Luke will find only what he takes with him. Unable to trust the Force's power, Luke takes his lightsaber and APPROACHES THIS INMOST CAVE. Inside, Luke faces his greatest fear, Darth Vader. Luke draws his lightsaber and physically conquers the vision, only to unearth an even greater fear. Luke's face lies beneath the SHADOW'S mask. This ORDEAL symbolizes how easy it is to fall to the Dark Side (his SHADOW) and foreshadows his dark legacy.

Having faced his ORDEAL of the Dark Side, Luke continues his training. The Force begins to flow through him. Luke can feel his connection with his surrounding SPECIAL WORLD, and can even levitate objects. But Luke can't see the full potential of the Force; resurrecting something as large as his X-wing is an impossible task. His wizened little MENTOR proves him otherwise, showing the positive potential of the Force. This MEETING OF THE MENTOR gives Luke renewed conviction to see his Journey through. The Force now becomes Luke's ALLY and REWARDS Luke with clairvoyance, and the horrifying vision of his friends in trouble. Faced with the possibility of the death of his friends, Luke prepares to sacrifice his training to save them. Both Yoda and the vision of Obi-Wan push Luke to complete his training. His Journey is dangerous at this junction and he can easily be tempted to the SHADOW of the Dark Side. Again impatience and recklessness threaten Luke's Journey. He REFUSES to turn his back on his friends and races to Cloud City and Darth Vader's trap.

Luke's and Han/Leia's Journeys converge at Cloud City and the ROAD BACK. Darth Vader prepares to use Han Solo to test the Carbon-Freezing Chamber. Seeing Han face deep-freeze and possible death (CRISIS OF THE HEART), Leia confesses her love to him, the REWARD of their Journey. He acknowledges her love and willingly sacrifices himself for her freedom. The freezing complete, we fear with Leia, Chewie and the rest that Han is dead. But he survives the frozen state, a RESURRECTION and REWARD for all, especially for Darth Vader. The SHADOW hands Solo over to Boba Fett and prepares the Chamber for Luke. Vader also double-crosses Lando and keeps Leia and Chewie as his prisoners.

Leia and Chewie are escorted away. But Leia's able to warn Luke of the trap, a REWARD that keeps Luke alert to the dangers ahead.

Lando turns the tables on the stormtroopers and frees Leia and Chewie. They can save Han, but they arrive at the landing platform moments too late. Leia watches Boba Fett's ship disappear.

An extensive RESURRECTION SEQUENCE begins as Luke confronts Darth Vader, while Leia, Lando and the gang battle stormtroopers to secure the *Millennium Falcon* and make their escape. Luke falls into Vader's trap but avoids carbon freeze, a REVERSAL that impresses Vader. Turning Luke to the Dark Side will be much harder than anticipated. Vader toys with Luke, breaking down his physical and emotional defenses, pushing him to embrace his anger and accept his SHADOW.

In a final duel along the gantry over the reactor shaft, Luke refuses to give in, and Vader severs the young HERO'S hand. Unable to fight, Luke must face his destiny. But MENTORS Obi-Wan and Yoda did not prepare him for Vader's revelation—that he and his SHADOW are the same flesh. Darth Vader is his father. Although Luke tries to deny it, he knows Vader speaks the truth, and all seems lost for our HERO. Vader offers allegiance to rule the galaxy, but Luke knows of one other way. He chooses the ultimate sacrifice (an emotional/spiritual RESURRECTION). Refusing to join his father and the Dark Side, Luke chooses death and releases himself to the abyss.

Luke miraculously survives his fall, clutching a weather vane. He calls for Obi-Wan, but unlike the previous episode's RESURRECTION, his MENTOR cannot help. However, like *Star Wars: A New Hope*, Luke's RESURRECTION comes from his humanity, his instinct and his love. He calls for Leia, and she hears him. She orders the *Falcon* back to rescue him, his physical RESURRECTION. The RESURRECTION SEQUENCE continues, as yet again, the *Falcon*'s hyperdrive fails. Before Vader can catch the *Falcon* and claim victory, Artoo helps the cause, reactivating the hyperdrive, granting the long-anticipated final RESURRECTION that sends the *Falcon* safely into light speed.

The Empire Strikes Back defies the "Happy Ending," leaving Han Solo in carbon freeze and Luke in a spiritual death, struggling with the DARK ELIXIR of his destiny as the son of Darth Vader. Luke's new mechanical hand brings him even closer to his father, who is more machine than human.

The ELIXIR OF HOPE exists for the HERO TEAM. Lando and Chewbacca are dispatched to find Jabba the Hutt and Boba Fett and prepare for their rendezvous with Luke at Tatooine. The rescue of Han Solo and the RESURRECTION of the HERO TEAM will have to wait for the next episode.

FADE OUT

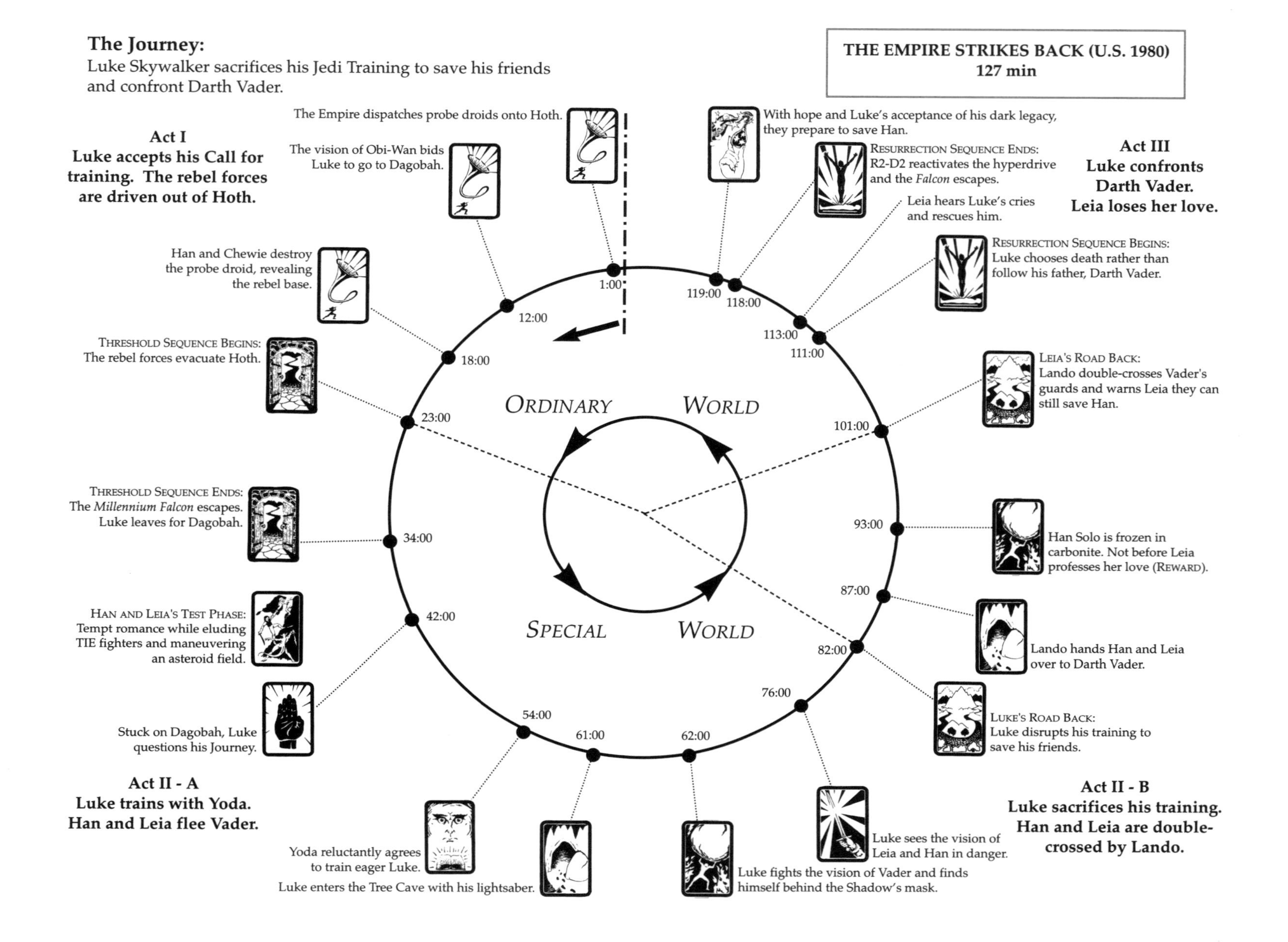
THE EMPIRE STRIKES BACK (U.S. 1980)
127 min
The Journey:
Luke Skywalker sacrifices his Jedi Training to save his friends and confront Darth Vader.
Act I
Luke accepts his Call for training. The rebel forces are driven out of Hoth.
The Empire dispatches probe droids onto Hoth.
The vision of Obi-Wan bids Luke to go to Dagobah.
Han and Chewie destroy the probe droid, revealing the rebel base.
Threshold Sequence Begins: The rebel forces evacuate Hoth.
Threshold Sequence Ends: The Millennium Falcon escapes. Luke leaves for Dagobah.
Han and Leia's Test Phase: Tempt romance while eluding TIE fighters and maneuvering an asteroid field.
Stuck on Dagobah, Luke questions his Journey.
Act II - A
Luke trains with Yoda. Han and Leia flee Vader.
Yoda reluctantly agrees to train eager Luke.
Luke enters the Tree Cave with his lightsaber.
Luke fights the vision of Vader and finds himself behind the Shadow's mask.
Luke sees the vision of Leia and Han in danger.
Act II - B
Luke sacrifices his training. Han and Leia are double-crossed by Lando.
Luke's Road Back: Luke disrupts his training to save his friends.
Lando hands Han and Leia over to Darth Vader.
Han Solo is frozen in carbonite. Not before Leia professes her love (Reward).
Leia's Road Back: Lando double-crosses Vader's guards and warns Leia they can still save Han.
Resurrection Sequence Begins: Luke chooses death rather than follow his father, Darth Vader.
Leia hears Luke's cries and rescues him.
Resurrection Sequence Ends: R2-D2 reactivates the hyperdrive and the Falcon escapes.
With hope and Luke's acceptance of his dark legacy, they prepare to save Han.
Act III
Luke confronts Darth Vader. Leia loses her love.
Ordinary World
Special World
1:00
12:00
18:00
23:00
34:00
42:00
54:00
61:00
62:00
76:00
82:00
87:00
93:00
101:00
111:00
113:00
118:00
119:00

EPISODE VI: RETURN OF THE JEDI
(U.S., 1983)

"You must confront Vader. Only then will you be a Jedi. And confront him you will."

—Yoda

Screenplay by Lawrence Kasdan and George Lucas
Story by George Lucas
Directed by Richard Marquand

As the Rebellion launches an attack on the Empire's more powerful Death Star, Luke Skywalker confronts the Dark Side and redeems his father.

LANDMARKS OF THE JOURNEY

Return of the Jedi recommits Luke and his Hero Team to the Cause, to defeat the Shadow and restore peace to the galaxy. It presents many parallels with *Star Wars*, including the power of the human spirit to vanquish the faceless technology of the Empire. Whereas in *Star Wars* Luke learned to trust the Force (his human intuition), now he chooses to trust his father's humanity that still resides in Darth Vader. Luke's sacrifice from the Hero Team to complete this spiritual quest is similar to Obi-Wan's sacrifice during *Star Wars*. The Hero Team has already been influenced by Luke's Heroic Journey. They can move on, choosing their Heroes' paths to complete the tasks at hand.

THE JOURNEY

The Gallactic Empire is secretly creating another armored space station, much more powerful than the Death Star. Darth Vader arrives at the space station to push construction back on schedule. This SHADOW/HERALD also announces the impending arrival of the Emperor to oversee its completion. Once activated, the space station spells doom for the Rebellion's efforts to restore peace in the galaxy (a Galactic CALL TO ADVENTURE). We later learn that the Emperor's arrival threatens Luke Skywalker, as the Emperor and Vader plot to turn the young Jedi to the Dark Side.

Meanwhile, Luke and his HERO TEAM return to Tatooine to rescue Han (OUTER PROBLEM). Still frozen in carbonite, Han Solo graces Jabba the Hutt's palace wall as the gangster's prized trophy. The rescue of Han Solo can be seen as the ROAD BACK, completing the previous episode's cliffhanger—a ROAD BACK that is also a mini-Journey. The droids, Artoo and Threepio, present themselves before Jabba with Luke's holographic CALL to negotiate Han's freedom, and to accept the droids as gifts. Jabba REFUSES Luke's offer and keeps the droids. Later SHAPESHIFTER/HERO Leia (disguised as a bounty hunter) collects a bounty on Chewbacca. Her BOLD APPROACH places her in Jabba's good graces, allowing her to secretly release Han from his carbonite cell—a miraculous physical RESURRECTION, as well as the RESURRECTION of their love.

But Jabba anticipated the trickery, a REVERSAL. He jails Han and enslaves Leia. Luke arrives with his mystical APPROACH, using his Jedi powers to easily bypass Jabba's THRESHOLD GUARDIANS. Jabba won't be influenced by Jedi mind tricks and throws Luke to the Rancor. Luke defeats the monster. The Jedi's survival of this ORDEAL enrages Jabba, who orders an agonizing death for the HERO TEAM in the Sarlacc pit. This ROAD BACK, Luke warns, will be Jabba's biggest mistake.

Aboard Jabba's Galleon, in the RESURRECTION SEQUENCE, the HERO TEAM finally works together to overcome all odds, and defeats Jabba and his legion. The TEAM earns the ELIXIR of REUNITING, a healing of the HERO TEAM. Additionally, Leia and Han finally claim the ELIXIR of their Love.

Having finally saved his best friend, Luke can return to Dagobah to finish his training as a Jedi Knight (OUTER PROBLEM). Master Yoda tells his protégé that he no longer needs a MENTOR'S training to complete his Journey to become a Jedi Knight. The HERALD warns Luke that only when he confronts Vader will he be a Jedi Knight, the CALL TO ADVENTURE. Preparing for his death, the 900-year-old MENTOR confirms Luke's fears that Darth Vader is his father. Yoda also confesses that there is another Skywalker, but he dies before he can say more.

Unprepared for the loss of his MENTOR, Luke feels alone and unable to complete his Journey (a REFUSAL). The spirit of Obi-Wan Kenobi visits Luke. This MEETING with his first MENTOR helps Luke overcome his fear of having to kill his own father. Obi-Wan insists that the good person who was his father, Anakin, is already dead. Obi-Wan also warns that Luke's REFUSAL to kill Vader means that the Emperor has already won. Obi-Wan allows Luke to search his inner feelings to realize that the other "hope" is Leia, his twin sister. This revelation gives Luke the strength, the reason, and the partnership with family to recommit to the Journey, entering his THRESHOLD into the final stage of his Journey.

He rejoins the Rebel Alliance and his HERO TEAM. Now aware of the Empire's new battle station, the Rebellion prepares an attack that requires precision timing. Although Intelligence reports that the battle station's weapons have yet to be activated, it is protected by an energy shield operated from a base on the nearby forest moon of Endor. A strike team, willingly comprised of Han, Leia, Luke, Chewbacca and the droids, must get to Endor to disable the shield generator, allowing Lando and his squadron to destroy the space station. Aboard a stolen Imperial shuttle, the strike team uses an old clearance code to land on Endor. As they await clearance, Luke can sense Darth Vader—and Vader senses his son. Luke realizes he has endangered their mission, but Vader allows them to pass so that he can deal with them on his own terms.

The TEAM has crossed the THRESHOLD. They land on Endor and enter their TEST PHASE. They CHASE down and defeat a band of stormtroopers (ENEMIES). With Threepio serving as a golden god and with some Jedi "magic," the TEAM also wins the valuable allegiance of the Endor natives, the Ewoks. Magical SHAPESHIFTERS with power over their natural habitat, the Ewoks will become HEROES in their own right; but for now, they celebrate the tales of the HERO TEAM. The TEAM APPROACHES THE INMOST CAVE, making final preparations for the ORDEAL. Luke privately confesses to Leia their heritage and his plans to hand himself over to Vader. He needs to protect the TEAM'S mission and to save the goodness of Anakin that he believes still resides in Darth Vader (Luke's INNER PROBLEM). He surrenders to Darth Vader, believing that the goodness of his father will not hand him over to the Emperor. But the SHADOW of Darth Vader has too much control over what may remain of Anakin Skywalker, and gives Luke to the Emperor.

The Strike Team makes their APPROACH on the shield-generator bunker, and Lando's squadron prepares its entrance out of lightspeed. But the Emperor was aware of the Rebellion's plan all along and reveals his trap to Luke, a REVERSAL that throws the HERO TEAM into an ORDEAL. On Endor, stormtroopers trap the Strike Team. With the Death Star's shields maintained, Lando's squadron appears out of hyperdrive and faces an armada of Imperial TIE fighters. The Emperor forces Luke to watch the destruction of his TEAM and the future of the Rebellion, using this ORDEAL to push Luke to his anger—and the Dark Side.

But the Emperor's plans didn't anticipate the role of the primitive Ewoks. Led by Threepio and inspired by the Hero Tales during the APPROACH, the Ewoks launch a surprise counter-attack, the REWARD. They overcome armored troops, Imperial walkers, and lasers with clubs, vines and stones. Lando tries to buy time for Han, trusting that the Strike Team will do their job. The Emperor reveals his last surprise; unbeknownst to the Rebellion, the Death Star is fully operational. The Emperor uses it to disintegrate an enormous Rebel cruiser. From Luke's perspective, the ROAD BACK seems bleak. Overtaken by his anger, Luke grabs his lightsaber and engages Darth Vader in a duel to the death.

While Luke surrenders himself down a dark ROAD BACK, signs of an extensive RESURRECTION is underway. On Endor, Chewie and several Ewoks hijack an Imperial walker. Han and the TEAM use the walker to trick the remaining Imperial squadron into giving up the bunker.

Back in the Emperor's throne room, Vader uses his empathic powers to search Luke's feelings, making him reveal the identity of his twin sister, Leia. This renews Luke's anger and determination to destroy Vader. The Emperor gleefully watches Luke sever his father's sword hand. The Emperor prods Luke to fulfill his destiny, and usurp his father's position by the Emperor's side. But Luke sees his father's mechanical appendage, similar to his own, as a sign of Luke's weakness to impatience and recklessness. Luke casts aside his lightsaber, granting Vader life and refusing the Emperor's dark plan, a RESURRECTION.

Meanwhile, the RESURRECTION continues on Endor. At last, the Strike Team destroys the shield-generator bunker, initiating the CHASE for Lando's strike on the Death Star's main reactor.

But the Emperor won't accept Luke's refusal and slowly destroys the boy. Luke's cries for his father's help finally RESURRECTS the humanity of Anakin. Overpowering the mechanical SHADOW of Darth Vader, Anakin rises, sacrifices himself and casts the Emperor into the abyss.

As the Death Star begins to quake from the Rebellion's attack, Luke tries to save his father, Anakin Skywalker. Anakin insists he take off his SHADOW MASK. Beholding this vulnerable man at death's door, Luke confesses that he wanted to save him. Anakin assures Luke that he has. Acknowledging the ELIXIR of his redemption at the hands of his son, Anakin dies. Luke escapes with his father's body as Lando's TEAM fires the deathblow, destroying the Death Star's main reactor, a RESURRECTION. The TEAM barely flees before the Space Station explodes.

The celebration spreads galaxy-wide. Societies everywhere enjoy the ELIXIR of freedom from the oppressive Galactic Empire. The revelry continues back on Endor. Leia and Han reaffirm the ELIXIR of their love. Luke reunites with his sister and his friends. And the Journey's final moment shows that death reunited friends as well. Luke acknowledges the redeemed spirit of Anakin, joining those of Obi-Wan and Yoda—a RESURRECTION of two Jedi knights with their Jedi master.

FADE OUT

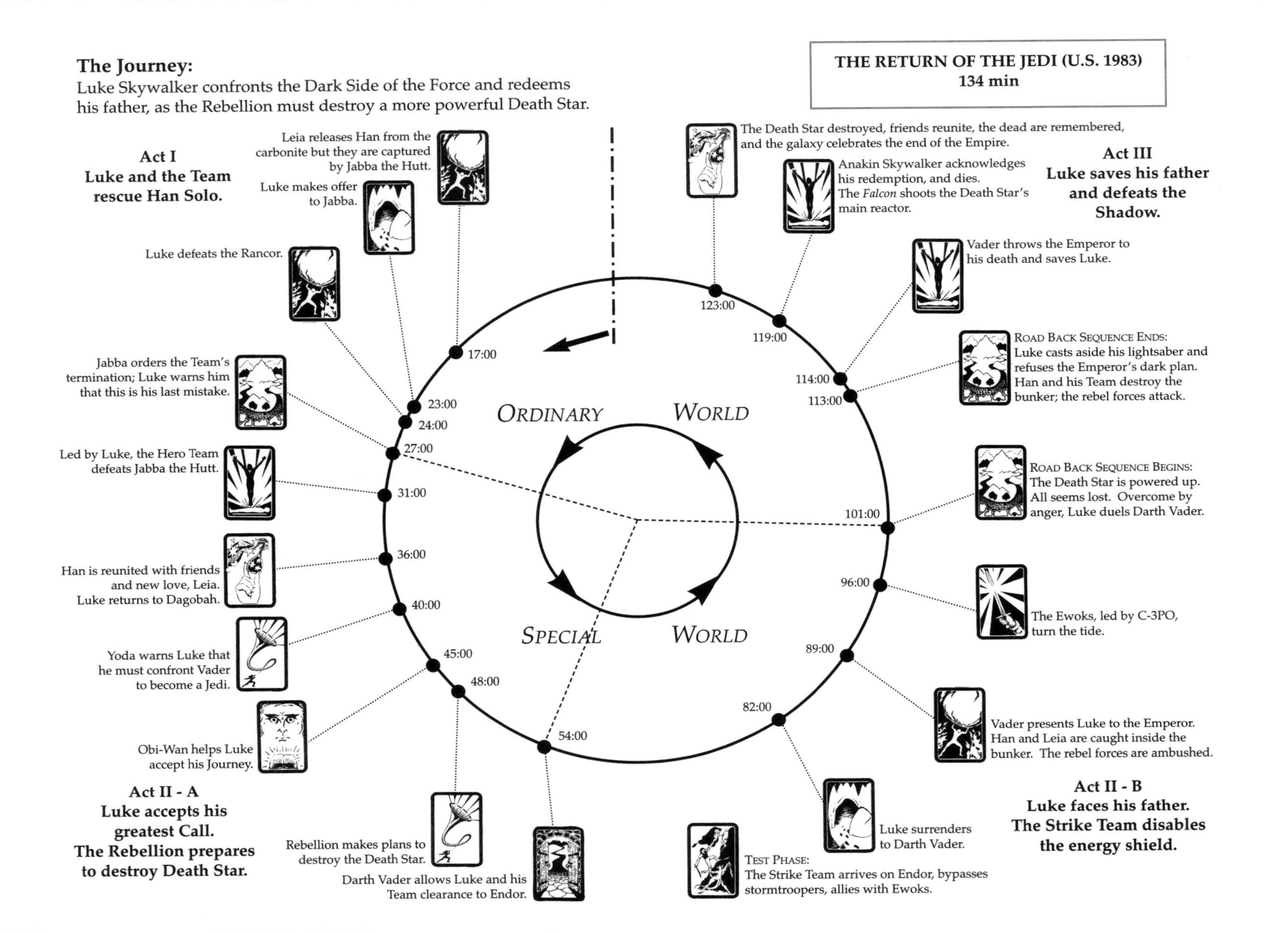
THE RETURN OF THE JEDI (U.S. 1983)
134 min
The Journey:
Luke Skywalker confronts the Dark Side of the Force and redeems his father, as the Rebellion must destroy a more powerful Death Star.
Act I
Luke and the Team rescue Han Solo.
Leia releases Han from the carbonite but they are captured by Jabba the Hutt.
Luke makes offer to Jabba.
Luke defeats the Rancor.
Jabba orders the Team's termination; Luke warns him that this is his last mistake.
Led by Luke, the Hero Team defeats Jabba the Hutt.
Han is reunited with friends and new love, Leia. Luke returns to Dagobah.
Yoda warns Luke that he must confront Vader to become a Jedi.
Obi-Wan helps Luke accept his Journey.
Act II - A
Luke accepts his greatest Call.
The Rebellion prepares to destroy Death Star.
Rebellion makes plans to destroy the Death Star.
Darth Vader allows Luke and his Team clearance to Endor.
TEST PHASE:
The Strike Team arrives on Endor, bypasses stormtroopers, allies with Ewoks.
Luke surrenders to Darth Vader.
Act II - B
Luke faces his father.
The Strike Team disables the energy shield.
Vader presents Luke to the Emperor. Han and Leia are caught inside the bunker. The rebel forces are ambushed.
The Ewoks, led by C-3PO, turn the tide.
ROAD BACK SEQUENCE BEGINS:
The Death Star is powered up. All seems lost. Overcome by anger, Luke duels Darth Vader.
ROAD BACK SEQUENCE ENDS:
Luke casts aside his lightsaber and refuses the Emperor's dark plan. Han and his Team destroy the bunker; the rebel forces attack.
Vader throws the Emperor to his death and saves Luke.
Anakin Skywalker acknowledges his redemption, and dies.
The *Falcon* shoots the Death Star's main reactor.
The Death Star destroyed, friends reunite, the dead are remembered, and the galaxy celebrates the end of the Empire.
Act III
Luke saves his father and defeats the Shadow.
ORDINARY WORLD
SPECIAL WORLD
17:00
23:00
24:00
27:00
31:00
36:00
40:00
45:00
48:00
54:00
82:00
89:00
96:00
101:00
113:00
114:00
119:00
123:00

THE JOURNEY OF LUKE SKYWALKER

Star Wars shows Luke's initial acceptance of his legacy, to become a Jedi Knight like his father before him. He crosses the Threshold into the Special World when he learns to trust the Force, and uses that trust to destroy the Death Star. Mentor Obi-Wan can take Luke only so far along his path of spiritual awakening. Although a Jedi himself, Obi-Wan holds only the Mentor's Special Power to introduce Luke to the Force, and to be the Herald of his Jedi Training at the hands of Jedi Master, Yoda. But Luke's Threshold issues a greater, more perilous Call to his Shadow, Darth Vader. Now aware of young Skywalker's potential, Vader seeks Luke to serve the Shadow's path. Luke's Special World of Training becomes a struggle between Light and Dark sides of the Force, as he is pulled between two opposing Mentors, Yoda and Darth Vader.

The Empire Strikes Back begins Luke's Test Phase, his training with Jedi Master Yoda. The episode completes Luke's central Ordeal, his acceptance of his dark legacy as the son of Darth Vader. To truly follow in his father's footsteps would mean taking the easy journey to the Dark Side. But Luke holds the power to shun this path. Hanging on to the Elixir of intuition and the lessons of Yoda, Luke refuses Vader's dark Call, the Resurrection of his Ordeal.

Return of the Jedi completes Luke's transformation. He provides the Road Back to resurrect his Hero Team and prepare them for a more powerful Death Star. *Return of the Jedi* also initiates Luke's Road Back to complete his training as a Jedi Knight. His final task is his most challenging—to confront Darth Vader. And Luke needs his two Mentors to push him ahead. Yoda presents his Road Back as his dying act. Obi-Wan completes the Road Back, giving Luke the warning that Darth Vader must be defeated. But Obi-Wan also gives Luke the strength to recommit to his Journey.

His Mentors may have passed from the corporeal world, but Luke is not alone; he still has his sister, Leia. Luke accepts his Road Back but instead of killing Darth Vader, he chooses to save his father's soul, which he believes still resides beneath Vader's mask. Perhaps the greatest Elixir that a Hero can provide is the ability to influence others to choose the heroic path. Luke's actions and deeds touch everyone: the self-serving Han Solo, the self-preserving Threepio, and finally his own father, Anakin. Defying the Emperor, Luke offers the greatest sacrifice of his life for his father's soul. And he receives the greatest boon. Anakin stands up to the Emperor and casts Evil to its death.

FINAL FADE TO BLACK

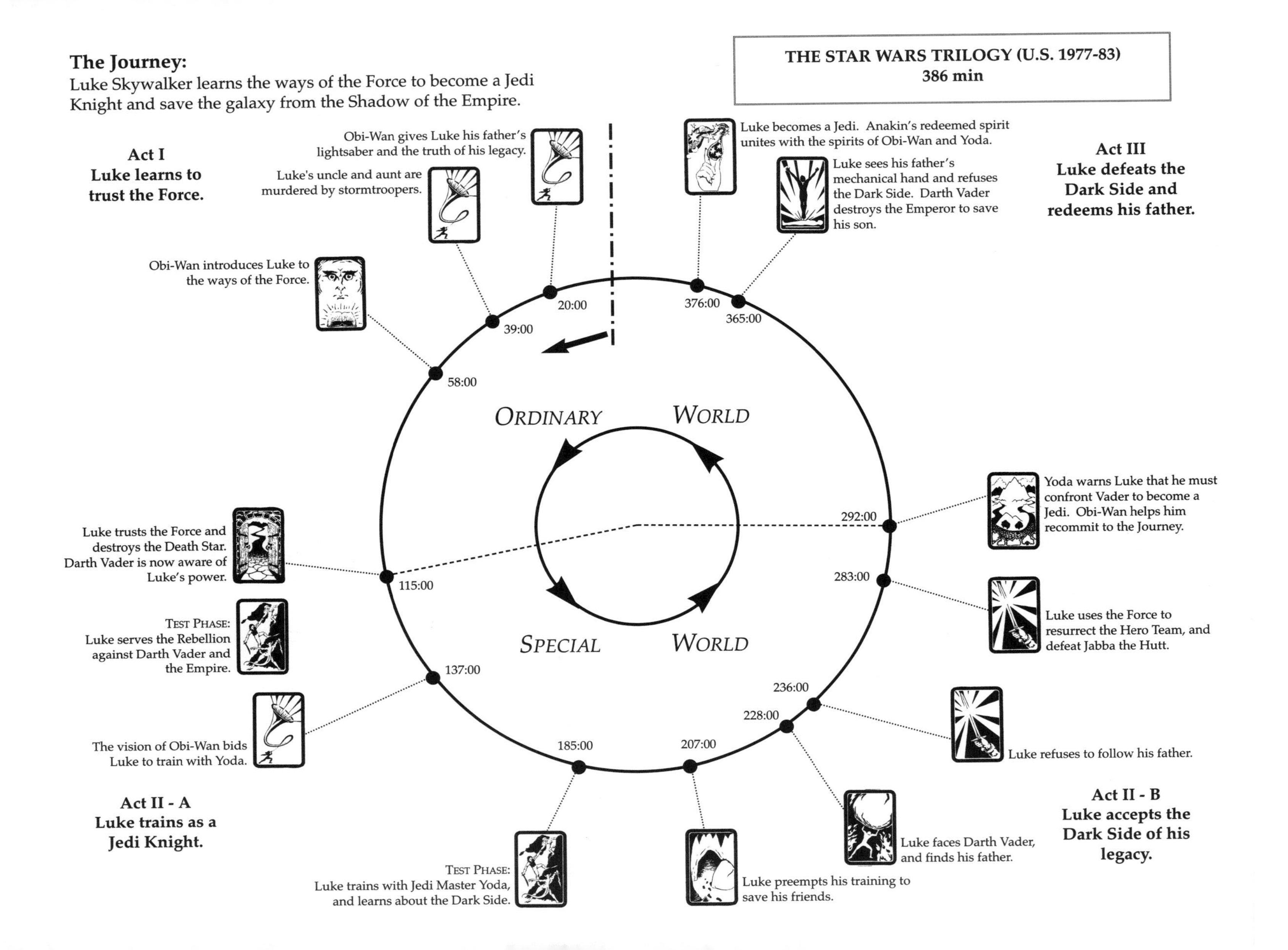

THE STAR WARS TRILOGY (U.S. 1977-83)
386 min
The Journey:
Luke Skywalker learns the ways of the Force to become a Jedi Knight and save the galaxy from the Shadow of the Empire.
Act I
Luke learns to trust the Force.
Obi-Wan gives Luke his father's lightsaber and the truth of his legacy.
Luke's uncle and aunt are murdered by stormtroopers.
Obi-Wan introduces Luke to the ways of the Force.
20:00
39:00
58:00
ORDINARY WORLD
SPECIAL WORLD
Luke trusts the Force and destroys the Death Star. Darth Vader is now aware of Luke's power.
115:00
TEST PHASE: Luke serves the Rebellion against Darth Vader and the Empire.
137:00
The vision of Obi-Wan bids Luke to train with Yoda.
Act II - A
Luke trains as a Jedi Knight.
185:00
TEST PHASE: Luke trains with Jedi Master Yoda, and learns about the Dark Side.
207:00
Luke preempts his training to save his friends.
228:00
Luke faces Darth Vader, and finds his father.
236:00
Luke refuses to follow his father.
Act II - B
Luke accepts the Dark Side of his legacy.
283:00
Luke uses the Force to resurrect the Hero Team, and defeat Jabba the Hutt.
292:00
Yoda warns Luke that he must confront Vader to become a Jedi. Obi-Wan helps him recommit to the Journey.
365:00
Luke sees his father's mechanical hand and refuses the Dark Side. Darth Vader destroys the Emperor to save his son.
376:00
Luke becomes a Jedi. Anakin's redeemed spirit unites with the spirits of Obi-Wan and Yoda.
Act III
Luke defeats the Dark Side and redeems his father.

EPILOGUE: REFLECTION ON THE JOURNEY

Movies entertain us, move us to tears or uncontrollable laughter; they inspire us to alter the way we act, the way we talk, the clothes we wear. Often movies address our darkest fantasies or answer our most mysterious questions about life. Movies today are as much a part of our mythmaking tradition as were the first storytellers who enthralled their audiences by the light of the campfire. Today's audience is bathed in the light of the cinematic screen, but the storyteller's role is no less magical or important.

Our society has lost touch with our old myths. Who remembers Parsifal's quest for the Holy Grail, the tragic love of Tristan and Isolde, or Persephone's sacrifice to the underworld? Yet today's young moviegoers can rattle off the tales of Luke Skywalker. And who doesn't know Rick and Ilsa's great love? The tragic fall of Charles Foster Kane? Or the redemption of Dr. Richard Kimble? Over the centuries, the stories may have changed, but the questions they pose and the needs they address haven't lost their significance.

I may gain understanding from a cynical pacifist holed up on Casablanca, while my two-year-old daughter gains insight from a silly old bear in the enchanted Hundred Acre Wood. We all have myths we live by, whether we find them in soap operas, television sitcoms, music videos, the latest Harlequin Romance or Clancy thriller. With the marketing and special effects that seem to pave cinema's road, it's all the more important that the screenwriter embrace the mythmaking power he holds.

What are these mythic questions that we want to answer? First, look within yourself. What are your own needs and desires? Your dreams and fears? Your triumphs and shortcomings? Second, look at the stories that attract you. What films are most significant in your life? What draws you to see them again and again? Is it that the elixir of love triumphs over all? Or perhaps that the fallen Hero armed solely with determination and integrity reclaims justice? Look within yourself to find the heart of your stories.

EMBRACE OUR MENTORS' LESSONS

My intention during this vast journey celebrating great motion picture storytelling was not to suggest that today's storytellers try to recreate past successes, but that they learn from them. Just as a painter studies the composition and brush techniques of Picasso or

Matisse, screenwriters can learn invaluable lessons in exposition and characterization from the works of William Goldman or Callie Khouri. We need to embrace our Mentors' lessons to guide us as we shape our stories.

USING THE HERO'S JOURNEY

I hope that all the analyses have provided inspiration, and answers as to why these films work so well, and have become some of our most cherished myths. Unfortunately, the Hero's Journey is sometimes seen as a stringent model that applyies to only some genres. In actuality, the Hero's Journey is an amazingly flexible set of tools that can liberate the storyteller beyond the perceived straitjacket of the "traditional" Three-Act structure.

I give you these film analyses to understand the universality of the Hero's Journey across many genres, to inspire your own writing, and to provide answers to your story problems. As you approach your own stories keep in mind that structure is the essential foundation of your story; you cannot create for structure alone. *Any* paradigm or model presents this problem. Writers (and studio executives) force the tools onto the story to serve the paradigm without first seeking the needs of the story. Yes, a great Romance like *The African Queen* has a similar structure to that of *Unforgiven;* yet each is a unique story, integrating the Hero's Journey tools to support its character and story needs. On the other hand, as we've seen in these analyses, one Journey may not need a particular stage, while another requires a repetition of stages. Structure must serve the story. Understand the power of the Hero's Journey stages and the functions of the archetypes; but when you face the blank piece of paper or computer screen, leave the tools in your subconscious and serve your gut, your heart, and your story.

Place these tools in your writer's bag of tricks as you resume your personal journey of storytelling. Feel free to apply them to your favorite films, the stories you've written or the ones you've yet to write. If you accept these tools that illuminate the mythic tradition underlying our greatest stories, not only will you meet your audience's expectations, you will exceed them.

BIBLIOGRAPHY

BOOKS AND ARTICLES:

Bouzereau, Laurent. *Star Wars: The Annotated Screenplays.* New York: Ballantine Books, 1997.

Campbell, Joseph. *The Hero with a Thousand Faces,* 2nd Edition. Bollingen Series no. 17. Princeton, N.J.: Princeton University Press, 1973.

Campbell, Joseph, with Bill Moyers. *The Power of Myth.* New York: Doubleday, 1988.

Gottlieb, Sidney. (ed.) *Hitchcock on Hitchcock.* Berkeley, CA: University of California Press, 1995.

Henderson, Mary. *Star Wars: The Magic of Myth.* New York: Bantam Books, 1997.

Hunter, Allan. (ed.) *Movie Classics.* Chambers Encyclopedic Guides. New York: W & R Chambers Ltd., 1992.

Katz, Ephraim. *The Film Encyclopedia,* 3rd Edition. Revised by Fred Klein and Ronald Dean Nolan. New York: HarperCollins Publishers, Inc., 1998.

Lucas, George, with Bill Moyers. "Of Myth and Men." Time, April 26, 1999.

Maltin, Leonard. (ed.) *Leonard Maltin's Movie & Video Guide,* 1998 Edition. New York: Signet, 1997.

Murdock, Maureen. *The Heroine's Journey.* Boston: Shambhala, 1990.

Pearson, Carol S. *Awakening the Heroes Within.* New York: HarperCollins Publishers, Inc., 1991.

________. *The Hero Within.* New York: HarperCollins Publishers, Inc., 1989.

Richie, Donald. *The Films of Akira Kurosawa.* Berkeley, CA: University of California Press, 1996.

Saks, Sol. *Funny Business: The Craft of Comedy Writing,* 2nd Edition. Los Angeles: Lone Eagle Publishing Company, 1991.

Thomas, Sam. (ed.) *Best American Screenplays: First Series.* New York: Crown Publishers, Inc., 1986.

________. *Best American Screenplays 2.* New York: Crown Publishers, Inc., 1990.

________. *Best American Screenplays 3.* New York: Crown Publishers, Inc., 1995.

Thomas, Tony. *The Great Adventure Films.* Secaucus, N.J.: Citadel Press Books, 1976.

Vogler, Christopher. *The Writer's Journey: Mythic Structure for Writers,* 2nd Edition. Studio City, CA: Michael Wiese Productions, 1998.

Vorhaus, John. *The Comic Toolbox.* Hollywood, CA: Silman-James Press, 1994.

INTERNET RESOURCES:

Berardinelli, James, *Movie Reviews.* http://movie-reviews.colossus.net/movies.html

Dirks, Tim. *The Greatest Films.* http://www.filmsite.org/home.html

Ebert, Roger. *Roger Ebert on Movies.* http://www.suntimes.com/ebert/ebert.html

The Internet Movie Database http://us.imdb.com

VIDEOCASSETTE:

New York Center for Visual History. *American Cinema.* In co-production with KCET and the BBC. Beverly Hills, CA: FoxVideo, Inc. (distributor), 1995.

THE SCREENWRITERS

THE DIRECTORS

THE FILMS

THE WRITER'S JOURNEY

MYTHIC STRUCTURE FOR WRITERS - 2ND EDITION

Christopher Vogler

Over 100,000 Sold

This new edition provides fresh insights and observations from Vogler's ongoing work with mythology's influence on stories, movies, and humankind itself.

Learn why thousands of professional writers have made THE WRITER'S JOURNEY a best-seller and why it is considered required reading by many of Hollywood's top studios! Learn how master storytellers have used mythic structure to create powerful stories that tap into the mythological core which exists in us all.

Writers of both fiction and nonfiction will discover a set of useful myth-inspired storytelling paradigms (e.g., The Hero's Journey) and step-by-step guidelines to plot and character development. Based on the work of Joseph Campbell, THE WRITER'S JOURNEY is a must for writers of all kinds.

New analyses of box office blockbusters such as Titanic, The Lion King, The Full Monty, Pulp Fiction, and Star Wars.

- A foreword describing the worldwide reaction to the first edition and the continued influence of The Hero's Journey model.

- Vogler's new observations on the adaptability of THE WRITER'S JOURNEY for international markets, and the changing profile of the audience.

- The latest observations and techniques for using the mythic model to enhance modern storytelling.

- New subject index and filmography.

- How to apply THE WRITER'S JOURNEY paradigm to your own life.

Book-of-the-Month Club Selection • Writer's Digest Book Club Selection
Movie Entertainment Book Club Selection

$22.95, 300 pages, 6 x 9
ISBN 0-941188-70-1
Order # 2598RLS

STEALING FIRE FROM THE GODS

A DYNAMIC NEW STORY MODEL FOR WRITERS AND FILMMAKERS

James Bonnet

STEALING FIRE will take readers beyond classical story structure to an extraordinary new story model that can demonstrate how to create contemporary stories, novels, and films that are significantly more powerful, successful, and real. James Bonnet reveals the link between great stories and a treasury of wisdom hidden deep within our creative unconscious selves — a wisdom so potent it can unlock the secrets of the human mind.

Great stories are created by powerful and mysterious inner processes. The stories are designed to guide us to our full potential and are as necessary to our well-being as fresh air. Understanding great stories means understanding these inner processes can lead to a profound understanding of ourselves and the world.

This book introduces two important new models:

• The Golden Paradigm — discovery of a new psychological model brought to light by the intriguing patterns hidden within great stories.
• The Storywheel — a cosmological view of story that brings all of the different types of story together into one grand design.

Movie Entertainment Book Club Selection
JAMES BONNET, founder of Astoria Filmwrights, is a successful Hollywood screen and television writer. He has acted in or written more than 40 television shows and features including *Kojak*, *Barney Miller*, and two cult film classics, *The Blob*, and *The Cross and the Switchblade*.

Available
September 1999
Advance Orders

$26.95, 300 pages, 6 x 9
ISBN 0-941188-65-5
Order # 38RLS

CALL 24 Hours a Day
1-800-833-5738

It's Finally Here!

- *All information is cross-referenced*
- *Look up by country, company, last name, market & region, & type of company*
- *$54.95 hard cover*
- *$99.95 online subscription*
- *Also available in mailing label format*

FILM BUYERS & DISTRIBUTORS FROM OVER 70 COUNTRIES

published by the ***HOLLYWOOD CREATIVE DIRECTORY***

www.hcdonline.com

Call for a free week's trial: 310-315-4815 / 800-815-0503

ORDER FORM

To order these products please call 1-800-833-5738 or fax (818) 986-3408 or mail this order form to:

MICHAEL WIESE PRODUCTIONS
11288 Ventura Blvd., Suite 821
Studio City, CA 91604
1-818-379-8799

BOOKS:

____
____
____
____

Subtotal $ _______
Shipping $ _______
8.25% Sales Tax (Ca Only) $ _______

TOTAL ENCLOSED _______________

Please make check or money order payable to *Michael Wiese Productions*

(Check one) ____ Master Card ____ Visa ____ Amex

Company PO# ____________

Credit Card Number __________________________
Expiration Date ______________________________
Cardholder's Name ___________________________
Cardholder's Signature ________________________

CREDIT CARD ORDERS

CALL 1-800-833-5738

or FAX 818-986-3408

OR E-MAIL
mwpsales@earthlink.net

SHIPPING
ALL ORDERS MUST BE PREPAID

UPS GROUND SERVICE
One Item - $7.00
For each additional item, add $2.00.

Special Reports-$2 ea.

EXPRESS DELIVERY
3 Business Days
Add an additional $12.00 per order.

OVERSEAS
Surface - $15.00 ea. item
Airmail - $30.00 ea. item

SHIP TO:

Name ____
Address ____
City ______________________________ State _____ Zip ________
Country ____________________ Telephone _________________

Ask about our free catalog

VISIT OUR HOME PAGE www.mwp.com

Please allow 2–3 weeks for delivery.
All prices subject to change without notice.